WHY I AM A
CHRISTIAN

WHY I AM A CHRISTIAN

LEADING THINKERS EXPLAIN WHY THEY BELIEVE

NORMAN L. GEISLER AND PAUL K. HOFFMAN, EDITORS

 Baker Books

A Division of Baker Book House Co
Grand Rapids, Michigan 49516

Published by Baker Books
a division of Baker Book House Company
P.O. Box 6287, Grand Rapids, MI 49516-6287

Second printing, October 2001

Printed in the United States of America

Library of Congress Cataloging-in-Publication Data

Why I am a Christian / Norman L. Geisler, Paul K. Hoffman, editors.
    p.   cm.
    Includes bibliographical references.
    ISBN 0-8010-1210-4
    1. Apologetics. I. Geisler, Norman L. II. Hoffman, Paul K., 1955–
BT1103.W49 2001
239—dc21   2001025170

For current information about all releases from Baker Book House, visit our web site:
http://www.bakerbooks.com

CONTENTS

INTRODUCTION

NORMAN L. GEISLER
AND PAUL K. HOFFMAN

Someone once said that there are two types of people in this world: those who divide people into types and those who don't. Most of us would have to admit that we are dividers. We categorize and label people not for the malicious purpose of fostering divisiveness but for the pleasure derived from cognitive order. Generalizations allow us to systematize knowledge into a pleasantly complete picture or tidy packets of truth. To be sure, labels and categories can occasionally be misleading, but they often present some important truth in a useful mode. They provide a handle on truth.

Sometimes a truthful generalization hurts. Take, for example, the statement "lawyers are liars." This is biting but true, and coeditor Paul K. Hoffman ought to know. He's made a living practicing law for the past two decades. He, of course, never lies, certainly never to judges, or opposing counsel, or juries, or his clients. But all this may depend on where the meaning of the word *lies* lies. If the truth is hurtful, discouraging, offensive, or otherwise problematic, he may simply elect to present the facts *in the light most favorable* to his clients' legal, emotional, and financial well-being. Be that as it may, one must admit that, in general, lawyers do have a nasty habit of bending the truth, even though some notable exceptions do exist. So there you have it. Though it smarts, we can take the truth.

"Lawyers are liars" is indeed a hurtful adage, but Mr. Hoffman's pain and status as an exception to the rule do not disprove its validity. If a given generalization is false or misleading, it is so not because it is hurtful or because one or more exceptions exist but only because it is, in most cases, simply not true. Indeed, a generalization by definition must have some exceptions. So it is that incidental pain and inaccuracies unavoidably arise from the valuable process of making useful generalizations.

As a thinking person, you too undoubtedly find it useful to divide and categorize people and their beliefs. It is likely that you already embrace some generalizations about the Christian faith. You may be a believer seeking to better understand what you believe. Or you may be a skeptic, doubtful but willing to keep an open mind. You may even be a thoroughgoing agnostic or atheist. In any case, you very likely already embrace generalizations of some kind about Christians and Christianity, which may include one or more of the following:

1. Christians are not very intellectual and are often anti-intellectual.
2. The exceptional "intellectual" Christian has, of necessity, adroitly compartmentalized his or her intellect and his or her faith so that never the twain shall meet.
3. Anyone who claims to have "the truth" (as Christians do) obviously doesn't.
4. The scientific evidence for evolution has rendered a Creator God superfluous.
5. The philosophical arguments for the existence of God were proven long ago to be false and invalid.
6. Even if God does exist, the evidence for his existence is not convincing and certainly not sufficient to compel religious obedience or justify eternal damnation for nonbelief.
7. The Christian faith, as with all religions, is irrational or at best non-rational.
8. Scientists and historians have proven that the Bible is full of myths and errors.
9. Jesus never claimed to be the Son of God but was mistakenly declared to be such by his followers.

Now we have seen that exceptions do not disprove a generalization, and we hope you will grant, as well, that your coeditors are quite able to accept a truthful generalization, painful though it may be. That being understood, we invite you to consider the possibility that these particular generalizations provide not a handle on truth but a grip upon a shield. Though useful in warding off uninvited or unappealing claims and propositions, they are not based in fact or on critical reasoning. They are simply not true.[1] This brings us to one of the central purposes of our book: to demonstrate that these and other commonly held beliefs about Christians and Christianity are false. We are confident we can prove this to you if you are willing to keep an open mind and hear us out. If what you genuinely desire is a useful handle on truth, please lay down your shield and read on.

NO DOGS OR GUNS ALLOWED

Paul Hoffman has the joy of practicing law and living in a terrific town in the Northwest. People are generally quite kind and neighborly in The Dalles, Oregon. Nevertheless, disputes do arise (for how else could a lawyer make a living?), and they are often settled in the Wasco County Courthouse, a stately and handsome, 1914 neoclassical, marble-floored, oak-paneled beauty.

Though this grand old courthouse is inspiring in its beauty, it is not without flaws. There have, on different occasions, been two signs near the entrance that have often brought a grin to passersby. The first said, "No dogs allowed, except for seeing-eye dogs." To whom was the second phrase directed: the blind man or his dog? The other, which is still there, says:

> No weapons of any kind are allowed in this courthouse. "Weapons" includes, but is not limited to, rifles, shotguns, pistols, knives, mace, and anything else capable of inflicting bodily injury.

Is this sign supposed to deter a gun-toting thug from carrying out his evil plan? Can you see it? *"Drat," said the well-armed litigant after carefully reviewing the threatening signs. Disheartened, he turned and walked away with his faithful pit bull, Chopper, by his side.*

Some things really ought to go without saying.

Still, other things do need to be said. So let us say that we welcome you, the reader, to another kind of courthouse, one in which coeditor Norman L. Geisler, having been an expert witness in noted court cases, is very much at home. It too is a dignified place where disputes are settled by presenting evidence and arguments. We treat each other here with respect and honor. No animals, please. Only civilized human beings are allowed to enter the courtroom of philosophy. And since no one carries any weapons, no one need carry a shield. So please, as we asked before, let us lay down our shields, both intellectual and emotional.

Imagine that you have been called for jury duty. You believe it is your responsibility as a thinking person to serve. As with most prospective jurors, you are probably half interested in the mysterious process of jury duty and half wishing you could get back to work. Five dollars a day just doesn't cut it. But here is a twist. The value of your service in this particular courthouse is potentially priceless. You could possibly gain everything, the true meaning of life, even eternal life.

Some of you are already skeptical. You may be like the juror in a car accident case who believes there is no such thing as whiplash. With crossed arms and a stern expression, you have firmly concluded that people fake it for whatever financial or psychological benefits they hope to gain. We can understand why, having never personally experienced whiplash, you may feel this way. Still, you should know that Paul Hoffman has had occasion to prove to incredulous jurors that whiplash is a genuine medical phenomenon. Religious faith is similar, for those who have never experienced it also find religious faith difficult to believe. But we assure you it is quite real.

Clearly, we shall fail in our efforts to persuade you if you are completely unwilling to believe. If your mind is closed, and if you have determined beforehand that no amount of evidence or expert testimony will change your mind, be advised that the law allows a trial attorney to have you removed from the jury panel. To serve as a juror you must promise, under oath, that you will keep an open mind and weigh the evidence set before you. Though you may be skeptical, can you nonetheless promise that you will keep an open mind, hear the evidence, weigh it, and make a fair and honest decision? That is all we can ask. We in return promise that our witnesses will not lie to you or attempt to trick you.

MAY IT PLEASE THE COURT

Ladies and gentlemen of the jury, we are here today representing our client, Christianity. Our client has been accused of making false statements and outrageous claims. The Christian faith has been maligned and defamed by its detractors for centuries. We are here not to seek retribution or remuneration for harm done but simply to set the record straight. We intend to prove to you that the Christian faith is both reasonable and true, and we shall do this by presenting expert and eyewitness testimony. Indeed, all our experts are also eyewitnesses to the truth and power of the gospel of Jesus Christ.

"Then they are biased!" you may object, and of course you are correct. But herein lies a problem. We have searched the world over, and we cannot find anyone who is unbiased in matters of religion. As a juror, you must therefore carefully examine their testimony to see if by their bias our witnesses have skewed the facts. If it appears they have, you are free to reject their testimony. But if the facts are presented plainly and straightforwardly, and if the facts support the claims of Christianity, you are duty-bound to give them their due weight.

Here then is what the evidence will show. Two thousand years ago a man lived in what is today the country of Israel. He was a Jew and a carpenter by trade. He never traveled far from home, never wrote a book, never raised an army, and never served in any political office. But amazingly, incredibly, he claimed to be the Messiah and Son of God. He lived a perfect life and performed miracles, healing the sick and lame, giving sight to the blind, walking on water, even raising the dead, the kinds of things one would expect the real Son of God would be able to do.

There were those who considered his claims blasphemous, and they executed him for this crime, just as he had predicted (along with the Old Testament prophets centuries before). Three days later he rose physically from the dead, proving convincingly that he was who he claimed to be, and that is how and why he is now our Savior. The person of the Son of God, by taking on a human

10

body and living a perfect life, by suffering with us and dying for us, and by overcoming death itself, has reunited us with our Creator. This is truly good news. God loves us, he knows our pain, and he has provided the means for sinful men and women to have true relationship with a holy God. These are the facts, and believing these facts is, in the most basic sense, what makes one a Christian.[2]

We recognize that there are many intellectual obstacles to such belief. In presenting our evidence in support of the facts described above, therefore, we shall also do our best to remove common obstacles to faith, obstacles that have given rise to the following questions and objections.

How can anyone claim to have *the* truth or to *know* the truth?

Aren't agnosticism and atheism sound positions, since no one can really prove the existence of God?

Even if a god is proven to exist, how does this prove that he (or it) is the God described in the Bible?

Honestly now, isn't believing in miracles silly?

Don't we know, from evolution, that the Bible story about creation is false?

How can we accept as historically reliable what the followers of Jesus wrote and obviously embellished in the Gospels? Isn't it just myth?

"Historically" reliable, maybe. But how can it be the true Word of God when it contains so many statements that are scientifically impossible?

There are many other holy books. What makes you Christians think your book is better than the others?

If Jesus Christ was the Messiah, then aren't the Jews all mistaken?

He may have been the promised Messiah. He may even have performed miracles. But the Son of God? Isn't that going a bit too far?

With all the evil and suffering in this world, don't you have to admit that your God is either weak or evil himself?

I believe in Jesus, but I'm just not as religious as some people are. Doesn't God understand and accept me, faults and all?

How could a good and loving God make faith in Jesus the only way to heaven and eternal life? Don't all religions lead ultimately to God?

We do not claim to have all the answers. But we have more than enough to show that our faith in an omnipotent, omniscient, holy, and loving Creator God, who bridged the gap between himself and humankind in the person of Jesus Christ, is not only reasonable but is, in fact, the most intellectually and existentially coherent option among all others. Christianity is both sensible to the head and satisfying to the heart.

Our expert witnesses are scholars and apologists. They are sophisticated defenders of the Christian faith. But in the end their purpose here is very personal. They have a story to tell, a wonderful story of how their lives were changed by encountering the Author of truth. Each contributor desires to share with you the good news by offering his reasoned contribution to this book.

And so, dear reader, as the angel said to the shepherds on that first Christmas night, we now bring you good tidings of great joy, which shall be to all people. For unto to you we present this day a Savior, which is Christ the Lord (see Luke 2:10–11 KJV).

PART 1

WHY
I BELIEVE
IN TRUTH

J esus said, "I am the way and *the truth* and the life" (John 14:6, emphasis added). He also said, "I am the *good* shepherd" (John 10:11, emphasis added). Our first order of business is to lay the groundwork not simply for proving Christ's unique and remarkable claims but for demonstrating the meaningfulness of these claims. Do the claims of Jesus have any objective and universal meaning? Are truth and goodness real and knowable, or are such matters ultimately beyond our grasp or simply matters of personal preference?

While genuine knowledge of truth and goodness has been questioned by skeptics for centuries, few seriously challenged the very *existence* of truth and goodness until the eighteenth-century's hopeful modernism collapsed into the twentieth-century's chaotic postmodernism. If God is unnecessary (as Darwinism seems to imply), or if God is in fact dead (as Nietszche boldly claimed), who is there to write the rules of life? Like a bratty child, may we not, with justification, incessantly reply to all claims and directives, "Says who?—says who?—says who?"

"Says the Bible" was a perfectly adequate reply for many a century ago. That is not the case today. Relativism so pervades our cultural consciousness that we have reached the very brink of our capacity for meaningful dialogue. We seem to have no way to express even the most basic directional concepts; there is no real "up" or "down" beyond that which exists in one's own mind. If up and down have no clear meaning, what can we possibly know of truth and goodness?

In beginning our examination of the Christian faith, it must be understood that Jesus was not a relativist. The man who walked on water had his feet grounded on moral and objective truth. He was not a to-each-his-own sort of guy. On the contrary, he was an emphatic and unequivocal absolutist. Of course he was loving, or as apostle John put it, "full of grace," but not grace alone. The man who knew Jesus intimately said he was "full of grace *and truth*" (John 1:14, emphasis added). Jesus boldly berated the religious leaders of his day, physically assaulted the activity of the money changers in the temple, discriminated against non-Jews in his ministry, and quoted the Old Testament with uncompromising zeal. He spoke and acted like a man who actually believed that he knew the truth, or indeed, that he *was* the truth, incarnate. And for this he was not well received in polite society. Imagine his reception today!

It is this very problem, our deeply ingrained cultural resistance to claims of truth, that is addressed in chapters 1 and 2. Dr. Francis J. Beckwith first explains why moral claims (e.g., "I am the good shepherd") are real and meaningful. He also shows that objective moral values do exist and that you—yes, you— hold such beliefs. Dr. Norman L. Geisler then shows that objective truth not only exists but is knowable and that you cannot live, let alone function productively, without first acknowledging that you know certain things to be true.

If you think we may be wrong, we ask you to ponder this question: Is it true that we are wrong?

ONE

WHY I AM NOT
A MORAL RELATIVIST

FRANCIS J. BECKWITH

In his influential work, *The Closing of the American Mind*, the late philosopher Allan Bloom made the observation that "there is one thing a professor can be absolutely certain of: almost every student entering the university believes, or says he believes, that truth is relative. . . . The students, of course, cannot defend their opinion. It is something with which they have been indoctrinated."[1] Bloom was talking about both *moral* relativism and *epistemological* relativism. The latter is the view that there is no such thing as objective truth, that knowledge is relative to one's self, culture, and/or point of view. This type of relativism will be addressed in the next chapter. In this chapter, however, I will focus on moral relativism, a view that is not limited to indoctrinated college freshmen but is dominant in North American culture.

Moral relativism is the view that when it comes to questions of morality, there are no absolutes and no objective right or wrong; moral rules are merely personal preferences and/or the result of one's cultural, sexual, or ethnic orientation. The fact that one believes there are exceptions or, to be more precise, exemptions to moral rules does not make one a moral relativist. For example, many people who believe lying is wrong nonetheless believe it is not wrong to lie in order to protect someone's life. These people are not moral relativists, for to permit certain exemptions to a rule one must first acknowledge the general validity of the rule. The moral relativist rejects the idea that any such moral rules exist at all.

Many people see relativism as necessary for promoting tolerance, non-judgmentalism, and inclusiveness, for they think if one believes one's moral position is correct and others' incorrect, one is closed-minded and intolerant. They typically consider moral relativism the indispensable cornerstone of our pluralistic and modern democratic society. Unless we all embrace relativism, they fear we will likely revert to a moralistically medieval culture.

In this chapter, we will see why the arguments for relativism fail and why relativism itself cannot live up to its own reputation. But why, you may ask, is a critical evaluation of relativism important to the case for the Christian faith? First, Christianity teaches that there are objective moral norms that apply to all persons in all places and at all times.[2] Relativism says that there are no such norms. If relativism is true, therefore, Christianity must be false. But if relativism is incorrect, Christianity cannot be dismissed on the grounds that it affirms objective moral norms. Second, if moral norms exist, then materialism as a worldview is false, because moral norms are nonmaterial things.[3] If materialism is false, then other nonmaterial things such as God, angels, and souls cannot be ruled out on the grounds that they are not material. Thus, the falsity of materialism helps support the truth of Christianity. Ultimately, the claim "I am not a moral relativist" is not based on the fact that I am a Christian. Rather, I am a Christian at least in part because I am convinced that moral relativism is completely false.

In this chapter, I will first briefly discuss how moral relativism has affected our ability to engage in moral discourse. Then I will present and critique two arguments for moral relativism. Finally, I will argue that given the existence of objective moral norms, the God of theism is the best explanation of the source of their existence.

MORAL RELATIVISM AND MORAL DISCOURSE

Moral relativism has stunted our ability to grasp the nature of moral claims. People in our culture often confuse *preference* claims with *moral* claims or reduce the latter to the former. To understand what I mean by this, consider two statements:[4]

1. I like vanilla ice cream.
2. Killing people without justification is wrong.

The first statement is a preference claim, since it is a description of a person's subjective taste. It is not a *normative* claim. It is not a claim about what one ought or ought not to do. It is not saying, "Since I like vanilla ice cream, the government ought to coerce you to eat it as well," or, "Everyone in the world ought to like vanilla ice cream too." A claim of *subjective* preference tells us nothing about what one *ought* to think or do. For example, if someone were to say, "I like to torture children for fun," this would tell us nothing about whether it is wrong or right to torture children for fun.

The second claim, however, is quite different. It has little if anything to do with what one likes or dislikes. In fact, one may *prefer* to kill another person without justification and still know that it is morally wrong to do so. This statement is a moral claim. It is not a descriptive claim, for it does not tell us what, why, or how things are, or how a majority of people in fact behave and think. Nor is it a preference claim, for it does not tell us what anyone's subjective preference may be or how one prefers to behave and think. Rather, it is a claim about what persons *ought* to do, which may be contrary to how persons in fact behave and how they prefer to behave.

Unfortunately, the espousal of moral relativism has made it difficult for many people in our culture to distinguish between preference claims and moral claims. Rather than pondering and struggling with arguments for and against a particular moral perspective, people sometimes reduce the disagreement to a question of personal preference or subjective opinion. Take, for example, the issue of whether parents and other concerned citizens have a right to boycott products that are advertised during television programs these citizens find to be morally inappropriate, especially for children. The usual reply to these citizens is, "If you don't like a particular program, you don't have to watch it. You can always change the channel." But does the person who employs this reply really understand what these citizens are saying?

These groups are not merely saying that they don't prefer these programs. In fact, these citizens and their children may actually be tempted to watch these programs; that is, in terms of sheer untutored appetite, they may actually *prefer* these programs, though they still may know these programs are not good for them, just as one may prefer a candy bar but still know it's not good for him or her. To put it another way, these citizens are saying something a bit more subtle and profound than their detractors are likely to recognize let alone admit: These programs convey messages and create a moral climate that will affect others, especially children, in a way that is adverse to the public good. Hence, what troubles these citizens is that *you* and *your children* will not change the channel. Furthermore, it concerns these people that there is probably somewhere in America an unsupervised ten-year-old who is, on a consistent basis, watching late night HBO or listening to radio shock-jock Howard Stern. Most of these people fear that their ten-year-olds, who are not watching or listening to such programs, may have to interact socially with the unsupervised ten-year-old. Others, who may not have young children, are concerned for the declining moral health of their communities, which is sometimes manifested in an increasing level of rudeness, disrespect, incivility, crime, or verbal and physical violence.

There are, in fact, many well-educated and reasonable people who believe that such a community concern is justified, especially in light of what we know about how certain forms of entertainment and media affect people, especially the young. Just as a concern for people's lungs and physical health has resulted in criticism of and reprisals against tobacco companies, concern for people's souls and spiritual health sometimes results in criticisms of and reprisals against different media. Thus, such concerns cannot be relegated to a question of one's personal preference. The real question is whether *any* community or social action is *ever* permissible and would best serve the public good. Moral relativists, to be consistent, must answer no, while common sense seems to tell us otherwise.

Consider another example: the debate over abortion rights.[5] Many who defend a woman's right to abortion (pro-choicers) sometimes tell those who oppose abortion rights (pro-lifers), "If you don't like abortion, then don't have one." The intent and effect of such rhetoric is to reduce the abortion debate to a mere preference claim. That is, the objective moral rightness or wrongness of abortion (i.e., whether or not it involves killing an innocent human person) is declared, without argument, to be irrelevant. But this is clearly a mistake, for those who oppose abortion do so because they believe that the fetus (during most if not all of a woman's pregnancy) is a human person with a right to life, and it is generally wrong, both objectively and universally, to violate a person's right to life. For this reason, when the pro-lifer hears the pro-choicer tell her that if she doesn't like abortion she doesn't have to have one, it sounds to her as if the pro-choicer is saying, "If you don't like murder, then don't kill any innocent persons." Understandably, the pro-lifer, committed to objective moral norms, finds such rhetoric perplexing as well as unpersuasive. Of course, a number of sophisticated pro-choice advocates are not moral relativists and recognize the error of substituting preference claims for substantive moral debate.[6] But it does seem that in the popular debate, pro-choicers tend to reduce the question of abortion to a question of preference, proving they have been more affected by moral relativism than have their opponents.

ARGUMENTS FOR MORAL RELATIVISM

Two arguments are often used to defend moral relativism. The first is the argument from cultural and individual differences and the second is the argument from tolerance.

THE ARGUMENT FROM CULTURAL AND INDIVIDUAL DIFFERENCES

In this argument, the relativist concludes that there are no objective moral norms because cultures and individuals disagree on moral issues. To defend this premise the relativist typically cites a number of examples, such as cross-cultural and intra-cultural differences over the morality of sexual practices, abortion, war, and capital punishment. Hadley Arkes, an opponent of moral relativism, has sardonically observed, "In one society, a widow is burned on the funeral pyre of her husband; in another, she is burned on the beach in Miami. In one society, people complain to the chef about the roast beef, in another, they send back the roast beef and eat the chef."[7] There are at least four problems with the argument from cultural and individual differences.

Relativism does not follow from disagreement. The fact that people disagree about something does not mean that there is no truth. For example, if you and I were to disagree on the question of whether the earth is round, our disagreement would certainly not be proof that the earth has no shape. Likewise, the fact that a skinhead (a type of neo-Nazi) and I may disagree on the question of whether we should treat people equally is certainly not sufficient reason to conclude that equality is not an objective moral value. Even if individuals and cultures hold no values in common, it simply does not follow that nobody is ever right or wrong about the correct values. Despite the existence of moral disagreement, it is still quite possible that an individual or an entire culture, such as Adolf Hitler and Nazi Germany, are simply mistaken.

If the mere fact of disagreement were sufficient to conclude that objective norms do not exist, we would then have to acknowledge that there is no objectively correct position on such issues as slavery, genocide, and child molestation, for the slave owner, genocidal maniac, and pedophile clearly have an opinion that differs from the one held by those of us who condemn their actions. In the end, moral disagreement is simply a sociological observation that proves nothing about the true nature of morality.

Disagreement actually counts against relativism. Suppose, however, that the relativist, despite the logical failure of his case, sticks to his guns and maintains that disagreement over objective norms proves the correctness of relativism. The relativist has set down a principle—disagreement means there is no truth—that unravels his own case. After all, some of us believe that relativism is a mistaken view. We, in other words, disagree with the relativist over the nature of morality. We believe that objective moral norms exist whereas the relativist does not. But according to the relativist's own principle (i.e., "disagreement means there is no truth"), he ought to abandon his own opinion that relativism is the correct position. To make matters worse for the relativist, his "disagreement" principle is a proposition for which there is no universal agreement and thus on its own grounds must be rejected. As Arkes points out, "My disagreement establishes that the proposition [i.e., disagreement means there is no truth] does not enjoy a universal assent, and by the very terms of the proposition, that should be quite sufficient to determine its own invalidity."[8]

Disagreement is overrated. Although it is true that people and cultures disagree on moral issues, it does not follow that they do not share the same values or that certain moral norms are not binding on all nations at all times and in all places. Take, for example, the Salem witch trials. During colonial days in Massachusetts, certain individuals were put to death as punishment for practicing witchcraft. We do not execute witches today, but not because our moral norms have changed. Rather, we don't execute witches because we do not believe, as the seventeenth-century residents of Massachusetts did, that the practice of witchcraft has a fatal effect on the community. But suppose we had evidence that the practice of witchcraft affects people in the same way that secondhand cigarette smoke affects nonsmokers. We would alter the practice of our values to take into consideration this factual change. We may set up non-witch sections in restaurants and ban the casting of spells on interstate airplane flights. The upshot of all this is that the good of the community is a value we share with the seventeenth-century residents of Salem, but we simply believe they were factually wrong about the actual effect of witches on the community.[9]

Philosopher James Rachels presents another example of how the knowledge of certain facts may help us understand why it *seems* other people have different values.[10] He points to the Eskimos' practice of infanticide (on primarily female babies). On the surface, this practice seems to show that the Eskimos have a radically different value of human life than we do. And because one's view of human life is so fundamental, it seems to follow from this that moral relativism is correct. Rachels does not agree. He explains that once one realizes that certain factual considerations have made the practice of infanticide a necessary evil for the Eskimos, one sees that the Eskimos' value of human life is not all that different from ours. Writes Rachels:

> But suppose we ask why the Eskimos do this. The explanation is not that they have less affection for their children or less respect for human life. An Eskimo family will always protect its babies if conditions permit. But they live in a harsh environment, where food is often in short supply. . . . Infant girls are readily disposed of because, first, in this society the males are the primary food providers—they are the hunters, according to the traditional division of labor—and it is obviously important to maintain a sufficient number of food gatherers. But there is an important second reason as well. Because the hunters suffer a high casualty rate, the adult men who die prematurely far outnumber the women who die early. Thus if male and female infants survived in equal numbers, the female adult population would greatly outnumber the male adult population. Examining the available statistics, one writer concluded that "were it not for female infanticide . . . there would be approximately one-and-a-half times as many females in the average Eskimo local group as there are food-producing males."
>
> So among the Eskimos, infanticide does not signal a fundamentally different attitude toward children. Instead, it is a recognition that drastic measures are sometimes needed to ensure the family's survival. Even then, however, killing the baby is not the first option considered. Adoption is common; childless couples are especially happy to take a more fertile couple's "surplus." Killing is only the last resort. I emphasize this in order to show that the raw data of the anthropologists can be misleading; it can make the differences in values between cultures appear greater than they are. The Eskimos' values are not all that different from our values. It is only that life forces upon them choices that the rest of us do not have to make.[11]

This is not to say that the Eskimos are right or that we should not try to persuade them to believe their practice is wrong. Rather, this example simply shows that so-called moral differences may not really be moral differences at all, after one carefully examines why a certain practice, such as female infanticide, is performed.

Consider again the issue of abortion. The conventional wisdom is that the moral and legal debate over abortion is a dispute between two factions that hold incommensurable value systems. But the conventional wisdom is mistaken, for these factions hold many values in common.

First, each side believes that all human persons possess certain inalienable rights regardless of whether their governments protect these rights. That is why both sides appeal to what each believes is a fundamental right. The prolife advocate appeals to "life" whereas the pro-choice advocate appeals to "liberty" (or "choice"). Both believe that a constitutional regime, in order to be just, must uphold fundamental rights.

Second, each side believes that its position best exemplifies its opponent's fundamental value. The pro-choice advocate does not deny that life is a value but argues that his position's appeal to human liberty is a necessary ingredient by which an individual can pursue the fullest and most complete life possible.

On the other hand, the pro-life advocate does not eschew liberty. She believes that all human liberty is limited by another human person's right to life. For example, one has a right to freely pursue any goal one believes is consistent with one's happiness, such as attending a Los Angeles Lakers basketball game. One has no right, however, to freely pursue this goal at the expense of another's life or liberty, such as running over pedestrians with one's car so that one can get to the game on time. The pro-life advocate argues that fetuses are persons with a full right to life. Since the act of abortion results in the death of the unborn, abortion, with few exceptions, is not morally justified.

The pro-choice advocate does not deny that human persons have a right to life. He just believes that this right to life is not extended to fetuses since they are not human persons. The pro-life advocate does not deny that people have the liberty to make choices that they believe are in their best interests. She just believes that this liberty does not entail the right to choose abortion since such a choice conflicts with the life, liberty, and interests of another human person (the fetus).[12]

Thus, when all is said and done, the debate over abortion is not really about conflicting value systems, for we all generally agree that life and liberty are fundamental values.

Absurd consequences follow from moral relativism. First, if it is true that no objective moral norms apply to all persons at all times and in all places, then the following moral judgments must be denied: Mother Teresa was morally better than Adolf Hitler; rape is always wrong; it is wrong to torture babies for fun. Yet to deny that these judgments are universally true certainly seems absurd.

21

Every instinct within us tells us that at least some moral judgments are absolutely correct regardless of what other cultures or individuals may think.

Second, if the relativist claims that morality is relative to the *individual*, what happens when individual moralities conflict? For example, Jeffrey Dahmer's morality apparently permitted him to cannibalize his neighbor; his unfortunate neighbor likely did not share Dahmer's peculiar tastes. What would the relativist suggest be done to resolve this moral conflict between the cannibal and his reluctant dinner? Since nobody's morality is in principle superior, should we then flip a coin or simply conclude that "might makes right"? In addition, if the moral life is no more than a reflection of people's individual tastes, preferences, and orientations, then we have no legitimate basis for telling young people that it is morally wrong to lie, steal, cheat, and kill their newborns.

Third, even if the relativist were to make the more modest claim that morality is not relative to the individual but to the individual's culture (i.e., that one is only obligated to follow the dictates of one's society), other problems follow.

First, the cultural relativist's position is self-refuting. J. P. Moreland explains what it means for a position to be self-refuting:

> When a statement fails to satisfy itself (i.e., to conform to its own criteria of validity or acceptability), it is self-refuting. . . . Consider some examples. "I cannot say a word in English" is self-refuting when uttered in English. "I do not exist" is self-refuting, for one must exist to utter it. The claim "there are no truths" is self-refuting. If it is false, then it is false. But if it is true, then it is false as well, for in that case there would be no truths, including the statement itself.[13]

How is cultural relativism self-refuting? The supporter of cultural relativism maintains that there are no objective and universal moral norms and for that reason everyone ought to follow the moral norms of his or her own culture. But the cultural relativist is making an absolute and universal moral claim, namely, that everyone is morally obligated to follow the moral norms of his or her own culture. If this moral norm is absolute and universal, then cultural relativism is false. But if this moral norm is neither absolute nor universal, then cultural relativism is still false, for in that case I would not have a moral obligation to follow the moral norms of my culture.

Second, since each of us belongs to a number of different "societies" or "cultures," there is no way to determine objectively which culture's norms should be followed when they conflict. For example, suppose a woman named Sheena is a resident of a liberal upscale neighborhood in Hollywood, California, attends a Christian church, and is a partner in a prestigious law firm. In her neighborhood, having an adulterous affair is considered "enlightened," and those who do not pursue such unions are considered repressed prudes. At her church, however, adultery is condemned as sinful, while at her law firm adultery is neither encouraged nor discouraged. Suppose further that Sheena chooses to commit adultery in the firm's back office with a fellow churchgoer,

Donald, who resides in a conservative neighborhood in which adultery is condemned. The office, it turns out, is adjacent to the church as well as precisely halfway between Sheena's neighborhood and Donald's neighborhood. Which society's morality should apply? If the cultural relativist responds that Sheena is free to choose, then we have regressed to individual relativism, which we have already determined to be absurd.

Third, if morality is reducible to culture, there can be no real moral progress. The only way one can meaningfully say that a culture is getting better or progressing is if there are objective moral norms that exist independently of the progressing culture. There must be some superior moral principles to which the progressing society may draw closer. However, if what is morally good is merely what one's culture says is morally good, then we can say only that cultural norms *change*, not that society is progressing or getting better. Yet who can reasonably deny that the abolition of slavery in the United States was an instance of genuine moral progress? Did America change for the better, or did it simply change?

In addition, if cultural relativism is true, there can be no true or admirable reformers of culture. Moreland writes:

> If [cultural] relativism is true, then it is impossible in principle to have a true moral reformer who changes a society's code and does not merely bring out what was already implicit in that code. For moral reformers, by definition, *change* a society's code by arguing that it is somehow morally inadequate. But if [cultural] relativism is true, an act is right if and only if it is in society's code; so the reformer is by definition immoral (since he adopts a set of values outside the society's code and attempts to change that code in keeping with these values). It is odd, to say the least, for someone to hold that every moral reformer who ever lived— Moses, Jesus, Gandhi, Martin Luther King—was immoral by definition. Any moral view which implies that is surely false.[14]

Thus, in order to remain consistent, the cultural relativist must deny that real moral progress or real moral reformers exist, for such judgments presuppose the existence of objective and absolute moral norms.

THE ARGUMENT FROM TOLERANCE

Many people see relativism as necessary for promoting tolerance, nonjudgmentalism, and inclusiveness. If you believe your moral position is correct and others' incorrect, you are viewed as closed-minded and intolerant, even bigoted. They usually base this premise on the well-known differences of opinion on morality between cultures and individuals. The moral relativist embraces the view that one should not judge other cultures and individuals, for to do so would be intolerant. There are at least four problems with this argument, all of which maintain that tolerance (rightly understood) and relativism are actually incompatible with each other.

Tolerance supports objective morality, not relativism. Ironically, the call to tolerance by relativists presupposes the existence of at least one nonrelative, universal, and objective norm: tolerance. Bioethicist Tom Beauchamp explains:

> If we interpret normative relativism as requiring tolerance of other views, the whole theory is imperiled by inconsistency. The proposition that we ought to tolerate the views of others, or that it is right not to interfere with others, is precluded by the very strictures of the theory. Such a proposition bears all the marks of a non-relative account of moral rightness, one based on, but not reducible to, the cross-cultural findings of anthropologists. . . . But if this moral principle [of tolerance] is recognized as valid, it can of course be employed as an instrument for criticizing such cultural practices as the denial of human rights to minorities and such beliefs as that of racial superiority. A moral commitment to tolerance of other practices and beliefs thus leads inexorably to the abandonment of normative relativism.[15]

If everyone ought to be tolerant, then tolerance is an objective moral norm. Therefore, moral relativism is false. Also, tolerance presupposes that there is something good about being tolerant, such as being able to learn from others with whom one disagrees or to impart knowledge and wisdom to others. But that presupposes objective moral values, namely, that knowledge and wisdom are good things. Moreover, tolerance presupposes that someone may be correct about his or her moral perspective. That is to say, it seems that part of the motivation for advocating tolerance is to encourage people to be open to the possibility that one may be able to gain truth and insight (including moral truth and insight) from another who may possess it. If that is the case, then objective moral truths exist that one can learn.

Relativism is itself a closed-minded and intolerant position. After all, the relativist dogmatically asserts that there is no moral truth. To illustrate this, consider a dialogue (based loosely on a real-life exchange) between a high school teacher and her student Elizabeth.[16] The teacher instructs her class, "Welcome, students. This is the first day of class, and so I want to lay down some ground rules. First, since no one has the truth about morality, you should be open-minded to the opinions of your fellow students."

The teacher recognizes the raised hand of Elizabeth, who asks, "If nobody has the truth, isn't that a good reason for me not to listen to my fellow students? After all, if nobody has the truth, why should I waste my time listening to other people and their opinions? What's the point? Only if somebody has the truth does it make sense to be open-minded. Don't you agree?"

"No, I don't. Are you claiming to know the truth? Isn't that a bit arrogant and dogmatic?"

"Not at all. Rather I think it's dogmatic as well as arrogant to assert that no single person on earth knows the truth. After all, have you met every person in the world and quizzed them exhaustively? If not, how can you make such a claim? Also, I believe it is actually the opposite of arrogance to say that

I will alter my opinions to fit the truth whenever and wherever I find it. And if I happen to think that I have good reason to believe I do know the truth and would like to share it with you, why wouldn't you listen to me? Why would you automatically discredit my opinion before it is even uttered? I thought we were supposed to listen to everyone's opinion."

"This should prove to be an interesting semester."

Another student blurts out, "Ain't that the truth," provoking the class to laughter.

Relativism is judgmental, exclusivist, and partisan. This may seem an odd thing to say since the relativist asserts that his viewpoint is nonjudgmental, inclusivist, and neutral when it comes to moral beliefs. But consider the following.

First, the relativist says that if you believe in objective moral truth, you are wrong. Hence, relativism is judgmental. Second, it follows that relativism excludes your beliefs from the realm of legitimate options. Thus, relativism is exclusivist. And third, because relativism is exclusive, all nonrelativists are automatically not members of the "correct thinking" party. So relativism is partisan.

Tolerance makes sense only within the framework of a moral order, for it is within such a framework that one can morally justify tolerating some things while not tolerating others. Tolerance without a moral framework, or absolute tolerance, leads to a dogmatic relativism, and thus to an intolerance of any viewpoint that does not embrace relativism.

The "tolerance" of moral relativism either condones barbarism or is self-refuting. As I pointed out above, some moral relativists embrace tolerance because they believe that such a posture is appropriate given the diversity of moral and cultural traditions in the world today. Humanist author Xiaorong Li points out the fallacy in this reasoning:

> But the existence of moral diversity does no more to justify that we ought to respect different moral values than the existence of disease, hunger, torture, slavery do to justify that we ought to value them. Empirical claims thus are not suitable as the basis for developing moral principles such as "Never judge other cultures" or "We ought to tolerate different values." . . .
>
> What if the respected or tolerated culture disrespects and advocates violence against individuals who dissent? When a girl fights to escape female genital circumcision or foot-binding or arranged marriage, when a widow does not want to be burned to death to honor her dead husband, the relativist is obligated to "respect" the cultural or traditional customs from which the individuals are trying to escape. In so doing, the relativist is not merely disrespecting the individual but effectively endorsing the moral ground for torture, rape and murder. *On moral issues, ethical relativists can not possibly remain neutral—they are committed either to the individual or to the dominant force within a culture.*
>
> Relativists have made explicit one central value—equal respect and tolerance of other ways of life, which they insist to be absolute and universal. *Ethical relativism is thus repudiated by itself.*[17]

25

GOD AND MORALITY

Given the failure of moral relativism, it must be the case that objective and universal moral norms exist.[18] But if they exist, what is their source? Where do they come from? I will argue that the God of theism best explains the existence of universal and objective moral norms. The case I will make here is certainly not irrefutable proof of God's existence. It is more like a prosecutor's legal argument for a defendant's guilt based on circumstantial evidence. In other words, given the "fingerprints" one finds on moral norms when one reflects on their nature, they are best explained as the result of the hand and mind of the God of theism. Although one may reject this conclusion (i.e., one may conclude that "reasonable doubt" exists), it is difficult to conceive of a better explanation for the evidence taken as a whole. In the words of philosopher Paul Copan, "Objective moral values are quite at home in a theistic universe. Given God's existence, moral realism is natural. But given an atheistic universe . . . , objective morality—along with its assumptions of human dignity, rights, and moral responsibility—is unnatural and surprising and 'queer.'"[19]

THE NATURE OF MORALITY

Given the existence of moral norms, there are some observations we can make about them. First, they are known, for if they were not known, then we would have to be moral skeptics. The above critique of moral relativism, however, shows that moral skepticism is not an option.

Second, moral norms are not physical. They have no physical properties such as extension, weight, height, and they do not consist of chemicals, particles, or other parts that can be measured by scientific instruments. We do not discover them by using our sense organs; rather, we encounter them through introspection and reflection. Thus, if moral rules exist and they are not physical, then materialism as a worldview is false.

Third, moral norms are a form of communication, an activity in which one mind through statements conveys meaning to another mind. Moral norms are found in imperatives (e.g., "One ought to keep one's promises"), commands (e.g., "Keep your promises"), and descriptions (e.g., "Keeping promises is good").

Fourth, there is an incumbency to moral norms. As Gregory Koukl puts it, moral norms "have a force we can actually feel *prior* to any behavior. This is called the incumbency, the 'oughtness' of morality. . . . It appeals to our will, compelling us to act in a certain way, though we may disregard its force and choose not to obey."[20]

Fifth, when we break a significant and clear moral rule, it is usually accompanied by feelings of painful guilt and sometimes shame, for we are cognizant of our moral failure and realize we deserve to be punished. Only sociopaths succeed in overcoming their conscience completely.

The Source of Morality

Moral norms, therefore, are known nonmaterial realities that are a form of communication for which we have a sense of incumbency and about which we feel painful guilt when we violate them. I believe there are only three possible sources of these moral norms: (1) They are an illusion; (2) they exist but are accidents, a product of chance; or (3) they are the product of an intelligence.

Morality is an illusion. This, of course, is the position of the relativist. As we have seen in this chapter, however, this position fails. Morality, therefore, is real; it is not an illusion.

Moral norms are accidents, products of chance. If moral norms are products of chance, then they are the result of unguided evolution. But this does not seem adequate, for if moral norms have no mind behind them, then there is no justification to obey them. Consider this illustration: If while playing Scrabble the letters randomly spell, "Go to Baltimore," should I obey the command, buy a plane ticket, make hotel reservations, and/or take up temporary residence in Baltimore? Of course not, for "the command" is a chance-created phrase and is thus really no command at all. As Koukl points out, "Commands are communications between two minds. Chance might conceivably create the appearance of a moral rule, but there can be no command if no one is speaking." A command created by accident "can be safely ignored."[21]

Suppose, however, that an evolutionist replies that morality exists because it is necessary for survival. According to this view, moral rules against adultery, murder, stealing, and so on are the result of the forces of natural selection "choosing" those genes that perpetuate traits that are more conducive to the preservation of the human species. In the words of Robert Wright:

> If within a species there is variation among individuals in their hereditary traits, and some traits are more conducive to survival and reproduction than others, then those traits will (obviously) become more widespread within the population. The result (obviously) is that the species' aggregate pool of hereditary traits changes.[22]

Behavioral patterns that help sustain these species-preserving traits are part of what we call "morality." There are several problems with this viewpoint.

First, since helping the weak, the genetically marred, and the needy are not evolutionarily helpful (i.e., they do not advance the "survival of the fittest"), why is it that we have a sense of duty and incumbency to help those less fortunate than ourselves? Suppose the evolutionist answers that we would not have this sense of duty and incumbency unless it were helpful to human evolution. That is, it must be helpful even if we do not know exactly how. There are at least two problems with this answer. (1) The question we are asking is whether evolution can *explain* all our moral senses. It is circular reasoning to presuppose that whatever moral senses we have must be the result of evolution. (2) Because it is clear that not every human being has a moral sense that he or she has a duty and incumbency to help those less fortunate, on what grounds could the evolutionist say that these human beings are mistaken in their moral viewpoint? After all, people who lack this moral sense have existed all over the globe for generations, and if they too are the products of evolution, perhaps having such people in our population is necessary for the preservation of the species. If that is the case, then "moral sense" is personally relative and is not universally binding. But this is pure relativism, and as we have seen, it fails as a moral theory. On the other hand, suppose the evolutionist bites the bullet and maintains that those who lack the moral sense to see that they have an obligation to those weaker than themselves are morally wrong regardless of what moral sense they may feel. Then there is a morality above evolution by which we can make moral judgments about the moral senses of different segments of our population that resulted from unguided evolution. Thus, evolution lacks explanatory power in accounting for morality.

Second, evolution is concerned only with the sorts of *behavior* that are conducive to the preservation of the species. But morality is more than just behavior, for it includes, among other things, motive and intent. In fact, a moral judgment is incomplete without taking these into consideration, for one can be immoral without any behavior, simply on the basis of motive and intent. For example, I can intend to carry out a murder and by my sloth or incompetence fail to do so. My bad intentions alone are clearly immoral. One can also be immoral simply on the basis of motive and intent even if the behavior has "good" results. For example, if I intend to trip someone in order to harm them, but it results in the person not being hit by a car and thus saving his or her life, the results are good even though what I did was clearly immoral.

"Bad" results may be part of a morally good act simply on the basis of motive and intent. For example, if a surgeon operates on a terminal patient with the intent to remove a cancer, but during the operation the patient dies of cardiac arrest, the surgeon has not acted immorally. Since evolution, at best, can only *describe* what behaviors are conducive to the preservation of the species and does not address the role of motive and intent in evaluating those behaviors, evolution is an inadequate explanation for the existence of moral norms.

Third, the evolutionary explanation of morality is merely *descriptive*. That is to say, it merely tells us what behaviors in the past may have been conducive to the survival of the species and why I may have on occasion moral feelings to act consistently with those behaviors. But evolution cannot tell me whether I ought to act on those feelings in the present and in the future. Granted, I am grateful that people in the past behaved in ways that made my existence possible. But why should I emulate only those behaviors that many people today say are "good"? After all, some people in the past raped, stole, and murdered. And I know of many people today who have feelings to rape, steal, and murder. Perhaps these behaviors are just as important for my existence and the preservation of the species as the "good" behaviors. Unless there is a morality above the morality of evolution, it is difficult to see how one can distinguish between morally good and bad actions if both types may have been conducive to the preservation of the species.

Moral rules are the product of intelligence. Since moral norms are neither illusory nor the product of chance, only one option remains: They have their source in an intelligent being. As C. S. Lewis explained in *Mere Christianity*, the existence of moral law implies a moral *lawgiver*. But what sort of intelligence is this being, this lawgiver?

It must be the sort of being who could be the ground of morality. It could not be a contingent intelligence, one whose existence and moral authority is dependent upon something else outside itself, for in order to be the *ground* of morality, a being must not receive its existence and moral authority from another, for that other being, if it is not contingent, would then be the ground of morality. Moreover, the source of morality must be the sort of being who has the moral authority to enforce universal moral norms. Therefore, the source of morality must be a self-existent, perfectly good being whose realm of authority is the entire universe. It seems fitting to call such a being "God."

CONCLUSION

Moral relativism is a philosophical failure. The two main arguments for moral relativism—the argument from disagreement and the argument from tolerance—are seriously flawed in numerous ways. Given the failure of moral relativism, we must conclude that objective moral norms do exist. Since they exist, morality cannot be an illusion, and if it is not an illusion, it is either a product of unguided evolution (i.e., chance) or a self-existent mind. We have seen that the second option clearly makes more sense. Thus, the objective moral norms that exist are best explained by a being we call God.

TWO

WHY I BELIEVE TRUTH IS REAL AND KNOWABLE

NORMAN L. GEISLER

T he nature and knowability of truth is crucial to the Christian faith. Christianity claims to possess the objective truth about God and about the way to God through Jesus Christ, the Son of God. If truth is not objective, real, and knowable, then the Christian faith is not only false but fraudulent. Christians hold that God made himself known and knowable through the historical figure of Jesus of Nazareth. This same Jesus claimed to be "the truth" (John 14:6). To see and know him is to see and know the truth, for he perfectly corresponds with truth. So it is that the unequivocal claims of Christianity imply a certain theory of truth, namely, a correspondence view of truth.

THE NATURE OF TRUTH EXAMINED

Truth can be understood both negatively and positively, that is, from what it is and from what it is not. First, a brief discussion about what truth is not.

WHAT TRUTH IS NOT

There are many views of the nature of truth. Most of these result from a confusion between the nature (definition) of truth and a test (defense) of truth, or from not distinguishing the result from the rule.[1]

Truth is not "that which works." One popular theory of truth is the pragmatic view of William James and his followers. According to this view, truth is what works. In William James's words, "Truth is the expedient in the way of knowing." A statement is known to be true if it brings the right results. It is the expedient as confirmed by future experience.[2]

This view is inadequate for several reasons. First, proponents of this theory believe their view is true because it corresponds to the facts, not because it works. But this is a correspondence view of truth, not a pragmatic one.

Further, the pragmatic view of truth confuses cause and effect. If something is true, it will work, at least in the long run. But simply because something works does not make it true. Lies often work, but that does not make them true.

What is more, the pragmatic view is narrow and restrictive. At best it refers to only practical truths, not to theoretical or mathematical truths (e.g., 7+3=10) or to factual truths (e.g., the tree has green leaves), for these are not true because they work but because they correspond to the way things are, whether in the abstract or in the concrete.

In addition, the pragmatic view is not how truth is understood in everyday life nor in court, where knowing the truth is a matter of life and death. No judge would accept the testimony of a person who says, "I swear to tell the expedient, the whole expedient, and nothing but the expedient, so help me future experience!"

Finally, results do not settle the truth question. Even when the results are in, one can still ask whether the initial statement corresponded to the facts. If it did not, then it is not true, no matter what the results were.

Truth is not "that which coheres." Some have proposed that truth is what coheres, or is internally consistent, or has self-consistency. But this is also an inadequate definition of truth for two basic reasons.

For one thing, the very statement "Truth is that which coheres" is offered by the coherentist as a statement that *corresponds* to reality. The coherence theory, therefore, depends on the opposing correspondence view of truth even to express itself. No coherentist wants us to accept his view simply because it coheres but because it is true (i.e., because it correctly represents the state of affairs to which it refers).

Further, empty statements cohere or hang together, even though they are devoid of content, i.e., they do not refer to anything in the real world. For example, "All husbands are married men" is internally consistent, but it is empty. It tells us nothing about reality. The statement would be so even if there were no husbands. It really means, "*If* there is a husband, then he must be married." But it does not inform us that there is a husband anywhere in the universe.

Additionally, a set of false statements can be internally consistent. Such is the case in a conspiracy to lie in court. Finally, at best, coherence is only a negative test of truth. That is, statements are wrong if they are inconsistent but not necessarily true because they are consistent.

Truth is not "that which was intended." Others have suggested that truth is found in intentions, not necessarily in affirmations. That is, a statement is true if the author intends it to be true and false if he does not intend it to be true. But there are also serious difficulties with this position.

For one thing, a proponent of the intentionalist view of truth has to use a correspondence view of truth to express his view. The very statement "The intentionalist view of truth is *true*" is true not because he intended to say it but only if it corresponds to its referent. The word *true* in that very sentence means "correct" or "corresponds" to its referent, otherwise the claim makes no sense.

For another thing, many statements do not agree with the intention of the author. Slips of the tongue occur, and they are often false. But if a statement was true because it was intended to be true, even if it was mistaken, then all such errors would be true. The reverse scenario also presents a problem. Some statements are accidentally uttered (such as Freudian slips), and they are true even though they do not agree with the intention of the speaker.

One final thought can be added. If something is true because someone intended it to be true, then all sincere statements ever uttered would be true— even those that were not correct! Many sincere people have been sincerely wrong. Hence, the intentionalist view of truth is inadequate.

Truth is not "that which is comprehensive." Others claim that truth is found in what is most comprehensive. That is to say, the view that explains the most data is true, while those that are not as comprehensive are not true. However, this theory of truth also falls far short of being a comprehensive definition of truth for several reasons.

First, the very claim that "the comprehensiveness view of truth is *true*" depends for its truth on the correspondence view of truth, for the word *true* in that sentence means that which corresponds to reality or to what is correct.

Second, comprehensiveness is at best only a *test* for truth, not the *definition* of truth. Certainly, a good scientific theory will explain all the relevant data. This is one way the theory can be tested. However, this is only a way to confirm whether something is true, not a way to define what truth is.

Finally, even as a test for truth a view is not necessarily true simply because it is more encyclopedic. If it were, then a comprehensive view of error would be true and a short presentation of truth would be in error.

Truth is not "that which is existentially relevant." Following Søren Kierkegaard[3] and other existential philosophers, some have insisted that truth is what is relevant to our existence or life. Truth is subjectivity, as Kierkegaard put it. As others put it, truth is livable, and it is found in persons, not in propositions. There are a number of problems with this definition of truth.

First, the very statement "Truth is not found in propositions" is itself a propositional truth claim. In other words, it is self-defeating.

Second, many existentialists confuse the *nature* of truth and the *application* of truth. Of course all applicable truth should be applied to one's life. That is, all objective truth should be appropriated subjectively where possible. But this does not mean that truth itself is subjective.

Third, this is too narrow as a definition of all truth. Even if some truth is existential (i.e., is truth about personal existence), not all truth fits into this category. There are many other kinds of truth, including physical, mathematical, historical, and theoretical truths. If truth by its very nature was found only in existential relevance, then none of these could be true. Thus, existential relevance fails as a definition of truth in general.

Finally, what is true will be relevant, but not everything relevant is true. A computer is relevant to an atheist writer, and a gun is relevant to a murderer. But this does not make them true. A truth about life will be relevant to life, but not everything relevant to one's life will be true.

Truth is not "that which feels good." A popular view of truth is that truth is what provides a satisfying feeling, and error is what feels bad. Truth is found in our subjective feelings. Many New Agers hold versions of this as well.[4] However, this view is faulty for several reasons.

For one thing, this view is self-defeating. The claim that "what feels good is *true*" is so only if this corresponds to the way things are. Thus, it depends on a correspondence view of truth to make sense of its claim, for it is claiming that its view of truth is correct only if it corresponds to the facts of the matter, not simply because it feels good.

For another thing, bad news that makes us feel bad can be true, but if what feels good is always true, then this would not be possible. Bad report cards do not make a student feel good, even though they may be true.

What is more, feelings are relative to individuals. What feels good to one person may feel bad to another. If so, then truth would be relative. But all truth cannot be relative. The truth claim that "all truth is relative" is offered as an absolute truth.

Finally, even if truth makes us feel good—at least in the long run—this does not mean that what feels good is true. There is a confusion here of the cart and the horse. The nature of truth is not the same as the result of truth.

WHAT TRUTH IS: CORRESPONDENCE

Now that the nature of truth has been examined, it remains to state the positive view. Truth is found in correspondence. Simply put, truth is what corresponds to its referent. As applied to the world, truth is telling it the way things really are. Truth is "telling it like it is."[5]

Of course, there can be truth about abstract realities as well as actual ones. For example, there are mathematical truths. There are also truths about ideas, such as the ideas in one's mind. But truth is what accurately expresses these states of affairs whatever they may be.

By contrast, falsehood is that which does not correspond to its referent. It does not tell it like it is but like it is not. It is a misrepresentation of the way things are. Statements are false if they are mistaken, even if one intended to say the correct things.

ARGUMENTS FOR A CORRESPONDENCE VIEW OF TRUTH

There are many reasons for supporting a correspondence view of the nature of truth. Consider the following:

First, non-correspondence views are self-defeating. As was shown above, all non-correspondence views of truth imply a correspondence view of truth in their very attempt to deny the correspondence view. For example, the claim that "the non-correspondence view is true" implies that this view corresponds to reality. If so, then the non-correspondence view cannot even express itself without using the correspondence view of truth.

Second, even lies are impossible without a correspondence view of truth. If one's statements need not correspond to the facts in order to be true, then any factually incorrect statement could be true. If this is the case, then even lies become impossible, for if any statement is compatible with any given state of affairs, then all statements can be true and none false.

Third, without correspondence there could be no such thing as truth or falsity. In order to know something is true as opposed to something that is false, there must be a real difference between things and the statements about the things. But this real difference between thought and things is precisely what is entailed in a correspondence view of truth.

Fourth, factual communication would break down without a correspondence view of truth. Factual communication depends on informative statements, but informative statements must be factually true (that is, they must correspond to the facts) in order to inform one correctly. Further, all communication seems to depend ultimately on something being literally or factually true, for we cannot know something (such as a metaphor) is not literally true unless we understand what is literal. If this is the case, it would follow that all communication depends in the final analysis on a correspondence view of truth.

Fifth, even the intentionalist theory of truth depends on the correspondence view. The intentionalist theory claims something is true only if the accomplishments correspond to the intentions. Without correspondence of intentions and accomplished facts there is no truth.

SOME OBJECTIONS TO A CORRESPONDENCE VIEW CONSIDERED

Objections to the correspondence view of truth come from many sources. The major objections include the following:

Objection 1. When Jesus said, "I am the truth" (John 14:6), he demonstrated that truth is personal, not propositional. This falsifies the correspondence view of truth in which truth is a characteristic of propositions (or expressions) and supports the existentialist view.

In response, what Jesus said does not refute the correspondence view of truth. A person can correspond to reality as well as a proposition can. As the exact image of the invisible God (Heb. 1:3), Jesus perfectly corresponds to the Father (John 1:18). He said to Philip, "Anyone who has seen me has seen the Father" (John 14:9). So a person can correspond to another in his character and actions. In this sense, persons can be true or express the truth.

Objection 2. Christians claim that God is truth, yet there is nothing outside himself to which he corresponds. According to the correspondence view, all truth is that which correctly represents reality. Since there is nothing outside God to which he can correspond, it follows that he is not true as the Bible says he is (Rom. 3:4).

In reply, truth as correspondence relates to God in several ways. First of all, God's words correspond to his thoughts, so God is said to be true in the sense that his word can be trusted.

Second, God's thoughts are identical to themselves, which is a kind of perfect correspondence. In this sense, God is true to himself.

Third, if truth is understood as what corresponds to *another*, then in this sense God would not be true. Nevertheless, God is in fact the ultimate reality to which all truth corresponds.

Finally, the basic fallacy in this objection is an equivocal use of the definition. If correspondence means to correspond to something *outside* one's self, then of course God cannot be truth but only that ultimate reality to which all truth must correspond. If, on the other hand, correspondence can also be *inside*, then God can correspond to himself in the most perfect way. In this sense, God is truth in a perfect way by self-identity. Consider the following fallacious thinking: (1) All who submit to the authority of the Pope are Roman Catholic; (2) but the Pope cannot submit to himself; (3) therefore, the Pope is not Roman Catholic. The mistake here is in the second premise. Contrary to the claim, the Pope can submit to himself. He simply has to follow the rules he lays down for all Roman Catholics. Likewise, God can and does live in accord with his own authority, and in this sense he is true to himself and, thus, cannot lie (Heb. 6:18).

In summation, truth may be tested in many ways, but it should be understood in only one way. There may be many different ways to *defend* different truth claims, but there is really only one proper way to *define* truth. The confusion between the nature of truth and the verification of truth is at the heart of the rejection of a correspondence view of truth.

Likewise, there is a difference between what truth *is* and what truth *does*. Truth is *correspondence*, but truth has certain *consequences*. Truth itself should not be confused with its results or with its application. The failure to make this distinction leads to wrong views of the nature of truth. Truth is that which corresponds to its referent, to the state of affairs it purports to describe. Falsehood is what does not correspond.

TWO HURDLES TO KNOWABLE TRUTH

Now that truth is understood as that which corresponds to its objects, there are two major hurdles to jump before we can affirm that truth is knowable: relativism and agnosticism. The former denies there are any absolute truths, and the latter denies that any truth is knowable.

RELATIVISM

Absolute truth stands in contrast to relative truth. *Relative* can mean any one of several things. First, the relativist may claim that some things are true only for some people but not for all. The relativist may also claim that some things are true only for some times but not for all times, or that some things are true only in some places but not in all places. By an *absolute* truth, then, we mean something that would be true for all people, at all times, and in all places.

The relativity of truth is a popular contemporary view. However, truth is not determined by majority vote. Let's take a look at the reasons people give for the belief that truth is relative.

First, some things appear to be true only at some times and not at others. For example, people once believed the world was square. Now we know that is not so. It would seem that this truth has changed with the times. Or has it? Certainly the world did not change from a cube to a sphere. What changed in this regard is our belief, not our earth. Truth did not change; rather, we changed from holding a false belief to holding a true one.

Second, other things appear to be true only for some people but not for others. For example, "I feel warm" may be true for me but not for you. You may feel cold. Isn't this an example of a relative truth? Not at all. Actually, the statement "I (Norman Geisler) feel warm" (said August 1, 2000) is true for everyone in the universe, for it is not true for anyone that Norman Geisler did *not* feel warm on August 1, 2000. In fact, it is not only true for everyone, but it is also true everywhere and at all times that Norman Geisler felt warm on August 1, 2000. It will be true in Moscow, Peking, Washington, and even in outer space that Norman Geisler felt warm on August 1, 2000. If it is true for all people, in all places, at all times, then it is an absolute truth. What at first looked like a relative truth turned out to be an absolute truth.

Let's take another example of a supposed relative truth. If a teacher facing her class says, "The door to this room is on my right," when it is on the left for the students, this truth would seem to be relative to the teacher since it is false for the class. But this is not so. The fact that the door is on the teacher's right is really an absolute truth, for it will never be true for anyone, anywhere, at any time that the door is on the teacher's left. It will always, everywhere, and for everyone be true that the door is on her right. Likewise, the other truth that the door is on the students' left will always be true for everyone everywhere. That is also an absolute truth.

It seems obvious enough that it is hot on the equator but cold at the North Pole. It appears, therefore, that some things are true for some places but not for other places. However, this is not the case. Whatever is true in one place will still be true everywhere else. For example, the statement "It is cold at the North Pole" is also true on the equator. It is true everywhere that "it is cold at the North Pole." Likewise, the statement "It is hot on the equator" is true at the North Pole and everywhere else. Truth is what corresponds to the facts, and the fact is that it is cold at the North Pole and hot at the equator. These truths are true everywhere, for there is nowhere that these statements do not correspond to the facts.

The truth of the matter is that all truth is absolute. There are no relative truths, for if something is true, then it is true everywhere, at all times, and for everyone. After all, 7+3=10 is not true just for mathematics majors. It is true for everyone. And it is true everywhere, not just in math class but in your workplace and in your home too.

Like an old apple, relativism may look good on the surface, but it is rotten at the core. Let's take a look at some of the problems.

Problems with Relativism

Relativism is self-defeating. Most relativists believe relativism is true for everyone, not just for them. But that is the one thing they cannot believe if they are truly relativists, for a relative truth is true for one person but not necessarily for everyone. Therefore, if a relativist thinks relativism is true for everyone, then he really believes it is an absolute truth. Of course, this being the case, he is no longer a relativist, since he believes in at least one absolute truth.

Relativism entails a world full of contradictions. If relativism were true, then the world would be full of contradictory conditions. If something is true for me but false for you, then opposite conditions exist. If I say, "There is milk in the refrigerator," and you say, "There is no milk in the refrigerator," and we are both right, then there must be milk in the refrigerator and no milk in the refrigerator at the same time and in the same sense. But that is impossible. If truth were relative, then the impossible would be actual. In the religious realm it would mean that the theist is telling the truth when he says "God exists" and the atheist is also correct in claiming "God does not exist." But these two statements cannot both be true. If one is true, then the other is false.

Relativism means no one has ever been wrong about anything. If truth is relative, then no one is ever wrong—even when they are. As long as something is true to me, then I am right even when I am wrong. The drawback to this situation is that I can never learn anything, because learning is moving from a false belief to a true one—that is, from an absolutely false belief to an absolutely true one.

Objections to Absolute Truth Considered

Relativists have leveled several objections to the view that truth is absolute. The following are the most important ones.

Some things are relative to others. One objection is that many things are relative to others—like relative sizes such as shorter and taller. As such, they cannot be absolute truths, since they change depending on the object to which they are relative. For example, some people are good compared to Adolf Hitler but evil compared to Mother Teresa.

Contrary to the claim of relativists, relative comparisons do not disprove absolutism. The facts that "John is short in relation to an NBA basketball player" and "John is tall compared to a jockey" are absolutely true for all times and all people. John is in between in size, and it depends on the one to which he is compared as to whether he is short or tall. Nonetheless, it is absolutely true that John (being 5'10") is short compared to Shaquille O'Neal and tall compared to jockey Willie Shoemaker. The same thing is true of other things, such as warmer or colder and better or worse.

No new truth (or progress) is possible. If truth never changes, then there can't be new truth. This would mean that progress is not possible. But we do come to know new truths. That is what scientific discovery is all about. In response to this, "new truth" can be understood in two ways. It might mean "new to us," as with a new discovery in science. But that is only a matter of us discovering an "old" truth. After all, the law of gravity existed long before Newton discovered it. Many truths have always existed, but we are just finding out about them. The other way we might understand "new truth" is that something new has come into existence that makes it possible to make a new statement about it that is only then true for the first time. That's no problem either. When January 1, 2050, arrives, a new truth will exist because it will not be true until that day to say, "This is January 1, 2050." Therefore, "old" truths don't change and neither do "new" truths when the conditions they describe come to pass. Once it is true, it is always true—for everyone everywhere.

Truth changes with our growth in knowledge. Relativists also object that knowledge of truth is absolute since we grow in truth. What is true today may be false tomorrow. The progress of science is proof that truth is constantly changing.

This objection fails to note that it is not truth that is changing but our understanding of it. When science truly progresses, it does not move from an old truth to a new truth but from error to truth. When Copernicus argued that the earth moves around the sun and not the reverse, truth did not change. What changed was our scientific understanding of the earth and the sun.

Absolute truth is too narrow. This objection is common but without basis. Of course truth is narrow. There is only one answer for the equation 4+5. It is not 1. It is not 2. It is not 3. It is not 4, 5, 6, 7, 8, or any other number from 10 to infinity. It is only 9 and nothing else. That's narrow! But it is true.

Non-Christians often complain that Christians are narrow-minded because they claim Christianity is true and all non-Christian systems are false. However, the same is true of non-Christians who claim that their view is true and all opposing beliefs are false. Their position is equally narrow. The truth of the matter is that if C (Christianity) is true, then it follows that all non-C is false. Likewise, if H (say, humanism) is true, then all non-H is false. Both views are equally narrow. That's the way the truth is. Whenever anyone makes a truth claim, he has thereby claimed that whatever opposes it is false. Christianity is no more narrow than any other belief system that claims to be true, whether atheism, agnosticism, skepticism, or pantheism.

Belief in absolute truth is dogmatic. The claim that those who believe in absolute truth are dogmatic misses the point. First, all truth is undeniably absolute, for, as we have seen, if something is true, then it is true for all people, times, and places. In this sense, everyone who claims something is true is "dogmatic." Even the relativist who claims that relativism is true is dogmatic.

Further, something important is overlooked in this charge of dogmatism. There is a big difference between the pejorative charge that belief in absolute truth is dogmatic and the manner in which someone may hold to this belief. No doubt the way in which many absolutists have held to and conveyed their belief in truth has been less than humble. However, no agnostic would consider it a telling argument against agnosticism that some agnostics have been held and communicated their agnosticism in a very dogmatic manner.

How can we know absolutely whether something is true? Many object to the idea that truth is absolute since we do not have an absolute knowledge of truth. Even most absolutists admit that most things are known only in terms of degrees of probability. How, then, can all truth be absolute?

This objection misses the mark for two reasons. First, we can be absolutely sure of some things. I am absolutely sure that I exist. In fact, my existence is undeniable, for I would have to exist in order to make the statement "I do not exist." I am also absolutely sure that I cannot exist and not exist at the same time. And that there are no square circles. And that 3+2=5.

Second, there are, of course, many more things of which I am not absolutely certain. But even here the relativists are misguided in rejecting absolute truth simply because we lack absolute evidence that some things are true. They fail to recognize that the truth can be absolute no matter what our grounds for believing it. For example, if it is true that Sydney, Australia, is on the Pacific Ocean, then it is absolutely true no matter what my evidence or lack of evidence may be. An absolute truth is absolutely true in itself no matter what evidence there is for it. Evidence (or the lack thereof) does not change a fact. And truth is what corresponds to the facts. The truth doesn't change just because we learn something more about it.

Of course, more basic yet is the objection that truth is not knowable at all. We turn now to consider the claims of agnosticism.

Agnosticism

Perhaps the most fundamental objection is that truth is altogether unknowable. This view is called agnosticism. The word comes from two Greek words (*a* meaning "no" and *gnosis* meaning "knowledge"). The term *agnosticism* was coined by T. H. Huxley and means literally "no knowledge." Thus, an agnostic is someone who claims not to know.

Immanuel Kant (an agnostic) was a rationalist until he was "awakened from [his] dogmatic slumbers" by reading David Hume (a skeptic). There is a formal difference between an agnostic and a skeptic. The former says, "I don't (or can't) know." The latter claims, "I doubt if I can know." In actual practice, however, both can be lumped together, since both claim the world is devoid of any sure knowledge of reality.

THE SKEPTICISM OF DAVID HUME

Technically, the views of eighteenth-century philosopher David Hume are "skeptical," but they serve well the agnostic aim. Hume claimed that there are only two kinds of meaningful statements. He wrote:

> If we take in our hands any volume; of divinity or school metaphysics, for instance; let us ask, Does it contain any abstract reasoning concerning quantity or number? No. Does it contain any experimental reasoning concerning matter of fact and existence? No. Commit it then to the flames: for it can contain nothing but sophistry and illusion.[6]

That is, any statement that is neither purely a relation of ideas (definitional or mathematical) on the one hand or a matter of fact (empirical or factual) on the other hand is meaningless. Of course, all statements about God fall outside these categories and, hence, knowledge of God becomes impossible.

Furthermore, all sensations are experienced as "entirely loose and separate." Causal connections are made by the mind only after one has observed a constant conjunction of things in experience. All one really experiences is a series of unconnected and separate sensations. Indeed, there is no direct knowledge even of one's self, for all we know of ourselves is a disconnected bundle of sense impressions. It does make sense of course to speak of connections made only in the mind a priori, or independent of experience. Hence, from experience there are no known and certainly no necessary connections. All matters of experience imply a possible contrary state of affairs.

According to Hume, "All reasoning concerning matters of fact seems to be founded on the relation of *cause and effect*. . . . By means of that relation alone can we go beyond the evidence of our memory and senses."[7] And knowledge of the relation of cause and effect is not a priori but arises entirely from experience. There is always the possibility of the post hoc fallacy, namely, that things happen after other events (even regularly) but are not really caused by them. For example, the sun rises regularly after the rooster crows but certainly not because the rooster crows. One can never know causal connections, and without a knowledge of the cause of this world, for example, one is left in agnosticism about such a supposed God.

Even if one grants that every event has a cause, we cannot be sure what the cause is. Hence, in his famous *Dialogues Concerning Natural Religion*,[8] Hume contends that the cause of the universe may be (1) different from human intelligence since human inventions differ from those of nature; (2) finite, since the effect is finite and one only need infer a cause adequate for the effect; (3) imperfect, since there are imperfections in nature; (4) multiple, for the creation of the world looks more like a long-range trial and error product of many cooperating deities; (5) male and female, since this is how humans generate; and (6) anthropomorphic, with hands, nose, eyes, and so forth, such as his creatures have. Hence, we are left in skepticism about the nature of any supposed cause of the world.

THE AGNOSTICISM OF IMMANUEL KANT

The writings of Hume had a profound influence on the thinking of Immanuel Kant.[9] Before reading them, Kant held a form of rationalism in the tradition of Gottfried Leibniz. Leibniz and Christian Wolfe following him believed reality was rationally knowable and that theism was demonstrable. It was the pen of Kant that put an abrupt end to most of this thinking in the philosophical world.

Kant granted to the rational tradition of Leibniz that there was a rational, a priori dimension to knowledge, namely, the form of all knowledge is independent of experience. On the other hand, Kant agreed with Hume and the empiricists that the content of all knowledge came via the senses. The "stuff" of knowledge is provided by the senses, but the structure of knowledge is attained eventually in the mind. This creative synthesis solved the problem of rationalism and empiricism. However, the unhappy result of this synthesis was agnosticism, for if one cannot know anything until it is structured by the a priori form of sensation (time and space) and the categories of understanding (such as unity and causality), then there is no way to get outside one's own being and know what it really was before he so formed it. That is, a person can know what something is to himself but never what it is in itself. We must remain agnostic about reality. We know that it is there, but we can never know what it is.[10]

Not only is there an unbridgeable gulf between knowing and being, between the categories of our understanding and the nature of reality, but there are also the inevitable contradictions that result once we begin to trespass the boundary line.[11] For example, there is the antinomy of causality. Not every cause can have a cause, or else a series of causes would never begin to cause—which they in fact do. Yet, if everything has a cause, then there cannot be a beginning cause, and the causal series must stretch back infinitely. But it is impossible for the series to be both infinite and also have a beginning. Such is the impossible paradox resulting from the application of the category of causality to reality.

These arguments do not exhaust the agnostic's arsenal, but they do lie at the heart of the contention that God cannot be known. However, even some who are unwilling to admit to the validity of these arguments opt for a more subtle form of agnosticism known as logical positivism. Logical positivists hold that the means whereby we *verify* a proposition determines the meaningfulness of the proposition. If a proposition (e.g., "God exists") cannot be verified (i.e., proven true) either through mathematics or through scientific observation, then the proposition is not simply false but meaningless.[12]

AN EVALUATION OF AGNOSTIC ARGUMENTS

There are two forms of agnosticism:[13] The weak form simply holds that God is unknown, that is, we do not know God. This, of course, leaves the door open that one may know God and indeed that some do know God. As such, this kind of agnosticism poses no threat to Christian theism. The second or strong form of agnosticism claims that God is unknowable, that is, that God cannot be known. Even here one must make an important distinction before embarking on a critique. There is unlimited and limited agnosticism about God. The former claims that God and all reality is completely unknowable. The latter claims only that God is partially unknowable because of the limitations of man's finitude and sinfulness.

This leaves us with three basic alternatives with respect to knowledge about God. First, we can know nothing about God; he is unknowable. Second, we can know everything about God; he is completely and exhaustively knowable. Third, we can know something about God but not everything; he is partially knowable. The first position we will call agnosticism; the second, dogmatism; and the last, realism. In the following critique, we will be concerned with only the complete agnostic who rules out in theory and practice all knowledge of God.

Agnosticism is self-defeating. Complete agnosticism is self-defeating because it reduces to the assertion that "one knows enough about reality in order to affirm that nothing can be known about reality." If one knows something about reality, then he surely cannot affirm in the same breath that all of reality is unknowable. And, of course, if one knows nothing whatsoever about reality, then he has no basis whatsoever for making a statement about reality. It will not suffice to say that his knowledge of reality is purely and completely negative, that is, a knowledge of what reality is not, for every negative presupposes a positive. One cannot meaningfully affirm that something is not "that" if he is totally devoid of a knowledge of the "that." It follows that total agnosticism is self-defeating because it assumes some knowledge about reality in order to deny any knowledge of reality.

Some have attempted to avoid the logic of the above critique by putting their skepticism in the form of a question: "What do I know about reality?" However, this does not avoid the dilemma but merely delays it. This question can and ought to be asked by both agnostic and Christian, but it is the answer that separates the agnostic from the realist. "I can know something about God" differs significantly from "I can know nothing about God." Once the answer is given in the latter form, a self-defeating assertion is made.

Of course, someone may be willing to grant that knowledge about finite reality may be possible but not willing to allow any knowledge about an alleged infinite reality, such as the God of Christian theism. If so, two things should be noted. First, the position is no longer complete agnosticism, for it holds that something can be known about reality. This leaves the door open to whether this reality is finite or infinite, personal or impersonal. Second, the latter discussion takes us beyond the question of agnosticism to the debate between finite godism and theism.[14] Before we take up some of the specific arguments of agnostics, it will be helpful to further illustrate how agnosticism involves a self-defeating assertion.

Reply to Kant's agnosticism. Kant's argument that the categories of thought (such as unity and causality) do not apply to reality is unsuccessful, for unless the categories of reality corresponded to those of the mind, no statements could be made about reality, including that very statement Kant made.[15] That is to say, unless the real world were intelligible, no statement about it would apply. A preformation of the mind to reality is necessary whether one is going to say something positive about it or something negative. We cannot even think that reality is unthinkable. Now, if someone should press the argument that the agnostic need not be making any statement at all about reality but simply defining the necessary limits of what we can know, it can be shown that even this is self-defeating. To say that one cannot know any more than the limits of the phenomena or appearance is to draw an unsurpassable line for those limits. But one cannot draw such firm limits without surpassing them. It is not possible to contend that appearance ends here and reality begins there unless one can see at least some distance on the other side. In other words, how can one know the difference between appearance and reality unless he already knows both so as to make the comparison?

Another self-defeating dimension is implied within Kant's admission that he knows that the noumenon is there but not what it is. Is it possible to know that something *is* without knowing something about *what* it is? Does not all knowledge imply some knowledge of characteristics? Even a strange creature one has never seen before cannot be observed to exist unless it has some recognizable characteristics such as size, color, or movement. One need not know the origin or function of something. However, one must observe something of *what* it is or else he could not know *that* it is. It is not possible to affirm that something *is* without simultaneously declaring something about *what* it is.

AGNOSTICISM AND GOD

Hume denied both the traditional use of causality and analogy as a means of knowing the theistic God. Causality is based on custom and analogy and would lead to either a finite humanlike god or to a totally different God than the God of theism. Let us examine each of these in turn.[16]

In response to Hume, it should be noted first of all that Hume never denied the principle of causality. In fact, he admitted it would be absurd to maintain that things arise without a cause.[17] What he did attempt to deny is that there is any philosophical way of *establishing* the principle of causality. If the causal principle is not a mere analytic relation of ideas but is a belief based on customary conjunction of matter-of-fact events, then there is no necessity in it and one cannot use it with philosophical justification. But we have already seen that dividing all contentful statements into these two classes is self-defeating. Hence, it is possible that the causal principle is both contentful and necessary. In point of fact, the very denial of causal necessity implies some kind of causal necessity in the denial, for unless there is a necessary ground (or cause) for the denial, then the denial does not necessarily stand. And if there is a necessary ground or cause for the denial, then the denial is self-defeating, for in that event it is using a necessary causal connection to deny that there are necessary causal connections.

Some have attempted to avoid the logic of the above objection by limiting necessity to the reality of logic and propositions but denying that necessity applies to reality. But this will not succeed because in order for this statement to accomplish what it intends to do, namely, to exclude necessity from the realm of reality, it must itself be a necessary statement about reality. That is, it must in effect be claiming that it is necessarily true about reality that no necessary statements can be made about reality. It must make a necessary statement about reality to the effect that necessary statements cannot be made of the real. This is clearly self-canceling, for it actually does what it claims cannot be done.

Likewise, there is no way Hume can deny all similarity between the world and God, for this would imply that the creation must be totally dissimilar from its Creator. It would mean that effects must be entirely different from their cause. In actuality this statement too is self-destructive, for unless there were some knowledge of the cause, there would be no basis for denying all similarity with its effect. Comparison, even a negative one, implies some positive knowledge of the terms being compared. Hence, either there is no basis for the affirmation that God must be totally dissimilar or else there can be some knowledge of God in terms of our experience, in which case God is not necessarily totally dissimilar to what we know in our experience.

One should be cautioned here about going beyond the conclusion of these arguments. Once it has been shown that total agnosticism is self-defeating, it does not ipso facto follow that God exists or that one has knowledge of God. These arguments show only that if there is a God, one cannot maintain that he *cannot* be known. From this it follows only that God *can* be known, not that we *do* know anything about God. The disproof of agnosticism is not thereby the proof of realism or theism. In other words, agnosticism only destroys itself and makes it *possible* to build Christian theism. The positive case for Christian knowledge of God must be built later.

Finally, in each of Kant's alleged antinomies there is a fallacy.[18] One does not end in contradictions when one begins to speak about reality in terms of the necessary conditions of human thought. For instance, it is a mistake to view everything as needing a cause, for in this case there would be an infinity of causes and even God would need a cause. Only limited, changing, contingent things need causes. Once one arrives at an unlimited, unchanging, necessary being, there is no longer a need for a cause. The finite must be caused, but the infinite being would be uncaused. Kant's other antinomies are likewise invalid.

THE TRUTH ABOUT TRUTH

Truth is what corresponds to reality. Even those who propose other views of truth assume their view corresponds to reality. Likewise, those who deny the absolute nature of truth do not believe their view is just another relative view. They claim, at least implicitly, that it is absolutely true. In short, total relativism is self-defeating. Relativism of truth cannot be affirmed as truth unless relativism is false, for it is self-defeating to affirm that it is objectively true for all that truth is not objectively true for all. Absolute truth, therefore, is literally undeniable.

Nonetheless, there is an important distinction to keep in mind: Truth is absolute, but our grasp of it is not. Just because there is absolute truth does not mean that our understanding of it is absolute. This fact in itself should cause the absolutist to temper his convictions with humility. As finite creatures, we grow in our understanding of truth.

Nonetheless, it is self-defeating to claim that no truth about reality is knowable, for this very claim is offered as truth about reality. In the end, truth is undeniably real, objective, and knowable. Any view to the contrary must assume that this is true in order to state its self-defeating claims.

PART 2

WHY
I BELIEVE
IN GOD

M ost of the world's people believe in some sort of supreme being. Now, we all know that majority vote is a poor way to determine truth. A majority of people once thought the earth was flat, slavery was acceptable, and the Rams could never win the Super Bowl. So the fact that approximately 90 percent of the world now believes in God means little in terms of proving his existence. On the other hand, the fact that this 90 percent figure seems to have held true for several millennia does carry some weight. How could it be that the overwhelming majority of all people who have ever lived have been mistaken about what is certainly one of the most important questions in the universe? Billions of people have lived in this world, this universe, and it is the rare exception who, after looking around, and looking inside, concludes that this is all a colossal accident.

To be sure, Darwin made the colossal accident thesis more viable. Evolution appears to many to provide a plausible mechanism for producing all that we see. But given Darwinism's overwhelming acceptance in the scientific community, indeed, in popular culture, why then do we not have more atheists among us?

The fact is that it takes some real effort to deny God's existence. Disbelief, like a bodybuilder's frame, does not come naturally. Dr. J. Budziszewski once practiced the intellectual and existential gymnastics required to obtain an atheistic physique. He now maintains his well-being by the more natural exercise of simply walking in the truth. He tells in chapter 3 why he is no longer an atheist.

Forgive us, for we have been ignoring many of you, those who believe in God but are highly skeptical that his existence can be proven. Many have changed their views on this issue after reading some of the works of Dr. William Lane Craig and Dr. Norman L. Geisler. The presentations that follow are not intellectual tricks; they are sound arguments based on observational facts and sound logic. Please keep in mind that neither contributor will suggest that by one's intellect alone a person can know God or in any sense embrace true religion. Faith is foremost, but at the same time it is not mindless. If Christianity is true, it cannot contradict logic, and it must withstand legitimate intellectual inquiry. If no sound arguments could be made for the existence of God, this would certainly be a valid basis for doubting the Christian faith. But good arguments do exist. In chapter 4, Dr. Craig presents some fresh approaches to the classic arguments for the existence of God. Dr. Geisler, in chapter 5, then demonstrates why the God who exists is one and the same with the God described in the Bible.

THREE

WHY I AM NOT AN ATHEIST

J. BUDZISZEWSKI

Because another contribution to this book is titled "Why I Believe God Exists," it may seem redundant to have a chapter titled "Why I Am Not an Atheist." After all, any reason to believe in God's existence is also a reason not to disbelieve in him. But there is no duplication, for one must also consider the point of view. For some years after deserting the Christian faith of my youth, I was an atheist, so I know the matter from the inside.

Of course, inside knowledge is not always superior to outside knowledge. Sometimes it is even inferior to it. A drug addict does not understand his addiction better than his doctor does, for he is in the grip of it. Nor do we recommend suicide for the better understanding of self-inflicted death; understanding and consciousness depart together. The self-understanding of the atheist has a drawback of much the same kind as the self-understanding of the addict or the person attempting suicide. Like the former, the atheist is self-deceived; like the latter, he cuts himself off from the means of understanding.

This blindness has become visible to me only in retrospect. I am not an atheist simply but a repented atheist. It is not from the experience of having been an atheist that I claim to understand something of atheism but from the experience of ceasing to be one. I have acquired an outside view of my inside knowledge.

Having disposed of one difficulty—why this chapter was written at all—I must now dispose of another. Although there are good and compelling reasons to believe in God, it was not from an account of these reasons that I began to believe in him. In fact, it was not until several years after my conversion that I was able to give a rational account of it at all. Why was that? The reason is simple. Every doctrine rests on certain first principles that cannot themselves be proven, because they are the means by which we prove and disprove everything else. Granted the first principles, it is easy to explain how one has reached new conclusions. But if it is the first principles themselves that one has reached, then by what route could one have arrived at them? To what deeper considerations could one have appealed? Was the decision, in the end, merely arbitrary? These questions have answers, but to develop them I must depend on the same inside-outside knowledge I mentioned before.

And so this chapter must be largely autobiographical, but it is not a conventional personal testimony.[1] My aim is not so much to tell my story as to present an analytical reconstruction of that story with a view toward illustrating why atheism is not a good idea. I speak of "illustrating" the point because behind every instance of atheism is a different story. My own self-deception was more extreme than most, yet at the bottom of all atheism is self-deception.

If you are an atheist, I hope you are not offended by this claim. It would distract us from the question of whether the claim is true. I can honestly say that when I was an atheist, I was not offended by what Christians thought of me. I merely considered them mistaken. Plainly, if they were right, then I was as foolish as they believed. Conversely, if I was right, then they were the foolish ones. The only question worth discussing is who is right.

I had best start by explaining what I mean by self-deception. First, though, let me say that I am not trying to prove the reality of God by calling atheists self-deceived. I am not trying to prove his reality at all, though proofs aplenty may be found elsewhere in this book. Some good reasons to believe in him appear in this chapter too, but they are merely incidental to it. Rather than trying to prove the reality of God, I simply recognize his reality and tell the story from the perspective of that recognition.

Self-deception means playing dumb. It means pretending to ourselves that we don't know what we really do; it means playing at being ignorant though we are really in the know. I suggest that we human beings play dumb with God. We lie to ourselves, and one of the things we lie about is our knowledge of his reality. Psalm 14 opens with a remark that is often misunderstood: "The fool says in his heart 'There is no God.'" The psalmist is not calling the man a fool for *thinking* there is no God but for *telling* himself there is no God, though deep in his mind he knows better. Unbelievers do not disbelieve, they reject.

Paul expresses the same view in the first chapter of his letter to the Romans.

For the wrath of God is revealed from heaven against all ungodliness and wickedness of men who by their wickedness suppress the truth. For what can be known about God is plain to them, because God has shown it to them. Ever since the creation of the world his invisible nature, namely, his eternal power and deity, has been clearly perceived in the things that have been made. So they are without excuse; for although they knew God they did not honor him as God or give thanks to him, but they became futile in their thinking and their senseless minds were darkened.

vv. 18–21 RSV

I am not at present concerned to explore Paul's general claim that those who deny the Creator are wicked but only his more particular claim that they are intellectually dishonest. Notice that he does not criticize nonbelievers because they do not know about God but ought to. Rather, he criticizes them because they *do* know about God but pretend to themselves that they don't. According to his account, we are not ignorant of God's reality at all. Rather, we "suppress" it; to translate differently, we "hold it down." With all our strength we try *not* to know it, even though we can't help knowing it; with one part of our minds we do know it, while with another we say, "I know no such thing." From the biblical point of view, then, the reason it is so difficult to argue with an atheist—as I once was—is that he is not being honest with himself. He knows there is a God, but he tells himself that he doesn't.

We have in this passage the beginning of the answers to the questions I posed in the opening paragraphs. How can a person explain how he reached new first principles? By what route could he have arrived at them? To what deeper considerations could he have appealed? If the biblical account is true, then it would seem that no one really arrives at new first principles; a person only seems to arrive at them. The atheist does not lack true first principles; they are in his knowledge already, though suppressed. The convert from atheism did not acquire them; rather, things he knew all along were unearthed.

If this is so, then the purported first principles of atheistic systems of thought are not what they appear; they are merely a covering for deeper knowledge the atheist is trying to keep from acknowledging. We might also expect that an atheist's effort to hold down what he "can't not know" would be only partially successful. Here and there, flotsam from the sunken knowledge would bob back up to the surface. Some of this flotsam might be incorporated into his system of thought—and, in fact, from these incorporated bits of flotsam would flow all the plausibility that his system of thought might possess. For example, the atheist might seek to affirm the moral law while denying God. The fact that he affirms one of the things he can't not know would make his denial of another of the things he can't not know more palatable. I'll call this sort of thing a "plausibility gambit."

The point is that everyone knows certain things to begin with, including the reality of God. This is the only reason plausibility gambits are needed in the first place, because on the face of it, denying what we really know is implausible in the extreme. For these reasons, an adequate explanation of conversion to belief in God must be not an explanation of how the convert acquired new first principles but of how he came to be honest with himself, of how he came to admit the first principles he already knew.

Before turning to my own story, I must briefly consider a possible objection to what I have said about self-deception. Can't it be turned on its head? In fact, don't some atheists turn it on its head, holding that believers are the ones who are self-deceived? How are we to judge this claim?

The test is forensic. If one coroner says, "There has been foul play," and another replies, "No, there hasn't," then to find out which one is correct we must look more closely at the body. In the same way, if a Christian says, "You are deceiving yourself," and an atheist says, "No, you are," then to know which is correct we must look more closely at their respective belief systems. We then ask about each person, "Where we find incoherencies in belief, which of the following best explains the incoherencies: the person is trying to gain truth, or the person is trying to evade it?" In this essay, I use this very question to consider the way I thought during my own atheist days.

THE PROBLEM WITH "PLAUSIBILITY GAMBITS"

I spoke above of the "plausibility gambits" that an atheist employs to make palatable his rejection of truths that he in fact knows are true. Such gambits have two great disadvantages. The first is that they do not bear close examination; the second is that they slip from one's control, taking on a life of their own.

To illustrate the first disadvantage, consider the plausibility gambit I mentioned earlier—affirming the moral law while denying God. One reason it does not bear close examination is because every law presupposes a lawgiver. How then can I affirm the moral law while denying God? Of course, sophisticated replies may be given to this question, for a good many contemporary moral thinkers regard morality as something other than real law. For instance, James Q. Wilson, author of the book *The Moral Sense*, makes it a central premise of his theory that morality is not about laws or rules but about "sentiments."[2] Yet over and over he slips back into the language of laws and rules—even to explain what he means by a "sentiment" in the first place.[3] The atheist faces similar difficulties.

The second disadvantage needs more explanation. Atheistic plausibility gambits slip from one's control because, at bottom, they are lies, and the universe is so tightly constructed that in order to cover up one lie, we must usually tell another. This applies with just as much force to the lies we tell ourselves as to the lies we tell other people. Deception begets deception, and self-deception begets more self-deception. For example, because of the difficulty of affirming the moral law while denying the moral lawgiver, I may just have to deny morality as well. Of course, that is not the only possible lie, but it is one of the most common.

Suppose I do use this gambit, and I deny morality (the very problem addressed in chapter 1 by Dr. Beckwith). Are my difficulties over? Far from it. My new position, that there is neither law *nor* lawgiver, is more self-consistent (and in that respect more plausible), but it is even farther from what everyone really knows (and in that respect less plausible). Not only that, but without either God *or* the moral law, my life is likely to become more and more disordered and, hence, more and more marked by pain. This too poses problems of plausibility, which prompt still more gambits, which produce still more problems. And so it goes. My atheistic life provides an example of this loss of control; eventually I denied not only God but the very distinction between good and evil.

Not many people disbelieve in God and then begin to sin; most atheists adopt some favorite sin and then find reasons to disbelieve in God. In this common sequence of intellectual events, an individual does not begin by denying God or even by denying the moral law. Rather, he begins by denying a *part* of the moral law, perhaps even a *single* moral law. Perhaps he denies only the precept of chastity—that sex is a privilege of a marital union. Perhaps he denies only the precept of fidelity—that vows are to be kept. Perhaps he denies only the precept of filial reverence—that parents are to be held in respect. Or perhaps he denies only the precept of justice—that one must not seek unfair advantage.

One eventually loses control of the "no to just a part" gambit because it is impossible to reject just a part of the moral law. To affirm that the unitive and procreative power of sexuality may be used outside matrimony is to deny a great many things about human nature besides. To affirm that a vow may be broken is to call into question the very idea of personal responsibility. To deny to one's parents their due respect is to reject the chain of obligation that links all generations. To maintain that one may seek unfair advantage is to unleash the gods of the jungle.

One may try to forestall these consequences by monkeying around with the meanings of "matrimony," "vows," "respect," or "fairness," but monkeying with meanings carries consequences too. To keep these consequences from swamping the rest of one's knowledge, one may build dikes between this thought and that, but dividing the mind is a radical deed that also has consequences. The very means by which we limit the flood causes flood; denial spills, it slops, it spreads. Eventually it may reach the knowledge of God—as it did with me. Because the plausibility gambit by which an individual protected his favorite sin has slipped out of his control, he now needs new gambits to fortify his disbelief in God.

MY VERSION OF PRACTICAL ATHEISM

Atheists come in several kinds. I was not a "theoretical" but a "practical" atheist. In other words, I didn't claim that I could prove there was no God;

I understood the near impossibility of proving a universal negative. In this sense, I conceded that there could be a God, and when the mood struck me, I called myself only an agnostic. But I did not think there were any good reasons to believe that God *did* exist, and I lived as though he did not.

Here again we meet an incoherency. My pretense, when the agnostic mood struck me, was that we cannot know anything about God or his existence. Now, there is a great difficulty in dogmatically asserting God's unknowability. To say that we cannot know anything about God is to say something about God; it is to say that if there is a God, he is unknowable. But in that case, he is not *entirely* unknowable, for the agnostic certainly thinks that we can know one thing about him: That nothing *else* can be known about him.

Unfortunately, the position that we can know exactly one thing about God—his unknowability in all respects except this—is equally insupportable, for why should this one thing be an exception? How could we *know* that any possible God would be of such a nature that nothing else could be known about him? On what basis could we rule out his knowability in all other respects but this one?

The very attempt to justify the claim confutes it, for the agnostic would have to know a great many things about God in order to know that he couldn't know anything else about him. In fact, doesn't he actually have a rather elaborate picture of God in his mind, full of all sorts of colorful details that render God either impossible, or unknowable, except for the colorful details themselves?

Details like what? First, the agnostic must suppose that any possible God is infinitely remote—because otherwise he couldn't be so sure that he couldn't know anything else about him. Second, the agnostic must suppose that any possible God is either powerless to make himself known, unwilling to make himself known, or unconcerned about whether he is known or not—because otherwise he would have provided the means for the agnostic to know him. Third, the agnostic must suppose that any possible God is completely unlike the biblical portrayal of him—because in that account, God is anything but remote. He desires to be known, he has already provided the means for the agnostic to know him, and in fact, the agnostic does know him.

You see why I prefer the term "practical atheist," for the so-called agnostic has a theology after all. In his theology, the heavenly Father is like so many absentee fathers of our own generation. He isn't there, he doesn't care, or he's impotent.

My own practical atheism focused on the first and third prongs of the doctrinal fork—that he isn't there or he's impotent. I began by asserting the same dilemma about myself, and then argued that God must be in the same boat. I was either not there or impotent. If to deny God's reality I had to deny my own, so be it. As in the proverb, I would cut off my nose to spite my face. My thinking went something like this.

First, I insisted that if the principle of causality is true, then the chain of causes and effects is an unbreakable fetter. It followed that free will must be nonsense. It would be useless to say, as the Stoics did, that what happens is foreordained but that I am free to choose my attitude toward it; my attitude would itself be foreordained. Nor would it make a difference whether causality were probabilistic or deterministic; the outcome of a coin toss is as adamant as fate, if it rules me.

Of course, this understanding of causality was completely mechanical. It amounted to treating myself—and everything else—as a machine. My mind, I supposed, was nothing more than an activity of my brain, my brain nothing more than a computational device. Of course, we do not experience ourselves as machines, but I told myself that we are machines under a double curse—the illusion of being more than machines and the desire for the illusion to be true.

How a machine could suffer such things as desires and illusions deeply troubled me. In fact, all of the phenomena of consciousness troubled me. I was troubled by the redness of red, the deliberateness of choice, the preciousness of my loves, the sense I sometimes had of exerting my will against an inclination—I was even troubled by the experience of being troubled. I knew that I could not fit these things inside the theory that I was a machine, and I knew that the intuition that I was more than a machine made a better fit with reality. To get around this fact, I told myself that a machine is something that I know, whereas a soul is something that I do not know—conveniently forgetting that I experience myself, unlike machines, directly. *What* it is that I experience when I experience myself is the question, and I was begging it. I had reached my conclusions not because of the data but in spite of it.

If I was in the grip of a blind causality, it followed that whether I thought something, did something, or felt something, I was merely executing a program. To be sure, it must be an "open" program because it could be reset by experience, but I was responsible neither for the experiences (for they just came) nor the programming (for I came with it). Psychologists might quarrel over whether nature or nurture was more important to the determination of behavior, but the argument seemed pointless; however such causes might interact, they would remain causes, with everything about me merely their effect. I had no free will, no personal responsibility, no self. All those things were part of the illusion. What I called "I" did not produce my activity; it was its product. In a sense, I thought, I did not exist.

Having asserted that the dilemma "he isn't there or he's impotent" applied to myself, it was but a short step to apply it to God. If God existed at all, then he couldn't escape what I called causality any more than I could. He was no more free than I.

That fact, I thought, showed that he was like me in another way too. If I had no free will, then I was no more responsible for what I believed than for what I did; I believed what I believed, not because I recognized its concordance with reality but because it was cranked out by a mental mechanism over which I had no control. To be sure, that mental mechanism may have evolved to accomplish certain functions, but there was no reason to think that arriving at the truth of things would be one of them; unlike narrower intellectual capacities, such as finding food or outwitting predators, such a capacity would make no contribution to its own survival.

And so, I thought, I was really in the dark about everything—and the same must be true of God. He too must be in the dark about everything. How could he make himself known if he did not even know himself? You see where this reasoning led me: Although I could not quite prove the nonexistence of God, I thought I could prove the nonexistence of a God who mattered. I pictured God as the blinded monarch in *King Lear*, helpless, raving, a pawn to fatalities he did not understand. It was not Satan who was frozen in the ice at the center of hell, as Dante would have it; it was God.

There were two great holes in this argument about the irrelevance of God. The first is that in order to attack free will, I supposed that I understood cause and effect; I supposed causation to be less mysterious than volition.

If anything, it is the other way around. I can perceive a logical connection between premises and valid conclusions. I can perceive at least a rational connection between my willing to do something and my doing it. But between the apple and the earth, I can perceive no connection at all. Why does the apple fall? We don't know. "But there is gravity," you say. No, "gravity" is merely the name of the phenomenon, not its explanation. "But there are *laws* of gravity," you say. No, the "laws" are not its explanation either; they are merely a more precise description of the thing to be explained, which remains as mysterious as before. For just this reason, philosophers of science shy away from the term *laws;* they prefer "lawlike regularities." To call the equations of gravity "laws" and speak of the apple as "obeying" them is to speak as though, like traffic laws, the "laws" of gravity are addressed to rational agents capable of conforming their wills to the command. This is cheating, because it makes mechanical causality (the more opaque of the two phenomena) seem like volition (the less). In my own way of thinking, the cheating was even graver, because I attacked the less opaque in the name of the more.

The other hole in my reasoning was cruder. If my imprisonment in a blind causality made my reasoning so unreliable that I couldn't trust my beliefs, then by the same token I shouldn't have trusted my beliefs about imprisonment in a blind causality. But in that case, I had no business denying free will in the first place.

Granted these ragged flaws in my reasoning, what made a mechanical picture of the universe so attractive in the first place? The answer is not simple. At one level, the explanation is that I had been strongly influenced by the mythology of our age that confuses scientific rationality with materialism or physicalism—with the view that matter is all there is. If that were true, then there *couldn't* be such things as minds, moral law, or God, could there? After all, none of those are matter.

Let us be clear what is at stake in materialism. "Matter alone" has always been a difficult slogan to swallow. If matter is the pure potentiality to receive form, as Aristotle thought, then at least, besides matter, there must be form.

56

The formula of the ancient materialists, who disagreed with him, was that the universe is nothing but particles of matter in motion. But this presupposed that matter moves, so there must be space and time in which the matter can move. Viewed another way, all matter has spatial and temporal properties—and numerical ones too, because "particles" denotes more than one. But in that case (to use Aristotle's language) the forms of space, time, and number are built into matter already; it is not a *pure* potentiality after all.

The materiality of matter has been even further compromised in our day. Once upon a time, materialists insisted that there is no such thing as action at a distance; to affect each other, particles must touch. It has been a long time since materialists gave up that battle. Today they routinely concede the reality of "forces" such as magnetism, a concession that by ancient standards means they are not materialists at all. It gets worse. Biological materialists speak of a genetic "code" that carries "information," and these concepts are plainly semantic. According to one standard interpretation of quantum mechanics, the theory cannot even be formulated without reference to conscious observers—observers who cannot be consistently explained within the system because the system itself depends on them.

It seems that these days materialism can concede anything a person wants it to—except the existence of God. Excluding him, which critics always suspected was materialism's main point, now seems to be its only one.

But such a materialism is self-destructing. Is nothing beyond matter real? When considering that not even the properties of matter are matter, it becomes difficult to believe in matter, and so it became for me. I realized that in my fondness for this self-destructing theory, I had committed yet another incoherency. Did I then reject it? Not in the way you would expect. I concluded that reality itself was incoherent and that I was pretty clever to have figured this out—even more so, because in an incoherent world, figuring didn't make sense either. I decided that the philosophy of what is real is a blanket too small for the sleeper. Too cold in one place, he shifts the blanket to cover a part of himself, only to expose another part. He can never get warm everywhere at once. If he reduces everything to matter, he leaves mind in the cold; if to mind, he leaves will in the cold; if to will, he leaves matter in the cold.

It never occurred to me to ask why my philosophy had to be reductionist in the first place—why I couldn't accept the equally basic existence of matter, mind, will, and any other realities that might cross my path. In retrospect, I know the answer. Matter, mind, and will require explanation. There must be a reason why there is something rather than nothing. Just beyond the passage I quoted earlier, in which Paul explains that nonbelievers are not ignorant of the truth about God but suppress it, he says that they exchange the truth for a lie, worshiping and serving the creature rather than the Creator. That was what I wanted. I was looking for something *within* the created order to which I could plausibly attribute the creative power that belongs only to God.

The materialistic mythology of the day did not make me an idolater; I was that already. It only offered me an idol. I used the idol of matter until it broke, and then made an idol of the breakage. Did nothing make sense? Then I would make an idol of nothing.

THE IDOL OF SELF

Though a million idols are adored by the sons of men, in the end there is only one—the million idols are all masks for the idol of self. Finding that we are made in God's image, we worship the image in place of God.

Our own time is unusual in that people tend to adore the self openly, according to its proper name. As a best-selling New Age writer recommends, "Let each person in relationship worry about *Self*—what *Self* is being, doing, and having; what *Self* is wanting, asking, giving; what *Self* is seeking, creating, experiencing. . . . Let each person in relationship worry not about the other, but only, only, only about Self."[4] The classical pattern, however, is to disguise the adoration of self under the adoration of some reflection or representative. The idol reason, beloved of the Enlightenment, is the self as represented by its rational powers; the idol Priapus, as represented by its animal powers; the idol duty, as represented by its moral powers; and the gods race and nation, as reflected in the group.

My idolatries of matter and nothing followed the classical rather than the New Age pattern. I did not consciously think "I shall adore myself"; nevertheless, the real significance of my idolatries was that they seemed to annihilate God so that I could be God. This explanation of their significance may seem unbelievable, for my road to deicide was through suicide—in order to annihilate God, I had to annihilate myself. The solution to the paradox is that we misunderstand what suicide is about.

Killing oneself is not an act of supreme self-resignation, as we suppose it to be, but of extreme self-assertion. G. K. Chesterton put it best:

> The man who kills a man, kills a man. The man who kills himself, kills all men; as far as he is concerned he wipes out the world. His act is worse (symbolically considered) than any rape or dynamite outrage. For it destroys all buildings: it insults all women. The thief is satisfied with diamonds; but the suicide is not: that is his crime. He cannot be bribed, even by the blazing stones of the Celestial City. . . . There is a meaning in burying the suicide apart—for it makes even crimes impossible.[5]

God may have called everything into being, but the person who commits suicide imagines that he can make it all go away. My suicide was just like that, but more violent still. A conventional suicide can destroy the universe only once, but for me each day was suicide. There was no need to bother with the taking of poison or the slashing of wrists, because it was all going on in my mind. In one long, interminable prolongation of nightfall, the light went out and went out and went out, all without the inconvenience of physical death.

Besides, to commit suicide *was* to commit deicide, symbolically. I said above that self-adoration is the worship of the image of God in the place of God. So strong was my own wish to replace him that I resented even his image in me. Visualize a man opening up the access panels of his mind and pulling out all the components that have God's initials on them. The problem is that they all have God's initials on them, so the man can never stop. No matter how much he pulls out, there is still more to remove. I was that man.

Because I pulled out more and more, there was less and less that I could think about. But because there was less and less that I could think about, I thought I was becoming more and more focused. Because I believed things that filled me with dread, I thought I was smarter and braver than the people who didn't believe them. I thought I saw an emptiness at the heart of the universe that was hidden from their gauzy eyes.

Nietzsche too had thought like this. This prophet of the "death of God" had written that given the meaninglessness of things, nothing was left but to laugh or be silent. Pop culture transcribes the two attitudes as that of the cool and the tough. The cool say that meaning is a drag and they prefer the world to be pointless. The tough say that meaning is indispensable—but they are brave enough to dispense with it.

Unfortunately for Nietzsche, he failed to carry his premises to their conclusions. He never seemed to recognize that both attitudes are poses. The cool don't really like life to be pointless; they seek meaning in seeming to like it that way. Nor can the tough really live without meaning; they seek it in the idea of being brave. For the former, the problem is that in a pointless life, being cool is as pointless as everything else; for the latter, the problem is that there is nothing to be brave about.

I thought I had outdone my master, for my fancy was that I carried his premises to their conclusions. Here in the void, I thought, not even laughter or silence are left. One has no reason to do or not do anything at all. This is a terrible thing to believe, but like Nietzsche, I imagined myself one of the few who had the strength to believe it—who could walk the rocky heights where the air is thin and cold. Which merely shows that I had not outdone him at all, that I too was adopting a pose. It was a bluff.

FROM ATHEISM TO FAITH

How then did I become undeceived? Not because anyone called my bluff. When I told the faculty of the University of Texas that there is no rationally knowable difference between good and evil and that we aren't responsible for our deeds anyway, they gave me a job teaching the young.

Nor was it through recognition of my own incoherence. I saw the holes in my arguments even at the time but covered them over with elaborate nonsense such as the need to take an ironic view of reality.

Nor through love. I loved my wife and children, but it is difficult to keep up a commitment to the true good of another person when one denies the reality of good, denies the reality of persons, and denies that his commitments are in his control.

Nor through learning. When I taught my students the theology of law of Thomas Aquinas, I wanted to weep for the beauty of the appearance of the truth. But I told myself that the very poignancy of that beauty came only from the fact that it was an illusion.

Nor even through the agony I had brought upon myself. "Truly . . . affliction is a treasure, and scarce any man hath enough of it," says John Donne, but such treasure was wasted on me. The greater the pain, the more it fed my pride. To be sure, there was a grain of justification in my stubbornness, because pain as such is not a logical argument; its usefulness lies not in proving things true or false but in moving us to reconsider. But supposing pain a refutation was not my temptation. Mine was supposing it a proof.

I did pray to God one night. I told him that I thought I was talking to the wall. I said that if he existed, he could have me, but he would have to show me because I couldn't tell. As the minutes ticked past, the wall looked more and more like a wall, and I felt a fool.

Yet he did hear my prayer. I came, months later, to feel a greater and greater horror about myself, not exactly a feeling of guilt, nor of shame, nor of inadequacy—just horror: an overpowering true intuition that my condition was objectively evil. I could not have told *why* my condition was horrible; I only perceived that it was. It was as though a man noticed one afternoon that the sky is blue, when for years he had considered it red.

Nothing like this had ever happened to me before, and I could not explain it. The intuition of the objective evil of my condition appeared as though from nowhere and contradicted everything I had been telling myself. I experienced it not as an inference but as direct knowledge. It had authority, commanding assent—and I assented. Though I did not know it at the time, it was what John's Gospel calls the conviction of sin. I believe that the Holy Spirit, in answer to my prayer, had been secretly cutting a door in the stone wall of my self-deception.

Augustine argued that although evil is real, it is derivative; the concept of a "pure" evil makes no sense, because the only way to get a bad thing is to take a good thing and ruin it. This does not make evil less horrible; it is *how* evil is horrible. Evil is a parasite on good. I had always considered this a neat piece of reasoning, with a defective premise. Granted the horrible, there had to exist a wonderful of which the horrible was the perversion. But I did not grant the horrible.

Now all that had changed. I had to grant the horrible; it was right behind my eyes. If there was evil, then there must be good, though I did not know what it was. The significance of this fact was not that it gave me a great deal of knowledge but that it humbled my mental censors.

I began to realize not only that my errors had been total but that they had not been errors at all, merely lies. Years earlier, when I had deserted the faith of my youth, I thought I had done so for good reasons. Yet search my memory as I might, I could not remember any. Had I forgotten them? On the contrary, as the days went by, I was *unforgetting* more and more of my past. I had never had good reasons to desert my faith. My desertion had taken place first; my reasons, as I called them, had been cooked up afterward. One after another, various pieces of repressed knowledge reasserted themselves: the good of this, the evil of that, the reality and goodness of God.

The final step of my recovery was the restoration of faith in Christ, for there is more to Christianity than mere theism, much more to faith in the Son than belief in the Father. The recognition that I had never had good reason to lose my faith was not enough to restore it; I also needed reason to return to it.

Did I then reason my way back to the Savior? No, and this used to puzzle me. Some years passed before I understood how this final step took place. It had been through misuse of intellect that I had deserted him; therefore, in his mercy, God chose a means of restoration that humbled my intellectual pride.

I do not mean that my restoration was against reason. On the contrary, what happened was a reinstatement of the good reasons for faith that I had possessed before. I had, after all, been a well-instructed Christian, and it had not been for ignorance of the grounds of faith that I had thrown them all away. Now, by the grace of God, I remembered them—and I recognized that their force was unimpaired.

My story is extreme. Yet in the essentials, I think my atheism was like all atheism. Not every atheist deceives himself about the same things, or as many things, or to the same degree as I deceived myself, yet there is no atheism without self-deception. There is a way to honesty, but it leads through Jesus Christ.

FOUR

WHY I BELIEVE GOD EXISTS

WILLIAM LANE CRAIG

W estern philosophy, observes James Collins, has carried the burden of God.[1] From the first glimmerings of philosophy among the ancient Greeks through the dawn of the third millennium after Christ, the world's greatest thinkers from Plato to Plantinga have wrestled with the question of God. Is there a personal, transcendent being who created the universe and is the source of moral goodness? I think there is and that there are good reasons to think so.

GOD MAKES SENSE OF THE ORIGIN OF THE UNIVERSE

Have you ever asked yourself where the universe came from? Why everything exists instead of nothing? Typically, atheists have said that the universe is just eternal, and that's all. But surely this is unreasonable. If the universe never had a beginning, that means the number of past events in the history of the universe is infinite. But mathematicians recognize that the idea of an infinite number of things leads to self-contradictions. For example, what is infinity minus infinity? Mathematically, you get self-contradictory answers. If you subtract all the odd numbers 1, 3, 5, . . . from all the natural numbers 0, 1, 2, 3, . . . , how many numbers do you have left? An infinite number. So infinity minus infinity is infinity. But suppose instead you subtract all the numbers greater than 2—how many are left? Three. So infinity minus infinity is 3! It needs to be understood that in both of these cases we have subtracted identical quantities from identical quantities and come up with self-contradictory answers. In fact, you can get any answer you want from zero to infinity! This shows that infinity is just an idea in one's mind, not something that exists in reality. David Hilbert, perhaps the greatest mathematician of this century, states, "The infinite is nowhere to be found in reality. It neither exists in nature nor provides a legitimate basis for rational thought. The role that remains for the infinite to play is solely that of an idea."[2] Therefore, since past events are not just ideas but are real, the number of past events must be finite. Therefore, the series of past events can't go back forever; rather, the universe at some point must have begun to exist.

This conclusion has been confirmed by remarkable discoveries in astronomy and astrophysics. The astrophysical evidence indicates that the universe began to exist in a great explosion called the big bang around fifteen billion years ago. Physical space and time were created in that event, as well as all the matter and energy in the universe. Therefore, as Cambridge astronomer Fred Hoyle points out, the big bang theory requires the creation of the universe from nothing. This is because, as one goes back in time, he reaches a point at which, in Hoyle's words, the universe was "shrunk down to nothing at all."[3] Thus, what the big bang model requires is that the universe began to exist and was created out of nothing.

This tends to be very awkward for the atheist, for as Anthony Kenny of Oxford University urges, "A proponent of the big bang theory, at least if he is an atheist, must believe that the . . . universe came from nothing and by nothing."[4] But surely that doesn't make sense. Out of nothing, nothing comes. In every other context, atheists recognize this fact. The great skeptic David Hume wrote, "But allow me to tell you that I never asserted so absurd a Proposition as that *anything might arise without a cause*."[5] The contemporary atheist philosopher Kai Nielsen gives this illustration: "Suppose you suddenly hear a loud bang . . . and you ask me, 'What made that bang?' and I reply, 'Nothing, it just happened.' You would not accept that. In fact you would find my reply quite unintelligible."[6] But what's true of the little bang must be true of the big bang as well. So why does the universe exist instead of just nothing? Where did it come from? There must have been a cause that brought the universe into being. As the great scientist Sir Arthur Eddington said, "The beginning seems to present insuperable difficulties unless we agree to look on it as frankly supernatural."[7]

We can summarize the argument thus far as follows:

1. Whatever begins to exist has a cause.
2. The universe began to exist.
3. Therefore, the universe has a cause.

Given the truth of the first two premises, the third necessarily follows.

From the very nature of the case, as the cause of space and time, this supernatural cause must be an uncaused, changeless, timeless, and immaterial being that created the universe. The being must be uncaused because we've seen that there cannot be an infinite regress of causes. It must be timeless and therefore changeless because it created time. Because it also created space, it must transcend space as well and therefore be immaterial, not physical.

Moreover, I would argue, it must also be personal, for how else could a timeless cause give rise to a temporal effect such as the universe? If the cause were a mechanically operating set of necessary and sufficient conditions, then the cause could never exist without the effect. For example, water freezes because the temperature (the cause) is below 0°C. If the temperature were below 0° from eternity past, then any water that was around would be frozen from eternity. It would be impossible for the water to *begin* to freeze just a finite time ago. So if the cause is timelessly present, then the effect should be timelessly present as well. The only way for the cause to be timeless and the effect to begin in time is for the cause to be a personal agent who freely chooses to create an effect in time without any prior determining conditions. For example, a man sitting from eternity could freely will to stand up. Thus, we are brought not merely to a transcendent cause of the universe but to its personal Creator.

What objections might be raised against this argument? Premise 1: The fact that whatever begins to exist has a cause seems obviously true—at least more so than its denial. Yet a number of atheists, in order to avoid the argument's conclusion, deny the first premise. Some say that subatomic physics furnishes an exception to premise 1, since on the subatomic level events are said to be uncaused. In the same way, certain theories of cosmic origins are interpreted as showing that the entire universe could have sprung into being out of the subatomic vacuum.

This objection, however, is based on misunderstandings. In the first place, not all scientists agree that subatomic events are uncaused. A great many physicists today are quite dissatisfied with this view (the so-called Copenhagen Interpretation) of subatomic physics and are exploring deterministic theories such as that of David Bohm.[8] Thus, subatomic physics is not a proven exception to premise 1. Second, even according to the traditional, indeterministic interpretation, particles do not come into being out of nothing. They arise as spontaneous fluctuations of the energy contained in the subatomic vacuum; they do not come from nothing.[9] Third, the same point can be made about theories of the origin of the universe out of a primordial vacuum.[10] Popular magazines touting such a theory as getting "something from nothing" simply do not understand that the vacuum is not nothing; it is a sea of fluctuating energy endowed with a rich structure and subject to physical laws. Philosopher of science Robert Deltete accurately sums up the situation: "There is no basis in ordinary quantum theory for the claim that the universe itself is uncaused, much less for the claim that it sprang into being uncaused from literally nothing."[11]

Other atheists have said that premise 1 is true for things *in* the universe, but it is not true *of* the universe itself. But this objection misconstrues the nature of the premise. Premise 1 does not state merely a physical law such as the law of gravity or the laws of thermodynamics, which are valid for things within the universe. Premise 1 is not a physical principle. Rather, premise 1 is a metaphysical principle, a principle about the very nature of reality: Being cannot come from nonbeing; something cannot come into existence uncaused from nothing. The principle therefore applies to all reality. It is thus metaphysically absurd that the universe should pop into being uncaused out of nothing. Even J. L. Mackie, one of the most prominent atheists of our day, admitted that he found such an idea incredible, commenting, "I myself find it hard to accept the notion of self-creation *from nothing*, even given unrestricted chance. And how *can* this be given, if there really is nothing?"[12] According to the atheistic view, the *potentiality* of the universe's existence didn't even exist prior to the big bang, since nothing is prior to the big bang. But then how could the universe become actual if there wasn't even the potentiality of its existence? It makes much more sense to say that the potentiality of the universe lay in the power of God to create it.

So what about premise 2: The universe began to exist? The typical objection raised against the philosophical argument for the universe's beginning is that modern mathematical set theory proves that an actual infinite number of things can exist. For example, there is an infinite number of members in the set {0, 1, 2, 3, . . . }. Therefore, there's no problem with an infinite number of past events.

But this objection does not work. First, not all mathematicians agree that actual infinities exist even in the mathematical realm.[13] They regard series such as 0, 1, 2, 3, . . . as merely *potentially* infinite; that is to say, such series approach infinity as a limit, but they never actually get there. Second, existence in the mathematical realm does not imply existence in the real world. To say that infinite sets exist is merely to postulate a realm of discourse, governed by certain axioms and rules that are simply presupposed, in which one can talk about such collections.[14] Given the axioms and rules, one can discourse consistently about infinite sets. But that's no guarantee that the axioms and rules are true or that an infinite number of things can exist in the real world. Third, the real existence of an infinite number of things would violate the rules of infinite set theory. As we saw, trying to subtract infinite quantities leads to self-contradictions; therefore, infinite set theory just prohibits such operations to preserve consistency. In the real world, however, there's nothing to keep us from breaking this arbitrary rule. If I had an infinite number of marbles, I could subtract or divide them as I please.

Sometimes it's said that we can find counter examples to the claim that an infinite number of things cannot exist, so this claim must be false. For instance, isn't every finite distance capable of being divided into 1/2, 1/4, 1/8, . . . on to infinity? Doesn't that prove that in any finite distance there is an infinite number of parts? The fallacy of this objection is that it once again confuses a potential infinite with an actual infinite. You can continue to divide any distance for as long as you want, but such a series is merely potentially infinite; infinity serves as a limit you endlessly approach but never reach. If you assume that any distance is *already* composed of an infinite number of parts, then you're begging the question. You're assuming what the objector is supposed to prove, namely, that there is a clear counterexample to the claim that an infinite number of things cannot exist.

As for the scientific confirmation of premise 2, it has been the overwhelming verdict of the scientific community that no theory is more probable than the big bang theory. The devil is in the details, and once you get down to specifics, you find that there is no mathematically consistent model that has been so successful in its predictions or as corroborated by the evidence as the traditional big bang theory. For example, some theories, such as the oscillating universe (which expands and re-contracts forever) or the chaotic inflationary universe (which continually spawns new universes), have a potentially infinite future but turn out to have only a finite past.[15] Vacuum fluctuation universe theories (which postulate an eternal vacuum out of which our universe was born) cannot explain why, if the vacuum was eternal, we do not observe an infinitely old universe.[16] The quantum gravity universe theory propounded by the famous physicist Stephen Hawking, if interpreted realistically, still involves an absolute origin of the universe even if the universe does not begin in a so-called singularity, as it does in the standard big bang theory.[17] In sum, according to Hawking, "Almost everyone now believes that the universe, and *time itself*, had a beginning at the Big Bang."[18]

In light of the evidence, premises 1 and 2 seem more plausible than their denials. Hence, it is plausible that a transcendent Creator of the universe exists. People sometimes resist this conclusion because they claim that it is a pseudo-explanation of the origin of the universe. "Just because we can't explain it doesn't mean God did it," they protest. But such a response misconstrues the argument. In the first place, this argument is a deductive argument. Therefore, if the premises are true and the logic is valid, the conclusion follows, period. It doesn't matter if it's explanatory or not. The conclusion is entailed by the premises, so you can't object to the conclusion once you have granted the premises. Moreover, in no place does the argument postulate God to plug up a gap in our scientific knowledge. The scientific evidence is used only to confirm the truth of premise 2, which is a religiously neutral statement that can be found in any textbook on astronomy. God's existence is implied only by the conjunction of premise 1 with premise 2. Finally, the hypothesis of God is, in fact, genuinely explanatory, though it is not a scientific but a personal explanation.[19] It explains some effect in terms of an agent and his intentions. We employ such explanations all the time.

For example, if you were to come into the kitchen and find the kettle boiling and ask me, "Why is the kettle boiling?" I might give you an explanation in terms of the kinetic energy communicated to the water by the flame by means of the heat-conducting metal used in the manufacture of the kettle, which causes the molecules of the water in the kettle to vibrate faster and faster until they are thrown off in the form of steam. Or I might say, "I put it on to make a cup of tea!" Both are equally legitimate explanations, and in many contexts, only a personal explanation will do. In the case of cosmic origins, as Oxford philosopher Richard Swinburne points out, there *cannot* be a scientific explanation of a first state of the universe, since there is nothing before it. Therefore, if a personal explanation does not exist, then there is simply no explanation at all—which is metaphysically absurd, since on that account the universe just popped into being uncaused out of nothing.

Other atheists have charged that the argument's conclusion is incoherent, since a cause must come before its effect, and there is no moment before the big bang. This objection, however, is easy to answer. Many causes and effects are simultaneous. Thus, the moment of God's causing the big bang is the moment of the occurrence of the big bang. We can then say that God existed alone without the universe before the big bang, not in physical time but in an undifferentiated metaphysical time, or that he is strictly timeless and entered into time at the moment of creation. No incoherence has been shown in either of these alternatives.

But people will say, "But if the universe must have a cause, then what is God's cause?" This question reveals an inattentiveness to the formulation of the argument. The first premise does not state, whatever *exists* has a cause, but rather, whatever *begins to exist* has a cause. The difference is important. The insight that lies at the root of premise 1 is that being cannot come from nonbeing, something cannot come from nothing. God, since he never began to exist, would not require a cause, for he never came into being. This is not a special pleading for God, since this is exactly what the atheist has always claimed about the universe: that it is eternal and uncaused. The problem is that the atheist's claim is now rendered untenable in light of the beginning of the universe.

Finally, someone might wonder, "But isn't God supposed to be infinite? Your argument shows that the infinite cannot exist. So how can God exist?" In fact, the argument was that an infinite number of things cannot exist. God is not a collection of an infinite number of things. As a nonphysical being, he doesn't even have parts. When theologians speak of God's infinity, they are thus using the term in a *qualitative* not a *quantitative* sense. They mean that God is absolutely holy, uncreated, self-existent, all-powerful, all-present, and so forth. It's not a mathematical concept. Thus, there's no contradiction.

In sum, we have a powerful reason based on the origin of the universe to believe that an uncaused, changeless, timeless, immaterial, personal Creator of the universe exists.

GOD MAKES SENSE OF THE COMPLEX ORDER IN THE UNIVERSE

During the last thirty years or so, scientists have discovered that the existence of intelligent life depends on a complex and delicate balance of initial conditions given in the big bang itself. Scientists once believed that whatever the initial conditions of the universe, eventually intelligent life might evolve. But we now know that our existence is balanced on a knife's edge. It seems vastly more probable that a life-prohibiting universe rather than a life-permitting universe such as ours should exist. The existence of intelligent life depends on a conspiracy of initial conditions that must be fine-tuned to a degree that is literally incomprehensible and incalculable. For example, Stephen Hawking has estimated that if the rate of the universe's expansion one second after the big bang had been smaller by even one part in a hundred thousand million million, the universe would have re-collapsed into a hot fireball.[20] British physicist P. C. W. Davies has calculated that the odds against the initial conditions being suitable for later star formation (without which planets could not exist) is one followed by a thousand billion billion zeroes, at least.[21] He also estimates that a change in the strength of gravity or of the weak force by only one part in 10,100 would have prevented a life-permitting universe. Roger Penrose of Oxford University has calculated that the odds of the big bang's low entropy condition existing by chance are on the order of one out of $10^{10(123)}$.[22] There are around fifty such quantities and constants present in the big bang that must be fine-tuned in this way if the universe is to permit life. And it's not just each quantity that must be finely tuned; their ratios to one another must be also finely tuned. Therefore, improbability is added to improbability to improbability until our minds are reeling in incomprehensible numbers. (For a more thorough presentation of the fine-tuning evidenced in nature and the improbability of our universe's appearance, as it is, by chance, see chapter 8 of this book by Hugh Ross.)

Three possibilities exist for explaining the presence of this remarkable fine-tuning of the universe: natural law, chance, or design. The first alternative holds that the fine-tuning of the universe is physically necessary. There is some unknown theory that would explain the way the universe is. It had to be the way it is, and there was really no chance or little chance of the universe not being life-permitting. By contrast, the second alternative states that the fine-tuning is due entirely to chance. It's just an accident that the universe is life-permitting, and we're the lucky beneficiaries. The third alternative rejects both of these accounts in favor of an intelligent mind behind the cosmos who designed the universe to permit life. Which of these alternatives is the most plausible?

On the face of it, the first alternative seems extraordinarily implausible. It requires us to believe that a life-*prohibiting* universe is virtually physically impossible. But surely it does seem possible. If the matter and antimatter had been differently proportioned, if the universe had expanded just a little more slowly, if the entropy of the universe were slightly greater—any of these adjustments and more would have prevented a life-permitting universe, yet all seem perfectly possible physically. The person who maintains that the universe must be life-permitting is taking a radical line that requires strong proof. But there is none; this alternative is simply put forward as a bare possibility.

Moreover, there is good reason to reject this alternative. First, there are models of the universe that are different from the existing universe. As John Leslie explains:

> The claim that blind necessity is involved—that universes whose laws or constants are slightly different "aren't real physical possibilities" . . . is eroded by the various physical theories, particularly theories of random symmetry breaking, which show how a varied ensemble of universes might be generated.[23]

If, as Leslie suggests, subatomic indeterminacy (or uncausedness) is real, then it must be possible for the universe to be different, since a number of physical variables depend on subatomic processes that are random in nature.

Second, even if the laws of nature were necessary, one would still have to supply initial conditions. As P. C. W. Davies states:

> Even if the laws of physics were unique, it doesn't follow that the physical universe itself is unique. . . . The laws of physics must be augmented by cosmic initial conditions. . . . There is nothing in present ideas about "laws of initial conditions" remotely to suggest that their consistency with the laws of physics would imply uniqueness. Far from it. . . .
> It seems, then, that the physical universe does not have to be the way it is: it could have been otherwise.[24]

The extraordinarily low entropy condition of the early universe would be a good example of an arbitrary quantity that seems to have been put in at the creation as an initial condition. We really do not know how much certain constants and quantities could have varied from their actual values, but this admitted uncertainty becomes less important when the number of the variables to be fine-tuned is high. For example, the chances of all fifty known variables being finely tuned, even if each variable has a 50 percent chance of being its actual value, is less than 3 out of 10^{17}.

Finally, if there is a single, physically possible universe, then the existence of this incredibly complex world-machine might be itself powerful evidence that a designer exists. Some theorists call the hypothesis that the universe must be life-permitting "the Strong Anthropic Principle," and it is often taken as indicative of God's existence. As physicists Barrow and Tipler write in their Anthropic Cosmological Principle, "The Strong Anthropic Principle . . . has strong teleological overtones. This type of notion was extensively discussed in past centuries and was bound up with the question of evidence for a Deity."[25] Thus, the first alternative is not plausible to begin with and is perhaps indicative of design.

What about the second alternative, that the fine-tuning of the universe is due to chance? The problem with this alternative is that the odds against it are so incomprehensibly great that they cannot be reasonably faced. Students or laymen who blithely assert that "it could have happened by chance" simply have no conception of the fantastic precision of the fine-tuning requisite for life. They would never embrace such a hypothesis in any other area of their lives. For example, they would not use such a hypothesis to explain how there came to be a car in one's driveway.

But it's important to understand that the probability is not the only thing at stake here. After all, fantastically improbable events happen every day. Your own existence, for example, is the result of an incredibly improbable union of a certain sperm and a certain egg, yet no one would infer that their union was therefore designed. Rather, what is at stake in eliminating the hypothesis of chance is what theorists call "specified probability": the demonstration that the event in question is not only improbable but also conforms to an independently discovered pattern.[26] Any sequence of letters hammered out by a chimpanzee seated at a typewriter is equally improbable. If we find that the chimpanzee has typed a beautiful sonnet, however, then we know this is not the result of blind chance, since the sonnet conforms to the independently given pattern of grammatical English sentences. In the same way, physics and biology tell us independently of any knowledge of the early conditions of the universe what physical conditions are requisite for life. We then discover how incredibly improbable such conditions are. It is this combination of a specified pattern plus improbability that serves to render the chance hypothesis implausible.

With this in mind, we can immediately see the fallacy of those who say that the existence of any universe is equally improbable, and therefore, there is nothing here to be explained. It is not the improbability of some universe or other's existing that concerns us; rather, it is the specified probability of a life-permitting universe's existence that is at issue. Thus, the proper analogy to the fine-tuning of the universe is not, as defenders of the chance hypothesis often suppose, a lottery in which any individual's winning is fantastically and equally improbable but which some individual has to win. Rather, the analogy is a lottery in which a single white ball is mixed into a billion black balls, and you are asked to reach in and pull out a ball. Any ball you pick will be equally improbable; nevertheless, it is overwhelmingly more probable that whichever ball you pick, it will be black rather than white. Similarly, the existence of any particular universe is equally improbable, but it is incomprehensibly more probable that whichever universe exists, it will be life-prohibiting rather than life-permitting. It is the enormous, specified improbability of the fine-tuning that presents the hurdle for the chance hypothesis.

How can the atheist get over this hurdle? Some thinkers have argued that we really shouldn't be surprised at the finely tuned conditions of the universe, for if the universe were no‹t fine-tuned, then we wouldn't be here to be surprised about it! Given that we are here, we should expect the universe to be fine-tuned. But such reasoning is logically fallacious. The statement "We shouldn't be surprised that we do not observe conditions of the universe incompatible with our existence" is true. If the conditions of the universe were incompatible with our existence, we couldn't be here to observe them. So it's not surprising that we don't observe such conditions. But from that statement it does not logically follow that "we shouldn't be surprised that we *do* observe conditions of the universe that *are* compatible with our existence." Given the incredible improbability of such finely tuned conditions, it is surprising that we observe them.

John Leslie provides an analogy to illustrate the fallacy of the objector's reasoning. Imagine you are traveling abroad, and you are arrested on trumped-up drug charges and dragged in front of a firing squad of one hundred trained marksmen, all with rifles aimed at your heart. You hear the command, "Ready! Aim! Fire!" and then the deafening roar of the guns. And then you observe that you are still alive, that *all* one hundred trained marksmen missed! What would you conclude? "I guess I really shouldn't be surprised that they all missed. After all, if they hadn't all missed, then I wouldn't be here to be surprised about it! Given that I am here, I should expect them all to miss." Of course not! You would immediately suspect that they all missed on purpose, that the whole thing was a setup, engineered for some reason by someone. You wouldn't be surprised that you do not observe that you are dead (since if you were dead, you wouldn't be there to observe it), but you would be quite rightly surprised that you do observe that you are alive (in view of the enormous improbability of all the marksmen missing). You wouldn't just write off your survival to chance.

Theorists who defend the alternative of chance have therefore been forced to adopt an extraordinary hypothesis: the many worlds hypothesis. According to this hypothesis, our universe is but one member of a greater collection of universes, all of which are real, actually existing universes, not merely possible universes. In order to ensure that somewhere in the world ensemble there will appear by chance a universe finely tuned for life, it is further stipulated that there are an infinite number of universes in the collection (so that every possibility will be realized) and that the physical constants and quantities are randomly ordered (so that the worlds are not all alike). Thus, somewhere in this world ensemble there will appear by chance alone finely tuned universes such as ours. We should not be surprised to observe finely tuned conditions, since observers like us exist only in those universes that are finely tuned.

The very fact that detractors of the design hypothesis have to resort to such a remarkable hypothesis underlines the point made earlier: Fine-tuning is not explicable in terms of natural law alone or in terms of sheer chance in the absence of a world ensemble. The many worlds hypothesis is a sort of back-handed compliment to the design hypothesis in its recognition that the fine-tuning cries out for explanation. But is the many worlds hypothesis as plausible as the design hypothesis?

It seems not. In the first place, the many worlds hypothesis is no more scientific, and no less metaphysical, than the hypothesis of a cosmic designer. As the scientist-theologian John Polkinghorne says, "People try to trick out a 'many universe' account in sort of pseudo-scientific terms, but that is pseudo-science. It is a metaphysical guess that there might be many universes with different laws and circumstances."[27] But as a metaphysical hypothesis, the many worlds hypothesis is arguably inferior to the design hypothesis because the design hypothesis is simpler. According to a principle known as Ockham's razor, we should not multiply causes beyond what is necessary to explain the effect. It is simpler to postulate one cosmic designer to explain our universe than to postulate the infinitely bloated collection of universes required by the many worlds hypothesis. Therefore, the design hypothesis is preferred.

Second, there is no known way for generating a world ensemble. No one has been able to explain how or why such a collection of universes could or should exist. Moreover, the attempts that have been made require fine-tuning themselves. For example, although some cosmologists appeal to so-called inflationary theories of the universe to generate a world ensemble, the only consistent inflationary model is Linde's chaotic inflationary theory, and it requires fine-tuning to start the inflation. As Robert Brandenburger of Brown University writes, "Linde's scenario does not address a crucial problem, namely the cosmological constant problem. The field which drives inflation in Linde's scenario is expected to generate an unacceptably large cosmological constant *which must be tuned to zero by hand*. This is a problem which plagues *all* inflationary universe models."[28]

Third, there is no evidence for the existence of a world ensemble apart from the fine-tuning itself. But the fine-tuning is equally evidence for a cosmic designer. Indeed, the hypothesis of a cosmic designer is again the better explanation because we have independent evidence of the existence of such a designer in the form of the other arguments for the existence of God.

Fourth, the many worlds hypothesis is guilty of what probability theorists call "multiplying one's probabilistic resources without warrant," that is to say, arbitrarily assuming that one has more chances than it appears just to increase the odds of getting some result. If we're allowed to do that, *anything* can be explained away. For example, a cardplayer who gets four aces every time he deals could explain this away by saying that there are an infinite number of universes with poker games going on in them, and therefore, in some of them someone always by chance gets four aces every time he deals, and—lucky me!—we just happen to be in one of those universes. This sort of arbitrary multiplying of one's probabilistic resources would render rational conduct impossible.

Thus, the many worlds hypothesis collapses and along with it the alternative of chance, which it sought to rescue. Both the natural law alternative and the chance alternative are therefore implausible.

We can summarize this second argument as follows:

1. The fine-tuning of the universe is due to either law, chance, or design.
2. It is not due to law or chance.
3. Therefore, it is due to design.

What objections might be raised to the alternative of design? According to this hypothesis, a cosmic designer exists who fine-tuned the initial conditions of the universe for intelligent life. Such a hypothesis supplies a personal explanation of the fine-tuning of the universe. Is this explanation implausible?

Detractors of design sometimes object that the designer himself remains unexplained. It is said that an intelligent mind also exhibits complex order, so that if the universe needs an explanation, so does its designer. If the designer does not need an explanation, why does the universe?

This popular objection is based on a misconception of the nature of explanation. It is widely recognized that in order for an explanation to be the best explanation, one needn't have an explanation of the explanation (indeed, such a requirement would generate an infinite regress, so that everything becomes inexplicable). If the best explanation of a disease is a previously unknown virus, doctors need not be able to explain the virus in order to know it caused the disease. If archaeologists determine that the best explanation of certain artifacts is a lost tribe of ancient people, the archaeologists needn't be able to explain the origin of the people in order to say justifiably that they produced the artifacts. If astronauts should find traces of intelligent life on some other planet, we need not be able to explain such extraterrestrials in order to recognize that they are the best explanation. In the same way, believing that the design hypothesis is the best explanation of the fine-tuning doesn't depend on our ability to explain the designer.

Moreover, the complexity in a mind is not really analogous to the complexity of the universe. A mind's *ideas* may be complex, but a mind itself is a remarkably simple thing, being an immaterial entity not composed of parts. Moreover, a mind, in order to be a mind, must have certain properties such as intelligence, consciousness, and volition. These are not contingent properties that it might lack but are essential to its nature. Therefore, it is difficult to see any analogy between the contingently complex universe and a mind. Detractors of design have evidently confused a mind's thoughts (which may be complex) with the mind itself (which is fairly simple). Postulating an uncreated mind behind the cosmos is thus not at all like postulating an undesigned cosmos.

Some people object to design by pointing to examples of alleged design that we regard as evil or hurtful. For example, a deadly bacterium or a tapeworm is a complex entity, but how could we ascribe such creatures to a divine designer?

This objection is simply irrelevant to the design hypothesis, which says nothing about the moral qualities of the cosmic designer. A bacterium or even a single flagellum (not to speak of a tapeworm) is so fantastically complex an organism that it cannot be explained in terms of natural law and chance alone.[29] What their existence appears to call into question is not the need of a designer but the goodness or benevolence of the designer. That is an issue for the next argument we shall consider, the moral argument. To think moral considerations call into question the hypothesis of design would be to say that thumbscrews or a torture rack does not require the existence of an intelligent designer!

Thus, the design hypothesis does not share in the implausibility of its competitors and is a familiar sort of explanation we employ every day. It is, therefore, the best explanation of the amazing fine-tuning of our universe.

God Makes Sense of Objective Moral Values in the World

If God does not exist, then objective moral values do not exist. When I speak of *objective* moral values, I mean moral values that are valid and binding whether anybody believes in them or not. Thus, to say, for example, that the Holocaust was objectively wrong is to say that it was wrong even though the Nazis who carried it out thought it was right and that it would still have been wrong even if the Nazis had won World War II and succeeded in exterminating or brainwashing everyone who disagreed with them. Now, if God does not exist, then moral values are not objective in this way.

Many theists and atheists alike concur on this point. For example, Bertrand Russell observed:

> Ethics arises from the pressures of the community on the individual. Man . . . does not always instinctively feel the desires which are useful to his herd. The herd, being anxious that the individual should act in its interests, has invented various devices for causing the individual's interest to be in harmony with that of the herd. One of these . . . is morality.[30]

Michael Ruse, a philosopher of science at the University of Guelph, agrees. He explains:

> Morality is a biological adaptation no less than are hands and feet and teeth. Considered as a rationally justifiable set of claims about an objective something,

ethics is illusory. I appreciate that when somebody says "Love thy neighbor as thyself," they think they are referring above and beyond themselves. Nevertheless, such reference is truly without foundation. Morality is just an aid to survival and reproduction . . . and any deeper meaning is illusory.[31]

Friedrich Nietzsche, the great atheist of the last century who proclaimed the death of God, understood that the death of God meant the destruction of all meaning and value in life.

But we must be very careful here. The question here is not, "Must we believe in God in order to live moral lives?" I'm not claiming that we must. Nor is the question, "Can we *recognize* objective moral values without believing in God?" I think that we can. Nor is the question, "Can we formulate an adequate system of ethics without reference to God?" So long as we assume that human beings have objective moral value, the atheist could probably draft a moral code with which the theist would largely agree.

Rather, the question is, "If God does not exist, do objective moral values exist?" Like Russell and Ruse, I don't see any reason to think that in the absence of God, the herd morality evolved by *Homo sapiens* is objective. After all, if there is no God, then what's so special about human beings? They're just accidental by-products of nature that have evolved relatively recently on an infinitesimal speck of dust lost somewhere in a hostile and mindless universe and that are doomed to perish individually and collectively in a relatively short time. According to the atheistic view, an action such as rape may not be socially advantageous, and so in the course of human development has become taboo, but such a view does absolutely nothing to prove that rape is really wrong. It follows, therefore, that there's nothing wrong with your raping someone. Thus, without God there is no absolute right and wrong that imposes itself on our conscience.

But the problem (as Francis Beckwith explains in chapter 1) is that objective values *do* exist, and deep down we all know it. There's no more reason to deny the objective reality of moral values than the objective reality of the physical world. As John Healey, the executive director of Amnesty International wrote in a fund-raising letter, "I am writing you today because I think you share my profound belief that there are indeed some moral absolutes. When it comes to torture, to government-sanctioned murder, to 'disappearances'—there are no lesser evils. These are outrages against all of us."[32] Actions such as rape and child abuse aren't just socially unacceptable behavior—they're moral abominations. Some things are really wrong. Similarly, love, equality, and self-sacrifice are really good. But if moral values cannot exist without God and moral values do exist, then it follows logically and inescapably that God exists.

We can summarize this argument as follows:

1. If God does not exist, objective moral values do not exist.
2. Objective moral values do exist.
3. Therefore, God exists.

Again, let us consider possible objections that might be raised against this argument. Some atheist philosophers, unwilling to bite the bullet and affirm that acts such as rape or the torture of a child are morally neutral actions, have tried to affirm objective moral values in the absence of God, thus in effect denying premise 1. Let's call this alternative atheistic moral realism. Atheistic moral realists affirm that moral values and duties do exist in reality and are not dependent on evolution or human opinion, but they insist that they are also not grounded in God. Indeed, moral values have no further foundation. They just exist.

I must confess that this alternative strikes me as incomprehensible, an example of trying to have your cake and eat it too. What does it mean to say, for example, that the moral value justice just exists? I understand what it is for a person to be just, but I draw a complete blank when it is said that, in the absence of any people, justice itself exists. Moral values seem to exist as properties of persons, not as abstractions—or at any rate, I don't know what it means for a moral value to exist as an abstraction. Atheistic moral realists, seeming to lack any adequate foundation in reality for moral values, just leave them floating in an unintelligible way.

Second, the nature of moral duty or obligation seems incompatible with atheistic moral realism. Let's suppose for the sake of argument that moral values do exist independently of God. Suppose that values such as mercy, justice, love, forbearance, and the like just exist. How does that result in any moral obligations for me? Why would I have a moral duty, say, to be merciful? Who or what lays such an obligation on me? As the ethicist Richard Taylor points out, "A duty is something that is owed. . . . But something can be owed only to some person or persons. There can be no such thing as duty in isolation."[33] God makes sense of moral obligation because his commands constitute for us our moral duties. Taylor writes:

> Our moral obligations can . . . be understood as those that are imposed by God. . . . But what if this higher-than-human lawgiver is no longer taken into account? Does the concept of a moral obligation . . . still make sense? . . . The concept of moral obligation [is] unintelligible apart from the idea of God. The words remain but their meaning is gone.[34]

As a nontheist, Taylor, therefore, thinks that we literally have no moral obligations, that there is no right or wrong. The atheistic moral realist rightly finds this abhorrent, but, as Taylor clearly sees, according to an atheistic view there simply is no ground for duty, even if moral values somehow exist.

Third, it is fantastically improbable that just the sort of creatures would emerge from the blind evolutionary process who correspond to the abstractly existing realm of moral values. This would be an utterly incredible coincidence. It is almost as though the moral realm *knew* that we were coming. It is far more plausible that both the natural realm and the moral realm are under the hegemony or authority of a divine designer and lawgiver than to think that these two entirely independent orders of reality just happened to mesh.

Thus, it seems to me that atheistic moral realism is not a plausible view but is basically a halfway house for philosophers who don't have the stomach for the moral nihilism or meaninglessness that their own atheism implies.

What, then, about premise 2: Objective moral values do exist? Some people, as we have seen, deny that objective moral values exist. I agree with them that *if* there is no God, then moral values are just the products of sociobiological evolution or expressions of personal taste. But I see no reason to believe that is the case. Those who think so seem to commit the genetic fallacy, which is an attempt to invalidate something by showing how it originated. For example, a socialist who tried to refute your belief in democratic government by saying, "The only reason you believe in democracy is that you were raised in a democratic society!" would be guilty of the genetic fallacy. Even if it were true that your belief is the result of cultural conditioning, that does absolutely nothing to show that your belief is false (think of people who have been culturally conditioned to believe that the earth is round!). The truth of an idea is not dependent on how that idea originated. It's the same with moral values. If moral values are *discovered* rather than *invented*, then our gradual and fallible apprehension of the moral realm no more undermines the objective reality of that realm than our gradual, fallible apprehension of the physical world undermines the objective reality of the physical realm. We know objective moral values exist because we clearly apprehend some of them. The best way to show this is simply to describe moral situations in which we clearly see right and wrong: the abuse of a child, incest, rape, ethnic cleansing, racism, witch burning, the Inquisition, and so forth. If someone fails to see the objective moral truth about such matters, then he is simply morally handicapped, like a color-blind person who cannot tell the difference between red and green, and there's no reason to think that his impairment should make us call into question what we see clearly.

From the truth of the two premises, the conclusion follows logically that, therefore, God exists. Many atheists have objected to basing moral values in God. Frequently a dilemma known as the Euthyphro Argument is presented: Either something is good because God commands it or else God commands something because it is good. If you say something is good because God commands it, this makes right and wrong arbitrary; God could have commanded that acts of hatred, brutality, cruelty, and so on be good, and then we would be morally obligated to do such things, which seems crazy. On the other hand, if God commands something because it is good, then the good is independent of God after all. Thus, morality can't be based on God's commands.

Plato himself saw the solution to this objection: You split the horns of the dilemma by formulating a third alternative, namely, God *is* the good. The good is the moral nature of God himself. That is to say, God is necessarily holy, loving, kind, just, and so on, and these attributes of God comprise the good. God's moral character expresses itself toward us in the form of certain commandments, which become for us our moral duties. Hence, God's commandments are not arbitrary but necessarily flow from his own nature. They are necessary expressions of the way God is.

The atheist might press, "But why think that God's nature constitutes the good?" In one sense, the answer to that question is that there just isn't anything else available. There has to be some explanatory ultimate, some stopping point, and we've seen that without God there are no objective moral values. Therefore, if there are objective moral values, they cannot be based in anything but God! In addition, however, God's nature is an appropriate stopping point for the standard of goodness, for by definition, God is a being who is worthy of worship. When you think about what it means to worship someone, then it is evident that only a being who is the embodiment of all moral goodness is worthy to be worshiped.

Thus, God makes sense of ethics in a way that atheism cannot. In addition to the metaphysical and scientific arguments for God, therefore, we have a powerful moral argument for God. This moral argument also helps to solve the problem raised by the design argument concerning the moral character of the designer of the universe. We now see that moral evil in the world does not disprove God's goodness; on the contrary, it actually *proves* it. We may argue:

1. If God does not exist, objective moral values do not exist.
2. Evil exists.
3. Therefore, objective moral values exist (some things are truly evil).
4. Therefore, God exists.

Thus, evil paradoxically helps to prove God's existence, since without God things would not be good or evil. Notice that this argument shows the compatibility of God and evil without giving a clue as to *why* God permits evil. That is a separate question that is addressed in chapter 14 by John S. Feinberg and has been addressed by many other theologians.[35] But even in the absence of an answer to the why question, the present argument proves that evil does not call into question but actually requires God's existence.

We thus have good grounds for believing in the existence of an all-good, uncaused, timeless, changeless, immaterial, personal creator and designer of the universe, which is what most people mean by "God." But what about people who lack the education, resources, or time to comprehend these sometimes abstruse reasons for the existence of God? Can they know that God exists wholly apart from arguments? I'm persuaded that they can, for God can be known through immediate experience. This was the way people in the Bible knew God, as Professor John Hick explains:

God was known to them as a dynamic will interacting with their own wills, a sheer given reality, as inescapably to be reckoned with as destructive storm and life-giving sunshine. . . . They did not think of God as an inferred entity but as an experienced reality. . . . To them God was not a proposition completing a syllogism, or an idea adopted by the mind, but the experiential reality which gave significance to their lives.[36]

For these people, God was not the best explanation of their religious experience and so they believed in him; rather, in their religious experience they came to know God *directly*.

Philosophers call beliefs such as this "properly basic beliefs." They aren't based on some other beliefs; rather, they are part of the foundation of a person's system of beliefs. Other properly basic beliefs include the belief in the reality of the past, the existence of the external world, and the presence of other minds such as your own. When you think about it, none of these beliefs can be proven. How could you prove that the world was not created five minutes ago with built-in appearances of age, such as food in our stomachs from the breakfasts we never really ate and memory traces in our brains of events we never really experienced? How could you prove that you are not a brain in a vat of chemicals being stimulated with electrodes by some mad scientist to believe that you are here reading this book? How could you prove that other people are not really automata who exhibit all the external behavior of persons with minds, when in reality they are soul-less, robot-like entities?

Although these sorts of beliefs are basic for us, that doesn't mean they're arbitrary. Rather, they are grounded in the sense that they're formed in the context of certain experiences. In the experiential context of seeing and feeling and hearing things, I naturally form the belief that there are certain physical objects that I am sensing. Thus, my basic beliefs are not arbitrary but appropriately grounded in experience. There may be no way to prove such beliefs, and yet it is perfectly rational to hold them. You would have to be crazy to think that the world was created five minutes ago or that you are a brain in a vat! Such beliefs are thus not merely basic but *properly* basic.

In the same way, belief in God is for those who seek him a properly basic belief grounded in our experience of God, as we discern him in nature, conscience, and other means. This has an important lesson. If, through experiencing God, we can know in a properly basic way that God exists, then a real danger exists that proofs for God could actually distract one's attention from God himself. The Bible promises, "Draw near to God and he will draw near to you" (James 4:8 RSV). We mustn't so concentrate on the proofs for God that we fail to hear the inner voice of God speaking to our own heart. For those who listen, God becomes an immediate reality in their lives.

Someone might object that an atheist or an adherent to some nonpersonal religious faith such as Taoism could also claim to know their beliefs in a properly basic way. Certainly, they could *claim* such a thing, but what does that prove? Imagine that you were locked in a room with four color-blind people, all of whom claimed that there is no difference between red and green. Suppose you tried to convince them by showing them colored pictures of red and green objects and asking, "Can't you *see* the difference?" Of course, they would see no difference at all and would dismiss your claim to see different colors as delusory. In terms of *showing* who's right, there would be a complete standoff. But would their denial of the difference between red and green or your inability to show them that you are right do anything either to render your belief false or to invalidate your experience? Obviously not!

In the same way, the person who has actually come to know God as a living reality in his life can know with assurance that his experience is no delusion, regardless of what the atheist or Taoist tells him.[37] Still, it remains the case that in such a situation, although the believer may *know* that his belief is true, both parties are at a complete loss to *show* the truth of his respective belief to the other party. How is one to break this deadlock? We should do whatever is feasible to find common ground, such as logic and empirical facts, by means of which we can show in a noncircular way whose view is correct. For that reason, arguments such as I have given above are important, for even if they are not the primary means by which we *know* that God exists, they may be the means by which we can *show* someone else that God exists. We may know that God exists in a properly basic way, and we may try to show that God exists by appeal to the common facts of science, ethics, and philosophy.

In summary, we've seen good reasons to believe God exists, but that conclusion is but the first step, albeit a crucial one. The Bible says, "Whoever would draw near to God must believe that he exists and that he rewards those who seek him" (Heb. 11:6 RSV). If we have come to believe that he exists, we must now seek him, with the confidence that if we do so with our whole heart, he will reward us with the personal knowledge of himself.

FIVE

WHY I BELIEVE THE GOD OF THE BIBLE IS THE ONE TRUE GOD

NORMAN L. GEISLER

The devout French philosopher and mathematician Blaise Pascal objected that "the God of the philosophers" was not "the God of Abraham, Isaac, and Jacob." Pascal rightly insisted that the one true God cannot be known (personally) through the intellect; only faith and divine revelation can offer the means for a saving relationship with the Almighty. As a philosopher himself, and a man of extraordinary intellect, Pascal seemed to personify a commonly held belief that a great gulf exists between faith and intellect. Are the God of reason and the God of revelation truly the same being, as Augustine, Anselm, and Aquinas claimed? Or is the God of faith in a different domain than the God arrived at by rational argument?

Believers and unbelievers alike have challenged the connection between faith and intellect. Tertullian, an early church father, cried out, "What indeed has Athens to do with Jerusalem? What concord is there between the academy and the church? What between heretics and Christians?"[1] Our task then is to see if the God of the Bible squares with the God of reason. I believe the evidence will demonstrate they are one and the same.

IDENTIFYING THE GOD OF THE BIBLE

The God of the Bible, as understood by orthodox Christians down through the centuries, possesses certain metaphysical attributes that make him readily identifiable: unity, infinity, eternality, immutability, necessity, pure actuality, simplicity (indivisibility), omnipotence, omnipresence, omniscience, transcendence, and personality (comprised of intellect, feeling, and will).[2]

In addition to these nonmoral (metaphysical) attributes, the God of the Bible is absolutely morally perfect, having perfect love, holiness, truthfulness, and justice. These all exist in one and only one God in absolute unity.

GOD'S PURE ACTUALITY

Pure actuality means that God is actuality and has no potentiality whatsoever. Everything he could be, he is and always was and always will be. He exists but has no potential not to exist. This attribute is derived from several others.

God is pure being with no potential for nonbeing. "God said to Moses, 'I AM WHO I AM'" (Exod. 3:14). "Jesus answered, 'before Abraham was born, I am!'" (John 8:58). He is pure I Am-ness, not "I was . . ." or "I will be . . . ," but simply "I AM."

God is also an independent existence who does not depend on anything else for his existence. "In the beginning God . . ." (Gen. 1:1); "He is before all things" (Col. 1:17); "Before the mountains were born or you brought forth the earth and the world, from everlasting to everlasting you are God" (Ps. 90:2); "I am the Alpha and the Omega" (Rev. 1:8); "I am the First and the Last" (Rev. 1:17); "And now, Father, glorify me in your presence with the glory I had with you before the world began" (John 17:5; cf. 17:24; Rev. 13:8; 17:8).

God gives existence to everything else that exists. "In the beginning God created the heavens and the earth" (Gen. 1:1); "So God created . . . every living and moving thing" (Gen. 1:21); "Through him all things were made; without him nothing was made that has been made" (John 1:3); "He himself gives all men life and breath and everything else" (Acts 17:25); "For by him all things were created: . . . all things were created by him and for him" (Col. 1:16); "You created all things, and by your will they were created" (Rev. 4:11).

Finally, God is a necessary existence. "He is not served by human hands, as if he needed anything, because he himself gives all men life and breath and everything else" (Acts 17:25); "For from him and through him and to him are all things" (Rom. 11:36); "There is but one God, the Father, from whom all things came and for whom we live; and there is but one Lord, Jesus Christ, through whom all things came and through whom we live" (1 Cor. 8:6); "He is before all things, and in him all things hold together" (Col. 1:17); "He has spoken to us by his Son, whom he appointed heir of all things, and through whom he made the universe" (Heb. 1:2); "It was fitting that God, for whom and through whom everything exists . . ." (Heb. 2:10); "By your will they were created and have their being" (Rev. 4:11).

In summation, God is a pure, independent, necessary existence who alone gives existence to everything else that exists. As such, his own nonexistence is impossible. That is, he has no possibility not to exist. God's pure actuality is derived from the fact that he is an uncaused being. God is the uncaused cause of all that exists.

GOD'S INFINITY

The biblical basis for God's infinity (limitlessness) is found in numerous texts: "In the beginning God created the heavens and the earth" (Gen. 1:1); "But will God really dwell on earth? The heavens, even the highest heaven, cannot contain you. How much less this temple I have built!" (1 Kings 8:27); "Great is our Lord and mighty in power; his understanding has no limit" (Ps. 147:5); "Can you probe the limits of the Almighty? They are higher than the heavens—what can you do? They are deeper than the depths of the grave—what can you know? Their measure is longer than the earth and wider than the sea" (Job 11:7–9); "In the year that King Uzziah died, I saw the Lord seated on a throne, high and exalted, and the train of his robe filled the temple" (Isa. 6:1); "Who has measured the waters in the hollow of his hand, or with the breadth of his hand marked off the heavens? Who has held the dust of the earth in a basket, or weighed the mountains on the scales and the hills in a balance?" (Isa. 40:12); "'For my thoughts are not your thoughts, neither are your ways my ways,' declares the LORD. 'As the heavens are higher than the earth, so are my ways higher than your ways and my thoughts than your thoughts'" (Isa. 55:8–9); "For this is what the high and lofty One says—he who lives forever, whose name is holy" (Isa. 57:15); "This is what the LORD says: 'Heaven is my throne, and the earth is my footstool. Where is the house you will build for me? Where will my resting place be? Has not my hand made all these things, and so they came into being?'" (Isa. 66:1–2); "Oh, the depth of the riches of the wisdom and knowledge of God! How unsearchable his judgments, and his paths beyond tracing out!" (Rom. 11:33); "He is before all things, and in him all things hold together" (Col. 1:17).

Theologically, God's infinity can be inferred from several other attributes. For example, infinity follows from pure actuality. Pure actuality has no potency. Potency is what limits actuality. Hence, pure actuality has no limits. Infinity also flows from God's uncausality, that is, the fact that he is the first uncaused cause.[3] Everything caused is limited, and everything uncaused is unlimited (since it has no cause to limit it to what it is). God is uncaused, and therefore, must be unlimited (infinite).

83

Further, infinity follows from omnipotence. What is omnipotent is infinite in power. But God's power is identical to his being since he is a simple being (see below). Therefore, God is infinite in his being. Infinity also follows from omniscience for the same reason, for an omniscient being has no limits on its knowledge. What it knows, it is. A simple being does not *have* knowledge; rather, it *is* knowledge. Thus, if his knowledge is unlimited, then his being must be unlimited, since his knowledge and his being are absolutely one.

GOD'S IMMUTABILITY

The Bible repeatedly declares that God is immutable (unchangeable). Compare the following verses: "God is not a man, that he should lie, nor a son of man, that he should change his mind" (Num. 23:19); "He who is the Glory of Israel does not lie or change his mind; for he is not a man, that he should change his mind" (1 Sam. 15:29); "They will perish, but you remain; they will all wear out like a garment. . . . But you remain the same, and your years will never end" (Ps. 102:26–27; cf. Heb. 1:10–12); "I the LORD do not change. So you, O descendants of Jacob, are not destroyed" (Mal. 3:6); "[They] exchanged the glory of the immortal God for images made to look like mortal man and birds and animals and reptiles" (Rom. 1:23); "God did this so that, by two unchangeable things in which it is impossible for God to lie . . ." (Heb. 6:18); ". . . resting on the hope of eternal life, which God, who does not lie, promised before the beginning of time" (Titus 1:2); "Every good and perfect gift is from above, coming down from the Father of the heavenly lights, who does not change like shifting shadows" (James 1:17).

The theological basis for God's immutability is firmly established by other attributes. For instance, immutability follows from his pure actuality, since pure actuality has no potentiality. Whatever changes has the potential to change. Therefore, God cannot change. Immutability also follows from his simplicity (see below), since a simple being cannot be divided. But what cannot be divided cannot change (since change entails adding or subtracting a part to or from a being). A simple being has no parts, and therefore, a simple being cannot change.

God's changelessness also follows from his infinity. An infinite being has no parts, since whatever has parts cannot add up to an infinity. No matter how many parts something has, there could always be one more. What has no parts cannot change, since to change, something must either gain or lose a part. Hence, an infinite being cannot change. Immutability also follows from God's necessity,[4] for what a necessary being has, it has necessarily. Therefore, a necessary being cannot change. God, then, by his very nature cannot change.

GOD'S ETERNALITY

The Bible declares that God is eternal. He was before time, and he created time. Hence, he cannot be a part of time, though he can relate to time as its

Creator in the way a cause relates to its effect. Many verses of Scripture support God's eternality: "God said to Moses, 'I AM WHO I AM'" (Exod. 3:14); "Before the mountains were born or you brought forth the earth and the world, from everlasting to everlasting you are God" (Ps. 90:2); "For this is what the high and lofty One says—he who lives forever" (Isa. 57:15); "No, we speak of God's secret wisdom, a wisdom that has been hidden and that God destined for our glory before time began" (1 Cor. 2:7); "This grace was given us in Christ Jesus before the beginning of time" (2 Tim. 1:9); "God, who does not lie, promised before the beginning of time" (Titus 1:2); "He has spoken to us by his Son, whom he appointed heir of all things, and through whom he made the universe" (literally, "framed the ages"; Heb. 1:2); "To the only God our Savior be glory, majesty, power and authority, through Jesus Christ our Lord, before all ages, now and for evermore! Amen" (Jude 25).

The theological grounds for God's eternality are found in several other attributes. For example, immutability implies eternality, for an immutable being cannot change. But whatever is in time changes. Hence, God cannot be in time. God's eternality can also be inferred from his infinity. An infinite being has no limits, whereas a temporal being has limits. Hence, God is not a temporal being. Pure actuality is also a ground for eternality. Pure actuality has no potentiality, but whatever is temporal has potentiality. Hence, God is not temporal but eternal.

GOD'S ONENESS

The biblical basis for God's unity is found in texts such as the following: "Hear, O Israel: The LORD our God, the LORD is one" (Deut. 6:4); "You shall have no other gods before me" (Exod. 20:3); "I am the LORD, and there is no other" (Isa. 45:18); "The most important [command] . . . is this: 'Hear, O Israel, the Lord our God, the Lord is one'" (Mark 12:29); "We know that an idol is nothing at all in the world and that there is no other God but one" (1 Cor. 8:4); "For there is one God and one mediator between God and men, the man Christ Jesus" (1 Tim. 2:5).

Theologically, the unity of God can be argued from other attributes as well. Infinity implies there is but one God, for there cannot be two or more infinite beings.[5] Likewise, pure actuality implies there is only one God. In order to have two or more such beings, there would have to be some potentiality or limiting factor by which they differed. A God of pure actuality has no potentiality whatsoever. Also, the nature of the cosmos implies there is only one God, for the cosmos is a uni-verse, not a multi-verse. This is supported by the Anthropic Principle, which affirms that from its very inception the entire cosmos was fine-tuned and tweaked so as to make the origin of human life possible.[6] That is, there is a oneness of the universe from the very beginning, and oneness of the universe implies one Creator.

GOD'S SIMPLICITY

God's simplicity is derived from many affirmations of Scripture, including those that say he is absolutely one (see Deut. 6:4; Isa. 45:18; 1 Cor. 8:4), pure actuality (Exod. 3:14; Isa. 40:13–28; Acts 17:25; Rev. 1:8), and essentially immortal (1 Tim. 1:17; 6:16).

God's absolute oneness means that he cannot be divided. But what cannot be divided is indivisible. Hence, God is a simple (indivisible) being. God is also pure actuality (no potentiality). But whatever has no potentiality cannot be divided (for there is nothing by which it can be divided). What cannot be divided is indivisible. Therefore, God is indivisible. Further, God alone is immortal. Our immortality is derived from him (2 Tim. 1:10); his is essential. Whatever is essentially immortal is indivisible. Therefore, God is indivisible (simple). God is also immutable or unchangeable. He cannot change (Mal. 3:6; Heb. 1:12; James 1:17). Whatever cannot change cannot be divided (for division changes a thing). Hence, God is indivisible. God is also infinite, and an infinite being cannot be divided. If it could be divided, then finite parts would add up to an infinity. But no amount of finite parts can equal an infinity (since one more part could always be added). It follows, therefore, that an infinite being cannot be divided; it is indivisible (simple).

GOD'S PERSONHOOD

The God of the Bible is a personal God. Personhood is generally understood to include three essential characteristics: intellect, feeling, and will. A person can think, feel, and choose.

GOD CAN THINK

The God of Scripture has a mind. He is an intelligent and knowing being. In fact, he is all-knowing (omniscient). His understanding is infinite. "Great is our Lord and mighty in power; his understanding has no limit" (Ps. 147:5); "Be assured that my words are not false; one perfect in knowledge is with you" (Job 36:4; cf. 37:16); "He determines the number of the stars and calls them each by name" (Ps. 147:4); "I make known the end from the beginning" (Isa. 46:10); "In him we were also chosen, having been predestined according to the plan of him who works out everything in conformity with the purpose of his will" (Eph. 1:11).

"You know when I sit and when I rise; you perceive my thoughts from afar. You discern my going out and my lying down; you are familiar with all my ways. Before a word is on my tongue you know it completely, O LORD" (Ps. 139:2–4); "Nothing in all creation is hidden from God's sight. Everything is uncovered and laid bare before the eyes of him to whom we must give account" (Heb. 4:13); "Do not be like them, for your Father knows what you need before you ask him" (Matt. 6:8); "Are not two sparrows sold for a penny? Yet not one of them will fall to the ground apart from the will of your Father. And even the very hairs of your head are all numbered" (Matt. 10:29–30); "Oh, the depth of the riches of the wisdom and knowledge of God! How unsearchable his judgments, and his paths beyond tracing out!" (Rom. 11:33); "How precious to me are your thoughts, O God! How vast is the sum of them! Were I to count them, they would outnumber the grains of sand. When I awake, I am still with you" (Ps. 139:17–18).

GOD CAN FEEL

Not only can the God of the Bible think, he can feel. He possesses feeling or emotion. Of course, since he is unchanging, his feelings are unchanging. For example, he has an unchanging feeling of anger toward evil, and he has an unchanging feeling of pleasure toward good. Consider these texts that depict the feelings of God: God's Spirit is grieved at sin. "And do not grieve the Holy Spirit of God, with whom you were sealed for the day of redemption" (Eph. 4:30). Indeed, God expressed his great anger at sin: "The LORD will never be willing to forgive him; his wrath and zeal will burn against that man. All the curses written in this book will fall upon him, and the LORD will blot out his name from under heaven" (Deut. 29:20); God's fury is poured out on sin: "This is what the LORD Almighty says: 'I am very jealous for Zion; I am burning with jealousy for her'" (Zech. 8:2).

Further, God takes pleasure in the death of the righteous. "Do I take any pleasure in the death of the wicked? declares the Sovereign LORD. Rather, am I not pleased when they turn from their ways and live?" (Ezek. 18:23). Compare Psalm 116:15: "Precious in the sight of the LORD is the death of his saints." God also hates evil and loves good: "You love righteousness and hate wickedness; therefore God, your God, has set you above your companions by anointing you with the oil of joy" (Ps. 45:7). God takes pleasure in our faith: "And without faith it is impossible to please God, because anyone who comes to him must believe that he exists and that he rewards those who earnestly seek him" (Heb. 11:6).

GOD HAS A WILL

In addition to being able to know and feel, God can will, thus completing the triad of personal characteristics. Here is a sample of the many verses of Scripture that declare God has free choice: "Then you will be able to test and approve what God's will is—his good, pleasing and perfect will" (Rom. 12:2); "All these are the work of one and the same Spirit, and he gives them to each one, just as he determines [wills]" (1 Cor. 12:11); "He predestined us to be adopted as his sons through Jesus Christ, in accordance with his pleasure and will" (Eph. 1:5); "Here I am—it is written about me in the scroll—I have come to do your will, O God" (Heb. 10:7); "You are worthy, our Lord and God, to receive glory and honor and power, for you created all things, and by your will they were created and have their being" (Rev. 4:11).

GOD'S TRANSCENDENCE

The Scriptures declare that God is transcendent over all his creation: "In the beginning God created the heavens and the earth" (Gen. 1:1); "But will God really dwell on earth? The heavens, even the highest heaven, cannot contain you. How much less this temple I have built!" (1 Kings 8:27); "Can you probe the limits of the Almighty? They are higher than the heavens— what can you do?" (Job 11:7–8); "O LORD, our Lord, how majestic is your name in all the earth! You have set your glory above the heavens" (Ps. 8:1); "Be exalted, O God, above the heavens; let your glory be over all the earth" (Ps. 57:5); "For you, O LORD, are the Most High over all the earth; you are exalted far above all gods" (Ps. 97:9); "In the year that King Uzziah died, I saw the Lord seated on a throne, high and exalted, and the train of his robe filled the temple" (Isa. 6:1); "Who has measured the waters in the hollow of his hand, or with the breadth of his hand marked off the heavens? Who has held the dust of the earth in a basket, or weighed the mountains on the scales and the hills in a balance?" (Isa. 40:12); "'For my thoughts are not your thoughts, neither are your ways my ways,' declares the LORD. 'As the heavens are higher than the earth, so are my ways higher than your ways and my thoughts than your thoughts'" (Isa. 55:8–9); "For this is what the high and lofty One says— he who lives forever, whose name is holy" (Isa. 57:15); "This is what the LORD says: 'Heaven is my throne, and the earth is my footstool. Where is the house you will build for me? Where will my resting place be? Has not my hand made all these things, and so they came into being?'" (Isa. 66:1–2); There is "one God and Father of all, who is over all and through all and in all" (Eph. 4:6); "He is before all things, and in him all things hold together" (Col. 1:17).

The transcendence of God is also grounded in several other attributes. For example, God is infinite, and creation is finite. But what is infinite is beyond the finite. Hence, God is transcendent (beyond the finite universe). God also has majesty, which means he is exalted beyond all else. What is exalted beyond all else is transcendent. Thus, it follows that God is transcendent. Furthermore, God has sovereignty, that is, he is in control of all creation. But to be in control of all creation God must be beyond all creation. What is beyond all creation is transcendent. Hence, God is transcendent.

GOD'S MORAL PERFECTION

The Bible declares that God is perfect in his nature (Matt. 5:48), knowledge (Job 36:4), law (Ps. 19:7), will (Rom. 12:2), beauty (Ezek. 16:13–14), work (Deut. 32:4), way (2 Sam. 22:31), home in heaven (Heb. 9:11), gifts (James 1:17), love (1 John 4:18), goal for believers (Phil. 3:12–14), and place in Christ for believers (Col. 1:28). In summation, the heavenly Father is perfect (Matt. 5:48).

Support in Scripture for God's moral perfection is plentiful: "He is the Rock, his works are perfect, and all his ways are just. A faithful God who does no wrong, upright and just is he" (Deut. 32:4); "As for God, his way is perfect; the word of the LORD is flawless" (2 Sam. 22:31); "It is God who arms me with strength and makes my way perfect" (2 Sam. 22:33); "Do you know how the clouds hang poised, those wonders of him who is perfect in knowledge?" (Job 37:16); "As for God, his way is perfect; the word of the LORD is flawless" (Ps. 18:30); "The law of the LORD is perfect, reviving the soul" (Ps. 19:7); "The LORD will fulfill [perfect] his purpose for me; your love, O LORD, endures forever—do not abandon the works of your hands" (Ps. 138:8); "O LORD, you are my God; I will exalt you and praise your name, for in perfect faithfulness you have done marvelous things, things planned long ago" (Isa. 25:1); "Be perfect, therefore, as your heavenly Father is perfect" (Matt. 5:48); "Then you will be able to test and approve what God's will is—his good, pleasing and perfect will" (Rom. 12:2); "But when perfection comes, the imperfect disappears" (1 Cor. 13:10); "Every good and perfect gift is from above, coming down from the Father of the heavenly lights, who does not change like shifting shadows" (James 1:17); "But the man who looks intently into the perfect law that gives freedom . . . will be blessed in what he does" (James 1:25); "There is no fear in love. But perfect love drives out fear" (1 John 4:18).

There is also a theological basis for God's moral perfection. First of all, knowledge of the imperfect implies the perfect. We know what is imperfect. But this would not be possible unless we knew what is perfect. Hence, there must be a perfect (called God). Likewise, God's metaphysical attributes demand that God's perfection is absolute. As we have seen, God's nature is morally perfect. But God is infinite and necessary by nature. Hence, God is infinitely and necessarily morally perfect.

In summation, according to the Bible there is one, transcendent, personal, infinite, eternal, self-existent, immutable, morally perfect God who is the first uncaused cause of everything else that exists.

DISTINGUISHING THE GOD OF THE BIBLE FROM OTHER VIEWS OF GOD

The God described in the Bible is the God of theism or monotheism. Certain characteristics distinguish him from the other major views of God, which are briefly described below.

Many pantheists deny the personhood of God, whereas the God of theism has a will. All pantheists deny his transcendence, reducing God to his immanence by claiming he is in the universe but not also beyond it. While theism affirms that God is *over* all, pantheism claims God *is* all. Unlike the God of pantheism, the theistic God does not create out of necessity but out of liberty. He did not make the world because he had to but because he wanted to. John wrote, "You are worthy, our Lord and God, to receive glory and honor and power, for you created all things, and by your will they were created and have their being" (Rev. 4:11).

In contrast to deism, the theistic God not only supernaturally created the world, he also supernaturally intervenes in the world. Because he is sovereign and transcendent over the world, he can by his omnipotence perform miracles in the world. Furthermore, unlike the God of deism the theistic God sustains the world in existence. "In him all things hold together" (Col. 1:17). Indeed, "the Son is the radiance of God's glory and the exact representation of his being, sustaining all things by his powerful word" (Heb. 1:3). By him all things *came to be*, and by him all things *continue to be* (Rev. 4:11).

Since the God of the Bible is infinite and all-powerful, he is distinct from all forms of finite godism and dualism. The theistic God is neither finite nor impotent.

While pantheists claim God *is* all, panentheists insist God is *in* all. They claim God is bipolar, having both an actual pole and a potential pole. Classical theists, by contrast, claim that God has only one pole—pure actuality. Likewise, the theistic God is immutable and eternal, whereas the panentheistic God is changeable and temporal.

The God of the Bible is one God, not many. He and he alone is God. There are no others. Thus, he stands uniquely and in stark contrast to polytheism, the belief in many gods.

In summary, the God of Scripture is unique. Only he possesses certain characteristics that no other being has, such as infinity, eternality, absolute simplicity, pure actuality, necessity, sovereignty, transcendence, and absolute oneness. With these biblical attributes of God in mind, we turn now to the final question: Is the God of the Bible the one true God? In other words, are there good reasons to believe that the God who exists is one and the same with the God described in the Bible?

IDENTIFYING THE GOD OF THE BIBLE AND THE GOD OF REASON

In order to show it is reasonable to believe the God of the Bible is the God who actually exists, two things are necessary: (1) to provide good reasons that a theistic God (who possesses the unique characteristics previously described) actually exists, and (2) to show that there cannot be two such beings.

The first of these two premises was demonstrated convincingly by William Lane Craig in chapter 4 of this book. We can be confident that the theistic God exists because there is good philosophical and scientific evidence for his existence. This evidence is commonly divided into three arguments for God's existence: the cosmological, moral, and teleological arguments.

THE COSMOLOGICAL ARGUMENTS FOR GOD'S EXISTENCE

This demonstration of God's existence begins with the cosmos and the cause of it. Two basic forms are used.

The horizontal cosmological argument. First, a horizontal form argues from a beginning of the universe to a beginner (cause). This is called the kalam (Arabic: eternal) cosmological argument.[7] It reasons as follows: (1) Whatever had a beginning had a cause; (2) the universe had a beginning; (3) therefore, the universe had a cause. In support of the second premise, it offers both scientific and philosophical arguments. Scientifically, it appeals to the evidence for the big bang origin of the universe such as the Second Law of Thermodynamics (the universe is running out of useable energy and, hence, cannot be eternal). Philosophically, it argues that there cannot be an infinite number of moments before today because an infinite cannot be traversed. If there were an infinite number of moments before today, then today would never have arrived, but it has.

The vertical cosmological argument. There are also vertical forms of the cosmological argument. Two noted ones are as follows.[8]

The argument from contingency begins with a contingent being that now exists. Since its nonexistence is possible, it needs something to account for the fact that it exists rather than does not exist. But it cannot depend on other contingent beings for its existence, for they too need a cause for their existence. Hence, there must be at least one noncontingent (i.e., necessary) being that exists as the cause of all contingent beings that exist. To put it another way, if only contingent beings exist—and they could all not exist—then nonexistence could be the cause of existence, which is absurd.[9] Nothing comes from nothing.

Another form of the vertical cosmological argument goes like this: (1) Changing beings exist; (2) whatever changes passes from potentiality to actuality; (3) but no potentiality can actualize itself; (4) therefore, there must ultimately be a first unactualized actualizer who actualizes the existence of everything else that exists. In other words, a supernatural first cause exists who brought this natural world into existence and keeps it in existence. That is to say, the entire space-time universe came into existence out of nothing and would go back into nothing were it not kept in existence by a cause that cannot cease to exist. In short, there is both an originator and sustainer of all else that exists.

From these arguments several things can be rationally inferred about God. First, he is *eternal* (beyond time), since he created time. Time had a beginning, since there cannot be an infinite number of moments before today. If there were, then today would never have come, since an infinite cannot be traversed. But today has come, and therefore, time had a beginning. God has no beginning, and therefore, is not in time. He is before all time. That is to say, God is eternal (not temporal).[10]

Second, he must be *infinite* since he made the entire finite universe. If everything finite has a cause, then the first cause of everything finite cannot be finite, otherwise it too would need a cause. The first cause has no cause. Hence, it must be infinite.

Third, the theistic God has *aseity* (self-existence), since he is the first uncaused cause for everything else that exists. He is also the necessary ground of all contingent beings.

Fourth, this God must also have *necessity*. An uncaused being must exist of necessity, since it does not depend on anything else for its existence. Indeed, it existed when nothing else did prior to creation. If a necessary being did not exist, then contingent beings could not exist, for everything cannot be contingent. If everything were, then everything could not exist, and since something does exist, then nothing could have caused something, which is absurd.

Fifth, the cause of all finite perfections must itself be *infinitely perfect*. It must be infinite, since all finite beings need a cause that is not finite. And it must be infinitely perfect, since whatever perfections it has, it must have perfectly. The only way perfection can exist in an infinite being is to exist infinitely, for everything must exist in a being in accordance with its mode of being. For example, perfections in a finite being must exist finitely, and perfections in an infinite being must exist infinitely. Therefore, God must be an infinitely perfect being.

There are two basic reasons why *perfection* must be attributed to God: (1) We know there is imperfection, but it is not possible to know what is imperfect unless there is a perfect by which we can measure it; (2) there are moral perfections in creatures (such as goodness, love, truthfulness), but the creature (effect) possesses only perfections the creator (cause) gives it. A cause cannot give what it hasn't got. It cannot produce any positive perfection it does not possess.[11] It cannot share what it does not have to share. Thus, he who causes good must be good. The creatures *have* goodness, but the Creator *is* goodness.

THE MORAL ARGUMENT FOR GOD'S EXISTENCE

The moral argument states: (1) There is an absolute moral law; (2) all absolute moral laws must have an absolute moral lawgiver; (3) therefore, there is an absolute moral lawgiver. In support of the crucial first premise, the theist points to the following evidence. (1) We cannot know injustice unless we know what justice is; (2) we cannot measure the progress (or lack of it) of society unless there is a standard outside society by which we can measure it; (3) if there is no objective moral law, then no real moral disagreement can ever be possible; (4) the fact that we do know Mother Teresa was better than Adolf Hitler reveals an objective standard by which we are making the comparison. In short, if there is even one absolute moral law, then there must be an absolute moral lawgiver.

The Teleological Argument for God's Existence

The teleological argument begins with design in the world and argues to a designer beyond the world. The traditional form of this argument, following William Paley, states: (1) Every watch has a watchmaker; (2) the world is more complex than a watch; (3) hence, the world must have had a world maker.[12]

Two important discoveries in modern science have given new life to this old argument: microbiology and the Anthropic Principle. Michael Behe has forcefully argued that there are several examples of cellular functions that could not have been formed gradually by any natural process, including cilium, vision, blood clotting, or any complex biochemical process.[13] "Other examples of irreducible complexity abound, including aspects of DNA reduplication, electron transport, telomere synthesis, photosynthesis, transcription regulation, and more."[14] From these facts, Behe makes a bold conclusion:

> The result of these cumulative efforts to investigate the cell—to investigate life at the molecular level—is a loud, clear, piercing cry of "design!" The result is so unambiguous and so significant that it must be ranked as one of the greatest achievements in the history of science.[15]

Good Reasons to Affirm the God of the Bible Is the God Who Truly Exists

Now that the God of the Bible and the God of theistic arguments are known to share many of the same unique characteristics, it remains to demonstrate that they must be one and the same God. Three arguments emerge, the first two of which are based on the unique characteristics of God held by all theists.

There Cannot Be Two Infinite Gods

Both the Bible and the cosmological argument used to establish God's existence show that he is infinite. But there cannot be two infinite beings. Therefore, both the God of the Bible and the God of rational theism are one and the same being. Further, the God of theism has been shown by good reason to actually exist. Hence, the God described in the Bible actually exists.[16]

The burden of this argument rests on the premise that it is impossible to have two infinite beings. To argue that there are two infinite beings is like claiming there are two alls. But there can only be one all. It is like claiming there are two supremes, when it is obvious that only one being can be supreme. Or more precisely, infinite means without limits. If there are two beings, then one is limited by the other in some way. But an infinite cannot be limited by another, since it is unlimited by its very nature. Hence, there can be only one infinite (limitless) being.

THERE CANNOT BE TWO ABSOLUTELY PERFECT GODS

In like manner, there cannot be two absolutely perfect beings. In order to have two beings, one must differ from the other, otherwise they would be the same. In order to differ in perfection, however, one being would have to have a perfection that the other did not have. The one that lacked this perfection would not be absolutely perfect, since it would be lacking in perfection. Therefore, there can be only one absolutely perfect being. If the God of the Bible is absolutely perfect as is the God of the moral argument, then they are one and the same God.

THERE CANNOT BE TWO PURE ACTUALITIES

Another attribute shared by both the God of the Bible and the God of rational theism is pure actuality. Reason demands that God cannot have any potentiality in his being. If he did, then he would need a cause, since no potency is self-actualizing. But he needs no cause, since he is the first cause. He is self-existent, independent of all other beings. Thus, the God of the cosmological argument must be pure existence (actuality), as the great theists claimed he was.[17]

Pure actuality is absolutely unique. There cannot be two such beings, for the only way for one being to differ in essence from another being is by potentiality. That is, one being has a potential (to be something) that the other does not have. But a being of pure actuality has no potentiality whatsoever.[18] Hence, it cannot differ from another being of pure actuality.

Thus, there can be one and only one being who is pure actuality, such as both the God of reason and the God of Scripture are known to be.

CONCLUSION

In response to Pascal, the God of revelation is the same as the God of reason. Revelation and reason are simply two different ways to approach the same God. As Paul Tillich observed, one is approaching the same ultimate in two different ways.[19] Two mountain climbers can approach the same peak from different directions. In reality, there is only one absolute "peak"—an infinite, absolutely perfect being. Thus, the God described in the Bible and the God concluded from the cosmological, moral, and teleological arguments are one and the same. And since these arguments give us good reason to believe that such a God exists, it is reasonable to conclude that the God of the Bible does indeed exist. We can know with confidence that the God of Abraham, Moses, the Prophets, and the New Testament writers is the one true God, the same one who is known to exist.

PART 3

WHY
I BELIEVE
IN MIRACLES

Miracles are reported in Scripture, at least in part, to bolster faith in God. Yet miracles are often deemed a serious problem, an intellectual obstacle to embracing the Christian faith. This is a curious irony. That which was intended to give birth to faith seems occasionally to hinder it.

One can understand how the authors of Scripture, as mere men, might have miscalculated the value of miracle accounts. But how could God have made such a clumsy mistake? And why would God begin his Gospels, his all-important good news to the human race, with the incredible story of a virgin birth, a huge stumbling block to so many would-be believers in Jesus? Wouldn't the story sell better if it were more plausible, a story with fewer miracles and more solid teaching? Perhaps the explanation for this problem lies in the fact that the story of Jesus was written for a bygone age, an age in which faith came easily, unlike our own. If this is the case, it would certainly make sense to modernize the story of Jesus by eliminating the miracles.

Denying miracles and rewriting the Gospels would make good sense if the record about Jesus were simply a story. But it's not. It's history, or so it clearly purports to be. The context, tone, and style of the accounts of miracles in the New Testament are undeniably those of a historian's report, not a storyteller's yarn. (See chapter 9.)

As such, miracles truly are a problem, for they are simply unavoidable to the person drawn to Jesus. There is no Jesus without miracles, no Christianity without the miraculous. And either God planned it that way or the Gospel writers were extraordinarily devious and/or evil men.

Naturally, we contend that God planned it that way. He requires thoroughgoing assent to his omnipotence and his active role in human history (i.e., a theistic worldview) as part and parcel of the salvation he freely bestows. The gift of salvation in Jesus, like a beautiful Christmas present, is tied up in a ribbon of miracles. Grab hold of Christ's miracles and salvation is at hand.

So it is that the importance of miracles in Christianity can hardly be overstated. Our task in this section of the book begins with demonstrating that miracles, in principle, are both possible and believable. Dr. R. Douglas Geivett explains in chapter 6 why the philosophical arguments against miracles don't stand up to serious scrutiny, and why belief in miracles is quite reasonable.

Dr. Gary Habermas provides historical and textual evidence for Jesus' miraculous healings, exorcisms, and nature miracles and then presents impressive evidence for the capstone of Christ's miracles, his resurrection from the dead. Focusing on the words and life of the apostle Paul, Habermas presents a fresh approach to analyzing the compelling historical evidence that Christ rose bodily from the dead.

Finally, astronomer Hugh Ross demonstrates in chapter 8 how recent scientific evidence for the first and greatest of miracles, divine creation, is so overwhelming as to make theism the most viable option for the scientifically astute. Upon closer examination of "the beginning," we find it is not Moses (the proponent of exquisite design) but Darwin (the proponent of colossal chance) who calls us to make a giant leap of faith.

SIX

WHY I BELIEVE IN THE POSSIBILITY OF MIRACLES

R. DOUGLAS GEIVETT

Though belief in the miraculous persists today, such belief is judged by many to be a scandal of prodigious proportions. The fact that belief in miracles is itself a kind of miracle is precisely what philosopher J. L. Mackie meant by the title of his book *The Miracle of Theism*. He explains:

> The word "miracle" originally meant only something surprising or marvellous.
> . . . [The title of my book] echoes Hume's ironic remark that the Christian religion cannot be believed without a miracle by any reasonable person. . . . Theistic belief in general is no miracle. . . . But I hope to show that its continuing hold on the minds of many reasonable people is surprising enough to count as a miracle in at least the original sense.[1]

Given the current climate of opinion, it would seem those bent on affirming the miraculous have some explaining to do. What accounts for this benighted outlook, this credulous propensity to believe that miracles actually happen?

Some conclude that continued belief in the supernatural is little more than a hankering for the mysterious, a quaint nostalgia for the spiritual, a grasping for respite from the sterilizing forces of modernity.[2] Bemused skeptics with this cast of mind reflexively assume the following posture: Supernaturalism among the unrefined is at best harmlessly—perhaps even pleasingly—old-fashioned; among the intelligentsia it is merely eccentric. In any case, it is not to be taken seriously. Belief in miracles is no more reasonable than belief in Sasquatch, Cyclops, Medusa, griffins, pixies, trolls, or the Loch Ness Monster.

This type of response does not bother with a consideration of the reasons one might have, even in our day, for believing in miracles. What these reasons might be holds no interest for this sort of skeptic. Rather, they see nothing more than a question for the sociologist or the psychologist to answer: Why do people believe such incredible things? Critics who adopt this attitude tend to engage in ridicule rather than to offer sober-minded argument when confronted with belief in the miraculous. For them, it is an ineluctable given that miracles do not happen. Thus, belief in miracles is a source of amusement; it is not something to investigate with an open mind.

Not all who marvel at belief in the miraculous are so casually dismissive. There are those who reckon that a real difference exists between the exotic mythological predilections shared by denizens of hickdom and sincere belief in miracles on the part of more with-it folk. Traditional believers in the miraculous are not in general myth-mongering types. They exhibit no conspicuous penchant for the bizarre. Their one peculiarity is their conviction that sometimes events happen, or have happened, that are, in the words of Christian philosopher William Alston, "acts of God in a way in which most happenings are not."[3] The rank of true believers includes otherwise sane, sensible, intelligent—even erudite—people. Some are even philosophers of high reputation, Alston being a notable example. At least *their* belief in miracles, even if ultimately unfounded, must be taken seriously. How do these people manage to sustain the solid conviction that miracles have happened? Here the sentiment is far from dismissive, and those who share this sentiment feel obliged to set forth reasons to doubt the reality of miracles.

Skeptics of our day, therefore, typically adopt one of two postures, each exhibiting in a different way the attitude that belief in miracles is unreasonable. One posture is dismissive; the other is argumentative.

My aim here is to defend what initially appears to be a very modest proposition, so modest, in fact, that some will no doubt wonder whether it is worthy of sustained effort. The proposition is this: Miracles are possible. I believe in the possibility of miracles. But the mere possibility of miracles is really not of much interest. The truly interesting and momentous question about miracles is whether they are actual. I accept that.

Still, in defense of my more limited project, I have three things to say. First, it is not "the mere possibility of miracles" that I wish to defend. What I mean by this will become clear later. Second, I am interested in the possibility that a miracle could actually be identified as such and thus function as a sign of God's action in the world.[4] Third, those who affirm the actuality of miracles should be prepared to answer the objector who argues that miracles are not so much as possible.

To appreciate the force of skepticism of the more respectable argumentative variety, we need to ask, What is it that is so bewildering about persistent belief in the miraculous by intelligent people? But first we need a finer-grained characterization of skepticism about the miraculous.

VARIETIES OF SKEPTICISM ABOUT MIRACLES

Of the many varieties of skepticism about miracles, I shall distinguish only five. Consider, first, the following two propositions:

1. Miracles are possible.
2. Miracles are actual (i.e., miracles have actually occurred).

For each proposition, an individual may either believe the proposition, deny the proposition, or withhold judgment and remain neutral or agnostic. In general, denials of and agnosticism about propositions are two different ways of being skeptical. Since we are dealing with two propositions here, there are several specific attitudes one could take about the two propositions in relation to each other. The most straightforward cases are:

- One may affirm (that is, believe) both 1 and 2.
- One may deny both 1 and 2.
- One may withhold judgment about both 1 and 2.

But there are other options as well:

- One may affirm 1 and withhold judgment about 2.
- One may affirm 1 and yet deny 2.
- One may affirm 1 and withhold judgment about 2.

Two theoretical possibilities are unlikely:

- That one would deny 1 and yet affirm 2 (or deny 1 and be agnostic about 2).
- That one would withhold judgment about 1 and yet affirm 2.

Of these various combinations of attitudes about propositions 1 and 2, five are cases of skepticism about miracles:

   a. the denial that miracles are possible, and the denial that they are actual
   b. the belief that miracles are possible, but the denial that they are actual
   c. agnosticism about whether miracles are possible, but the denial that they are actual
   d. the belief that miracles are possible, but agnosticism about whether they are actual
   e. agnosticism about whether miracles are possible, and agnosticism about whether they are actual

In the first three cases, the actuality of miracles is patently denied. Of these, the strongest variety of skepticism is the first, in which the very possibility of miracles is denied. This denial may well figure into the denial of the actuality of miracles.

Notice, however, that denial of the actuality of miracles in cases b and c does not at all depend on the attitude taken with respect to the possibility of miracles. Cases b and c have something in common with each other that distinguishes them from case a: Both deny that miracles are actual, and both hold that *if* miracles are possible then they are *merely* possible. What distinguishes b and c is degree of conviction about the possibility of miracles. But in their agreement that miracles are not actual, they also agree about the sense of the term *possible* in proposition 1. Type-b and type-c skepticism both hold that miracles are *no more than possible*.

So we could say that proposition 1 is ambiguous. It may mean two different things because the term *possible* has more than one sense. We may, as it were, "dis-ambiguate" proposition 1 by specifying a different sense of *possible* in each case as follows:

   1a. Miracles are possible, and it remains an open question whether they are actual.
   1b. Miracles are merely possible, such that they are not actual.

In type-b cases of skepticism about miracles, 1b is affirmed. But 1b entails that 1a is false. So anyone who affirms 1b implicitly denies 1a. The type-b skeptic will deny 1a.

In type-c cases of skepticism, things are a bit more complicated, but a parallel point can be made. In type-c cases, 1b is not affirmed, but neither is it denied. Rather, judgment about 1b is withheld. But remember, in type-c cases, proposition 2 *is* denied. This means that the type-c skeptic affirms the following conditional proposition:

   3. If miracles are possible, then they are merely possible, such that they are not actual.

So whether the skeptic affirms 1b or 3, he holds that miracles are, at best, merely possible. Type-c skeptics are not free to affirm 1b, as type-b skeptics do. But type-b skeptics are free to affirm 3. This is because type-b skeptics and type-c skeptics are both committed to the thesis that miracles are no more than possible at best. Thus, I shall hereafter treat type-b and type-c skepticism together, under the label "type-b/c skepticism." Though this is not equivalent to denying the very possibility of miracles, it nevertheless is a pretty robust form of skepticism about miracles.

Varieties of skepticism d and e are special and more moderate than the others I have described. And d is more moderate than e. In contrast to skepticism of types a, b, and c, neither d-type nor e-type skepticism denies that miracles are actual.

With type e, skepticism extends to both propositions 1 and 2, but it is skepticism of the agnostic variety. Type-e skepticism resembles type-c skepticism in being agnostic about the possibility of miracles. The peculiarities of this dimension of type-e skepticism resemble those of type-c agnosticism about proposition 1, and for our purposes requires no further elaboration here. With respect to its agnosticism about proposition 2, type-e skepticism can be subdivided. But since the same sort of division results for type-d skepticism, and since the distinction to be made in this regard is more salient with respect to type-d skepticism, this division is explained next in the exposition of type d. (The reason why this division is more salient in the case of type-d skepticism is that type-e agnosticism about proposition 2 is of little practical significance given its agnosticism about proposition 1. And because its attitude toward proposition 1 parallels that of type-c skepticism, type-e skepticism has little to commend itself as a peculiar variety of skeptical challenge to belief in miracles.)

Skepticism of variety d is also agnostic, but its scope is more limited than that of type-e skepticism. Type-d skepticism about miracles subdivides. The first variety, type d_1, is incorrigibly committed to agnosticism about 2. In other words, the type-d_1 skeptic is resolved to remain agnostic about proposition 2. This sort of skeptic is an intransigent agnostic. But this intransigence is principled rather than merely a feature of the type-e skeptic's psychology. His agnostic intransigence regarding proposition 2 has to do with the conditions he stipulates for rational belief in miracles and his judgment that these conditions cannot be satisfied. I'll return to this point later.

The other variety, type-d_2 skepticism, is less severe in its attitude toward proposition 2, remaining open to the possibility of rational belief in the actuality of miracles. The type-d_2 skeptic does not foreclose on the possibility of eventually rationally concluding that miracles have occurred. His outlook is that although belief in the actuality of miracles is not presently justified, it could come to be justified, or it could in principle be justified even if it never in fact comes to be justified.[5]

One more point of clarification is needed. Earlier I pointed out that it is no part of my objective to defend "the mere possibility of miracles." It should now be clear what I mean by that. I am interested in defending what I shall call *the serious possibility of miracles*.

In summation, type-a skeptics deny the very possibility of miracles. Type-b and type-c skeptics concur in affirming the mere possibility of miracles; it is their joint claim (that miracles are no more than possible) that is most poignantly at stake in assessing both of these types of skepticism. The primary force of type-e skepticism is indistinguishable from the special force of type-c skepticism. It turns out, then, that three general types of skepticism are most worthy of close attention, if belief in the serious possibility of miracles, not to mention belief in their actuality, is to be deemed rational. In descending order of severity, they are: type a (Miracles are not even possible; still less are they actual); type b/c (Miracles are at best merely possible; they certainly are not actual); and type d (Miracles are possible, but it is uncertain whether they are actual).

THE SCIENTIFIC MOTIVATION FOR SKEPTICISM ABOUT MIRACLES

Let us now return to that imperious question posed earlier. What is so bewildering about persistent belief in the miraculous by intelligent people? Some answers that come to mind don't take us very far. It isn't just that our ordinary powers of perception are too limited to be able to detect a miracle. And it isn't primarily that testimonial evidence is unable to justify acceptance of miracle reports contained in ancient documents.

The problem goes deeper. It has to do with a significant shift in habits of mind. In particular, it has to do with the rise, development, and success of science. As social anthropologist Claude Lévi-Strauss, speaking of the progress of science during the twentieth century, has observed, "Not only has [science] enlarged and transformed our vision of life and the universe enormously: it has also revolutionized the rules by which the intellect operates."[6]

More than anything else, the revolutionary transformation of intellectual life, brought about by the steady advance of science, threatens to make a casualty of religious belief, and especially belief in the miraculous. Modern men and women march stridently into the twenty-first century armed with the means of explaining, predicting, and controlling the phenomena of the natural world to a previously unimaginable degree. As Roger Trigg remarks, the impressive track record of science tempts us to suppose that "success in reasoning can only be obtained through science."[7]

When science first came to be perceived as the singular source of knowledge, intellectual humility was limited to the acknowledgment that scientific progress may have to be sustained interminably, that the ideal of a complete science will always lie beyond our reach. Even if science is the sole means of tracking the truth, the ideals of science may not be completely realizable, given the vastness of the world yet to be understood and explained. T. H. Huxley wrote in 1887, "The known is finite, the unknown infinite; intellectually we stand on an islet of an illimitable ocean of inexplicability.

Our business in every generation is to reclaim a little more land."[8] The envisioned means of reclamation, of course, is science. But for Huxley, living back in the nineteenth century, the ideal of a comprehensive scientific explanation for everything was very nearly a pipe dream. The prospect of charting all unknown territory was jinxed by the sheer infinitude of the unknown.

Today, the spell is all but broken. Almost exactly one hundred years after Huxley's remark, Stephen W. Hawking—with the publication of his book *A Brief History of Time*—dreamily announced the real prospect of eventually discovering a theory of everything.[9] With such a discovery, Hawking said in an interview at the time his book was released, continued work in physics would be "like mountaineering after Everest."[10]

True, not all physicists expect the end of physics as forecast by Hawking, and Hawking himself is now more guarded in his optimism that we will one day come to "know the mind of God" through science.[11] Still, incautious forecastings of a scientific theory of everything intensify suspicion of the miraculous and spread it to the masses, who are little prepared to assess the force of these extravagant claims.

Whatever one makes of the realizability of the scientific ideal, there is widespread suspicion that belief in miracles conflicts with our commitment to the ideals of science. This is the primary inspiration for skepticism about the miraculous. But we are still left with a pretty vague idea about what it is that engenders the sort of skepticism delineated in the previous section. For the requisite clarification, we must look to the philosophical underpinnings of a-type, b/c-type, and d-type skepticism.

THE PHILOSOPHICAL BASIS FOR SKEPTICISM ABOUT MIRACLES

H. D. Lewis has written, "Few will doubt that the idea of miracle presents many problems. The main way in which philosophy comes into these appears when we ask what could be meant by a 'miracle' or how would anyone recognize a miracle if one were to happen?"[12]

These two questions get to the heart of the matter. They put us in touch with the basic rationale for a-type, b/c-type, and d-type skepticism. And they are indeed philosophical. Science is in no position to speak authoritatively on these questions. Indeed, which branch of science could provide answers to these questions?

The two questions stated by Lewis are closely related. Martin Curd clarifies their relation:

There are two distinct kinds of philosophical questions about miracles: (1) What are miracles? and (2) When, if ever, would we be rationally justified in believing of an event that it is miraculous? Any answer to the second, epistemological, question presupposes an answer to the first, conceptual, question. Similarly, adopting a particular conception of the miraculous is likely to have epistemological implications.[13]

Curd calls the first question the conceptual question; the second he calls the epistemological question. There are at least two constraints on a satisfactory answer to the conceptual question. First, miracles must be defined in a way that is conceptually coherent. Second, miracles must be defined in such a way that it is in principle possible to identify an event as miraculous if it is indeed miraculous.

This second constraint pinpoints the crucial interface of the two philosophical questions formulated by Lewis and by Curd. As atheist philosopher J. L. Mackie has said:

> If miracles are to serve their traditional function of giving spectacular support to religious claims—whether general theistic claims, or the authority of some specific religion or some particular sect or individual teacher—the concept [of miracle] must not be so weakened that anything at all unusual or remarkable counts as a miracle.[14]

This constraint explains why one particular conception of miracle has come to be regarded as standard. That conception has two components. First, a miracle is an event that is specially caused by God. Second, a miracle is a violation of one or more of the laws of nature. Mackie explicitly says that in order to satisfy the second constraint on producing an adequate definition of miracle, "we must keep in the definition the notion of a violation of natural law."[15]

The notion of miracle as a violation of natural law relates directly to the three versions of skepticism described above. Consider, first, type-a skepticism, which denies the very possibility of miracles. As R. F. Holland writes, "Most people think of a miracle as a violation of natural law; and a good many of those who regard the miraculous in this way incline to the idea that miracles are impossible and that 'science' tells us this."[16] Thus it is that the philosophical basis for a-type skepticism about the miraculous connects with the scientific inspiration for that same species of skepticism.

Alastair McKinnon is perhaps the best-known recent sponsor of this objection.

> The core of our objection is quite simple: the idea of a suspension of natural law is self-contradictory. This follows from the meaning of the term. . . . Natural laws . . . are simply highly generalized shorthand descriptions of how things do in fact occur. Hence there can be no suspensions of natural law rightly understood. Or, as here defined, *miracle* contains a contradiction in terms.
>
> Once we understand natural law in this proper sense we see that such law, as distinct from our conception of it, is inherently inviolable. Hence anything which happens, even an apparent miracle, happens according to law. Or, neg-

atively, no actual event could possibly violate a law of nature. Hence there can be no miracles in that sense of the term with which we are now concerned. Or, less misleadingly, it is in the nature of the case impossible that there should be an event which could be properly described by this term.[17]

Unfortunately, McKinnon's formulation of the objection depends on a dubious conception of natural laws as descriptive of anything that happens.

Martin Curd expresses the argument for type-a skepticism in a manner that seeks neutrality about the nature of laws of nature.

> We can analyze the difficulty in understanding miracles as violations of law by noticing that the following four statements form a logically inconsistent set.
>
> 1. E is a miracle.
> 2. If E is a miracle then there is at least one law of nature, L, such that E violates L.
> 3. If E violates L then E is a counterinstance of L.
> 4. If L is a law of nature then L has no counterinstances.
>
> If statements 2, 3, and 4 are true, then there are no miracles. Moreover, if 2, 3, and 4 were necessary truths (because they are conceptual or definitional truths), then this would show not merely that 1 is false, but also that it is logically impossible for any event to be miraculous. This is the core argument against the possibility of miracles as violations of law.[18]

For reasons that we will explore in the next section, many thinkers demur. They are not prepared to follow McKinnon, Curd, and others in drawing from the standard conception of miracles the implication that miracles are impossible.

Nevertheless, the same basic conception of miracle is thought by some to pose a problem when attempting to get beyond the mere possibility of miracles. For them the standard conception is an inducement to skepticism of type b/c. Mackie maintains that the standard conception of miracles is coherent, such that "their possibility is not ruled out a priori, by definition."[19] But he goes on to argue, in the spirit of David Hume (d. 1776), that we can never have good reason to believe that miracles have occurred. Therefore, rational belief in miracles is out of the question.

> Where there is some plausible testimony about the occurrence of what would appear to be a miracle, those who accept this as a miracle have the double burden of showing both that the event took place and that it violated the laws of nature. But it will be very hard to sustain this double burden. For whatever tends to show that it would have been a violation of natural law tends for that very reason to make it most unlikely that it actually happened. Correspondingly, those who deny the occurrence of a miracle have two alternative lines of defence. One is to say that the event may have occurred, but in accordance with the laws of nature. Perhaps there were unknown circumstances that made it possible; or perhaps what were thought to be the relevant laws of nature are not strictly laws; there may be

as yet unknown kinds of natural causation through which this event might have come about. The other is to say that this event would indeed have violated natural law, but that for this very reason there is a very strong presumption against its having happened, which it is most unlikely that any testimony will be able to outweigh. . . . The *fork*, the disjunction of these two sorts of explanation, is as a whole a very powerful reply to any claim that a miracle has been performed.[20]

Now, the conviction that we can never have good reason to believe that miracles have occurred is, strictly speaking, compatible with agnosticism about proposition 2. But Mackie is not really agnostic on this point. For one thing, he is an atheist and therefore denies the existence of the very being required by the first component in the standard conception of miracles. But he also apparently takes the availability of his "fork" for every alleged miracle as an adequate explanation for what is alleged. What he offers in response to miracle reports is not the equivalent of a proof that miracles have never happened. And yet he explicitly says that the two lines of defense that he describes are available to "those who *deny* the occurrence of a miracle."[21] He is saying, in effect, that since one may always have recourse to one or the other "explanation," one should deny that miracles are actual. On this interpretation, Mackie is a b/c-type skeptic.[22]

Nevertheless, the argument that Mackie develops—again, in the spirit of Hume—may also be deployed, with little modification, by skeptics of type d_1, and even by skeptics of type d_2 with a bit more modification. It is very possible, in fact, that one of these two alternatives was David Hume's own orientation.

What modification of "Mackie's fork" is required for its use by the type-d_1 skeptic? The d_1 skeptic stresses that the availability of Mackie's two explanation-types is never a guarantee that miracles do not occur. One would be justified only in denying the occurrence of miracles if one could be sure that one of Mackie's two explanations for an alleged miracle was the correct explanation. But that may sometimes be indeterminate. Merely having these explanations at one's disposal never justifies one in denying the actuality of miracles. Still, the type-d_1 skeptic may concur with Mackie that the two sorts of explanation he describes will always be available for any miracle claim whatsoever. One can be sure that one will never be justified in affirming the actuality of miracles. This accounts for our d_1 skeptic's intransigent agnosticism about proposition 2.

Mackie's fork must be further modified if it is to be used by the type-d_2 skeptic, for such a skeptic remains open to the possibility that there is an event that cannot plausibly be accounted for in either of the two ways Mackie describes. Such a skeptic may hold that one cannot decide in advance that for any miracle claim whatsoever it will always be plausible to suppose that either the event does not violate the laws of nature or the event did not occur. It is possible that some miracle claim will not be so readily susceptible to explanation in either of Mackie's two ways. Having duly noted that possibility, however, the d_2 skeptic may be impressed by the alternative *possibility* that for any miracle claim whatsoever, one or the other of Mackie's two explanations will prove plausible. But for the d₂ skeptic, this is only a possibility and never a sure thing.

In review, the standard conception of miracle as a special act of God that violates or suspends nature's laws is the basis for each of the three main varieties of skepticism explored in this chapter.

Theologian John Macquarrie appears to be as impressed as any atheist or agnostic by philosophico-scientific skepticism about miracles:

> The way of understanding miracles that appeals to breaks in the natural order and to supernatural interventions belongs to the mythological outlook and cannot commend itself in a post-mythological climate of thought. . . .
>
> The traditional conception of miracle is irreconcilable with our modern understanding of both science and history. Science proceeds on the assumption that whatever events occur in the world can be accounted for in terms of other events that also belong within the world; and if on some occasions we are unable to give a complete account of some happening—and presumably all our accounts fall short of completeness—the scientific conviction is that further research will bring to light further factors in the situation, but factors that will turn out to be just as immanent and this-worldly as those already known.[23]

It is difficult to pin Macquarrie down to a single specific form of skepticism. His remarks certainly appear to be an expression of type-b/c skepticism. He is unmistakably clear, however, in crediting science with providing the basis for his confident abandonment of the traditional conception of miracles. Macquarrie, McKinnon, and other recent theologians—Rudolf Bultmann comes to mind—have jettisoned the traditional conception in favor of an anemic concept of miracle that they consider both religiously meaningful and yet compatible with the ideals of science. Unfortunately, what they propose is also compatible with metaphysical naturalism. Any claim that a concept of miracle fashioned out of deference to metaphysical naturalism is nevertheless religiously meaningful is dubious in the extreme.

Must the concept of miracle be so radically reconceived in order for belief in miracles to escape the clutches of skepticism? That is the question to which we turn in the next section.

WHAT ABOUT THE POSSIBILITY OF MIRACLES?

We are able to make reasonable predictions about what will or will not happen in the physical world, based on what we understand to be the physical conditions of our environment together with what we believe to be the laws of nature within that environment. We consider events to be of the same general type when they occur under similar conditions and in accordance with the laws that have been formulated to explain their occurrence. The predictability of an event of a certain description depends in part on our ability to recognize the recurrence of relevant conditions that serve as causal antecedents for such events. Our success in making reliable predictions of this kind explains much of the respect we accord the scientific enterprise.

Let us imagine, however, an event whose occurrence would be most improbable, given the purported laws of nature and conditions in the physical environment. This would be an event we could not predict. If anything, we would predict that the event would not take place. We would, in fact, predict an utterly different state of affairs.

Now suppose we witness the occurrence of just such an event. Let us, in keeping with scientific practice, call this an "anomalous" event. What might we do to make sense of this event?

We first might suspect that we had overlooked salient conditions in the causal nexus of which the event is a part. We might surmise that the unpredictability of the event was due to a failure to notice these conditions. In order to make sense of the event, therefore, we might explore the possibility that there are, consistent with the laws with which we are familiar, other (perhaps deeper) laws that explain the occurrence of this event. This type of strategy reveals a desire to find an explanation that will be minimally disruptive to our existing scientific understanding of the world. Any explanation of this sort will specify the conditions under which the event has occurred and express a law or set of laws according to which events of that type will occur when the specified conditions recur. A successful explanation will enable us to predict future occurrences of the same type of event whenever the specified conditions are known to prevail. But such an explanation must be able to identify hitherto unnoticed conditions that feature in the causal nexus that includes the event.

Suppose that nothing can be found in the causal nexus of the event that would enable us to predict the occurrence of the event. Suppose that all the relevant conditions we can specify would, if known, still prevent us from predicting the occurrence of the event. And suppose that at any other time when these same conditions are known to obtain, nothing satisfying the description of our anomalous event ever occurs. At all other times when just these conditions occur, our existing beliefs about the laws of nature are confirmed. The only disconfirming instance we have is our anomalous event. And we have no way of specifying in terms of antecedent conditions a relevant difference between this anomalous event and what otherwise happens with perfect regularity and predictability.

Under these circumstances, we should be reluctant to abandon our current understanding of the laws of nature. We presently have no other laws to rely on in explaining either the events that customarily occur under the specified conditions or the troublemaking anomalous event. Meanwhile, we have a perfectly satisfactory lawlike explanation for all events occurring under the specified conditions, except for the one. The natural laws featured in this explanation predict that our anomalous event will not happen under the specified conditions. But *ex hypothesi*, the event does happen under the specified conditions. It is, therefore, a counterinstance to the laws of nature.[24]

Now, if the scenario described above is at least possible, then counterinstances of the laws of nature are possible. This spells trouble for Martin Curd's argument for the impossibility of miracles. Recall that his argument required that premise 4—"If L is a law of nature then L has no counterinstances"—be a necessary truth. If the standard definition of miracles as violations of the laws of nature simply means that miracles are counterinstances to the laws of nature of the kind described in the above scenario, then it seems that such violations are at least possible. Hence, miracles, so defined, are possible. Type-a skepticism is unsupported.

What about "Mackie's fork" and the other varieties of skepticism? Mackie explicitly acknowledges that the standard definition of miracles is coherent and that miracles, based on that definition, are possible.[25] It is surprising, therefore, that he adopts the stance of b/c-type skepticism and confidently denies the actuality of miracles. His own argument seems much better suited to the more moderate d-type skepticism that remains agnostic about the actuality of miracles. His willingness to take the harder line is due to his conviction that for any alleged miraculous event, one will be able to devise a naturalistic explanation, or, failing that, conclude that the event has not occurred. Mackie apparently is open to the possibility that a reported event will actually resist naturalistic explanation. But if that should happen, he would remain convinced that miracles do not happen, for he is prepared, in that circumstance, to deny that the event occurred. But if the occurrence of such an event is logically possible, the mere fact that an alleged event of that kind has no naturalistic explanation cannot count so decisively against there being an event of that kind.

Mackie concedes the coherence of the concept of a miracle. Thus, if he were presented with the report of an event that has no naturalistic explanation, he would be left with a disjunction: Either the event did not happen, or else it was a miracle. If he accepts the disjunction on the grounds that miracles are possible, then his choice of one disjunct over the other should not be decided on the basis of purely conceptual considerations. And yet his denial of the actuality of miracles seems to be based on purely conceptual factors. As far as he is concerned, it makes no difference how much evidence there is that a miracle has actually occurred. It is a peculiar liability of skepticism b/c that it seeks to resolve the question of the actuality of miracles on conceptual grounds only. These grounds seem better suited to d-type skepticism.

Recall that the d-type skeptic is agnostic about the actuality of miracles. One sort of d-type skeptic is resolute in his agnosticism. He is convinced that the case for a purported miracle will never be strong enough to rule out the possibility that the event in question either does conform to natural law or did not happen. Mackie mistakenly thinks he can rule out the actuality of miracles; the d_1-type skeptic thinks the alternatives of Mackie's fork can never be ruled out, even if one of them cannot ever be decisively ruled in. He is an intransigent agnostic about the actuality of miracles. But the d_1 skeptic is no more justified than Mackie in supposing that he can, on conceptual grounds alone, rule out in advance the possibility that an event will be so well attested that it should not be denied and so recalcitrant to naturalistic explanation that it must be a miracle.

The most reasonable of skeptical outlooks, then, is d_2 skepticism. For the d_2 skeptic, there always remains the possibility that a purported miracle really is a miracle and may yet be identifiable as a genuine miracle. It may turn out that neither a naturalistic explanation for the event nor denial that the event occurred will do justice to the available evidence. He is thus prepared to believe that a miracle has occurred, if evidence of the right sort should become available.

CONCLUSION

I conclude that miracles are possible. The only sort of skepticism that could be warranted on strictly philosophical grounds is the extremely moderate d_2 skepticism, which really is more aptly regarded as a variety of agnosticism about miracles. For the d_2 skeptic, no less than for the believer, miracles are a serious possibility. Science does not support any of the other versions of skepticism we have considered in this chapter, neither does philosophical reasoning about the nature and implications of the laws of science. In fact, the mounting successes of science put us in a much better position to recognize a genuine miracle when one occurs, to move from d_2 skepticism to belief. The more we learn from science about the laws of nature and their operation, the better we shall be able to know whether or not a particular event happened in accordance with natural laws.

I can think of no better candidate for miraculous status than the historically well-attested event of the resurrection of Jesus Christ. It is difficult to imagine how such an event could be explained in terms of the known laws of cell necrosis. It is equally unimaginable that the laws of cell necrosis, which predict the permanence of physical death, should be revised so as to accommodate, in an intelligible manner, both the general irreversibility of death and the singular exception of the resurrection of Jesus.

Of course, one may agree with this conclusion and yet remain skeptical about the miracle of the resurrection on the grounds that the historical evidence simply is not strong enough to warrant the verdict that a miracle occurred. But if God exists and had good reason to raise Jesus from the dead, and if he desires that we know and enjoy the benefits of his intervention in history, then the availability of adequate historical evidence is to be expected. These matters reach beyond the scope of this chapter. I trust that the argument developed here will at least discourage an anti-supernaturalism that would poison one's inquiry into the historical evidence. This is the unfortunate effect of a-type and b/c-type skepticism. To those d_2 skeptics who remain open to the miraculous but skeptical about the historical basis for the New Testament report of the resurrection, I especially commend the next chapter in this book.[26]

SEVEN

WHY I BELIEVE THE MIRACLES OF JESUS ACTUALLY HAPPENED

GARY R. HABERMAS

Once we know that miracles are possible, we turn to the question of historical evidence. Do we have enough data to argue that miracles have, in fact, occurred? In this chapter, we will investigate a particular portion of this topic: the case for Jesus' miracles. We will begin by asking two questions: (1) What general evidence is there for Jesus' miracles? (2) What specific evidence is there for Jesus' resurrection, in particular?

The subject of the historical Jesus is perhaps the most prominent theme in recent New Testament studies. One important category has to do with the Gospels' claims that Jesus performed miracles. As Jarl Fossum points out, "That Jesus was a miracle worker is central to the Christology of the New Testament."[1] For more than two hundred years, critical scholarship has frequently frowned on miraculous claims. Can it still be said that Jesus performed miracles? Surprisingly, the most recent studies of Jesus have reassessed the answer to this question.

A word about my methodology may be helpful before we begin. I will not take the more common route employed by many Christian apologists who argue from a trustworthy biblical text to supernatural events in that text. Even though I will argue in chapter 9 that the New Testament is indeed a historically reliable document, I will not rely on that final conclusion here. Rather, I will utilize another approach, building only on those historical facts that have two characteristics: They are attested to in multiple sources, and virtually all critical scholars who study the subject acknowledge that they are historical.

JESUS' MIRACLES

At first thought, one might wonder what sort of case might be made for the miracles of Jesus, excluding his resurrection. How much evidence is there for the Gospel proclamations? After addressing the phenomena of other miracle reports in the ancient world, we will investigate whether Jesus actually performed supernatural feats, as attested to in the Gospels.[2]

ANCIENT PARALLELS

As I will detail in chapter 9, supernatural reports in ancient writings are quite common, even in Roman histories from roughly the same period as Jesus. Omens and portents, prophecies, healings, demons, and interventions of the gods and fate were regular fare. Further, at least three groups of religious figures were said to have performed miracles: magicians, Hellenistic divine men, and Jewish holy men. A few of these instances might even bring to mind Jesus' miracles.

For example, the Talmud recounts the case of Rabbi Hanina ben Dosa, who prayed for healing for a boy who was not present but who was sick with a high fever. Then he pronounced that he was cured. The boy's father confirmed that the healing had occurred.[3] This is somewhat reminiscent of Jesus healing the centurion's servant in Capernaum (Matt. 8:5–13; Luke 7:1–10).

Another instance comes from the best known of the Hellenistic divine men, Apollonius of Tyana. Philostratus, his biographer, tells that Apollonius cast out a demon from a young man and ordered it to provide a sign that it had left. A nearby statue promptly fell down.[4] This case perhaps reminds us of Jesus expelling the demon from the Gadarene man (Mark 5:1–20).

Could any of these stories, or simply the supernatural mind-set of the times, have influenced the Gospel writers when they were composing their accounts of Jesus' miracles? Could the non-Christian reports have encouraged these writers to invent the Gospel accounts concerning Jesus?

There are multiple problems with such a charge, no matter what degree of influence is alleged. First, Jesus was obviously Jewish and was probably even widely considered by some to be a Jewish holy man. We are told that he was sometimes addressed as Rabbi (John 1:38, 49; 3:2; 6:25), as was John the Baptist (3:26). Still, we have no clear signs of mimicry. The ancient definition of magician, one who was involved in such practices as incantations, sorceries, spells, and trickeries, hardly seems to have applied any influence on the Gospel depiction of Jesus. Adjusting the concept more generally simply makes it relate to too many ancient persons. There is also a lack of clarity in the very notion of Hellenistic divine men, which makes this category difficult to compare to the Gospel rendition of Jesus.[5] Even Rudolf Bultmann, who popularized demythologization of the Gospel texts, says that "the New Testament miracle stories are extremely reserved in this respect, since they hesitate to attribute to the person of Jesus the magical traits which were often characteristic of the Hellenistic miracle worker."[6]

Second, there are few parallels between the magicians, divine men, and Jesus. Clearly, the Gospels are much more closely aligned with the Old Testament, Palestinian Judaism, and rabbinic literature. But given this, it becomes very difficult to establish the influence of pagan ideas on the Gospels. As historian Michael Grant points out, Judaism strongly opposed pagan beliefs, helping us understand why these ideas never gained much of a foothold in first-century Palestine.[7]

Third, and more importantly, most of the major cases associated with the three groups of miracle workers (magicians, Hellenistic divine men, and Jewish holy men) are dated later than the New Testament. The earliest portions of the Misnah date no earlier than roughly A.D. 200, becoming part of the Talmud even later. Josephus relates other cases of Jewish holy men, but his account was written perhaps A.D. 93–94, at the very end of the New Testament period. Philostratus's account of Apollonius was written in the third century A.D. Reginald Fuller explains that most of the data concerning these divine men is later than the New Testament. Additionally, he judges that similar Hellenistic concepts are not found until the second century A.D.[8] Barry Blackburn, who specializes in the subject, has scoured ancient Hellenistic literature and concludes that "I can adduce only three stories formally reminiscent of the Gospel accounts."[9] But even the presence of similar stories cannot prove any specific influence on the Gospels.[10]

Fourth, perhaps even more crucial, Christianity centers on the death and resurrection of Jesus, and this message is not borrowed from the beliefs of others. Martin Hengel asserts, "The Christian message fundamentally broke apart the customary conceptions of atonement in the ancient world and did so at many points."[11] Fuller comments, "The idea of resurrection in the biblical sense appears to be foreign to antiquity."[12]

Fifth, even though some nonbiblical miracle claims predated Christianity, there is no historical evidence that any of them actually occurred. To the contrary, there are myriads of problems with the accounts. Perhaps the best case of this is Apollonius of Tyana, although his account wasn't written until more than a century after the New Testament. Philostratus wrote more than a century after Apollonius lived. While this interim isn't insufferable for ancient accounts, it is long enough to make us cautious. Serious historical inaccuracies also taint the work, such as Apollonius's prolonged discussions with the kings of Nineveh and Babylon. Not only were these cities nonexistent in his time, but they had been destroyed long before! Apparently Philostratus did not know this.

Making matters even worse, Philostratus explains that his chief source was Damis, a disciple of Apollonius, but Damis also came from nonexistent Nineveh. Many scholars have concluded that Philostratus's work is chiefly romantic fiction, a popular style in the second century A.D. There are a number of reasons for this conclusion.[13] Further, similarities between Philostratus and Jesus may be explained in that Philostratus's patron was Domna, the wife of Roman emperor Septimus Severus. The popular view is that Severus arranged for this work to be written as "a counterblast to Jesus."[14] Philostratus is known to have embellished his account with miraculous claims.[15]

Admittedly, these problems with Philostratus's account do not condemn all other ancient accounts of miracles. But given that this is perhaps the most celebrated ancient record of miracles outside the Old or New Testaments, we should be somewhat suspicious of the others. Tough questions need to be asked of all ancient miraculous texts, even as they have been directed many times at Christian examples. Miracle *claims* are insufficient to establish such events.[16]

Sixth, on the other hand, and unlike their ancient counterparts, there is much historical evidence for the Gospel miracles, some of which I will point out below. This is widely recognized, even in the critical community, and is especially true concerning Jesus' resurrection. Therefore, whatever ancient accounts of miracles exist, one major question concerns whether there is sufficient evidence to establish the Christian miracle claims. If so, then the issue of outside influence is successfully sidetracked.

HISTORICAL EVIDENCE

Today it is common to categorize Jesus' Gospel miracle claims into three groups: healings, exorcisms, and nature miracles. It may be surprising that the community of critical scholars appears to have adjusted its stance toward at least the first two divisions. Usually, these are recognized as historical and explained cognitively. Both sick individuals as well as those who thought they were possessed by demons get better when they *believed* they were well. Jesus manifested a powerful personality and was able to convince them that they were healed. Marcus Borg provides three reasons why "it is virtually indisputable that Jesus was a healer and exorcist."[17]

Yet it is often denied that Jesus actually healed any organic sicknesses. Jesus Seminar cofounder John Dominic Crossan is bold in his declaration that Jesus "did not and could not cure that disease or any other one."[18] Further, many scholars deny that Jesus ever performed any nature miracles. Again, it is

Crossan who asserts, "I do not think that anyone, anywhere, at any time brings dead people back to life."[19] Fossum agrees that the belief that Jesus could raise the dead is due to "fundamentalist naivete."[20] Crossan believes that Jesus' resurrection would be the "supreme 'nature' miracle."[21]

But Borg is not so fast to rule out actual miracles, even those that affect nature. He points out that in the Gospels not all of Jesus' miracles were dependent on the person exercising faith, so it is perhaps not always possible to show that faith healing was the cause. Concerning whether or not Jesus could raise the dead, "a clear historical judgment is impossible."[22]

Given such stances by critical scholars, what sort of historical evidence is available regarding Jesus' miracles? In the process of answering this question, I will provide examples of each critical rule that I will introduce in chapter 9. Seven areas will be mentioned in defense of the Gospel narratives, addressing Jesus' healings, exorcisms, and even his nature miracles.

First, many critics doubt or reject the supernatural aspect of Jesus' miracles because they doubt the historical value of the Gospel accounts.[23] In chapter 9, I will discuss the reliability of these texts, presenting a number of strong reasons to accept their historicity. I will simply note here that such evidence can support a case for Jesus' miracles.

Second, for ancient historians, "two or three sources in agreement generally render the fact unimpeachable."[24] Even the Jesus Seminar argues that "two independent sources" are significant for determining early data.[25] Accordingly, a very impressive argument for Jesus' miracles is that some of them are attested to in each of the five independent traditions that critical scholars find in the Gospels.[26] More specifically, certain miracles are found in more than one source as well. Such multiple attestation in textual evidence is overwhelming in terms of ancient documents. Borg calls attention to this "widespread attestation in our earliest sources" for Jesus' healings and exorcisms.[27]

Third, another critical test is enemy attestation, which occurs when one's opponent admits something even though it is not in their best interest to do so. Maier states that "positive evidence within a hostile source is the strongest kind of evidence."[28] The Gospels tell us that those who most strongly opposed Jesus witnessed both his healing miracles and exorcisms (Mark 2:1–12; Luke 11:14–15; 13:10–17), as well as his nature miracles (Matt. 28:11–15; Mark 5:40–42; John 11:47–48). Their conclusion was that Jesus performed his miracles by the power of Satan (Mark 3:22; John 7:20–21; 10:19–21), thereby admitting the supernatural nature of these events. Borg thinks this is significant: "Even his opponents did not challenge the claim that powers of healing flowed through him. . . . They claimed that his powers came from the lord of the evil spirits."[29]

Before moving to the next piece of evidence, we might draw a preliminary conclusion here. Given Borg's statement that Jesus' exorcisms and healings are "virtually indisputable,"[30] why shouldn't the nature miracles be accredited by Borg on the same grounds? Since the nature wonders are also attested to in all five of the independent Gospel traditions, and Jesus' enemies also witnessed them but couldn't explain them away, it would seem that strong grounds exist for accepting them as historical. Plus, we have still more grounds on which to accept all three families of miracles.

Fourth, critical researchers have located in the Gospel texts numerous means of identifying healing and exorcism accounts that probably portray historical events. After several extensive studies, Graham Twelftree has noted dozens of such indications that many of Jesus' exorcisms and healings bear the historical and textual marks of authenticity, separating Jesus from the exorcists and miracle workers of his day. For example, the element of surprise or embarrassment is at times manifest, such as when Jesus appears to have limited knowledge (Mark 5:9; Luke 8:30) or especially when the healing doesn't seem to work the first time (Mark 8:23–25). Almost all of the healing or exorcism accounts that Twelftree judges as historical fulfill several of these critical criteria.[31] Jesus Seminar fellow Bruce Chilton is impressed with the early, pre-Markan status of the exorcism recorded in Mark 1:21–28, pointing to authenticity.[32]

Fifth, judging by a variety of these critical earmarks, scholars have also located numerous indicators that Jesus performed nature miracles. Again, Twelftree has done comprehensive work here. Although concluding that some of these Gospel accounts of nature miracles cannot be demonstrably established as historical, several others are quite probable. Factors include the likely presence of early and eyewitness reports, some of which are indicated by texts that employ Aramaic terms, Semitisms, or intimate knowledge of details (Mark 5:41; 7:31–37; Luke 7:11–17). Other miracles pass the test of dissimilarity (Mark 5:40–42), or cohere well with Jesus' other teachings and actions (Matt. 17:24–27). Here, each case deemed historical is supported by more than one of these criteria.[33] Other scholars have provided more reasons to seriously consider the historicity of several of Jesus' nature wonders.[34]

Sixth, the next section of this chapter addresses the incredible amount of historical evidence that exists for what Crossan terms the "supreme 'nature' miracle"[35]—the resurrection of Jesus. I will simply note here that if Jesus' resurrection happened, this event, in its context, would raise questions concerning the overall philosophical objection to the occurrence of miracles. Further, as the supreme miracle claim, this would also provide strong motivation for believing Jesus performed truly supernatural acts.

Seventh, another common objection to Jesus' miracles is that we don't see the same sort of phenomena today, especially since we suspect that medical science could explain these curiosities.[36] But would our perspective of the Gospel miracles change if we witnessed cases today that medical science could not explain naturally? Perhaps there are situations such as these, but we are not looking in the right places. Two examples may supply some clues.

In order to research the relationship between prayer and healing, physician Randolph C. Byrd conducted a double blind experiment in a California hospital, with almost four hundred coronary patients participating. Neither the patients nor the persons who were praying knew each other, and the former did not even know whether or not they were being prayed for. Still, there was a statistically positive result in twenty-one of twenty-six monitored categories for those patients who received prayer. The experimental design insured that the results could not be adequately explained by faith healing.[37]

Psychiatrist M. Scott Peck notes his attempt, along with a team of health professionals, to study and explain contemporary possession and exorcism cases. Yet, there were two situations that they could not explain by normal scientific means.[38] Citing this study, Borg notes "the provocative and illuminating" nature of Peck's admission, presumably as a caution against too hastily drawing conclusions concerning what can be known through modern scientific means. Borg goes on to remark that we cannot know whether or not Jesus actually performed nature miracles.[39]

Based on the above discussion, we can conclude that Jesus was a miracle worker, and there are many critical reasons[40] to support such a conclusion. We have early and eyewitness reports, multiple source attestation, negative confessions, admissions by antagonistic witnesses, Aramaic words and other Palestinian details, coherence with Jesus' teachings, indications of dissimilarity, as well as agreement by diverse contemporary researchers.[41]

A majority of recent scholars believes that Jesus was at least a healer and an exorcist. Borg, for example, states that this is "virtually indisputable."[42] But the data argue for more than this: Many of the Gospel texts that record Jesus' exorcisms, healings, and even the nature wonders possess numerous, specific earmarks indicating their historicity.[43] Additionally, the same characteristics that make the first two categories so "indisputable" also establish the third, making it difficult to disallow the nature miracles. In brief, there is a surprisingly large amount of evidence for Jesus' miracles.

THE RESURRECTION OF JESUS

Jesus' chief miracle claim is his resurrection, and the evidence for it is significant enough to occupy the remainder of this chapter. However, due to the intricacies of the historical case, I will only be able to summarize perhaps the best argument for the resurrection of Jesus, plus pursue a few side avenues. Along the way, I will also apply the critical rules that I used above and will detail in chapter 9 to see how the resurrection fares.

THE EARLIEST TESTIMONY TO JESUS' APPEARANCES

Chapter 9 addresses the question of the earliest apostolic preaching prior to the writing of the first New Testament books. I will explain the characteristics and importance of early creeds, or traditions, which circulated as oral teachings before being written down, zeroing in on the most famous creed in the New Testament.[44] That text is 1 Corinthians 15:3–8:

> For I delivered to you as of first importance what I also received, that Christ died for our sins according to the Scriptures, and that He was buried, and that He was raised on the third day according to the Scriptures, and that He appeared to Cephas, then to the twelve. After that He appeared to more than five hundred brethren at one time, most of whom remain until now, but some have fallen asleep; then He appeared to James, then to all the apostles; and last of all, as it were to one untimely born, He appeared to me also. (NASB)

Virtually all scholars who have studied the subject agree that in this passage the apostle Paul recorded an ancient creed, or tradition, regarding the death, resurrection, and appearances of Jesus. This proclamation actually took place long before the date of the book in which it appears.

There are many reasons for the conclusion that this is creedal material, predating 1 Corinthians. To begin with, Paul uses the technical terms *delivered* and *received* (as in 11:23), meaning that he passed on oral tradition to the Corinthians. Additional indicators include the parallelism and stylized content of the material, as if it had been repeated in a specific form, not arranged that way for the first time by Paul. A number of non-Pauline words (words not used by Paul in his epistles) show that he probably wasn't the original author of the material. The proper names of two other apostles (James and Cephas, or Peter) point to their own testimony. Other signs of traditional material include the Aramaic name Cephas in 15:5 (cf. the parallel in Luke 24:34), the possibility of an Aramaic original, and the threefold "and that" (which is similar to the Mishnaic Hebrew narrating method), along with two references to the Scriptures being fulfilled. Since Aramaic was Jesus' language, these examples point to an older substrata for this report.[45]

How early is this traditional material? Even critical scholars usually agree that it has an exceptionally early origin. Ulrich Wilckens declares that this creed "indubitably goes back to the oldest phase of all in the history of primitive Christianity."[46] Joachim Jeremias calls it "the earliest tradition of all."[47] The majority of scholars who comment think that Paul probably received this information about three years after his conversion, which probably occurred from one to four years after the crucifixion. At that time, four to eight years after Jesus died, Paul visited Jerusalem to speak with Peter and James, each of whom are included in the list of Jesus' appearances (1 Cor. 15:5, 7; Gal. 1:18–19).[48] Most scholars who provide a date as to when Paul received this teaching locate it two to eight years after Jesus' crucifixion. This places it at roughly A.D. 32–38.[49]

Paul's use of *historeo* in Galatians 1:18 in speaking of his visit with Peter provides some confirmation for this view. One of the most authoritative studies on the word concludes that Paul's purpose was an investigative inquiry for the purpose of getting information from Peter. In all probability, the details

Paul was most interested in had to do with Peter being "an eyewitness and . . . informant about the teachings and ministry" of Jesus.[50]

William Farmer agrees that this term signifies that Paul acted as an examiner or observer of Peter.[51] The topic in the immediate context both before (Gal. 1:11–17) and after (2:1–10) Paul's first trip to Jerusalem is the nature of the gospel. In 2:1–10, fourteen years later, Paul specifically states that his purpose in coming back to Jerusalem was to check the content of his gospel message with the other apostles (2:1–2).[52] It makes sense, therefore, that in the earlier meeting, Paul was also speaking with Peter and James concerning the gospel message (1:18–19). In a well-known comment, C. H. Dodd explains, "At that time he stayed with Peter for a fortnight, and we may presume they did not spend all the time talking about the weather."[53]

Paul's testimony in 1 Corinthians 15 presents an authoritative foundation for the truth of the Christian gospel message. Critical scholars almost unanimously recognize its importance. German historian Hans von Campenhausen maintains concerning this report, "This account meets all the demands of historical reliability that could possibly be made of such a text."[54] A. M. Hunter adds that this early tradition is "open to testing."[55] Dodd charges that "Paul's preaching represents a special stream of Christian tradition which was derived from the main stream at a point very near to its source."[56]

THE RELIABILITY OF PAUL'S TREATMENT OF THE RESURRECTION

Most scholars are quite willing to grant the value of Paul's treatment of Jesus' resurrection due to its exceptionally early date and his status as an eyewitness and apostle. But as important as these points are, the chief issue here is not when, where, and from whom Paul received the tradition in 1 Corinthians. Rather, the more crucial matter is Paul's own reliability in reporting what he does about Jesus' resurrection appearances. In other words, wherever the tradition came from, does Paul accurately narrate it? Happily, this is where his material is at its strongest. There are four indications that the content of Paul's report was trustworthy. Further, there are five additional areas of non-Pauline confirmation, corresponding to each of the first four.

First, to repeat the summary above, Paul recorded early material that he himself received, recounting the eyewitness appearances of Jesus to many of his followers (1 Cor. 15:4–7). Many scholars think he probably obtained the creed directly from Peter and James, in Jerusalem, just a very few years after Jesus' crucifixion (Gal. 1:18–19). But even if we cannot be absolutely sure of the creed's exact origin, we may postulate that Paul received the material from what he considered to be a trustworthy source. Since Paul is almost unanimously seen by critical scholars as a reliable guide to early Christian beliefs, even this last conclusion is quite significant.

But perhaps we have overemphasized the importance of Paul receiving this creed from others. The second indication of the trustworthiness of Paul's account is that he didn't have to rely merely on others' testimony, for he was an apostle, an eyewitness to an appearance of the risen Jesus (1 Cor. 9:1; 15:8). Critics readily admit the strength of this argument. Even philosophical atheist Michael Martin acknowledges Paul's status as an eyewitness to Jesus' appearances,[57] as does G. A. Wells.[58] This is amazing, since these scholars are two of the very few who doubt whether it can be determined that Jesus even lived in the first century.[59]

Third, Paul returned to Jerusalem fourteen years after his initial interview with Peter, specifically to check out the nature of his gospel preaching (Gal. 2:1–2). After Paul met with the apostolic leadership, Peter, James, and John confirmed that the content of Paul's message was accurate. On this apostolic consensus, Hans Dieter Betz notes that "the event had an official and legally binding character."[60] The Jerusalem leaders offered to Paul and Barnabas their fellowship (Gal. 2:1–10), with Betz informing us that the "gesture of the handshake here formally concludes an agreement."[61]

Paul had always been careful to assert that preaching the gospel necessarily included the theme of Jesus' resurrection. In fact, without the resurrection, there was no gospel faith at all.[62] This apostolic stamp of approval on Paul's message, therefore, communicated that the leaders were both aware of and appreciated the content of his gospel preaching. Given the centrality of the resurrection message both in Paul's preaching and in the early church, it would be inconceivable that the other apostles didn't know what Paul preached on this subject.

Fourth, after he finished his recitation of the early creed by listing some of the other key witnesses who saw Jesus' appearances (1 Cor. 15:3–8), Paul made a crucial declaration. He announced that all the other apostles were currently preaching the same gospel message he was with regard to Jesus' death and resurrection appearances (15:11–15). We are clearly told on Paul's authority that the resurrection appearances he just finished listing were also being proclaimed by the other apostolic eyewitnesses.

Especially given Paul's authority in current critical discussions, these four arguments regarding the reliability of his resurrection proclamation are powerful. They are further confirmed by five more non-Pauline arguments, corresponding to the Pauline claims just made.

First, confirmation that Paul received this message from others, just as he reported, comes from the large number of indications (like those mentioned above) that this material was not his. It has many marks of a formalized tradition, meaning that it is an early, pre-Pauline report. There is also literary substantiation of Paul's claim to have received it from someone else, and the critical acclaim here is almost overwhelming. In fact, Jewish scholar Pinchas Lapide attests that the grounds for this creed are so firm that this testimony "may be considered as a statement of eyewitnesses."[63]

Second, additional reports of Jesus' appearance to Paul are located in the Book of Acts, where it is reported three times (9:1–8; 22:6–11; 26:12–18).

This is as close as we get to a description of what happened to him. The fact that Paul's conversion was not a natural event is strongly evidenced by a number of factors.[64]

Third, in Acts 15:1–35, a discussion that is reminiscent of the one in Galatians 2 takes place. Again, it concerns the nature of Paul's gospel proclamation, and once again, Peter and James are both involved. The apostolic decree again is that Paul's gospel preaching was accurate (vv. 6–21).

Some scholars believe this meeting in Acts 15 is roughly a duplicate of the dialogue Paul describes in Galatians 2. This issue, however, makes little difference here. If the incidents are the same, then we have a second confirmation of Paul's earlier account. If these are separate occasions, then we have two different situations that both verify our point. The apostolic leaders, eyewitnesses to Jesus' resurrection appearances themselves, clearly confirmed the accuracy of Paul's gospel message.

Fourth, we also have two kinds of non-Pauline corroboration for Paul's assertion that the other apostles were teaching the same thing he was regarding Jesus' appearances. The apostolic message is confirmed by early creedal material contained in Acts, and several important details emerge from these texts with regard to Jesus' resurrection, including Jesus' appearances to groups of people.[65] Many scholars think that these passages in Acts manifest an early layer of proclamation, since the material is concise, with little theological enhancement, and could well be translations of Aramaic originals.

Critical scholars have pointed out that these textual characteristics signify a reliable portrayal of early preaching. Although not all scholars agree, Dodd has noted "a large element of Semitism" along with "a high degree of probability" that there was an Aramaic original for at least some of these portions. Additionally, there is a lack of suspicious signs that would signal the presence of later strata here. Though Luke uses his own language, these speeches represent "the *kerygma* of the Church at Jerusalem at an early period" and provide reminiscences of the message the apostles preached.[66]

For reasons such as these, John Drane is another scholar who agrees:

> The earliest evidence we have for the resurrection almost certainly goes back to the time immediately after the resurrection event is alleged to have taken place. This is the evidence contained in the early sermons in the Acts of the Apostles. . . . But there can be no doubt that in the first few chapters of Acts its author has preserved material from very early sources.[67]

Fifth, another reason to hold that the other apostles, like Paul, preached the resurrection appearances is found in the Gospel accounts. (Although I cannot go into detail here, I will point out some good reasons to trust these writings in chapter 9.[68]) After using critical methods, Dodd explains that several of the Gospel resurrection texts report early traditions. In particular, the appearance narratives in Matthew 28:8–10, 16–20, John 20:19–21, and, to a lesser degree, Luke 24:36–49 are all based on early material. But Dodd thinks that even the other Gospel portrayals of Jesus' appearances lack typical mythical tendencies and should receive careful consideration.[69]

A further perspective here comes from the application of the critical rules (to be discussed in chapter 9) as they are applied to the resurrection texts. The resurrection reports are unquestionably *early*, as seen in Paul's writings, Mark 16:1–8, and especially in the pre–New Testament creeds.[70] *Eyewitness* reports come at least from Paul but also, in all likelihood, from Peter, James, and any appropriate testimony from the Gospels. *Multiple attestation* of independent sources is derived from at least four Gospel sources[71] plus Paul's epistles. Perhaps the most evident example of *embarrassment* or *negative report* is the often-stated reports of the disciples' doubts after Jesus' resurrection.[72] Other examples of this include the disciples' disbelief when Jesus predicted his resurrection[73] and Jesus' rebuke of Peter for denying him (John 21:15–18).

Enemy attestation comes from the recognition of the Jewish leaders that Jesus' tomb was empty (Matt. 28:11–15) and from the reported conversions of many Jewish priests (Acts 6:7). The conversions and testimonies of former skeptics Paul and James, the brother of Jesus, are also crucial here. The principle of *dissimilarity* or *discontinuity* applies to the facts that Jesus' resurrection did not fit either the Jewish understanding of what would happen to the Messiah (Mark 9:31–32; Luke 24:20–21; John 20:9) or the Jewish understanding that the resurrection of the dead would only occur corporately and at the end of time. *Coherence* involves the extraordinary consistency of Jesus' resurrection with his unique life and teachings, including his predictions of his death and resurrection.[74] The use of *recognized historical facts* is seen in the overall method used in this chapter, that of building a case based on critically accepted data.[75] The resurrection texts in the New Testament measure incredibly well against criteria such as these, fulfilling basically whatever standards commentators require.

I have presented four arguments that Paul is a reliable source when he speaks about the resurrection appearances of Jesus, in addition to five non-Pauline points that confirm his testimony. Regarding Jesus' appearances, then, the apostles checked out Paul's message, and all parties taught that Jesus appeared to them after his resurrection from the dead. Together, nine arguments indicate that the earliest apostles declared they had witnessed the risen Jesus. The sources are apostolic, eyewitness, and, hence, authoritative.

The overall case is multifaceted as well. It isn't based on Paul alone but builds on creedal passages such as those in 1 Corinthians 15 and Acts, as well as utilizes specific reports from the Gospels and Acts. Yet, Paul is admittedly the center of the case. But here we are on the strongest possible ground (I will point out reasons for this in chapter 9). Paul is enjoying a time of perhaps unparalleled positive attention from critical scholars. His admittedly genuine epistles, the reliability of the Book of 1 Corinthians in particular, the early date and apostolic attestation of his writings, his personal knowledge of the leaders among the other apostles, and the care with which he made sure of the truth (as in Galatians 1–2) all combine to indicate that the four arguments based on Paul are well grounded.

Few scholars question Paul's authority in these matters. Dodd argues that Paul's account of the earliest Christian gospel is so close to the original source that "anyone who should maintain that the primitive Christian gospel was fundamentally different from that which we have found in Paul must bear the burden of proof."[76]

Few critical scholars will reject all nine of the arguments presented in this chapter. To be sure, some points carry more weight than others. But the total approach is exceptionally strong, especially since Jesus' resurrection follows from the truth of almost any of the nine arguments. As a result, critics need to show that there are no credible historical arguments for the resurrection, which would be very difficult indeed.

Consequently, Paul's testimony is an invaluable report of the original eyewitnesses' experiences: It helps us piece together what the earliest apostles thought they actually perceived. We conclude that these are potent reasons for arguing that these believers thought they had seen the resurrected Jesus alive after his death. It is not surprising that most critical scholars agree. The disciples' experiences were definitely visual in nature. This appears to be the only conclusion that accounts for all the data.

Reginald Fuller declares that the disciples' belief that Jesus rose from the dead is "one of the indisputable facts of history." Fuller then states that the disciples had some sort of visionary experiences, which "is a fact upon which both believer and unbeliever may agree."[77] This is perhaps the same grounds on which James Dunn concludes, "It is almost impossible to dispute that at the historical roots of Christianity lie some visionary experiences of the first Christians, who understood them as appearances of Jesus, raised by God from the dead."[78] Similarly, Michael Grant points out that a historical investigation can actually "prove" that the earliest Christians thought they had seen the risen Jesus.[79] Carl Braaten claims that even skeptics agree that for the early believers Jesus' appearances were real events in space and time.[80] Wolfhart Pannenberg agrees with these assessments, maintaining that "few scholars, even few rather critical scholars, doubt that there had been visionary experiences."[81] More recently, even skeptic Gerd Luedemann argues that the language of the New Testament is the language of sight: Jesus' disciples certainly thought they had seen the risen Jesus.[82]

OTHER HYPOTHESES

Due to both space limitations as well as the strength of the above evidence, we will consider only one naturalistic hypothesis here. The majority of natural hypotheses usually don't take direct aim at Jesus' appearances.[83] The one that is most specifically directed at the disciples' belief that they had seen the risen Jesus is the hallucination (or subjective vision) thesis.[84] Can such sub-jective phenomena satisfactorily explain all the data? The following critique should sufficiently reveal some of the glaring problems with this attempt. Addi-tional aspects can be gleaned from the notes.

(1) Hallucinations are private events, experienced by one person alone.[85] Yet, there is strong evidence that Jesus appeared to groups of people.[86] (2) Per-haps the major predicament for this hypothesis is that Jesus appeared to a vari-ety of persons, at various times, places, and under different circumstances. The belief that all of these people were candidates for such a rare combination of hallucinatory phenomena (visual, auditory, and so on) multiplies the improb-able and borders on gullibility. (3) Moreover, while hallucinations generally develop from hopeful anticipation, the disciples despaired after Jesus' death and did not expect him to rise. (4) Further, it is highly unlikely that subjec-tive experiences could inspire the disciples' radical transformations, even being willing to die for their faith. (5) What grounds do we have to think that James, the family skeptic, was in the right frame of mind to see Jesus? (6) What grounds do we have to think that Paul the persecutor yearned to see Jesus? (7) Hallucinations cannot explain the empty tomb.[87]

Therefore, it is not surprising that numerous critical scholars of varied theo-logical persuasions have rejected these subjective hypotheses.[88] Pannenberg concludes, "These explanations have failed to date."[89]

Comparatively few scholars today pursue naturalistic hypotheses against the resurrection. Some hypotheses are periodically revived, but it is generally con-ceded that the known facts are sufficient to refute these alternative views. For example, Dunn states that "alternative explanations of the data fail to provide a more satisfactory explanation."[90] Most of the time, these attempts are even disdained by scholars. Raymond Brown explains that "the criticism of today does not follow the paths taken by the criticism of the past. No longer respectable are the crude theories of fraud and error popular in the last century."[91]

Since hallucinations and other subjective hypotheses fail in their attempts to explain the data, we need to return to our earlier thesis. The core elements of the original disciples' experiences indicate that they witnessed appearances of the risen Jesus.[92] We conclude that the pre-Pauline report in 1 Corinthians 15:3ff. and the additional arguments above clearly link the eyewitness con-tent of the gospel with its later proclamation, and with the evidence showing that the participants actually saw the risen Jesus, both individually and in groups. A fair analysis of the historical record strongly supports the conclu-sion that Jesus Christ did in fact physically and literally rise from the dead.

EIGHT

WHY I BELIEVE
IN THE MIRACLE
OF DIVINE CREATION

HUGH ROSS

For me, the evidence for creation was the starting point of my coming to faith in Christ. My strong interest in astronomy began when I was seven years, and from the age of eight, I knew my future career would lie in that field. During my teenage years I pursued a vigorous program of variable star observations. In the midst of that program I began a serious study of cosmology.

Even then, in the early 1960s, it seemed obvious to me that the observations uniquely supported the theory of general relativity and the big bang explanation for the universe. That being the case, the universe must be exploding. If it is exploding, it must have a beginning. If there is a cosmic beginning, there must exist a cosmic Creator. Thus, from the age of sixteen onward I never doubted God's existence.

Though God's existence and the reality of a transcendent creation event ceased to be a matter of doubt, I was highly skeptical that the God who created a hundred billion trillion stars would want to communicate through a book to humans on an insignificant speck we call earth. Nevertheless, for the sake of academic honesty, I launched into a critical study of the holy books of the world's great religions. Except for the Bible, my suspicions were confirmed that they were penned from the limited space-time perspective of human beings and reflected the limited and often incorrect scientific knowledge of the times in which they were written. Only the Bible leaped beyond the dimensions of length, width, height, and time. Only the Bible successfully predicted future scientific discoveries. Only the Bible accurately described cosmic origins and the anthropically fine-tuned nature of the universe and solar system. These discoveries, the obviously superior moral message of the Bible, and its uniquely complete solution to the human moral dilemma led me at age nineteen to sign my name in the back of a Gideon Bible, indicating my commitment to make Jesus Christ my Lord and Savior.[1]

Eight years later, I finally met other Christians with whom I could discuss spiritual matters. I found that the lack of strong evidence for creation was what kept most Christians from discussing with their friends and associates the truth claims of Jesus Christ and the Bible. At that point, I began to spend significant time researching the evidence for the accuracy of the biblical creation doctrine and developing tools to assist both scholars and laypeople in communicating the evidence. What follows is a brief summary of the latest scientific evidence that the God of the Bible transcendently created the universe for the benefit of the human race. Readers will find much more complete discussions in my other writings and videos.[2] Also, I am omitting here evidence that God created the first life-forms, all the life-forms seen in the fossil record, and human species. Such evidence, too, I discuss elsewhere.[3]

Astronomy's Unique Perspective

Unlike other science disciplines, astronomy directly observes and measures the past. Because light travels at a fixed, finite velocity (the constancy of light's velocity throughout all cosmic history and geography is easily proven), we see—and measure—conditions on an astronomical object as they were when that object's radiation began moving toward us (that the radiation came from the object rather than from some distance between us and the object is also well established). When we look at the sun, for example, we see its conditions eight minutes ago, when the visible light and other radiation we now detect left the sun. When we map the Orion Nebula, we see it as it was twelve hundred years ago. When we examine the center of our galaxy, we discover what was happening there thirty thousand years ago. When we study the core of the Andromeda Galaxy, we observe what took place two million years ago, given light's travel time.

In a sense, astronomers can claim to witness the past. To see how the creation was taking shape a certain number of years ago, we need only focus our instruments on objects the appropriate distance away. With recent technological advances, we can actually see all the way back to when light first separated from darkness and even to a split second after the cosmic explosion with which all the universe's time, space, matter, and energy began.

Early Evidence for a Transcendent Cause

The first clue that a causative agent operating from beyond matter, energy, and the space-time dimensions of the universe must be responsible for the existence of the universe came via Einstein's theory of general relativity. The picture that emerges from the equations defining the theory is that a finite time ago the entire cosmos burst forth and is still expanding from an infinitely (or nearly infinitely) dense state. Actually, this same picture can be derived from Newtonian mechanics. On the condition there exists a star and a planet of the type needed for physical life, stable orbits of planets about stars will be possible only in a universe described by three very large, rapidly expanding dimensions of space.

Whether or not the universe is expanding in the manner predicted by general relativity and Newtonian mechanics can be tested through measuring relative to us the velocities of galaxies at various distances. The first such systematic measures, completed in 1929,[4] verified that the universe indeed was expanding from a beginning. This conclusion was supported by confirmations of all three predictions Einstein deduced from his theory, namely, the bending of light, the shifting of certain spectral lines, and the orbital behavior of inner solar system planets.[5]

Space-Time Theorem of General Relativity

In a 1970 research paper, Stephen Hawking and Roger Penrose proved a new theorem: If the equations of general relativity reliably describe the dynamics of the universe, and if the universe contains any measurable mass, then space and time must have originated concurrently with matter and energy.[6] Also, the cause of the universe must bring it into existence independent, or transcendent, of matter, energy, and all the space-time dimensions that can be associated with matter and energy. A corollary to this theorem is that time itself is finite. It had a beginning outside the universe's boundaries.

Obviously, the universe contains mass. However, in 1970, a tiny shadow of doubt still hovered over the extent of general relativity's reliability, leaving room for at least a little speculation. Ten years later, however, a NASA rocket experiment all but erased that shadow—demonstrating that the reliability of general relativity exceeded 99.99 percent.[7] In 1994, a team led by radio astronomer Joseph Taylor used twenty-one years of measurements on the orbital periods of binary pulsar PSR 1913+16 (two neutron stars orbiting one another) to confirm general relativity's reliability to better than 99.999999999999 percent.[8] In Roger Penrose's words, this research data made Einstein's general relativity "the most accurately tested theory known to science."[9]

General relativity is also the most exhaustively tested principle in physics. In addition to the three tests proposed by Einstein, modern-day physicists and astronomers have developed nine more:

1. retardation of radar and laser signals bounced off various solar system bodies[10]
2. dragging and twisting of the space-time fabric by rapidly rotating neutron stars and black holes[11]
3. oscillation rates of X-ray radiation from disks of gas and dust orbiting black holes[12]
4. population statistics of black holes at different masses[13]
5. infall velocities of accretion disks surrounding supermassive (exceeding a million solar masses) black holes[14]
6. diameters and intensities of Einstein rings (the rings formed around quasar images when massive bodies lie exactly between us and the quasars thereby setting up gravitational lenses)[15]
7. Lense-Thirring effect (slight alterations in the orbits of tiny bodies orbiting a massive body that is generated by the spin of the massive body)[16]
8. marginally stable orbits of matter being accreted onto neutron stars from normal stars that happen to be in close orbits about the neutron stars[17]
9. hypernova gamma ray bursts generated by the simultaneous merger of several black holes[18]

Until recently, the last eight of these tests lay beyond the measuring limits of our best instruments. Since 1998, however, all nine tests have been successfully performed, and all nine demonstrate the applicability and reliability of general relativity.

Now that the reliability of general relativity has been established beyond any reasonable doubt, all uncertainty in the space-time theorem of general relativity has been removed. This establishes a singular origin of matter, energy, space, and time and that the act, or cause, of the universe arises from some context (dimensions, realm, or other) independent of the space-time dimensions of our universe. Of all the holy books of the religions of the world, only the Bible's claims about cosmic creation are consistent with general relativity's space-time theorem.

EXTRA-DIMENSIONAL CREATION

The Creator's transcendence received dramatic verification and extension in 1996, as physicists and astronomers tackled two seemingly intractable problems plaguing the big bang models.

The first dilemma was this: Treating fundamental particles as point entities (the traditional view) made unification of any of the four forces of physics

impossible. Since we have both complete theoretical and complete experimental proof that this unification can and did occur for the weak nuclear force
and the electromagnetic force, some new approach or explanation is necessary, one allowing more flexibility. That new something proved to be lines or
loops of energy called "strings." When theoreticians treated fundamental particles as highly stretched, vibrating, rotating elastic bands in the extreme heat
of the first split second of creation, the dilemma disappeared. For all practical purposes, they behave as points under the cooler conditions since then,
but not in the crucial beginning moment. Strings, however, require more than
three spatial dimensions. They need more room to operate; they need at least
a few dimensions beyond the ones we experience.

The second dilemma was that in the easily recognized four space-time
dimensions of the universe, all gravitational theories imply that quantum
mechanics is impossible and all quantum mechanical theories imply that gravity is impossible. Andrew Strominger hypothesized a brilliant resolution in
the form of "extremal" (i.e., very small) black holes, which become massless
at critical moments.[19] At first, however, he seemed merely to have traded one
dilemma for another. Black holes are massive objects so highly collapsed that
their gravity attracts anything within proximity. How can a black hole be
massless without violating the definition of a black hole or without violating
the principles of gravity? Simply put, how can there be gravity without mass?

The answer lay, once again, in extra-dimensionality. Strominger discovered
that in six spatial dimensions, the mass of an extremal black hole is proportional
to its surface area. As the surface shrinks, the mass eventually becomes zero. The
resolution works given the existence of exactly six extra spatial dimensions.

One theory solves the two great dilemmas. Here's what that theory tells us:
The universe was created with ten rapidly expanding space-time dimensions.
When the universe was just 10^{-43} seconds old, the moment when gravity separated from the strong-electroweak force, six of these ten dimensions ceased
to expand. Today, these six dimensions still remain as a component of the universe, but they are as tightly curled up as when the cosmos was only 10^{-43} seconds old. Their cross sections are only 10^{-33} centimeters, so small as to be unde-
tectable by direct mesurement.

Six sets of evidences indicate that this theory is correct.[20] Perhaps the most
convincing is that string theory produces, as a bonus by-product, all the equations of special and general relativity. In other words, if we had known nothing at all about relativity, this ten-dimensional string theory would have
revealed relativity theory in complete form. Therefore, the precise experimental confirmation of special and general relativity establishes to the same
degree the creation of ten space-time dimensions. Such profound, precise corroboration is both rare and wonderful in the world of science research. And
from the Christian's perspective, its magnificence cannot be overstated.

God's transcendence of ten space-time dimensions and operation within
those ten dimensions explain certain mysteries of Christian theology, para-

doxes that have puzzled biblical scholars for centuries. The very existence of such paradoxical doctrines in the Bible yields a powerful proof that the Bible must be divinely rather than humanly inspired. No one can visualize phenomena in more dimensions than what he or she are able to experience. For example, mathematicians can easily show that in four dimensions of space a basketball can be turned inside out without making a cut or a hole in the skin of the basketball. However, because we are confined to just three space dimensions, we cannot gain a complete visual picture of the operation.

This dimensional limitation in our capacity to visualize explains a key distinctive of the Bible among all holy books. Holy books other than the Bible contain only those doctrines that can be conceptualized within the dimensions of length, width, height, and time. Their lack of any content that would demand the operation of being transcendent to our four space-time dimensions raises the strong suspicion that their words were merely humanly inspired. The Bible alone contains doctrines (e.g., the Trinity, the simultaneity of human free choice and divine predetermination, eternal security, the atonement, evil and suffering in the context of God's power and love, heaven, and hell) that are impossible in our space-time dimensions but are all resolvable given that a being powerful enough to create transcendently ten space-time dimensions exists. Such content in the Bible (see table 1) establishes that its words must be inspired by the being that transcends ten space-time dimensions.

Table 1: Biblical Cosmology Confirmed via Trans- and Extra-Dimensionality

1. God existed before the universe. God exists totally apart from the universe and yet can be everywhere within it (Gen. 1:1; Col. 1:16–17).
2. Time has a beginning. God's existence and cause-and-effect activities precede time (2 Tim. 1:9; Titus 1:2).
3. Jesus Christ created the universe. He has no beginning and was not created (John 1:3; Col. 1:16–17).
4. God created the universe from what cannot be detected with the five senses (Heb. 11:3).
5. After his resurrection Jesus could pass through walls in his physical body, an evidence of his extra-dimensionality (Luke 24:36–43; John 20:26–28).
6. God is very near, yet we cannot see him, a further suggestion of his extra-dimensionality (Exod. 33:20; Deut. 30:11–14; John 6:46).
7. God designed the universe in such a way that it would support human beings (Genesis 1–2; Neh. 9:6; Job 38; Ps. 8:3; Isa. 45:18).

CREATION RADIATION

In the 1940s, George Gamow, Ralph Alpher, and Robert Herman, on the condition that the universe expands rapidly from a singularity, that is, from a transcendent creation event, calculated that a faint background radiation from that event of just a few degrees above absolute zero must exist everywhere in the sky astronomers look.[21] The predicted radiation was discovered in 1964.[22]

In 1965, astronomers noted that for a star like the sun and a planet like earth to be possible so that physical life could survive, the radiation left over from the creation event must be very homogeneous on large scales and must match the energy spectrum of a perfectly radiating body. In the 1970s, several independent teams of astronomers observed that the cosmic background radiation indeed had these properties.[23]

Immediately following these discoveries in the 1970s, astronomers calculated that for galaxies and stars to form out of a hot big bang creation event tiny differences in the temperature of the cosmic background radiation must exist everywhere across the heavens at a level of slightly less than one part in a hundred thousand. In 1992, the COBE satellite,[24] and later several other instruments,[25] detected the temperature differences at exactly the level predicted by the creation model. It was this discovery that caused science historian Frederic Burnham to comment that the idea God created the universe had become more credible for scientists than at any time in the past hundred years.[26]

Later, in 1993, COBE satellite measurements showed that the cosmic background radiation (the radiation remaining from the Gen. 1:1 event) fits the spectral profile of a perfect radiator to better than 0.03 percent precision over the entire range of wavelengths.[27] This established that the universe is a half billion times more entropic, that is, more efficient in radiating heat and light, than a burning candle. Only one scientific explanation accounts for this extreme entropy measure: The universe must have started from a nearly infinitely hot and infinitely compact volume.

This cosmic entropy measure eliminated any possibility for a reincarnating or oscillating universe (the Hindu-Buddhist-New Age idea of a universe cycling through a sequence of beginning, growth, contraction, and re-beginning).[28] Eliminated, too, is the possibility of stretching the bang of the creation event over a tightly spaced succession of "little" bangs.[29] The universe must have erupted from a single explosive event that by itself accounts for at least 99.97 percent of the radiant energy in the universe.

As far back as the 1940s, physicists noted that cosmic creation from a hot big bang implied that the background radiation would measure hotter and hotter as we look farther and farther away in the universe (hence, farther and farther back in time). In 1994, using the newly built Keck telescope, astronomers determined that the cosmic background radiation affecting very distant gas clouds was hotter than the cosmic background radiation we see today by exactly the amount predicted from a hot big bang creation event.[30]

The fifth prediction concerning the cosmic background radiation arising from the hot big bang creation event, noted in 1992, was that the amplitude of the temperature differences in the cosmic background radiation would have different values at different angular resolutions. That is, a telescope only able to distinguish temperature details ten moon diameters apart would see temperature differences a certain value smaller than a telescope capable of seeing temperature details one moon diameter apart, which in turn would see temperature differentiation a certain value larger than a telescope able to resolve details just a tenth of moon diameter apart. This prediction was proven true by several independent teams of observers in 1999 and 2000.[31]

On April 25, 2000, the long-anticipated maps of the temperature differences in the cosmic background radiation from the Boomerang observations were released at a NASA press conference and published in a subsequent issue of *Nature*.[32] The maps made the front pages of newspapers and television news programs all around the world. The reason for all the excitement surrounding the Boomerang results is that the measurements were made at so many different angular resolutions and with such precision that not only was the creation prediction proven correct but the quality of the observations permitted for the first time an accurate determination of the geometry of the universe.

MOST PROFOUND FINE-TUNING

What made the accurate measurement of the geometry of the universe theologically significant is that astronomers had already determined a relatively precise measure of the mass density of the universe. This mass density measure was for the total mass of the universe, including both ordinary matter (matter that strongly interacts with radiation, e.g., protons, neutrons, and electrons) and exotic matter (matter that very weakly interacts with radiation, e.g., neutrinos). It was 28 percent (upper limit = 33 percent) of the density that would have been necessary for matter alone to determine a flat geometry for the universe (for a flat geometry universe the shortest distance a beam of light can travel between two far apart galaxies will be a straight line).[33]

The Boomerang results showed that the total density of the universe (matter density plus space energy density) added up to a value somewhere between 88 and 112 percent of what would be necessary for a flat geometry cosmos. Thus, the space energy density contribution (the cosmological constant that describes a self-stretching property of the space-time fabric of the universe such that as the fabric becomes more and more stretched by the expansion of the universe it gains progressively more energy to accelerate the expansion) must be about 70 percent of what is needed for a flat geometry.

The fact that there was a space energy density contribution for the universe was not new news. An international team of thirty-one astronomers published in a June 1999 issue of the *Astrophysical Journal* their discovery that the velocities of distant supernovae definitely indicated the presence of a space energy density contribution to the dynamics of cosmic expansion.[34] The problem, though, was that a few astronomers expressed some concerns over how well the supernova yardstick that was used for the discovery held up at extreme distances.[35] Though other astronomers quickly produced additional reassurances in the quality of the supernova yardstick,[36] several skeptics still demanded independent confirmation.

The skeptics' concerns were largely taken care of when the requested confirmation was made just three months after the discovery. That confirmation was achieved through measuring by how much the velocities of different galaxies over a broad range of distances departed from the big bang expansion velocity of the universe.[37] None of the energy density measures at that time, however, were precise enough to attach anything other than the rough conclusion that the cosmic energy density term was within a factor of four or five of the value attached to the matter density term. The Boomerang discovery changes all that. We now have a measurement so accurate that any reasonable doubt in the existence of a space energy density term has been removed. We not only have more than adequate confirmation but the measurement establishes that most of the mass of the universe is exotic in nature and most of that exotic matter is "cold," that is, it is made up of particles that move at much less than relativistic velocities. All this extra detail in pinning down the characteristics of cosmic creation, of course, strengthens the support for a biblical creation model.

More support for a biblical creation model comes from the values now determined for the cosmic density terms. Establishing that the expansion of the universe from the creation event is governed by two factors, a mass density term plus a space energy density term, means that both the mass density and the space energy density of the universe must be fine-tuned to an extremely high degree for the universe to have any capacity to support physical life. In fact, the value of the mass density term must be fine-tuned to better than one part in 10^{60}, and the value of the space energy density term to better than one part in 10^{120}. In the words of the nontheistic astrophysicist Lawrence Krauss, this is "the most extreme fine-tuning problem known in physics."[38] Other nontheistic astronomers have written that "this type of universe requires a degree of fine tuning of the initial conditions that is in apparent conflict with 'common wisdom'"[39] and that "we are confronted with a disturbing cosmic coincidence problem."[40] Why the discovered fine-tuning is so disturbing to nontheists becomes evident when the measure of fine-tuning is compared to the best example of human engineering design, namely, a gravity wave telescope that has just been put into operation. The cosmic fine-tuning in the cosmic density terms establishes that the cause or God of creation, at a minimum, is ten trillion trillion trillion trillion trillion trillion trillion times more intelligent, more knowledgeable, more creative, and more powerful than human beings.

The sixth prediction about the cosmic background radiation from the hot big bang creation model has not yet been confirmed by observations. This prediction states that more precise measurements of the temperature differences of the cosmic background radiation at many more different angular resolutions should reveal not just one well-defined peak in the amplitude of the temperature differences but rather several. Two experiments are scheduled to test this sixth prediction. One that should produce results as early as 2003 is a more advanced Boomerang study. The other, which promises unprecedented precision, is a NASA satellite scheduled for launch in 2007 with the first results due as early as 2008.

Given how spectacularly the first five predictions about the cosmic background radiation from the hot big bang creation model have been confirmed, and given all the other confirmed predictions from the hot big bang creation model,[41] no astrophysicist doubts that the sixth prediction will be proven true. In fact, some hints of at least a second peak are showing up in the data that is already available.[42] What is building anticipation for the confirmation of the sixth prediction is that an accurate measurement of the positions and the amplitudes of all the peaks will also produce precise determinations of the age of the universe, cosmic expansion rates with respect to various epochs after creation, the mass density of the universe, the space energy density of the universe, how much of the various forms of ordinary and exotic matter exist, and whether or not the universe manifests any "quintessence" (see next section). Such an accurate and detailed proof of cosmic creation, I believe, will do much to promote a Christian theistic interpretation of nature in secular society and to settle creation interpretation differences and disputes within the Christian community.

We need not really wait, however. Thanks to the latest advances in our understanding of the cosmic background radiation, we already have the necessary tools to challenge secularists with the truth claims of our Creator as well as the tools for resolving creation disputes that exist among Christians.

QUINTESSENCE

Two paragraphs ago I slipped in the term *quintessence* without defining it. *Quintessence* is a word used by certain cosmologists to refer to a hypothesized phenomenon they hope might possibly reduce the extremely high level of design apparent in the cosmic density terms.

There are a few different ways to explain quintessence. One way is to define it as a hypothesized variation over time of the term that describes the pressure of the universe divided by the term that describes its density. If one carefully chooses the initial value of this ratio and sets its rate of variation to a specific value, then a significant amount of the apparent design in the cosmic density terms is removed.

Is there any evidence for cosmic quintessence? So far, none. The only shred of hope is that we know the universe contains exotic matter. If the right kind of exotic mass particles exist and if they exist in just the right abundance with just the right distribution, then the desired quintessence becomes possible.

Obviously, this appeal to quintessence is simply one of trading design for design. The design eliminated in the cosmic density terms, at least in part, is replaced by new design in the pressure to density ratio or in the kind, amount, and distribution of exotic mass particles. In fact, as one group of astronomers has pointed out, the possible discovery of quintessence may actually confront the nontheists with even more evidence for design.[43] Unless the quintessence takes on a particular value, and unless it takes on a specific rate of change, not only does all the apparent design in the cosmic density terms still stand but additional design from the quintessence factor must be added in as well.

One thing we must keep in mind is that we will never gain a measure of the total extent of God's design in the universe or a perfect measure of one of the design attributes of the universe. Because of our human limitations, we will always be overlooking some characteristics for cosmic design. Because of the same limitations, we will either underestimate or overestimate the actual level of design in any given characteristic for which design is evident. However, the more we learn about the universe, the more design characteristics we will discover. Also, the more we learn about the universe, the more accurate will our estimates be of the level of design in each characteristic. The strength of the case for the God of the Bible can be judged by the fact that in 1989, the total list of cosmic design characteristics published by my ministry organization, Reasons To Believe, numbered sixteen.[44] In my latest book publication on the subject (1998), the list stood at thirty-four, and the quality of most of the design measures had vastly improved.[45]

A Special Time, a Special Place

In 2000 in the *Astrophysical Journal*, Lawrence Krauss and Glenn Starkman, astronomers at Case Western Reserve University, wrote what was for them a depressing assessment of the future of astronomy now that we know the universe has a significant space energy density term.[46] They point out the value of the space energy density term is such that from now on the universe will expand faster and faster. What this increasingly more rapid expansion of the universe implies is that more and more objects in the universe will disappear from our view. Presently observable distant sources will move beyond the theoretical limit of any possible telescope (the age of the universe in years times one light-year). Thus, astronomers will have less and less of the universe to look at and eventually (not any time soon!) we will be forced to close down all the observatories.

As a Christian I can put a positive spin on Krauss and Starkman's deduction. God designed the universe in such a way, created us at the precise moment in the history of the universe, and granted us the necessary standard of living and technology so that we humans have the opportunity to see the greatest possible extent of his creation glory. If we were created any earlier in cosmic history, the age of the universe would limit our view both in terms of the distance we could look out to and in the numbers and kinds of objects that would have formed. If we were created any later, the space energy density of the universe would have sped an increasingly larger portion of the universe beyond our limits of possible observation.

The current moment in cosmic history is also the just right time to observe the cosmic background radiation. As the universe continues to expand, the cosmic background radiation will become progressively fainter and fainter. Meanwhile, the dimmest stars, the red dwarfs and brown dwarfs, are still forming in large numbers throughout the universe. These dim stars have the capacity to burn for tens of billions of years. With the universe only fourteen or fifteen billion years old, this means that none of them have yet burned out. Also, during their burning phase, they get progressively brighter. The net result is that as the universe ages, the background radiation from dim stars will overwhelm the radiation from the cosmic creation event. The problem with trying to observe the cosmic background radiation any earlier than the present epoch is that stars like the sun and planets like the earth (necessary for observers to be possible) would not yet exist.

It is not just that we were created at a special time. We were created in a special location. Our galaxy has the good fortune of being situated in one of the least populated parts of the universe. Whereas most galaxies find themselves in one of millions of dense clusters of galaxies, our Milky Way galaxy resides in a tiny well-dispersed galaxy group that lies far from any giant cluster of galaxies. As such, our neighboring galaxies do not block our view of the universe.

We also possess a unique window seat within our galaxy. Our solar system is located between two spiral arms of our galaxy that are loaded with gas and dust. If we were located within a spiral arm, as is the vast majority of our galaxy's stars, such gas and dust would block our view of anything but the nearby stars and gas and dust clouds. Only our position between spiral arms permits us to see the other parts of our galaxy and any of the other several hundred billion galaxies in the universe.

As a new piece of research demonstrates, however, it is not enough for our solar system to be positioned between two spiral arms. Two Russian astronomers recently determined that the sun remains for billions of years situated between spiral arms because it is one of those exceptional stars that is at the "galactic corotation radius."[47] Typically, the stars in our galaxy orbit about the center of our galaxy at a rate different from that of the spiral arm pattern. This means that if a star is located between spiral arms, it will not stay there for very long. With the star revolving around the galaxy's center at a rate different from the spiral arm structure, it is just a matter of time before the star is swept inside a spiral arm. Only at the corotation radius could a star remain for a long time period between two spiral arms.

What does all this mean? It means that earth is the best place and right now is the best possible time to be an astronomer. Earth is the only place and right now is the only possible time to uncover the secrets of creation embedded in the cosmic background radiation and in the distant stars, galaxies, and gas clouds. Right now is when and on earth is where "the heavens [are declaring] the glory of God" (Ps. 19:1). Moreover, there is no need to be depressed about the future. God, the Creator, has promised us in the Bible that as soon as he completes the conquest of evil, he will replace this vast universe with one far more glorious, wonderful, and good than the one in which we presently reside (Revelation 21–22).[48]

DESIGN PARAMETERS

As helpful as big bang cosmology has been in affirming both the Creator's existence and transcendence, it has provided what may be considered an even greater service in attesting to the Creator's personal characteristics. The more we learn about the physics of the universe, the more clearly we see reflected not only the awesome power but also the mind and heart of the one who planned and initiated and continues to sustain all things, inanimate and animate. Big bang cosmology is showing us both the universe's limits and its characteristics. More of both are coming within the measuring capacity of researchers, and as they do, the indications of exquisite design are becoming irrefutable. Astronomers and physicists, even the few who still hesitate to call themselves theists, widely acknowledge that the only reasonable explanation for the intricately harmonious features of the universe, our solar system, our planet—all ingeniously focused on the requirements for life—is the action and ongoing involvement of a personal, intelligent designer.[49]

Princeton University physicist Robert Dicke, in 1961, was the first to suggest that gravity required fine-tuning if life, any conceivable kind of life, were to be possible anywhere and at any time in the universe.[50] Carl Sagan calculated two more characteristics requiring fine-tuning, namely, the mass of the star and the distance of the planet from its star, which he published in 1963.[51] In the first printing of The Fingerprint of God in 1989, I listed sixteen characteristics of the universe and another nineteen of the solar system that must be fine-tuned to make life possible and sustainable.[52] By the time of the most recent printing of the second edition of The Creator and the Cosmos (1995), those lists had grown to twenty-six characteristics for the universe and forty-one for the solar system.[53] In the past few years, the pace of new discoveries demonstrating design in the universe and solar system has escalated dramatically. I am attempting to publish a quarterly update. The most recent of these updates describes thirty-five characteristics for the universe and 122 for the solar system.

A summary of the thirty-five characteristics of the universe that must be fine-tuned for any kind of physical life to be possible appears in table 2. Table 3 gives a conservative calculation of the probability that all 122 characteristics of our galaxy and solar system, acknowledged as fine-tuned for life, could

Table 2: Evidence for the Fine-Tuning of the Universe

1. strong nuclear force constant
   if larger: no hydrogen; nuclei essential for life would be unstable
   if smaller: no elements other than hydrogen

2. weak nuclear force constant
   if larger: too much hydrogen converted to helium in big bang, hence, too much heavy element material made by star burning; no expulsion of heavy elements from stars
   if smaller: too little helium produced from big bang, hence, too little heavy element material made by star burning; no expulsion of heavy elements from stars

3. gravitational force constant
   if larger: stars would be too hot and would burn up quickly and unevenly
   if smaller: stars would be so cool that nuclear fusion would not ignite, thus no heavy element production

4. electromagnetic force constant
   if larger: insufficient chemical bonding; elements more massive than boron would be unstable to fission
   if smaller: insufficient chemical bonding

5. ratio of electromagnetic force constant to gravitational force constant
   if larger: no stars less than 1.4 solar masses, hence, short and uneven stellar burning
   if smaller: no stars more than 0.8 solar masses, hence, no heavy element production

6. ratio of electron to proton mass
   if larger: insufficient chemical bonding
   if smaller: insufficient chemical bonding

7. ratio of number of protons to number of electrons
   if larger: electromagnetism would dominate gravity preventing galaxy, star, and planet formation
   if smaller: electromagnetism would dominate gravity preventing galaxy, star, and planet formation

8. expansion rate of the universe
   if larger: no galaxy formation
   if smaller: universe would collapse prior to star formation

9. entropy level of the universe
   if larger: no star condensation within the proto-galaxies
   if smaller: no proto-galaxy formation

10. mass density of the universe
    if larger: too much deuterium from big bang, hence, stars would burn too rapidly
    if smaller: insufficient helium from big bang, hence, too few heavy elements forming

11. velocity of light
    if faster: stars would be too luminous for life support
    if slower: stars would not be luminous enough for life support

12. age of the universe
    if older: no solar-type stars in a stable burning phase in the right part of the galaxy
    if younger: solar-type stars in a stable burning phase would not yet have formed

13. initial uniformity of radiation
    if smoother: stars, star clusters, and galaxies would not have formed
    if coarser: universe by now would be mostly black holes and empty space

14. average distance between galaxies
    if larger: insufficient gas would be infused into our galaxy to sustain star formation for a long enough time.
    if smaller: the sun's orbit would be too radically disturbed

15. galaxy cluster density
    if too rich: galaxy collisions and mergers would disrupt solar orbit
    if too sparse: insufficient infusion of gas to sustain star formation for a long enough time

16. average distance between stars
    if larger: heavy element density too thin for rocky planets to form
    if smaller: planetary orbits would become destabilized

17. fine structure constant (a number used to describe the fine structure splitting of spectral lines)
    if larger: no stars more than 0.7 solar masses
    if smaller: no stars less than 1.8 solar masses
    if larger than 0.06: matter is unstable in large magnetic fields

18. decay rate of the proton
    if greater: life would be exterminated by the release of radiation
    if smaller: insufficient matter in the universe for life

19. ^{12}C to ^{16}O nuclear energy level ratio
    if larger: insufficient oxygen
    if smaller: insufficient carbon

Table 2: Evidence for the Fine-Tuning of the Universe (continued)

20. ground state energy level for ^{4}He
    if larger: insufficient carbon and oxygen
    if smaller: insufficient carbon and oxygen

21. decay rate of ^{8}Be
    if slower: heavy element fusion would generate catastrophic explosions in all the stars
    if faster: no element production beyond beryllium and, hence, no life chemistry possible

22. mass excess of the neutron over the proton
    if greater: neutron decay would leave too few neutrons to form the heavy elements essential for life
    if smaller: proton decay would cause all stars to rapidly collapse into neutron stars or black holes

23. initial excess of nucleons over anti-nucleons
    if greater: too much radiation for planets to form
    if smaller: not enough matter for galaxies or stars to form

24. polarity of the water molecule
    if greater: heat of fusion and vaporization would be too great for life to exist
    if smaller: heat of fusion and vaporization would be too small for life; liquid water would be too inferior of solvent for life chemistry to proceed; ice would not float, leading to a runaway freeze-up

25. degree of uncertainty in the Heisenberg uncertainty principle
    if greater: too much quantum tunneling, which would disrupt life-essential protein chemistry
    if smaller: too little quantum tunneling, which would disrupt life-essential protein chemistry

26. size of the relativistic dilation factor
    if greater: certain life-essential chemical reactions would not function properly
    if smaller: certain life-essential chemical reactions would not function properly

27. supernovae eruptions
    if too close: radiation would exterminate life on the planet
    if too far: not enough heavy element ashes for the formation of rocky planets
    if too infrequent: not enough heavy element ashes for the formation of rocky planets
    if too frequent: life on the planet would be exterminated
    if too soon: not enough heavy element ashes for the formation of rocky planets
    if too late: life on the planet would be exterminated by radiation

28. white dwarf binaries
    if too few: insufficient fluorine produced for life chemistry to proceed
    if too many: disruption of planetary orbits from stellar density; life on the planet would be exterminated
    if too soon: not enough heavy elements made for efficient fluorine production
    if too late: fluorine made too late for incorporation in protoplanet

29. ratio of the mass of exotic matter to ordinary matter
    if smaller: galaxies would not form
    if larger: universe would collapse before solar-type stars can form

30. ratio of number of dwarf galaxies to number of large galaxies
    if smaller: significant star formation would shut down too soon
    if larger: life-candidate galaxies would become too unstable

31. number of effective dimensions in the early universe
    if smaller: quantum mechanics, gravity, and relativity could not coexist and life would be impossible
    if larger: quantum mechanics, gravity, and relativity could not coexist and life would be impossible

32. number of effective dimensions in the present universe
    if smaller: electron, planet, and star orbits would become unstable
    if larger: electron, planet, and star orbits would become unstable

33. mass of the neutrino
    if smaller: galaxy clusters, galaxies, and stars would not form
    if larger: galaxy clusters and galaxies would be too dense

34. big bang ripples
    if smaller: galaxies would not form; universe would expand too rapidly
    if larger: galaxy clusters and galaxies would be too dense; black holes would dominate; universe would collapse too quickly

35. cosmological constant
    if smaller: inadequate inflation in early history of the universe
    if larger: universe would expand too quickly for solar type stars to form

Table 3: Probability Estimate for Attaining the Necessary Parameters for a Life Support Planet

Parameter	Probability of Galaxy, Star, Planet, or Moon Falling in Required Range	Parameter	Probability of Galaxy, Star, Planet, or Moon Falling in Required Range
local abundance and distribution of dark matter	.1	period and size of eccentricity variation	.1
galaxy size	.1	period and size of inclination variation	.1
galaxy type	.1	number of moons	.2
galaxy location	.1	mass and distance of moon	.01
local dwarf galaxy absorption rate	.1	surface gravity (escape velocity)	.001
star distance relative to galactic center	.1	tidal force	.1
star distance from corotation circle of galaxy	.005	magnetic field	.01
star distance from closest spiral arm	.1	rate of change and character of change in magnetic field	.1
z-axis extremes of star's orbit	.1	albedo	.1
proximity of solar nebula to a supernova eruption	.01	density	.1
timing of solar nebula formation relative to supernova eruption	.01	thickness of crust	.01
number of stars in system	.7	oceans-to-continents ratio	.2
distance/mass of nearby stars	.1	rate of change in oceans-to-continents ratio	.1
star birth date	.2	global distribution of continents	.2
star age	.4	frequency, timing, and extent of ice ages	.1
star metallicity	.02	frequency, timing, and extent of global snowball events	.1
star orbital eccentricity	.1	asteroidal and cometary collision rate	.1
star's distance from galactic plane	.1	change in asteroidal and cometary collision rates	.1
star mass	.001	rate of change in asteroidal and cometary collision rates	.1
star luminosity change relative to speciation types and rates	.00001	mass of body colliding with primordial earth	.002
star color	.4	timing of body colliding with primordial earth	.05
star's carbon to oxygen ratio	.01	location of body's collision on primordial earth	.1
star's space velocity relative to Local Standard of Rest	.05	position and mass of Jupiter relative to Earth	.01
star's short-term variability	.05	major planet eccentricities	.1
star's long-term variability	.05	major planet orbital instabilities	.1
H3+ production	.1	drift and rate of drift in major planet distances	.05
supernovae rates and locations	.01	number and distribution of planets	.01
white dwarf binary types, rates, and locations	.01	atmospheric transparency	.01
location, timing, and rate of stellar encounters	.01	atmospheric pressure	.01
planetary distance from star	.001	atmospheric viscosity	.1
inclination of planetary orbit	.5	atmospheric electric discharge rate	.1
axis tilt of planet	.3	atmospheric temperature gradient	.01
rate of change of axial tilt	.01	carbon dioxide level in atmosphere	.01
period and size of axis tilt variation	.1	rate of change in carbon dioxide level in atmosphere	.1
planetary rotation period	.1	rate of change in water vapor level in atmosphere	.01
rate of change in planetary rotation period	.05	rate of change in methane level in early atmosphere	.01
planetary orbit eccentricity	.2	oxygen quantity in atmosphere	.01
rate of change of planetary orbital eccentricity	.1	chlorine quantity in atmosphere	.1
rate of change of planetary inclination	.5	cobalt quantity in crust	.1

Table 3: Probability Estimate for Attaining the Necessary Parameters for a Life Support Planet (continued)

Parameter	Probability of Galaxy, Star, Planet, or Moon Falling in Required Range	Parameter	Probability of Galaxy, Star, Planet, or Moon Falling in Required Range
arsenic quantity in crust	.1	quantity and timing of vascular plant introductions	.01
copper quantity in crust	.1		
boron quantity in crust	.1	quantity, timing, and placement of carbonate-producing animals	.00001
fluorine quantity in crust	.1		
iodine quantity in crust	.1	quantity, timing, and placement of methanogens	.00001
manganese quantity in crust	.1		
nickel quantity in crust	.1	quantity of soil sulfur	.1
phosphorus quantity in crust	.1	quantity of sulfur in the life planet's core	.1
potassium quantity in crust	.1	quantity of water at subduction zones	.01
tin quantity in crust	.1	hydration rate of subducted minerals	.1
zinc quantity in crust	.1	tectonic activity	.1
molybdenum quantity in crust	.05	rate of decline in tectonic activity	.1
vanadium quantity in crust	.1	volcanic activity	.1
chromium quantity in crust	.1	rate of decline in volcanic activity	.1
selenium quantity in crust	.1	viscosity at Earth core boundaries	.01
iron quantity in oceans	.1	viscosity of lithosphere	.2
tropospheric ozone quantity	.01	biomass to comet infall ratio	.01
stratospheric ozone quantity	.01	regularity of cometary infall	.1
mesospheric ozone quantity	.01		
water vapor level in atmosphere	.01	dependency factors estimate 1,000,000,000,000,000,000,000.	
oxygen to nitrogen ratio in atmosphere	.1		
quantity of greenhouse gases in atmosphere	.01	longevity requirements estimate	.0000001
rate of change of greenhouse gases in atmosphere	.01	Probability for occurrence of all 122 parameters $\approx 10^{-160}$	
quantity of forest and grass fires	.01	Maximum possible number of planets in universe $\approx 10^{22}$	
quantity of sea salt aerosols	.1		
soil mineralization	.1	Much less than 1 chance in 10^{138} (thousand trillion trillion trillion trillion trillion trillion trillion trillion trillion trillion) exists that even one such planet would occur anywhere in the universe.	
quantity of decomposer bacteria in soil	.01		
quantity of mycorrhizal fungi in soil	.01		
quantity of nitrifying microbes in soil	.01		

be met without invoking divine design. References to the discoveries on which these tables and calculations are based are presented in my books and booklets on the subject.[54]

Thirty-five years of research on the Anthropic Principle (the universe's tendency to provide every necessity for human life and sustenance) has built an expanding, rather than diminishing, body of evidence for divine design. What we see is the opposite of the old "God of the gaps" notion. As knowledge and understanding of the natural realm has advanced, the need to invoke a supernatural explanation has only increased. The thirty-five-year trend line moves so conclusively in one direction that nontheistic astronomers must own up to the nonscientific basis for their position. As cosmologist Ed Harrison says, an honest look at the cosmos's finely tuned features leads to a moment of truth:

Here is the cosmological proof of the existence of God—the design argument of Paley—updated and refurbished. The fine tuning of the universe provides *prima facie* evidence of deistic design. Take your choice: blind chance that requires multitudes of universes, or design that requires only one. . . . Many scientists, when they admit their views, incline toward the teleological or design argument.[55]

To place one's confidence in neo-Darwinist cosmology (i.e., blind chance) and the unknowable existence of a virtually infinite number of universes is to commit a form of the gambler's fallacy, a logic error so blatant as to expose irrationality. Let me illustrate. One could argue that a single coin flipped ten thousand times, coming up heads all ten thousand times, is not evidence that the coin has been designed to favor heads over tails on flips. After all, there might be $2^{10,000}$ coins, $2^{10,000}$ different coin flippers, producing $2^{10,000}$ outcomes different from the observed result of 10,000 consecutive heads. But if one had no evidence for the existence of $2^{10,000}$ coins, $2^{10,000}$ coin flippers, or $2^{10,000}$ distinct outcomes, then a form of the gambler's fallacy indeed will have been committed because one would be assuming the benefit of an extremely large sample size when, in fact, the sample size is only one. Given one coin and one flipper and a finite number of flips, the rational interpretation is that someone has fixed either the coin or the toss to come up with heads 10,000 times in a row.

In the case of the universe, we have one and only one to consider. General relativity tells us that since the first split second of the cosmos's existence, the space-time manifold of the universe has been "thermodynamically closed." This description means the space-time envelope of our universe cannot possibly overlap the space-time envelope of any other hypothetical universes. Therefore, we can either place our bets on the only universe we can ever possibly know, or we can speculate about hypothetical universes that will forever remain outside our realm of knowledge. To bet that the universe fell together exactly the way it is, precisely suited for life, by innumerable quirks of fate in innumerable universes makes even less sense than to bet that on the 10,001st toss, that same coin that has come up heads on the previous 10,000 observed tosses will come up tails.

CONCLUSION

The community of believers has no reason to fear and every reason to anticipate the advance of scientific research into the origin and characteristics of the cosmos. The more we learn, the more evidence we accumulate for the existence of God and for his identity as the God revealed in the Bible. Those who fight hardest against a supernatural, or theistic, explanation for the cosmos often produce the most powerful new evidence for it. As technology produces new measuring tools and theoretical capacities increase, the clearer the case for Christ the Creator will grow. Though not many scholars who write about these new measurements acknowledge Jesus as Lord and Savior, they do admit that the best, perhaps the only, explanation for the universe we observe is the work of an entity beyond the space-time continuum of the universe capable of exquisite design and of carrying out that design. Whether they know it or not, in their admission they have testified eloquently of the God who made us and wants to be known by us.

PART 4

WHY I BELIEVE THE BIBLE IS THE WORD OF GOD

It all comes down to this. If the Bible is not reliable, then Christianity is a hoax. And unlike any other religion, Christianity stands or falls based on the historical truth of an event in history: the resurrection of Jesus Christ. If this event did not happen as reported in the New Testament, if Jesus did not truly, literally, and physically rise from the dead (not figuratively, and not spiritually, but literally), then, as the apostle Paul put it, "Your faith is worthless. . . . We [Christians] are of all men most to be pitied" (1 Cor. 15:17, 19 NASB).

Christians believe in the resurrection of Jesus because the apostles, the eyewitnesses, recorded the event in the New Testament. No other religion stakes everything—*everything*—on the historicity of its holy book. But then again, no other religion offers the good news that God himself actually entered history as a human being to save a fallen humanity. Christianity is historical, it is grounded, it is physical, it is literal, it is thoroughly down-to-earth. And there are no secrets, no lofty bits of special knowledge for a privileged few. The good news is easily accessible to everyone; just pick up the book, in whatever language you speak, and read.

Reading the Bible works, that is, it truly changes lives, only because it truly is the Word of God. God, of course, is perfect, so that which is truly his Word must also be perfect. It must never fail to state accurately the facts asserted, and it certainly must never hold out as true something that is not or cannot possibly be true. In short, it must be historically and scientifically reliable.

We have now arrived at a point that, for Christians, constitutes one of the greatest academic battlefields of our day: the reliability of Scripture. Like the offensive line of a football team, the next three contributors have done the gritty and fundamental work of defending the Bible. They are strong and capable scholars who together create a hole in the line of attack so that others can run through and advance the Word.

Starting at center, we again have Dr. Gary R. Habermas, a religious historian and philosopher. In chapter 9, he demonstrates that the historical reliability of the New Testament far exceeds that of any other document from the ancient world. In addition to a few more customary strategies, he shows how four recent approaches regularly employed even by critical scholars enhance greatly the historical reliability of the New Testament.

At right guard is Dr. Walter Bradley, a scientist and professor of mechanical engineering. He addresses the most common objections to the scientific reliability of the Bible. With clarity and precision, he shows that though the Bible is not a science text, it is nonetheless reliable and sound when it makes statements that can be tested by science.

Finally, at tackle, is Dr. Winfried Corduan, a professor of philosophy and religion. In chapter 11, he undertakes the politically incorrect task of explaining why the Bible alone is the Word of God. You will see that there are actually few serious contenders for *the* Word of God and that the Bible is the winner, hands down.

NINE

WHY I BELIEVE THE NEW TESTAMENT IS HISTORICALLY RELIABLE

GARY R. HABERMAS

The credibility of Scripture is certainly a multifaceted issue. In this chapter, I will examine one specific angle—whether the New Testament is a *historically* reliable document. Topics such as precise textual issues, genre considerations, specific critical methodologies, scientific concerns, and the doctrine of inspiration are beyond the focus here.[1] Instead, I will examine several areas that indicate that the New Testament speaks accurately when it makes historical claims that can be checked. I will begin by assessing some conventional areas of consideration.

CUSTOMARY STRATEGIES

Typically, defenses of the reliability of the New Testament have emphasized several items: the superior manuscript numbers, early dating of these copies, as well as the authoritative authorship and dating of the original compositions. I will respond briefly to each, since they all still have an important part to play. Since these defenses have received much attention, however, I will only highlight a number of relevant issues.

MANUSCRIPT EVIDENCE

To start, are we even able to ascertain whether the text of the Bible is that of the original authors? While this issue relates strictly to the reliability of the text rather than to the historicity of its contents, the issue is still important in the overall scheme of this discussion. Generally, several qualities enhance manuscript value, assisting textual scholars in arriving at the best reading of the original text. The strongest case is made when many manuscripts are available, as close in time to the original autographs as possible. Wide geographical distribution of the copies and their textual families are likewise crucial. Of course, having complete texts is essential.

In light of these criteria, the New Testament is the best attested work from the ancient world. First, it has by far the greatest number of existing manuscripts. Ancient classical works are attested to by very few full or partial manuscripts—usually less than ten. In comparison, over five thousand full or partial Greek manuscripts of the New Testament exist. Thousands of additional texts exist in other languages, especially Latin. This overwhelming number of copies yields a much stronger base for establishing the original text.

Concerning the date between the original writing and the earliest copies, ancient classical works generally exhibit gaps of at least seven hundred years. The interval significantly lengthens to twice this amount (or longer) with certain works by a number of key writers such as Plato and Aristotle. In contrast, the Bodmer and Chester Beatty Papyri contain most of the New Testament, dating about 100–150 years later than the New Testament, using an approximate date of A.D. 100 for its completion. The Codex Sinaiticus is a complete copy of the New Testament, while the Codex Vaticanus is a nearly complete manuscript, both dating roughly 250 years after the originals. These small gaps help to ensure the accuracy of the New Testament text.

Further, significant portions of some ancient works are missing. For example, 107 of Livy's 142 books of Roman history have been lost. Of Tacitus's original *Histories* and *Annals*, only approximately half remain.

The fact that there is outstanding manuscript evidence for the New Testament documents is even admitted by critical scholars.[2] John A. T. Robinson succinctly explains, "The wealth of manuscripts, and above all the narrow interval of time between the writing and the earliest extant copies, make it by far the best attested text of any ancient writing in the world."[3] Even Helmut Koester summarizes:

> Classical authors are often represented by but one surviving manuscript; if there are half a dozen or more, one can speak of a rather advantageous situation for reconstructing the text. But there are nearly five thousand manuscripts of the NT in Greek. . . . The only surviving manuscripts of classical authors often come from the Middle Ages, but the manuscript tradition of the NT begins as early as the end of II CE; it is therefore separated by only a century or so from the time at which the autographs were written. Thus it seems that NT textual criticism possesses a base which is far more advantageous than that for the textual criticism of classical authors.[4]

The result of all this is an incredibly accurate New Testament text. John Wenham asks why it is that, in spite of the "great diversity" in our copies, the texts are still relativity homogeneous. He responds, "The only satisfactory answer seems to be that its homogeneity stems from an exceedingly early text—virtually, that is, from the autographs."[5] The resulting text is 99.99 percent accurate, and the remaining questions do not affect any area of cardinal Christian doctrine.[6]

AUTHORSHIP AND DATE

The above described quality of manuscript data shows that the New Testament manuscripts were careful copies of what the original authors produced. However, this does not necessarily guarantee that the contents of these writings are historically accurate. The traditional strategy has been to argue that the Gospels and Acts were written by eyewitnesses, or those writing under their influence, thereby ensuring as much as possible the factual content. A somewhat more cautious position is that these five books were at least influenced by eyewitness testimony.[7]

Evangelical scholars often date each of the synoptic Gospels ten or so years earlier than their critical counterparts, who usually prefer dates of roughly A.D. 65–90. There is widespread agreement on placing John at roughly A.D. 95. This places the writing of the manuscripts thirty-five to sixty-five years after the death of Jesus, close enough to allow for accurate accounts.

Perhaps the most promising way to support the traditional approach is to argue backward from the Book of Acts. Most of this book is occupied with the ministries of Peter and Paul, and much of the action centers in the city of Jerusalem. The martyrdoms of Stephen (7:54–60) and the apostle James (12:1–2) are recorded, and the book concludes with Paul under arrest in Rome (28:14–31). Yet Acts says nothing concerning the deaths of Paul and Peter (mid-60s A.D.), or James, Jesus' brother (about A.D. 62). Moreover, accounts of the Jewish War with the Romans (beginning in A.D. 66) and the fall of

Jerusalem (A.D. 70) are also strangely absent. Further, the book ends enigmatically with Paul under house arrest, without any resolution to the situation.

How could the author of Acts not mention these events or resolve Paul's dilemma, each of which is centrally related to the text's crucial themes? These events would even seem to dwarf many of the other recorded occurrences.[8] It is difficult to resist the conclusion that the author did not record these items simply because they had not yet occurred. These omissions argue persuasively for an early date for the composition of Acts, before the mid-60s A.D.

If it is held that Luke was written prior to Acts but after Mark and Matthew, as perhaps most critical scholars do, then all five books may be dated before A.D. 65. It is simply amazing that Acts could be dated A.D. 80–85 and the author not be aware of, or otherwise neglect to mention, any of these events.[9]

ADDITIONAL SUPPORT

Extra-biblical sources are another avenue worth pursuing when determining whether the New Testament texts speak reliably concerning historical issues. While less frequently used by scholars, a number of ancient secular sources mention various aspects of Jesus' life, corroborating the picture presented by the Gospels.[10] The writers of these sources include ancient historians such as Tacitus, Suetonius, and Thallus. Jewish sources such as Josephus and the Talmud add to our knowledge. Government officials such as Pliny the Younger and even Roman Caesars Trajan and Hadrian describe early Christian beliefs and practices. Greek historian and satirist Lucian and Syrian Mara Bar-Serapion provide other details. Several nonorthodox, Gnostic writings speak about Jesus in a more theological manner.[11]

Overall, at least seventeen non-Christian writings record more than fifty details concerning the life, teachings, death, and resurrection of Jesus, plus details concerning the earliest church. Most frequently reported is Jesus' death, mentioned by twelve sources. Dated approximately 20 to 150 years after Jesus' death, these secular sources are quite early by the standards of ancient historiography.

Altogether, these non-Christian sources mention that Jesus fulfilled Old Testament prophecy, performed miracles, led disciples, and that many thought he was deity. These sources call him a good teacher or a philosopher and state that his message included conversion, denial of the gods, fellowship, and immortality. Further, they claim he was crucified for blasphemy but rose from the dead and appeared to his disciples, who were themselves transformed into bold preachers.[12]

A number of early Christian sources also report numerous details concerning the historical Jesus. Some, such as the writings of Clement of Rome, Ignatius, and Polycarp, date from A.D. 95–110, or just ten years after the last New Testament book.[13]

Information of a different sort can be derived from archaeological artifacts. While few provide direct confirmation of Jesus, they do provide helpful background information. Places such as the Bethesda and Siloam pools, the foundations of Herod's temple, possible locations of Pilate's Praetorium, and the general vicinity of Golgotha and the Garden tomb all enlighten modern readers. Much information has been gained about ancient Jewish social customs, and many details have been revealed concerning the cities, towns, coinage, commerce, and languages of first-century Palestine.[14] A. N. Sherwin-White has furnished a remarkable amount of background information corroborating many details of the trial of Jesus, as well as other legal scenes in the New Testament.[15]

In a few cases, more specific data is available. For example, the Latin inscription "Titulus Venetus" helps to illumine Augustus's census. A Latin plaque mentions "Pontius Pilatus, Prefect of Judaea." The bones of a first-century A.D. crucifixion victim, Yohanan, tell us much about the gruesome spectacle of crucifixion. The Nazareth Decree, perhaps circulated by Emperor Claudius between A.D. 41 and 54, threatens tomb robbers with death.[16]

In summary, those who use traditional strategies to support the historical reliability of the New Testament assert that superior manuscript evidence shows we have essentially what the authors wrote. By linking closely the authors and composition dates to the events themselves, it is argued that the writers were in the best position to know what actually occurred. Additional data are provided by extra-biblical and archaeological sources, showing that, when these details are checked, the New Testament fares well.

A surprising amount of traditional data corroborates the life and teachings of Jesus. Many questions remain, to be sure, but the available evidence indicates that believers are on strong ground when reporting the general reliability of the New Testament reports of the historical Jesus.

RECENT STRATEGIES

Scholarship in recent years, however, has moved in other directions. While not necessarily denying the traditional arguments just discussed, scholars are frequently less interested in the question of the New Testament's reliability. Nonetheless, among the contemporary tendencies to which critics gravitate, there are still many gems to be mined—treasures that point in additional ways to the historical trustworthiness of the New Testament. Some of the prizes turn out to be powerful tools. Four such approaches are outlined below.

CRITICAL RULES

The trend among recent critical scholars is not to accept the reliability of the Gospels in a wholesale manner. Rather, the tendency is to apply certain analytical principles to ascertain which individual texts or portions of texts have the greatest likelihood of being historically accurate. In so doing, these biblical scholars are following the trend set by historians in their own examination of ancient texts.[17] Following is a brief inventory of some of the rules that apply to written sources.

(1) Early evidence is strongly preferred, and in reference to Jesus, data from A.D. 30 to 50 would be exemplary.[18] If these sources can be drawn from (2) the accounts of eyewitnesses to the occurrences, this would provide two of the strongest evidences possible. Historian David Hackett Fischer dubs this last criterion "the rule of immediacy" and terms it "the best relevant evidence."[19]

(3) Independent attestation by more than one source significantly strengthens a factual claim from antiquity. As historian Paul Maier notes, "Many facts from antiquity rest on just one ancient source, while two or three sources in agreement generally render the fact unimpeachable."[20] Even the highly skeptical Jesus Seminar emphasizes items "attested in two or more independent sources."[21]

Some details are enhanced by additional criteria. (4) The principle of embarrassment, negative report, or surprise reveals disparaging remarks made by the author about himself, another person, or event toward which the author is *friendly* and has a vested interest.[22] (5) Precisely the opposite can also provide a different sort of evidence: when an antagonistic source agrees about a person or event when it is *not* in the source's best interests to do so. Maier even thinks that "such positive evidence within a hostile source is the strongest kind of evidence. . . . If Cicero, who despised Catiline, admitted that the fellow had one good quality—courage—among a host of bad ones then the historian correctly concludes that Catiline was at least courageous."[23]

(6) A skeptical criterion of historicity is that of dissimilarity or discontinuity. A saying, for instance, can be attributed to a person only if it cannot be plausibly attributed to other contemporary sources. In the case of Jesus, the chief issue is whether a Gospel teaching can be ascribed to either Jewish thought or to the early church. Historian Michael Grant calls this the "principal valid method of research."[24]

(7) Another criterion specifically applied to Gospel studies is the presence of Aramaic words, substrata, or other indications of a Palestinian origin. Such conditions are thought to bring us closer to Jesus' teachings.[25]

An overall test is (8) coherence. Does an event or teaching fit well with what is known concerning other surrounding occurrences and teachings?[26] Even better, does the proposed event illuminate other known incidents, thereby making them more intelligible?

Certainly one of the strongest methodological indications of historicity occurs when (9) a case can be built on accepted data that are recognized as well established by a wide range of otherwise diverse historians. Historian Christopher Blake refers to this as the "very considerable part of history which is acceptable to the community of professional historians."[27]

Combining a number of these critical rules of evidence, I propose what I call the "minimal facts" historical method, using precisely those data that satisfy at least two major standards. (1) Each event must be exceptionally well attested on several grounds, as indicated by criteria such as those listed above, and

(2) the events must be admitted as historical by the vast majority of scholars who treat this specific topic. Of these two tests, the first one (strong confirmation for multiple reasons) is clearly the most significant. In chapter 7, we viewed Jesus' miracles and his resurrection in light of these criteria.[28]

Other historical rules could be mentioned,[79] but those described above are sufficient for our current purposes. The functional value of critically applied rules such as these can be seen in many contemporary studies. They are often the decisive tests that are applied to the Gospel accounts in order to derive much of the basis for what is perhaps the major emphasis of current New Testament scholars today, the study of the historical Jesus. Other considerations may also be employed,[30] some of which will be pursued below, as we attempt to build a case for the historicity of the New Testament.

THE GOSPELS AND ANCIENT HISTORIOGRAPHY

A second trend among a few scholars today is to defend the Gospels based on standards derived from ancient historiography. Both because the study of the historical Jesus is so prominent today and because too many analyses simply miss the benefits of such a comparison, I will devote a little more room to this discussion, but from a historical perspective only.[31]

R. T. France takes this approach regarding the authorship of the Gospels. While he thinks a plausible case can be made for the traditional writers, he suggests a different tack. He contends that "authorship . . . is not a major factor in our assessment of the reliability of the gospels."[32] France insists that we evaluate the Gospels by the same criteria that are used in studying ancient writings. Not only are the Gospels the earliest sources for Jesus, but the nature of the tradition behind them should cause us to treat them seriously.[33]

Some scholars still approach the Gospels in terms of authorship,[34] but France's point is noteworthy. Rather than view the Gospels as largely nonhistorical, religious propaganda, as do some critics, ancient historians and classical scholars often treat the Gospels quite seriously. These writings are frequently viewed as important sources for information concerning Jesus, opposing the more radical versions of criticism encouraged by some contemporary New Testament scholars. In fact, ancient historians regularly detect an adequate basis for historical data, especially in the Gospels. Roman historian Sherwin-White leveled the following accusation at modern biblical scholarship:

> So, it is astonishing that while Greco-Roman historians have been growing in confidence, the twentieth-century study of the Gospel narratives, starting from no less promising material, has taken so gloomy a turn in the development of form-criticism . . . that the historical Christ is unknowable and the history of his mission cannot be written. This seems very curious.[35]

Although the reference to form criticism is a bit outdated, Sherwin-White's chief point is clear. Because the Gospel narratives are "no less promising" than

Greco-Roman sources, the same standards commonly applied to ancient non-religious history can also be applied to the New Testament records. The result yields a significant amount of factual content.

Michael Grant is another ancient historian who reaches similar conclusions. By employing normal historical techniques in regard to the New Testament, he concluded that much can be known about the historical Jesus.[36] Grant specifically rejects the methodology of radical theologians who insist that the New Testament is guilty until it is proven innocent, since "that also is too extreme a viewpoint and would not be applied in other fields."[37] The key, therefore, is the application of the same historiographical principles to both the Gospels and ancient documents.

At this point, critics often raise two major objections to the comparison of the New Testament writings to ancient Greco-Roman sources. (1) The Gospels contain many reports of supernatural events, which militates against their claim to be historical documents. (2) Further, the Gospels cannot be compared to ancient, nonreligious writings, since the latter recorded history while the former were written by authors whose religious doctrines significantly colored their perspectives. In short, we are told that the Gospels are of a different genre. The writers were not as concerned with discerning history as with relating miracles and composing religious propaganda written for the purpose of indoctrination.

Regarding the charge of miraculous claims, the critic is simply mistaken to separate the Gospels from ancient historical documents. Ancient histories regularly recounted supernatural reports of all sorts, including omens and portents, prophecies, healing miracles, various sorts of divine interventions, as well as demonic activity. Examples are literally too numerous to miss. For instance, in his widely recognized account of Alexander the Great, Plutarch begins by noting Alexander's likely descent from Hercules. Later he tells how the gods favored and assisted Alexander in his battles and how Alexander talked with a priest who claimed to be the son of the god Ammon and then with Ammon himself. Near the end of his life, Alexander took almost every unusual event to be supernatural, surrounding himself with diviners and others who foretold the future.[38]

But such is quite normal fare in ancient historical writings. Tacitus reports worship of the caesars, even by the Roman Senate, and that people saw normal occurrences such as crop failure as omens.[39] Suetonius provides a wider range of examples, including the working of fate, sightings of spirits and ghosts of deceased emperors, prayers to the gods, prophecies, rulers who read horoscopes and animal entrails, as well as an entire host of omens and portents manifest in comets, lightning, dreams, and even birds. Strangely, some of the caesars, convinced by signs that their death was imminent, awaited their demise in a dire state of mind.[40]

It is true that these ancient writers may have at times simply recorded what certain people believed or thought they saw. In fact, on occasion they questioned whether certain occurrences were truly supernatural.[41] But there can be no doubt that at other times these same writers clearly accepted the supernatural reports.[42]

These examples are sufficient to assist us in reaching a verdict regarding the supernatural reports in ancient histories. These reports do not keep us from proclaiming their texts to be reliable historical accounts, as modern historians explicitly recognize.[43] So why should the Gospels be treated far more severely for the same reasons, especially when they report the supernatural perhaps even less commonly?

Another objection might also be raised here. Why should *any* ancient report of supernatural activity be accepted today? This question involves several philosophical issues, as well as the subject of historical evidence.[44] We are justified in rejecting the Greco-Roman supernatural claims precisely because they are not accompanied by a sufficient amount of evidence. On the other hand, many New Testament miracles, and the resurrection of Jesus in particular, are surrounded by exceptional evidence. Even critical scholars such as those in the Jesus Seminar think that the best data indicate that Jesus performed healings of some sort. Marcus Borg concedes that there are some "very strong" historical reasons that favor this conclusion. But can truly supernatural events be excluded? Borg thinks that we cannot rule them out.[45] (See chapter 7, which discusses Jesus' miracles and resurrection in detail.)

What about the second charge, that religious purposes kept the Gospel authors from recording history? Numerous responses to this complaint are found in the writings of A. N. Sherwin-White, Michael Grant, and other historians.[46] (1) Several prominent writers in antiquity composed works with purposes fairly similar to the intent exhibited in the Gospels. One example is Plutarch, who even declared that "my design was not to write histories, but lives."[47] Grant explains that the Gospel authors "would have applauded" many of these ancient efforts. The secular sources are still well recognized as historical, so why should the Gospels not be treated similarly?[48]

(2) The sort of thoroughgoing propaganda literature that some critics believe the Gospels to be was actually nonexistent in ancient times. Sherwin-White declares, "We are not acquainted with this type of writing in ancient historiography."[49]

(3) The Gospels are dated a maximum of several decades after the life of Jesus, while other ancient authors often recount events that took place even centuries earlier. For instance, Livy comments on Rome's beginnings by relating accounts from hundreds of years before his time.[50] Plutarch, too, writes extensively about persons who lived centuries before him.[51] But modern historians are able to reconstruct the ancient past, even in cases in which their sources report events that are vastly earlier.

(4) Critics sometimes point out what they believe are discrepancies in the Gospels that undermine their claim to historicity. From one angle, each case could be examined on its own grounds.[52] Yet, ancient histories sometimes "disagree amongst themselves in the widest possible fashion," but this fails to deter the modern scholar from reconstructing the past.[53] In answering the

same question about the Gospels, Maier states, "The earliest sources telling of the great fire of Rome, for example, offer far more serious conflicts. . . . Yet the fire itself is historical: it really happened."[54]

(5) Contemporary theologians are too often satisfied simply to discuss the religious experiences of the earliest Christians, as if this were an end in itself. However, historians pursue adequate causes behind these experiences.[55]

(6) One New Testament writing that has been confirmed by surprising amounts of external data is the Book of Acts. As Sherwin-White argues, "For Acts the confirmation of history is overwhelming." Although he thinks that Acts is no less given to propaganda than the Gospels, Sherwin-White still concludes that "any attempt to reject its basic historicity even in matters of detail must now appear absurd. Roman historians have long taken it for granted."[56]

(7) Even if radical criticism is applied to the Gospels, this still should not thwart the discovery of much historical data in these works. Although the Gospel writers' primary concern may have been theological in nature, it does not automatically follow that they would thereby have been unable to preserve the relevant historical facts in the process. Theological or moralizing motives can coexist with the reporting of facts.[57]

For many reasons, then, historians see a number of weaknesses in the critical methodology that is so popular with certain contemporary theologians. In sum, if the same criteria that are regularly applied to other ancient writings are also implemented by New Testament scholars, a solid historical basis emerges for the life and teachings of Jesus.[58]

However, it is far from the case that all New Testament scholars have adopted the stance of radical criticism. A. M. Hunter maintains that there are several reasons for believing that the Gospel presentation of Jesus is essentially reliable. (1) The earliest believers were Jews who were very careful about faithfully preserving the initial traditions of Jesus' life and teachings; (2) the Gospel authors were "in a position to know the facts about Jesus"; (3) Jesus taught in such a manner that his teachings could be more easily remembered; (4) all four Gospels correctly reflect the first-century Palestinian mileau; and (5) in spite of differences, the same portrait of Jesus emerges from each of the four Gospels.[59]

By applying the same methods to the Gospels that are applied to other ancient documents, then, scholars have shown that these four volumes provide accurate depictions of Jesus' life.[60]

THE WRITINGS AND THOUGHTS OF THE APOSTLE PAUL

At present, next to the historical Jesus, perhaps the most popular New Testament area of research is the writings and thoughts of the apostle Paul. Due to the exceptionally high respect given to Paul by critical scholars, his epistles are therefore one of the best ways to approach aspects of the historicity of Jesus and the reliability of the New Testament.

The majority of critical scholars question or reject a few of the epistles that bear Paul's name—usually some of the prison and/or pastoral epistles.[61] But Romans, Corinthians, Galatians, and Philippians are rarely questioned, even by skeptics, and 1 Thessalonians and Philemon are widely respected. At least the first five, and often the last two, belong to the corpus that recent scholars refer to as Paul's "undisputed letters."[62] In spite of his critical approach, Helmut Koester states that all seven books are "generally accepted as genuine without doubt."[63] Even G. A. Wells acknowledges that a group of writings is unanimously considered Pauline, while personally admitting as genuine eight of Paul's epistles—the above seven plus Colossians.[64]

Therefore, scholars can trace historical paths from Paul's accepted epistles to the historicity of Jesus or early Christian beliefs. What might such approaches look like? Three are described below.

One route is to list the historical data about Jesus—both the events of his life and his teachings—that are specifically found in Paul's accepted epistles. Jesus was born as a Jew (Gal. 3:16) from the family of David (Rom. 1:3) and lived under Jewish law (Gal. 4:4). Jesus had brothers (1 Cor. 9:5), one of whom was James (1 Cor. 15:7), as well as twelve disciples (1 Cor. 15:7). Paul knew that at least some of Jesus' brothers and apostles had wives (1 Cor. 9:5). In fact, Paul knew personally James, as well as apostles Peter and John, having spent time with at least the first two on more than one occasion (Gal. 1:18–2:16).

Paul also relates a few personal qualities about Jesus. He was poor (2 Cor. 8:9),[65] a servant who acted with humility (Phil. 2:5, 7–8), meekness, and gentleness (2 Cor. 10:1). Though he did not act on his own behalf, he was still abused by others (Rom. 15:3). Further, Paul also knew a number of Jesus' teachings and encouraged believers to obey them. This is clearly indicated when he specifically refers to Jesus' words (1 Cor. 7:10; 9:14; 11:23–25). A number of times, his point seems to been taken from one of Jesus' sayings in the Gospels. Some of these instances include the topics of divorce and remarriage (1 Cor. 7:10–11), ministers being payed wages (1 Cor. 9:14), paying taxes (Rom. 13:6–7), the duty to love our neighbors as we do ourselves (Rom. 13:9), and ceremonial cleanliness (Rom. 14:14). On topics such as women, the treatment of sinners, and society's outcasts, Paul also seems to have been aware of Jesus' attitudes and teaching. His assertions about specific titles reflecting Jesus' deity are another important area for comparison with Jesus' own teachings (Rom. 1:3–4; 10:9). Paul also encourages believers to be vigilant in light of Jesus' second coming (1 Thess. 4:15), which would happen like the thief that comes in the night (1 Thess. 5:2–11).

Paul provides the most details concerning the last week of Jesus' life, speaking frequently of these events due to their centrality to the gospel. He gives particulars concerning the Lord's Supper, even citing the words Jesus spoke on this occasion (1 Cor. 11:23–25). Paul speaks often of Jesus' death (Rom. 4:25; 5:8), specifying crucifixion (Rom. 6:6; Gal. 2:20) and mentioning Jewish instigation

(1 Thess. 2:14–15). He tells how Jesus was buried, rose again three days later, and appeared to numerous people, both individually and in groups (1 Cor. 15:3–8). He is now at God's right hand (Rom. 8:34).[66]

Paul's recognized epistles, as accredited sources, provide a rough outline of Jesus' life and teachings. When Paul's authorship is granted to other epistles, we gain additional sources from which we can draw information.[67]

Another direction is provided by C. H. Dodd, who argued forcefully that "a comparison, then, of the Pauline epistles with the speeches in Acts leads to a fairly clear and certain outline sketch of the preaching of the apostles."[68] As such, critical investigation can establish the "essential elements" of "apostolic Preaching" [sic] back to an early date.[69]

A somewhat similar but more radical approach is taken by New Testament historian Paul Barnett. Totally apart from the Gospels and Acts, he argues that we can gain an understanding of the earliest apostolic activity before and after Easter from Paul's epistles alone. Suffice it to say, he outlines such a case, arguing from "passing references in Paul's letters" to "our earliest window" of primitive apostolic teachings, soon after Jesus' ministry.[70]

In all three of these approaches, Paul's writings provide the primary historical groundwork from which we may reconstruct the central portions and the overall contours of the early Christian message.

Critics seldom provide any additional grounds for their positive approach to Paul, apparently thinking that this is unnecessary. But such reasons are not difficult to find. In the earliest period after the close of the New Testament canon, at the end of the first century, at least three writers knew his books well. Clement of Rome (c. A.D. 95–96), Ignatius (c. A.D. 107), and Polycarp (c. A.D. 110) quote or otherwise refer to statements in twelve of the thirteen letters traditionally attributed to Paul. Only Philemon is exempted, probably because of its brief, nontheological nature. The other twelve epistles are cited almost ninety times! Of this total, 1 Corinthians is mentioned over thirty times, the most referenced of Paul's letters from this early date.[71] Clement testifies to the early belief in the authenticity and inspiration of Paul's first letter to Corinth: "Take up the epistle of the blessed Paul the Apostle." In it, Paul spoke "in the Spirit."

Very rarely do even skeptics doubt the Pauline authorship of this work. In fact, we could hardly hope for more critical consensus. Not even G. A. Wells protests the authorship of 1 Corinthians, including it among those texts that "are universally accepted as genuinely Pauline."[72] Scholars are equally agreed on the approximate date of 1 Corinthians. Paul first visited the city of Corinth roughly A.D. 51–52 (cf. Acts 18:1–18). His first epistle to them was written between 53 and 57,[73] approximately twenty-five years after Jesus' death.[74]

We are on solid critical ground, therefore, in accepting 1 Corinthians as the apostle Paul's work, dating from a comparatively short time after Jesus' death. On matters concerning the historical Jesus, Paul was an authoritative source, an eyewitness who was close to the data he records.

CREEDS OR TRADITIONS

What was the content of the earliest apostolic preaching before the first New Testament book was written? The vast majority of people in the first-century Mediterranean world were illiterate, so it was necessary for them to learn orally.[75] This requirement meant that the easiest way for the central elements of a message to be remembered long after they were heard was for them to be presented in a brief, easily retainable manner.

In the New Testament, we find numerous statements that actually predate the texts in which they are embedded. These creeds or traditions are often concise, catchy sayings that are packed with meaning in a minimal number of words. They provide the clearest examples of the apostolic teaching that occurred in the earliest years after Jesus' death but prior to the first canonical writings. As such, this is one of the most important, as well as most exciting, topics in New Testament studies.[76] Scholars have pointed out several textual indicators that these creeds are present.[77]

The clearest indication of a creedal statement occurs when a writer specifically tells us that he is passing on such a tradition. The best example is Paul, who distinctly states on various occasions that he is repeating teachings or traditions, sometimes explaining that they have been given to him by others.[78] Other indicators include the presence of a stylistic rhythm, a repetitive word pattern that shows up elsewhere in the New Testament, a different syntactical configuration from the immediate context, the inclusion of vocabulary or style that are not the author's normal speech patterns, along with the presentation of a fairly simple, unevolved theology.[79]

In these early creedal statements, we find numerous reports about Jesus. He was born in the lineage of David, came from the town of Nazareth, was preceded by John the Baptist, had twelve disciples, preached, performed miracles, and fulfilled Old Testament Scripture. Several other details are narrated concerning the Last Supper, Jesus' appearance before Pilate, and the confession he gave before this Roman ruler. Multiple creeds also report that Jesus was crucified and died in Jerusalem and was buried. But he was resurrected three days later and appeared to many of his followers, both individually as well as in groups. Later, he ascended to heaven and was glorified. His miracles and especially his resurrection showed that God vindicated him along with his message, and many believed in him. These early confessions also ascribe to Jesus the titles of deity, such as Son of God, Lord, Christ or Messiah, and Savior.[80]

The value of these creedal statements can hardly be overestimated. Not only do they report significant aspects regarding Jesus' life, but they do so from an exceptionally early time period that is very close in date to the events themselves. Perhaps even more crucial, they reflect the preaching and teaching of those who were closest to Jesus, from the earliest period of the church. While a number of these traditions are reported by Paul, many others are not. These latter examples fill in even more details concerning Jesus' life, death, and resurrection.[81]

CONCLUSION

This chapter reveals that the New Testament fares exceptionally well in terms of its historical reliability, actually exceeding what is often expected of an ancient text. We have in the New Testament essentially what the authors originally penned, and the texts have been confirmed time and again by various means. Tough questions will always have to be addressed, but we have a highly evidenced document from which to proceed.

TEN

WHY I BELIEVE THE BIBLE IS SCIENTIFICALLY RELIABLE

WALTER BRADLEY

During my thirty-five years of teaching at universities, I have had many opportunities to talk to skeptical students and colleagues about Christianity. Often these discussions have been in the context of a lunchtime or evening discussion for the purpose of exploring the bigger questions about life. I have found that scientists and engineers can much more easily accept the existence of God than they can biblical Christianity. Why is this so, and should it be the case?

The scientific discoveries of the past fifty years have dramatically changed the view of many scientists concerning the existence of God. Science historian Frederick Burnham recently commented that for scientists belief in God is more "respectable" today than at any time in the past hundred years.[1] Michael Shermer, editor of *Skeptics Magazine*, indicates that he believes the natural world provides the best evidence for belief in God. In his recent book, *How We Believe: Search for God in an Age of Science*,[2] Shermer uses empirical results from a survey of twenty thousand people to demonstrate that, of those people who base their belief in God more on reason than on experience, the majority cite the evidence for a carefully crafted universe as their first reason. Over the past fifteen years, I have seen a dramatic increase in the acceptance of the design argument as I have had the opportunity to give a talk entitled "Is There Scientific Evidence for an Intelligent Creator of the Universe?" to over thirty thousand students on over sixty major university campuses around the country. In the past ten years, *Time* and *Newsweek* magazines have run major stories summarizing the scientific evidence that seems to point to a Creator God.

Ironically, while scientific discoveries have strengthened belief in a Creator, the confidence that the public has in the Bible has been systematically eroded by highly publicized "conflicts" between science and the Bible during the past 150 years, beginning with the seminal work of Charles Darwin. The 1927 Scopes "Monkey Trial" was a huge milestone in this controversy, with the biblical position argued by William Jennings Bryan being effectively ridiculed by Clarence Darrow. The popular movie *Inherit the Wind* based on the book by the same name reminded the next generation of this controversy, unfairly portraying Bryan as an ignorant bigot. Edward J. Larson documents the historical distortions in the movie *Inherit the Wind* in his Pulitzer Prize–winning book, *The Summer of the Gods: The Scopes Trial and America's Continuing Debate over Science and Religion*.[3]

Not all the heat for the Bible-science controversy came from advances in science, however. Higher criticism of the Bible and the rejection by liberal theologians in the nineteenth and twentieth centuries of supernatural events portrayed in the Bible created internal pressure within the church to deny the validity of any statement in the Bible that implied supernatural activity. For example, German theologian Franz Delitzsch at the beginning of the twentieth century wrote, "All attempts to harmonize our biblical story of the creation of the world with the results of natural science have been useless and must always be so."[4]

Any evaluation of the supernatural events of the New Testament must necessarily be philosophical and historical, as these unique events would have left no imprint in natural history for science to investigate. On the other hand, the events of the creation and early history of humankind recorded in Genesis 1–11 make claims that most certainly should be evident in natural history. It is these controversial claims that form the core of the Bible-science controversy.

The supposed contradictions between the Bible and science have been popularized by well-known television personalities and writers such as Steve Allen and Isaac Asimov. In his popular critique of the Bible, Steve Allen argues that the worldwide flood described in the Bible is impossible to reconcile with geological history.[5] Asimov, who is an accomplished science popularizer and science fiction writer, has written a best-selling commentary on the Bible.[6] He interprets Genesis 1 as saying that the sun, the stars, and the moon were created after light, after the water cycle, and after plants.[7] His interpretation of Genesis 2 places the creation of plants and animals between the creation of Adam and the creation of Eve. This then provides the basis for his labeling Genesis 1 and 2 "folktales."[8]

The approach of the National Academy of Sciences of the United States has been to make religion and science mutually exclusive domains of knowing with its statement, "Religion and science are separate and mutually exclusive realms of human thought whose presentation in the same context leads to misunderstanding of both scientific theory and religious belief."[9] This sounds like a restatement of the often quoted comment by Galileo Galilei that the intention of the Bible is to teach us how to go to heaven, not how the heavens go.[10] However, Francis Schaeffer has warned against developing such an "upper story/lower story" mind-set wherein religious and spiritual truth is placed safely in the upper story where it cannot be tested and validated as other truth claims about matters of fact.[11] While this puts religious truth claims safely beyond disproof, it leaves one with no evidential basis for belief, making belief in the Christian truth claims an exercise in "blind" faith.

To be fair, I must acknowledge that the challenges to the scientific reliability of Genesis 1–11 are partly intrinsic to the text itself. Was the earth really created in six days some six thousand years ago? Has the earth had a flood since the beginning of the human race that covered the tallest mountain peaks? Is man as recent a development in natural history as the Bible suggests? Did early men live to be more than nine hundred years old? It is to these questions that we must now turn our attention to see what the Bible seems to say about these matters and what science seems to suggest at this point in our progressive understanding of natural history. My goal is to demonstrate that these two sources of information about creation and the early history of the human race can be harmonized to a much greater degree than most people, and especially most scientists, generally think they can. The fact that we cannot at present answer precisely all the questions raised by Genesis 1–11 is no doubt due to our limited understanding of the natural world and almost certainly to our misinterpretations of some of the Genesis 1–11 passages.

I will first consider various approaches to the interpretation of Genesis 1–11 to try to determine the breadth of interpretations that are permissible. Then I will consider what we know from science about these same subjects to see whether the scientific view of natural history can be harmonized with the biblical picture. In particular, I want to address the age of the universe, the process whereby the tremendous variety of flora and fauna came into existence, the origin of the human race and the life span of the earliest human beings, and the Genesis flood.

GENERAL ISSUES IN UNDERSTANDING GOD'S ROLE IN CREATION AS PRESENTED IN GENESIS 1–11

In this section, I will consider various issues related to the interpretation of Genesis 1–11. In particular, the relationship of God to nature as presented in the Bible must be defined as a backdrop for interpreting God's creative work in

Genesis. The use of "phenomenal" language will be discussed, as unnecessary conflicts between the Genesis account and scientific understanding result when this principle is not applied during interpretation. Finally, I will describe the three most common interpretative frameworks applied to a study of Genesis 1–11, and I will indicate the one to be utilized in this chapter.

RELATIONSHIP OF GOD TO NATURE

It is important to note that Christians are theists, not deists, which means they see God as being immediately responsible for the regular patterns we see in nature (usually called the laws of nature, or "natural" processes) as well as the irregular events we see in nature (often called signs or miracles). Thus, the only issue for a Bible-believing Christian is how God did his creative work, not whether he did it. The Bible teaches that God's creation is purposeful (as distinct from accidental and purposeless), and that he not only created the physical universe but is also immediately responsible moment by moment for this physical reality in which we exist. Isaac Newton for one understood this and claimed that while the attraction of celestial bodies to each other was described by Newton's law of gravity, the ultimate (versus proximate) cause for gravity was God's providential care for his creatures.[12]

Many of the early practitioners of modern science shared the worldview that God was immediately responsible for nature.[13] It was this belief that caused them to disregard the scientific tradition of the Greeks, in which experimentation was shunned, and begin to test their theoretical ideas with experiments, which opened the door to the rapid advance of modern science.

THE USE OF PHENOMENAL LANGUAGE IN GENESIS 1–11

One of the most common mistakes when reading Genesis 1–11 is a failure to recognize the legitimacy and appropriateness of "phenomenal language."[14] By phenomenal language, I mean wording that represents things as they appear to a casual human observer on the face of the earth. Biblical critics often interpret such phrases as "the four corners of the earth" or "from the rising of the sun to the going down thereof" as implying that the Bible teaches there is a flat, rectangular earth and rejects a heliocentric (sun-centered) theory of the solar system. Such criticisms are usually framed in complete disregard for contextual factors and distinctive characteristics of literary genres such as poetry. Matters of common sense and contemporary practice at the time a book of the Bible was written are largely ignored, resulting in amazingly naive and oversimplified interpretations of the text. Several examples will help to illustrate this point.

We use the terms *sunrise* and *sunset* each day in the weather portion of the newspaper and television news. It would be utterly absurd for some future generation of scientific savants to conclude that we were a terracentric, backward, primitive culture. A second more important example is the interpretation of Genesis 1:14–19, which describes "day" four of creation. Biblical critics such as Isaac Asimov, to make the Genesis account look ridiculous, purposely claim that the Bible teaches that the sun, the moon, and the stars were created after the creation of light and after the creation of plants. There are at least four reasons to reject this interpretation of Genesis 1:16.

First, day and night were created during the first "day" (see Gen. 1:3–5), and the wording in Genesis 1:14 and 1:18 parallels that in Genesis 1:3–5, reaffirming God's initial creation of these celestial bodies. Second, the Hebrew word *asa*, translated "made" in Genesis 1:16, appears in the appropriate form for completed action. Genesis 1:17–18 indicates that Genesis 1:16 is simply reconfirming God's creation of these bodies, as previously noted in Genesis 1:3–5. Third, there is no reference to light anywhere in the Bible except in conjunction with the sun, the stars, the moon, or combustion.[15] Thus, the creation of light on the first "day" must be the consequence of the creation of the sun and other stars. Fourth, one must ask how the earth could possibly maintain an orbit in the absence of the sun.

What are the innovative features that appear in "day" four that were not already mentioned in "day" one? They are the first appearance of the seasons and the first opportunity to be able to use the celestial bodies to make a calendar. Clearly, "day" four is the period in natural history during which the earth's atmosphere was transformed from translucent (light-diffusing) to transparent (light-transmitting). It is generally accepted that the earth's early atmosphere was rich in carbon dioxide, which would have created a greenhouse effect. This greenhouse effect of "days" one through three would have provided a more uniform climate over the entire earth (which is consistent with fossil evidence of lush vegetation covering the entire earth in the past), and would have muted seasonal variations in weather. This greenhouse effect was probably the consequence of a high concentration of carbon dioxide. The creation of plant life in "day" three would result in the gradual conversion of the atmosphere from one that was carbon dioxide rich to one that is oxygen rich, since plants consume carbon dioxide and give off oxygen. Beginning with a carbon-dioxide-rich atmosphere would benefit the development of flora, while the transformation to an oxygen-rich atmosphere would help to stimulate the development of more complex animal life. It is clear that the Bible teaches that God created the sun, the moon, and the stars in "day" one but made them appear for the first time to observers on the earth in "day" four. This is an excellent example of the Bible's use of phenomenal language, describing natural phenomena as they would appear to a casual observer on the earth rather than describing them in a scientifically exact way.

THREE INTERPRETATIVE FRAMEWORKS FOR GENESIS 1–11

There are essentially three interpretative frameworks that various Christian groups have used to expound the meaning of Genesis 1–11, and they differ in their view of the way God accomplished his creative work, as described in Genesis 1: (1) all fiat miracles, (2) all "natural" processes, and (3) fiat miracles plus "natural" processes.[16]

Young earth creationism. Some Christians believe that God worked entirely through fiat miracles to complete his creative work in six solar days. Proponents of this view sometimes suggest a long period of time between Genesis 1:1 and Genesis 1:2, the so-called gap theory. Alternatively, some young earth creationists assume that the earth is recent in origin but appears to be old. Both approaches attempt an accord with the scientific indications of an old earth and universe. However, most young earth creationists believe that the appearance of age can be accounted for entirely by the Noachian flood. Attempts to harmonize the biblical creation story with modern science are seen as fruitless, since science deals with natural processes and creation was accomplished entirely by fiat miracles.

Progressive creationism. Progressive creationists believe that God used a combination of miracles plus processes to create the universe, earth, and plant and animal life. They believe that Genesis 1–11 presents real space-time natural history and that the "days" of Genesis are something other than solar days. For example, some progressive creationists believe the "days" of Genesis 1 are epochs or eras of time during which development occurred by natural processes between times of specific fiat creation. Other progressive creationists believe that the "days" of Genesis 1 might be revelatory days, with the arrangement being more topical than chronological. The major types of plant and animal life, especially the human being, are considered to be special creations of God in both the young earth creationist and progressive creationist views. Progressive creationists believe that an essential harmony between Genesis 1–11 and modern scientific understanding is possible and to be expected, God being the author of both.

Theistic evolution. According to this view, God works entirely through process. The miracle of creation is implicit in the intrinsic design (laws of nature, universal constants, and so on) and initial conditions that allowed creation to unfold seamlessly through "natural" processes. This essential nonliteral view of the Genesis 1–11 account assumes divine authorship but would argue that the purpose of Genesis 1–11 is something other than to inform us about twentieth-century scientific theories. Scientific descriptions of origins are seen as complementary to theological descriptions of origins. The biblical record is thought to be a divinely inspired story or parable that attributes creation to God and provides a basis for understanding the enmity between humankind and God. Proponents of this view accept the development of all plant and animal life, including human beings, through "natural" processes. More recently, some advocates of this position have suggested that "fully gifted creation" is a better description of the position than "theistic evolution," which carries baggage they do not accept. Like young earth creationists, advocates of a fully gifted creation have no problem harmonizing the biblical account with science, since the biblical account is not taken literally.

At the beginning of this section, I said that the three interpretative frameworks could be distinguished by how they explain God's work in creation: by fiat miracles, by fiat miracles plus "natural" processes (also attributed to God), or entirely by "natural" processes (again attributed to God). A second way to distinguish these three positions is based on interpretations of Genesis 1–11: entirely literally, essentially literally, and essentially nonliterally.[17] Gleason Archer has some keen insights into the question of biblical literalism that bear mentioning:

> The examples cited above lead us to the guiding principle that applies to the valid interpretation of any literary production, whether secular or sacred: the concern of the interpreter is to discover as accurately as possible what the original author meant by the words that he used, rather than imposing on his text meanings attached to terms used for translation purposes in some foreign language. Even earlier English works, such as those of Chaucer or Shakespeare, may be improperly construed by twentieth-century speakers of English who have not taken the trouble to discover what men of the fourteenth or seventeenth century meant or connoted by the words used differently than from what they signify today. A careful study of parallel usage elsewhere in Scripture is absolutely vital for valid interpretation of any biblical text. It should also be perfectly evident that it is wrong to take figuratively what the original author meant literally, or to take literally what the author intended in a figurative way. It is, therefore, ill-advised for any evangelical Bible teacher to urge the necessity of "taking the Bible literally." Anyone who takes literally what God means figuratively is right on the brink of heresy![18]

In trying to harmonize the details of the Genesis account of creation and the early history of the human race, I will utilize the progressive creationist framework, since it is the only one that seeks to harmonize what we can know from both science and theology. I also believe it is the correct framework. In the next section, I will explore what the Bible seems to say about earth and early human history and then evaluate whether the biblical scenario is contradicted by scientific observations.

CAN ONE HARMONIZE THE BIBLICAL ACCOUNT OF EARTH AND EARLY HUMAN HISTORY WITH SCIENTIFIC OBSERVATIONS?

In this section, I will consider the four key events described in Genesis 1–11 that touch areas that modern science has also studied: the age of the earth, the development of flora and fauna, the early history of the human race, including the alleged longevity of human beings in Genesis 1–11, and the Noachian flood.

THE AGE OF THE EARTH

The age of the earth is the poster child for the conflict between the Bible and science. The most derisive comments about biblical creationism are usually directed at the six-day creation that is alleged to have occurred six thousand years ago. Science has provided overwhelming evidence of a universe, solar system, and planets that are all between four and fifteen billion years old. Big bang cosmology and our expanding universe allow one to estimate the moment of the birth of the universe as approximately ten to fifteen billion years ago.[19] Radiometric dating of the earth, moon, and meteorites gives clear and consistent evidence that the earth is 4.5 to 4.7 billion years old, using the relative concentrations of several different parent/daughter pairs of elements.[20] Coral reefs around the world,[21] seafloor spreading,[22] and the rate of sedimentation in the Gulf of Mexico[23] give more than ample additional, independent evidence of an ancient earth, one that must be much greater than six thousand years old. The most popular arguments proposed to justify belief in a young earth have been found to be wanting.[24] These include the decaying earth's magnetic field, the missing mass in the universe, the quantity of dust on the moon, the rate of accumulation of various elements in the ocean, and the cooling rate of the earth. In view of the overwhelming evidence for an old universe and earth, it is understandable that scientists would ridicule the biblical teaching of a six-day recent creation story. But does the Bible really require such a belief? Does the Bible necessarily teach young earth creationism?

English Bibles translate the Hebrew word *Yom* as "day." It is worth noting that the Hebrew language has many fewer words than English, and thus has greater ambiguity. The term *Yom* is used in the Bible not only to refer to a twenty-four-hour solar day but also to refer to an indeterminate period of time, as in the many references to the coming "day" of the Lord (e.g., Isa. 2:12; 13:6, 9; Jer. 46:10; Ezek. 13:5; Amos 5:18, 20). In the creation account in Genesis, *Yom* refers to at least two different lengths of time; namely, the six *Yoms* of creation in Genesis 1 and the use of the same word in Genesis 2:4 to refer to the entire period of creation. Thus, it is quite reasonable to believe that the *Yoms* of Genesis 1 were indeterminate periods of time rather than the twenty-four-hour solar days that are often assumed by some Christians and some critics of the biblical account of creation.

The biblical evidence further commends this interpretation of the Hebrew word *Yom* in Genesis 1. Genesis 2 is an amplification of some of the creation events previously described in Genesis 1 for the sixth *Yom*, or period of time in Genesis 1, focusing especially on the creation of Adam and Eve, the first human couple. Genesis 1 places the creation of Adam and Eve in the sixth *Yom*. Yet Genesis 2 puts activities between the creation of Adam and Eve, such as Adam naming the animals and feeling lonely, that do not fit into a single sunrise-to-sunset scenario.[25]

In summarizing this section, it is clear that the interpretation of the *Yoms* of Genesis 1 as indeterminate periods of time is clearly supported by the Bible itself. Such an interpretation eliminates the most glaring example of a contradiction between the Bible and science.

THE DEVELOPMENT OF FLORA AND FAUNA—
EVOLUTION VERSUS CREATION

Here we address the classical creation-evolution debate. The Hebrew action verbs used in Genesis 1 to describe the creative activity of God are *bara* (Gen. 1:1, 21, 27), translated "create," and *asah* (1:7, 16, 25, 31), translated "make." The Hebrew word *bara* is used only thirty other times in the entire Old Testament, always implying at least some supernatural activity on the part of God, usually God creating something out of nothing. In contrast, the Hebrew word *asah* is used 620 additional times in the Old Testament, usually referring to the normal activities of people forming something from preexisting materials, refashioning something as it were. When *asah* is used elsewhere in the Old Testament to describe an activity of God, it often refers to God's providential care for his creatures in his customary way, such as when he makes the storm clouds bring the rain (Zech. 10:1). The use of both of these terms in the Genesis account seems to suggest that God used a combination of miracles plus "natural" processes to accomplish his creative purposes. Furthermore, the repeated reference to "plants and animals being made to reproduce after their own kind" in Genesis 1 seems to suggest natural limits to change.

If one takes the popular arguments for evolution at face value, then one might be persuaded that the Bible is indeed wrong about God using anything but "natural" processes to create the various types of plant and animal life found on earth. When people claim that evolution is a "fact," they are noting that simple things are found in the earliest part of the fossil record and more complex things are found in more recent strata. While it is assumed that mutation/natural selection can account for this progression in the fossil record, this is still a matter open to debate.

A distinction between microevolution and macroevolution needs to be made. By microevolution, I mean changes of existing characteristics or components in living systems by mutation/natural selection. This is both conceptually reasonable and appears to be supported by examples of speciation in the fossil record. What is not so clear is the origin of phyla and families in both the plant and animal kingdom. Macroevolution is the term used to describe change at this level, where new systems are brought into play. It is less obvious that changes that result in new systems requiring multiple component parts can occur in the same way that more modest changes occur, through mutation/natural selection generating the innovations.

Michael Behe, in his book *Darwin's Black Box*,[26] argues persuasively that multicomponent systems cannot be adequately explained by neo-Darwinian evolution (i.e., random mutation guided by natural selection). He gives a simple example of the mousetrap, which requires five to six parts to function in catching mice, and yet it cannot possibly be guided in its incremental development by natural selection. The component parts individually offer no selective advantage until all the necessary components reach a complex level of development that allows them to begin to function as a unit. Citing examples in nature that are exceedingly more complex than a mousetrap, Behe describes black boxes in nature that are irreducibly complex. Once such a system is functional, natural selection can guide in the incremental improvements of the system, but the neo-Darwinian theory of evolution leaves unanswered the question of the origin of such systems.

The well-known atheist Richard Dawkins, in his book *Climbing Mount Improbable*,[27] posits that the backside of Mount Improbable has a "foot path" that leads from the bottom to the top of the mountain in small, easily manageable steps. He also acknowledges that if this path has major discontinuities (i.e., large steps), then mutation/natural selection cannot get one to the top of Mount Improbable. It is the nature of this path from simplicity to complexity, then, that holds the key to the efficacy of blind, undirected mutations in combination with natural selection to account for the plethora of flora and fauna we see today.

The ultimate example of irreducible complexity in natural history may be the origin of life.[28] Every cell of every living plant and animal requires extremely complex organic molecules such as DNA, RNA, and a variety of proteins to take care of minimal life functions. Yet the formation of these molecules under abiotic conditions is so challenging that it is difficult to imagine how it might have happened. The production and isolation of the mers, or organic building blocks, is very difficult, but getting the building blocks assembled to give function is so improbable as to defy logic or statistics regarding how it might have happened. The highly complex arrangements necessary for life might be quantified as information. Generating this information in an abiotic system is difficult to imagine. Remember, until these molecules are formed and arranged in a cell-like structure, there is no reproduction on which natural selection might work. Thus, the key to abiotic or chemical evolution must be something other than what is alleged for biological evolution.

There are two ways we can imagine God generating irreducibly complex innovations in natural history. First, God might use the process of evolution, but with the caveat that the mutations are no longer random but are guided by God in some miraculous way. It is worth noting here that claims by atheistic scientists that evolution by mutation/natural selection is "blind and undirected with no purpose" are nothing more than philosophy masquerading as scientific fact. There is simply no scientific basis for such a claim. A second way that God could have produced innovation is by using occasional fiat miracles to generate new plants or animals. The Cambrian explosion, during which almost all the major animal phyla appeared suddenly, might be the best example of a fiat miracle. In either case, the natural reproductive limits suggested by Genesis 1 could be exceeded only by God's direct intervention.

God's creative activity ceases after the creation of Adam and Eve at the end of the sixth *Yom* according to the biblical account. God rested in the seventh *Yom*, or period of time, which continues to our present time (Gen. 2:1–3;

Heb. 4:1–6). It is interesting to note that since the appearance of the human race, the extinction rate of species has increased significantly[29] due to human activity, whereas the formation of new species seems to have come to a halt. For example, biologists Paul and Anne Ehrlich of Stanford University claim that "the production of a new animal species in nature has yet to be documented."[30] Thus, the biblical inference that creation of the various types of animal and plant life in some way involves God's creative activity is not without warrant. It is difficult to explain the tremendous variety of animal and plant life that we see today if the rate of innovation has always been what it has been in the last thirty thousand years. Thus, it is perfectly plausible to posit that the much more dynamic innovation in natural history in the past was the consequence of God's activity, whether by fiat miracle or by guiding the process of mutation/natural selection so that we are not left with only random mutations.

OVERALL CHRONOLOGY OF GENESIS 1 COMPARED TO GEOLOGICAL HISTORY

Creation of the universe (Gen. 1:1). One of the most remarkable features of the Genesis 1 account, despite the fact that it was written almost four thousand years ago, is its accord with "natural" history that has been written in the past two hundred years. Genesis 1:1 begins by claiming that the universe has not eternally existed but was created by God at a point in time. From the time of the Greeks, it has been fashionable to believe that the universe has eternally existed. Until the twentieth century, the idea of an eternal universe was supported by the scientific theories of conservation of energy and conservation of mass, which stated that neither energy nor mass could be created or destroyed. The big bang cosmology that has become almost universally accepted by cosmologists in the last third of the twentieth century clearly describes our universe as one that began, just as Genesis 1:1 indicates. It should be further added that the creation of the earth is explicitly mentioned in the account of this initial creation. Earth's formation almost certainly required a combination of miracle (the initial big bang) and natural processes (or God working in his customary way), as described by modern cosmology, thus the use of the Hebrew verb *bara*, translated "created." Stars that formed subsequent to the big bang by condensation burn via nuclear fusion to create the various elements, explode and recondense as new stars and planets, but with a much greater variety of elements than the first stars, which were largely hydrogen and helium.[31] Unless God chose to miraculously sustain it in some other way, the earth could not simply float freely in space. Thus, the explicit mention of the creation of the earth in Genesis 1:1 implies also the creation of the sun during this initial creative episode.

Initial condition on planet earth (Gen. 1:2). Genesis 1:2 clearly implies that the creation account is to be taken as the point of view of an observer on the face of the earth. The early earth is described as being "formless and void," without the shapes of oceans and land masses that we see today, and devoid of life-forms and light. Hugh Ross describes the usual situation for newly formed planets, based on observations of astronomers during the past decade, as follows:

> The theory and observations both confirm that all planets start with opaque atmospheres. Thick layers of such gases as hydrogen, helium, methane and ammonia surround them. Giant, cold planets such as Jupiter and Saturn perpetually retain their primordial opaque atmospheres. This gas cloud, combined with a dense shroud of interplanetary dust and debris, guarantees that no sunlight (or starlight) can reach the surface of a primordial planet such as early Earth. . . . The rule of thumb in planetary formation is that the greater a planet's surface gravity and the greater a planet's distance from its star, the heavier and thicker its atmosphere. Yet Earth departs from that rule. Theoretically, Earth should have an atmosphere heavier and thicker than that of Venus, but in fact it has a far lighter and much thinner atmosphere.[32]

Thus, the biblical account is quite consistent with the conditions scientists would tell us should have existed on the early earth.

Earth's atmosphere becomes translucent (Yom 1: Gen. 1:3–5). If Genesis is written from the point of view of an observer on the face of the earth and the sun has already been created in Genesis 1:1, then Genesis 1:3–5 must describe the first appearance of the sun's light on the face of the earth. Over time, gravity removed dust and weightier material from the earth's atmosphere. Furthermore, a very fortuitous set of circumstances allowed the earth's atmosphere to become translucent, retaining just the right amount of water and carbon dioxide to keep the temperature moderate on the face of the earth.[33] Assuming that the earth is already spinning on its axis from the time of its creation, the first penetration of sunlight through the dense atmosphere also brings the first cycles of day and night to the surface of the earth.

Formation of the water cycle (Yom 2: Gen. 1:6–8). The formation of a perfectly balanced water cycle is crucial to life on planet Earth. If there were too much carbon dioxide and/or water in the atmosphere, then the temperature of the surface of the earth would rise monotonically, giving off more evaporation and causing a greater increase in temperature by trapping more heat and further increasing the temperature until the oceans were boiled dry. On the other hand, if the earth had insufficient greenhouse gases (e.g., water vapor and carbon dioxide), then the residual water might have condensed out of the atmosphere in the form of ice and snow. Since ice and snow have a high luminescence, the greater reflectivity of the radiant energy from the earth's surface combined with the lower energy-trapping efficiency of the dry atmosphere would have caused all the water on the surface of the earth to be converted to ice and snow. Thus, the final product of an earth with just the right balance of water and carbon dioxide in the atmosphere and water in the oceans to maintain a moderate temperature over much of the earth (2°C–40°C) is quite remarkable.[34]

Formation of land (Yom 3: Gen. 1:9–10; Ps. 104:1–9). The formation of dry land is described next, again in a way consistent with known earth history. The dry land mass increased monotonically from 0 percent to the current 29 percent in the first four billion years of earth's history through volcanic activity and plate tectonics.[35] During the past five hundred million years, the forces of erosion seem to have been balanced by the dry land-generating forces of volcanic activity and plate tectonics, giving us a relatively constant land mass. Particularly interesting is the recent scientific evidence that the percentage of land mass appears to be crucial to making earth a suitable habitat for life, and we now have just the optimal amount.[36] The Hebrew verbs used in Genesis 1:9–10 do not imply fiat miracle, so the implication of God working in his customary way through process is consistent with our scientific description of land mass formation by volcanic activity and plate tectonics.

Formation of plant life on land (Yom 3: Gen. 1:11–13). Consistent with geological history, the formation of dry land is followed by the beginning of plant life on this dry land. Hugh Ross has noted that the Hebrew words *zera, es,* and *peri* mean, respectively, "semen or embryos of any plant species," "any large plant containing woody fiber," and "the food and/or embryos produced by any living thing."[37] English translations normally render these words "seed," "trees," and "fruit." Thus, criticism that some plants mentioned in the third *Yom* in the Genesis account come later in geological history is due to the translation of general Hebrew terms for plants into very specific English terms that refer to some plants that do indeed occur later in geological history. Furthermore, the biblical account does not say that all plant life came into being during this third *Yom*, or period of time. Some additional plant life may have developed in the fourth, fifth, or sixth *Yoms*. Thus, the alleged inconsistencies between the biblical account and "natural" history are due to questions having to do with translation and interpretation, and these questions are resolvable.

The transformation from a translucent to a transparent atmosphere (Yom 4: Gen. 1:14–19). This passage has already been discussed in detail in the section on phenomenal language, and it is clear that this passage cannot possibly be describing the creation of the sun, the moon, and the stars. The first appearance of the sun, the moon, and visible stars is the natural consequence as the earth's atmosphere is transformed from a translucent to a transparent state. The creation of plant life in the third *Yom* would take the carbon-dioxide-rich atmosphere and convert it into an oxygen-rich atmosphere with a concurrent translation from translucency to transparency. This would set the stage for the development of animal life. With the significant reduction of the greenhouse gases from the atmosphere, the sun, the moon, and the stars could be used for keeping calendars for the first time, as described in Genesis 1:14.

The creation of sea animals and birds (Yom 5: Gen. 1:20–23) and land mammals (Yom 6: Gen. 1:24–25). The introduction of sea animals, including sea mammals and birds, is reported in the fifth *Yom* and the introduction of land mammals in the sixth *Yom*. The development of more complex animal life after the conversion of the carbon-dioxide-rich atmosphere to an oxygen-rich atmosphere is exactly what historical geology and geochemistry reveal. The only potential problem in this passage is the indication of sea mammals prior to land mammals, assuming the Hebrew word *nephesh* implies mammals, or creatures with more relational behavior. However, only a few land mammals are explicitly identified as having been created in the sixth *Yom*, leaving open the exact time for the emergence of other land mammals. Furthermore, recent discoveries of fossils of whales as far back as fifty-two million years ago seem to eliminate any credible challenge to the placement of sea mammals in the fifth *Yom*.[38] We will deal with human evolution in the next section.

Comparison of Genesis 1 chronology with other ancient writings. One of the most compelling arguments for the supernatural origin of the Genesis 1 account of creation may be made by comparing it to other ancient origin stories. In contrast to the very straightforward, factual, and accurate chronology of creation given in Genesis 1, the other accounts are clearly fanciful. A more detailed comparison than space will allow in this chapter may be found in the *The Genesis Connection* by Hugh Ross.[39]

ORIGIN AND EARLY HISTORY OF THE HUMAN RACE: GENESIS 2–11

In this section, I will review details about the creation of Adam and Eve and try to see how these might be reconciled with anthropological findings. Then I will consider the possibilities for the long lives reported for early members of the human race. Finally, I will consider the spread of the human race after the flood.

Special creation of Adam and Eve (Gen. 1:26–27; 2:21–23). The Bible seems to clearly teach that Adam and Eve are real, historical people. Genealogies from the Old Testament and the New Testament trace human lineage back to Adam and Eve, which is difficult to imagine if Adam and Eve were only mythological or symbolic heads of the human race, as some have suggested they were. Giving God ultimate credit for creation and affirming a real, historical Adam and Eve are Francis Schaeffer's two nonnegotiables in his interpretation of Genesis 1 in his book *No Final Conflict*.[40]

How might we distinguish the descendants of Adam and Eve from other prehistoric hominids? The key is in understanding what is meant by the fact that we are made in the likeness of God (Gen. 1:26–27). In the areas of moral conscientiousness, creativity, intelligence, and imagination, the human race shares unique traits in common with God and is God-conscious. Evidence for these characteristics includes the development and use of complex tools, the creation of symbolic art and artifacts, and burial of the dead.

What window of time might bracket the appearance of Adam and Eve? If the genealogies of the Bible are all first-person (father/son) genealogies, then

Adam and Eve would have been created approximately seven thousand years ago. However, the genealogies do not include identical lists of names, although they are similar. It seems that the genealogies must be important-person rather than first-person genealogies. Thus, Adam and Eve could potentially have lived much earlier in history. It is easy to imagine them living as far back as fifty thousand years, but it would be a stretch to put them as far back as five hundred thousand years. While bipedal, tool-using primates with large brains roamed the earth between five hundred thousand and one million years ago,[41] religious relics including idols, altars, temples, art, and tombs for the dead have been found only as far back as about twenty-four thousand years ago.[42] It appears that bipedal primates except for Neanderthals all became extinct before the advent of human beings,[43] and a biological link between Neanderthals and human beings has been ruled out.[44] Thus, the creation of spiritual beings Adam and Eve seems to fit what we know from anthropology.

The creation story in Genesis 2 is sometimes seen as conflicting with the one in Genesis 1. However, this is unnecessary. The obvious intent of the creation story in Genesis 2 is to amplify the creation account of Adam and Eve, emphasizing their spiritual relationship with God. Only the most wooden interpretation of Genesis 2 would put the creation of man before the creation of plants and animals. The planting of the Garden in Genesis 2 is distinct from the creation of plant life in Genesis 1, which occurs much earlier in geological history. God's creation of various kinds of animals and his act of bringing them to Adam in Genesis 2:19 should not be interpreted to imply that Adam was created first. Genesis 1 has already clearly given the creation chronology. Genesis 2:19 alludes to the prior creation of animals, which God now brings to Adam in the Garden to be named.

The indication in Genesis 2:21–22 that Eve was fashioned from a rib of Adam (figuratively speaking) does not imply that Eve was fashioned only from Adam's rib. A better interpretation might be that God used Adam's rib like a DNA blueprint (as in genetic engineering) with appropriate modifications so that Eve was genetically related to Adam but distinctively different as well. Eve's formation, however, almost certainly required other "construction materials" besides the proverbial rib.

Long lives of human beings before the flood. One of the most vexing questions involves accounting for the long lives—more than nine hundred years—of the early descendants of Adam and Eve. Other ancient writers also indicate similarly long lifetimes for their ancestors.[45] I used to wonder if they were counting full moons as years, in which case these numbers would be reduced by a factor of twelve to a more reasonable seventy-five to eighty years of life. However, a careful reading of Genesis 5, taking into account this hypothesis, would have the early patriarchs beginning their families when they were between five and ten years of age, which is clearly unrealistic. Furthermore, God imposes a new restriction on the lives of human beings in Genesis 6:3, limiting them to 120 years to control their wickedness, which seemed to grow worse with age. After a short transition period (see Gen. 11:10–25), the life spans of biblical characters all seem to fall within this 120-year limit (e.g., Joseph dies at the age of 110, Moses at 120). It is interesting to note that people to this day do not seem to live longer than 120 years and seldom live to be older than 100 years.

Why is it that in Genesis 1:29 God commends to Adam and Eve a vegetarian diet, while in Genesis 9:3, after God has reset the limits on human longevity, he now includes meat in their diet? If one eats meat, one ingests a much higher concentration of heavy elements that over time can accumulate in the body.[46] If one lives nine hundred years, this would become a serious problem. If one lives 120 years or less, the accumulation never reaches levels that would adversely affect one's health. Thus, this change in diet is also consistent with the dramatic change in longevity of human beings indicated in the Bible.

The Bible does not indicate how God reset the biological clocks of human beings to reduce life spans to the current levels. However, recent scientific findings suggest some intriguing possibilities.[47] It is well known that high intensity radiation can dramatically shorten the life span of a human being, as evidenced by the aftermath of Hiroshima, Nagasaki, and Chernobyl. If the level of background radiation for the earth changed significantly around the time of the Noachian flood, this might account for the change in life spans noted in the Genesis account. The most likely candidate to have provided such radiation is the Vela supernova, which produces more than thirty times the radiation on earth of the next most intense supernova.[48] It has been dated to have exploded between ten thousand and thirty thousand years ago, a time period that brackets the dates one would expect for the Noachian flood.

A second possibility is a cell phenomenon called apoptosis that ultimately limits longevity.[49] Human cells are apparently designed to reproduce only a fixed number of times, after which the reproductive process shuts down. This would set an absolute limit on longevity, assuming one does not die for other reasons first. Recent research suggests that apoptosis may be a powerful force in countering the growth of cancer cells. If this is the case, then the introduction of apoptosis, which limits life to 120 years, may have been essential to mediate the greater incidence of cancer that the Vela radiation would surely have produced over time.[50]

Spread of the human race after the flood. If all members of the human race except Noah's family died during the flood, then all members of the human race today should be descendents of Noah. Furthermore, the spread of the human race to its present geographical distribution should have occurred after the flood. We know that the migration of human beings from East Asia to North America occurred roughly 10,000 B.C.,[51] since the Bering Strait was passable by land for a brief time between 9,000 and 12,000 B.C. During this same period of time, a lower ocean level would have made passage between the various Indonesian islands and on to Australia much easier either by land or by a short boat journey in waters that were much warmer than the Bering

Sea. A subsequent increase in the ocean levels due to the melting of ice would have restricted subsequent migration to or from these locations. This would positively date the Noachian flood prior to 10,000 B.C., which is consistent with the dating of the flood and the concurrent reduction of life spans of human beings ten thousand to thirty thousand years ago. Anthropological data previously cited put Adam and Eve at possibly twenty-four thousand years ago. Thus, the biblical events of the history of the human race are quite consistent with relevant scientific data.

THE FLOOD OF NOAH

The flood of Noah is one of the greatest events of Genesis 1–11, and, like young earth creationism, is the source of considerable scorn regarding the reliability of the Bible. But as with the question of the age of the earth, the controversy here is unnecessary if one reads and interprets the passage carefully. The fundamental question is whether the Noachian flood was global or local.

The terminology used in Genesis 6–9 seems to favor a global flood. For example, Genesis 7:19–23 says, "The water prevailed more and more upon the earth, so that all the high mountains everywhere under the heavens were covered. . . . Thus He blotted out every living thing that was upon the face of the land, from man to animals to creeping things and to birds of the sky, and they were blotted out from the earth" (vv. 19, 23 NASB). The use of such biblical language in other stories may help us to understand the intention here. In Genesis 41:56, we are told, "The famine was spread over all the face of the earth" (NASB). We normally interpret this famine as devastating the lands of the ancient Near East around Egypt and do not assume that American Indians and Australian aborigines came to buy grain from Joseph. First Kings 10:24 states that "the whole world sought audience with Solomon to hear the wisdom God had put in his heart." Surely Inca Indians from South America or Maoris from New Zealand had not heard of Solomon and sought his audience.

The Hebrew word *erets* used in Genesis 7:19 is usually translated "earth" or "world" but does not generally refer to the entire planet.[52] Depending on the context, it is often translated "country" or "land" to make this clear. References to the entire planet are found in Genesis 1:1; 2:1; and 14:22, for example. However, more typical references might be Genesis 1:10; 2:11; or 2:13, where *erets* is translated "land." In Genesis 12:1, Abram was told to leave his *erets*. He was obviously not told to leave the planet but rather to leave his country. Genesis 41:56 describes the famine as being over all the face of the *erets*, which could be translated "land," "country," or (entire) "earth." Obviously, the famine did not literally cover the entire earth. Again, in Exodus 10:5, 15, we are told the locusts covered the surface of the *erets*. Translating *erets* as "earth" here would not make sense. We see once again, as with the Hebrew word *Yom*, that the small and limited vocabulary of the Hebrew language requires that many Hebrew words have multiple meanings, with the actual meaning determined by the context. A final helpful comparison to obtain a proper interpretation of Genesis 7:19 involves Deuteronomy 2:25, which talks about all the nations "under the heavens" being fearful of the Israelites. Obviously, all nations "under the heavens" was not intended to mean all on planet Earth.

The Hebrew word translated "covered" in Genesis 7:19 is *kasah*. It can mean "residing upon," "running over," or "falling upon."[53] Twenty feet of water running over or falling upon the mountains (or hills) is quite different from that amount residing upon them, although either event could destroy human and animal life in its path. The Hebrew word *har* translated "mountain" in most English translations of Genesis 7:19 also means "hill" or "mount."[54] Thus, we might as easily translate Genesis 7:19 to say that "all the high hills in the region of the Mesopotamian valley were covered with water to a depth of more than twenty feet." This is very different from the usual rendering that "all the highest mountains on the earth were covered with water to a depth of twenty feet."

In the New Testament, Paul claimed that the faith of the Roman church was being proclaimed "throughout the whole world." Peter notes in 2 Peter 3:6, "By . . . waters also the world of that time was deluged and destroyed." The Greek word here is *kosmos*, otherwise translated "whole universe," "whole planet Earth," the "whole of humanity," or a "portion of the earth." Obviously, Paul meant the world of the Roman Empire, or a portion of the entire earth. Peter's intent was clearly all of humanity.[55]

In Genesis 1–9, the only geographical references are to the region of Mesopotamia. If the ancestors of Noah had elected to stay in this general region rather than spread throughout the earth as God had commanded, then God's judgment would require only a flood in this region, and this appears to have been the case.

If the entire Mesopotamian valley was flooded and the water receded slowly, then Noah might have seen only water, with distant mountain ranges being over the horizon. God's use of wind in Genesis 8:1 to cause the flood to subside would be reasonable for a local flooding of this huge valley. It would not make sense for a flood that left water to a depth of thirty thousand feet, sufficient to cover Mount Everest. Genesis 8:4 indicates that the ark came to rest on the hills or mountains of Ararat, not specifically Mount Ararat, which is seventeen thousand feet tall. This complex mountain range extends north and east of Mount Ararat down to the foothills skirting the Mesopotamian plain. If the ark had landed near the top of Mount Ararat, it is difficult to imagine how Noah and his family as well as the animals would have been able to descend to the base of the mountain, given the considerable difficulty mountain climbers have today attempting to reach the locations where the ark is thought (I believe, incorrectly) to have landed.

Further evidence for a local flood is found in Genesis 8:5, where it is noted that the water receded until the tenth month when the tops of mountains (or hills) became visible for the first time. The reference here seems to be what Noah could see, not the entire world. In Genesis 8:11, the dove returns with an olive leaf. Since olive trees don't grow at higher elevations, a flood that covered all the mountains would not give this type of evidence of receding.

One can estimate the total amount of water that would be needed to cover all the mountains on the face of the earth and compare this to the total water reserves that we know of on planet Earth, both in lakes and oceans and in subterranean aquifers. A flood that covered all the mountains on earth would require 4.5 times the total water resources that exist on planet Earth. Furthermore, such a worldwide flood would be pointless if the descendants of Adam lived only in the region of Mesopotamia.

While scientific evidence for a worldwide flood is clearly missing, there is considerable evidence from both geology and archaeology of one huge and several smaller floods in the region of Mesopotamia during the time period of the Noachian flood. Fredrick A. Filby, in *The Flood Reconsidered*, summarizes his chapter on this topic as follows:

> Some time after the Ice Age and before the rise of the great dynasties, a great flood caused by either a close approach of some heavenly body, or by the movement of the continents, or both swept from the Atlantic, the Mediterranean, and the Indian Oceans over much of Europe and Asia. During this period Paleolithic man disappeared, the entire climate of Siberia was radically changed, herds of mammoths were completely eliminated, some being apparently almost instantaneously frozen to death by unprecedented cold, and the sabre-tooth tiger, the woolly rhinoceros and a hundred million other creatures perished. Herds of animals in Europe and Western Asia were trapped by rising water and many were dashed to pieces, their bones being swept into great cracks, which had appeared in the earth. Lesser risings and fallings of certain local areas have continued, giving rise to raised beaches, shifting levels of fens in England, or various flood levels in Mesopotamia, but these are obviously small compared with the event which drowned a hundred million animals and exterminated an ancient race of men. The great oceanic tide, accompanied in the Middle East by torrential rain, and in Siberia by intensely frozen snow, capable of floating and indeed of driving a 10,000 ton wooden barge, probably from Mesopotamia to the regions of the mountains (or hills) of Ararat . . . that Flood which Genesis describes so minutely, was surely unique in history, and, by the promise of God was not to be repeated—and in fact, never has been.[56]

It should be noted that Filby's account, which was completed before 1970, would place the flood between four thousand and ten thousand years ago, but after the last ice age. Hugh Ross's more recent treatment of this topic would place it somewhat earlier, with humans bridging the Bering Sea to populate North and South America about eleven thousand years ago, before the ice melted and the sea levels rose.[57] This would put Noah's flood between probably ten thousand and twenty thousand years ago.

THE FALL OF ADAM AND EVE AND THE RAINBOW

A couple of minor details need to be addressed before we conclude this chapter. Some claim that Genesis 2:5–6 in combination with the rainbow mentioned for the first time in Genesis 9 should be interpreted to mean that rain never fell before the flood. However, both Filby and Ross argue convincingly that God always takes something familiar and gives it a special significance when he makes a covenant (e.g., bread, wine, and water).[58] Thus, there is no reason to assume that the rainbow appeared for the first time in Genesis 9. Rather, it was given a special significance for the first time in Genesis 9.

Second, some speculate that the curse on nature after the fall was the introduction of the Second Law of Thermodynamics. This cannot possibly be the case since the capacity of nature to utilize energy flow is made possible by the Second Law of Thermodynamics. Furthermore, transport phenomena that are essential for life would not be possible without the Second Law of Thermodynamics. It is certain that nature changed in some way at the time of the fall, but it is unclear what that change might have been physically.

CONCLUSION

The Bible may be interpreted to give the following scenario for the origin of the universe (including earth), the origin of plants and animals, the origin of human beings, and the early history of the human race:

- The universe was created with a miraculous big bang followed by processes described by cosmology that resulted in stars and planets some twelve billion years ago.
- The earth originally had an opaque atmosphere and was covered with water and in complete darkness.
- The atmosphere eventually became translucent, allowing diffuse light to reach the surface of the spinning earth, giving for the first time day and night on the surface of the earth.
- Land began to form through the processes of volcanism and plate tectonics, again by God working in his customary way.
- The origin of the first life was not mentioned specifically in the Genesis account but almost certainly would have required miraculous intervention on God's part.
- Plant life developed on the newly formed land mass, possibly by process or by God-directed mutations.

- Subsequently, sea and land animals appeared, with the verbs indicating a combination of miracle plus process (maybe events such as the Cambrian explosion are evidence of God's creative activity).
- Since the creation of humankind, God has withdrawn from his creative activity, and, not surprisingly, the introduction of new family or phyla (maybe even species) seems to have come to a halt since the appearance of man.
- Human beings appear to be a special creation of God and not the end product of hominid evolution.
- Human beings are distinguished by their spiritual aptitude and practice and appear to be relatively recent, possibly coming into existence twenty-five thousand years ago.
- Early human beings apparently lived for nine hundred or more years, but radiation from a supernova may have shortened life spans to their current roughly one-hundred-year maximum, or God may have reset our cellular clocks to the current limit at about the time of the flood.
- The flood appears to have occurred between ten thousand and twenty thousand years ago and was local.
- The earth was populated by the descendents of Noah and his family since the flood.

Amazingly enough, this picture from Genesis is extremely consistent with what we know from science. The alleged contradictions of the Bible by science are the result of an improper reading of the Bible (e.g., *Yoms* of Genesis 1 are solar days; the flood was worldwide, covering all the mountains with water) and/or an exaggerated inference from science about the creative powers of nature alone (e.g., the origin of life and macroevolution are easily explained by natural processes alone).

ELEVEN

WHY I BELIEVE THE BIBLE ALONE IS THE WORD OF GOD

WINFRIED CORDUAN

Imagine yourself as a visitor from another planet. For some reason, you are conversant with human languages, but you know little else about human culture. You have been given the task by your commander to report on which books are considered sacred by earthlings and whether any of them are actually divinely inspired. How would you go about compiling this report?

You might begin by visiting a public library. After you examined each of, say, one hundred thousand books, however, you would be convinced that this is no way to get your job done. The books do not necessarily tell you whether people accept them as sacred or not. Anthologies are always selective, and no two anthologies of sacred writings contain the same assortment. It dawns on you that you need to approach your task more systematically.

So you come up with a plan. You create a list of criteria to determine whether a writing might qualify as sacred. This is no easy task, and it is somewhat precarious because you might accidentally eliminate a bona fide contender, but you have to start somewhere. And so you come up with the following list. In order to be deemed sacred, a book has to

- belong to an established community of faith
- be regarded by the members of that community as sacred
- address the spiritual issues on which the community focuses
- have integrity as a text and in its function within that community (viz., not be produced fraudulently or used frivolously)

Alas, this procedure still does not yield unequivocal results. Some scriptures are clearly on the borderline of these criteria, and worse yet, the religious communities themselves do not always agree on what specific writings should be included in their sacred scriptures. Further, you have to contend with the fact that what particular communities mean by such words as *sacred* or *inspired* varies wildly, ranging from accepting the writings as divinely dictated to venerating them without necessarily paying much attention to their actual teaching.

So you need to push your method a little farther. Now that you have a rough list of those books that are generally considered sacred, you need to clarify the best understanding of the term *sacred*. Then you need to study all the eligible writings (to which you might have access) to determine how they fit with your understanding.

Unfortunately, this again is not a very likely scenario, assuming that you, as an alien visitor, have abilities not too much greater than human beings. Not only is the list extremely long, but the eligible writings coming out of some of the traditions are huge. Thus, you are not only up against a lifetime of reading, but at the same time, you have to learn what the religion is all about so that you can understand what you are reading, for the essence of a religion is not always contained in its writings.

At this point, you might be tempted to claim that all the writings are equally sacred and inspired. However, you know that many of the writings clearly contradict each other, and so you cannot logically claim they are all equally inspired. If some of them are inspired, others cannot be inspired.

Clearly, you need to turn the process around if you ever wish to accomplish your mission. Rather than attempting to survey every possible sacred writing and then drawing conclusions, you decide to begin with a likely candidate, draw conclusions concerning it, and then apply what you have learned to the other writings. Since you have landed in a nominally Christian culture, you begin with the Bible.

A LOOK AT THE BIBLE

The point of the above scenario is to show how difficult, almost impossible, it is to sort through all the allegedly sacred writings in the world and single out

183

which, if any, are truly inspired. From time to time I hear people say, "I studied all the scriptures in the world, and then I decided that such-and-such was true." I suspect that "true" in such an instance meant "appealed to me the most," but in any event, the person is claiming to have done something that is not really possible to do to its full extent. The person probably studied *some* selections of *some* of the writings representing *some* of the religions in the world, and this is commendable, but he or she could not possibly have done an exhaustive study.

Let us not pretend, therefore, to do something that is clearly impossible. We need to begin with information that is accessible and then expand our study from there. As suggested above, let us begin with the Bible and then apply what we conclude to the other religious writings in the world. Thus, before making a case as to why I believe the Bible alone is the Word of God, I need to make a case as to why I believe the Bible is the Word of God at all. Then I will make the contrast with other writings.

My argument is going to move in three steps: First, I am going to show that the New Testament is a reliable source for historical information. Second, I will show that the New Testament makes an argument that Christ is God. The argument concludes with the observation that Christ endorsed the Bible as inspired. In short:

1. The New Testament as history shows that
2. it is reasonable to believe in the deity of Christ, who
3. taught us to accept the Bible as the Word of God.

In chapter 9, Gary Habermas made the case for the historical reliability of the Bible. For now, I want to briefly reexamine some of his arguments. We have seen that by applying normal historical procedures, we can justifiably treat the New Testament as a valid source of historical information because

- the authors of the four Gospels were directly acquainted with the events they depict and the people who were a part of those events.
- we have reliable reproductions of the original manuscripts written by the authors.
- the Gospels do not report logical impossibilities.
- the Gospels do not show evidence of such systematic bias as to be unbelievable.
- writers outside the New Testament corroborate the essential points of the Gospel reports.[1]

Thus, it is legitimate to use the New Testament as a source of historical truth. We can trust the factual information it conveys as well as its historical information.

One piece of information the New Testament conveys is the deity of Christ. Again, I need only summarize the argument here because Peter Kreeft addresses this point in chapter 13. There are two startling facts that come together in the person of Jesus Christ: (1) his unique claims about himself, and (2) his unique life, particularly his purity and his miracles. He claimed that he was God, and his life leaves no reasonable alternative but that he actually was who he claimed to be. Consequently—and this is not a point anyone can accept casually—Jesus Christ actually is God, who became incarnate as Jesus of Nazareth.

Now we come to the thrust of this argument. When Christ came into the world, he came into a culture that accepted a particular set of writings as Scripture, namely, the Jewish writings commonly called the Old Testament by Christians, referred to as the tanakh within Judaism.[2] Granting that Jesus is who he claimed to be, namely, God incarnate, he clearly could have gone in one of three directions:

1. He could have told his fellow Jews that they ought not to accept their Scriptures as inspired writings.
2. He could have conformed his work and teaching to Jewish practice and used their Scriptures simply to accommodate himself without actually accepting them.
3. He could have actually accepted the Jewish Scriptures as inspired writings.

How can we decide which of the three options corresponded with Christ's own view of the Scriptures? The only thing we can do is look at how he used Scripture in his ministry on earth, and when we do so, we find that he embraced the third option: He accepted the Scriptures as inspired.

Let's look at one episode in Christ's teaching ministry, as recorded in Mark 7:1–13.[3] This episode begins with the Pharisees[4] observing some of Christ's disciples eating their supper with unwashed hands. Because doing so violated one of their many traditional points of law, they berated Christ for tolerating his disciples' laxity. However, Jesus turns the tables on the Pharisees. He accuses them of being hypocritical because, even though they pay a great amount of attention to human traditions, in the process they wind up neglecting the law of God. He twice refers to the Old Testament law as "the commandment of God" (vv. 8–9) and as "the word of God" in verse 13. In fact, he cites the Scriptures in order to reprove the Pharisees.

Note what is going on here. First of all, Jesus refers to the Scriptures as coming from God, in the sense that where the Scriptures speak, God speaks. This is what we mean when we say that a piece of writing is inspired—it reveals to us the will and word of God. Now, it helps to know a little bit about first-century Jewish culture to put the right framework around Christ's statement. When Christ referred to the law and the Scriptures, he was referring specifically to those books (the tanakh) that were accepted as holy writings among the Jews of his day and today make up the Christian Old Testament.

Second, Christ makes a crucial distinction here between the command-ments of God and the human traditions, ruling out the possibility that Jesus was simply accommodating himself to his human hearers when he referred to their sacred Scripture. If that had been the case, he would not have made a distinction between the Word of God and human tradition because it would all have been human tradition. Jesus scolds the Pharisees precisely because they did not observe this distinction but mingled human tradition with divine revelation. In the process, Christ emphasizes that the Scriptures themselves are not derived from human beings but from God himself. And it seems rea-sonable to argue that if the Son of God taught this, then we ought to accept it as true as well.

It follows from this line of reasoning, which could be duplicated with many other Gospel passages, that Christ not only accepted the Old Testament as God's Word but even taught the same. Obviously the same argument cannot be repeated for the New Testament because this collection had not been writ-ten by the time of his teaching ministry. Nonetheless, it is again Christ's author-ity that we can use to defend the New Testament as inspired writing.

This time the argument focuses on Jesus' own disciples. In John 15:26–27, Jesus says:

> When the Helper comes, whom I will send to you from the Father, that is the Spirit of truth, who proceeds from the Father, He will bear witness of Me, and you will bear witness also, because you have been with Me from the beginning. (NASB)

Again, we can make two important points. First, Jesus exhorts his disciples to bear witness of him. This task would, of course, include propagating Christ's teaching, a point he specifically makes in Matthew 28:19–20 (the so-called Great Commission) and Acts 1:8. Second, Jesus promises that the disciples would be able to carry out this mission with the aid of God, the Holy Spirit. In the passage above, he is referred to as the Spirit of truth and as the Helper. Clearly, the point is that the Holy Spirit would enable the disciples to remem-ber Christ's teaching, and they would be guided by the Holy Spirit in pro-claiming it. This is also stated plainly in John 14:25–26:

> These things I have spoken to you, while abiding with you. But the Helper, the Holy Spirit, whom the Father will send in My name, He will teach you all things, and bring to your remembrance all that I said to you. (NASB)

Thus, we have twin facts: The disciples were to continue the teaching min-istry of Christ, and they were to do so with the aid of God himself. But we need to take one further step.

Much confusion exists today concerning the compilation of the New Testament. I know a number of people who are troubled by the fact that several writings were produced during the early years of the Christian church that did not make it into the New Testament, while others obviously did. Isn't that arbitrary? Why choose one set of books over another? The apparent arbitrariness goes away, however, when we look at what the church was doing, and it was a very straightforward project: They were collecting the writings of the apostles. The church recognized that the former disciples, now apostles, were continuing the teachings of Jesus and were doing so with divine authority, and they understood that the apostolic writings were simply further continuations of this mission. When the apostles grew old and it became apparent that the church would survive them, the church began to collect their writings, knowing that the apostolic teachings came with the authority of Christ himself and that this teaching was now embodied in their writings. The church also understood that this authority ended with the disciples. As we saw in the passage from John 15, Jesus was addressing those who had been with him "from the beginning." In other words, the authority to write inspired Scriptures began and ended with the original disciples. No one can write anything afterward and legitimately claim that it is on a par with the writings of the apostles.

Thus, we see that the authority of the New Testament also rests on Christ's own authority. He, as the Son of God, saw to it that his disciples preserved his divine teachings, which are now retained in the New Testament. There is every reason, therefore, for us to accept the New Testament as divinely inspired.

And so we have arrived at an important conclusion—we can accept the Bible as inspired writing—which rests squarely on the shoulders of Christ. As the Son of God, he has given his endorsement to both testaments, the Old by authoritatively using it as God's Word, and the New by endowing his apostles with both the task and the spiritual assistance to continue his teachings.

We now have a base from which to continue our quest. It is indeed reasonable to believe that the Bible is inspired writing. If this is so, then what about all the other writings of the world's religions? Can one not make a similar argument for the Vedas, the Lotus Sutra, or the Qur'an? Our quest continues.

A Crucial Principle

How can we proceed from here? Most easily, we can attempt to show that, once we believe the Bible is inspired, all other writings are automatically ruled out. "My Scriptures are the right ones; thus, all others must be false." Admittedly, this sounds tremendously arrogant and presumptuous. Consequently, we must make sure this statement gets as much support as we can muster. The foundational support comes from the basic laws of thought. Then we can also illustrate our contention by means of illustrations drawn from other representative religious scriptures.[5]

187

Here is the key to this phase of the discussion. There is a basic law of thought, known as the law of noncontradiction, that states that two contradictory statements cannot both be true. If it is true that there is a tree in my yard, it cannot also be true that there is no tree in my yard. If it is false that I am presently in my office, then it must be true that I am not in my office.

There seems to be a great deal of confusion concerning this principle. For one thing, it is not a law of omniscience. Countless statements exist and I have no idea whether they are true or false (e.g., "the tree in my backyard has exactly 3,798 leaves"), and so I cannot tell whether their contradictions are true or false either. In order to apply the law of noncontradiction meaningfully, I need to begin with a statement that I know either to be true or false, and then I can know that its contradiction is either true or false.

Second, as Norman Geisler showed in chapter 2, the law of noncontradiction is unavoidable. Epistemological relativism (i.e., "nobody can know *the* truth") is not a viable position, for sooner or later one has to affirm certain statements as true and their contradictions as false. If you claim that the law of noncontradiction is false, you are asserting that it is true that it is false, and it is false that it is not false. Even to say that it is questionable that it is true implies that it is true that it is questionable and it is false that it is not questionable. One cannot dispense with the law of noncontradiction at will. It is inescapable.

We can apply this principle to the issue of scriptures. Having given good reasons why we can accept the Bible as inspired Scripture, and since it is a given that an inspired piece of writing tells the truth, any writing that contradicts the statements of the Bible must be false. Again, we need not be able to claim that we can compile everything asserted in the Bible, but we can certainly accumulate quite a few biblical assertions. If we know that these assertions in the Bible are true, then a scripture that proclaims the opposite of that information cannot also be true.

Is there information in the Bible that would logically exclude other scriptures in this way? Perhaps almost ironically, the Bible makes the answer to this question fairly easy (at least as long as a person accepts it for what it says and not for what he or she thinks it should say). The Bible makes exclusive claims concerning the God and the religion it advocates. "I am the LORD your God. . . . You shall have no other gods before Me" (Exod. 20:2–3 NASB) is the first commandment. This statement is followed with God's avowal, "I, the LORD your God, am a jealous God" (Exod. 20:5). Throughout the Old Testament all worship of any other purported deity is reproved and oftentimes judged. The same thing is true for the New Testament. Jesus declares, "I am the way and the truth and the life. No one comes to the Father except through me" (John 14:6). The apostle Peter declares before the council, "Salvation is found in no one else; for there is no other name under heaven given to men by which we must be saved" (Acts 4:12). This is just a small sampling of some of the best-known verses in the Bible that claim exclusive truth and salvation.

The law of noncontradiction dictates that we can go only in a limited number of directions on the basis of these verses.

1. Theoretically, it is possible that these statements are false. Then there could be other truthful scriptures relating other valid deities and ways of salvation.
2. It is possible that these statements are true. In that case, any other scripture that advocates any other god or any other way of salvation must be false.

The first option is logically possible, but we have already shown why it must be rejected. This book as a whole and this chapter in particular have provided good reasons to believe the Bible is truthful in matters of fact as well as inspired on the authority of the Lord Jesus himself. The first option then is plainly eliminated since the Bible cannot be true and false at the same time.

Consequently, we are left with the conclusion that the Bible is true—and that it must be exclusively so. If a book advocating salvation through faith in Christ alone is true, then any book advocating any other means of salvation cannot also be true. To quibble with this statement is to fall back into the morass of relativism from which Francis Beckwith and Norman Geisler liberated us in the first two chapters.

Though the preceding argument, based as it is on simple logic, is cogent and compelling, the great importance of our task compels us to do at least a little more homework. Sometimes straightforward logical arguments seem suspect precisely because of their simple nature. So let us now take a look at a number of scriptures from around the world in order to provide a little more content for this argument.

SOME CRITERIA REVISITED

At the outset, when our poor alien was attempting to make an inventory of all the potential scriptures of the world, we tried to help him out by giving him a list of criteria. We said that candidates for recognition as scripture ought to, at the very least,

- belong to an established community of faith
- be regarded by the members of that community as sacred
- address the spiritual issues on which the community focuses
- have integrity as a text and in its function within that community (viz., not be produced fraudulently or used frivolously)

To begin with an obvious example, I am not now writing holy scripture. Even though I am writing as a member of the Christian community, the community as a whole would hardly accept ownership of this piece of writing. It would be even less likely that the Christian community at large would recognize my writing as inspired. It is true that this piece (hopefully) addresses spiritual issues central to the church, but it certainly would not be given an integral place in the functioning of the community.

What applies so obviously to my writings ought also apply to many other writings. You cannot invent your own scripture. You can pen writings that are very important to you and others in your faith and, consequently, are inspiring, but that does not make them inspired. It is thoroughly unreasonable to expect every last piece of writing to be eligible for such consideration.

Let me add a further consideration to these reflections by referring to another important principle of human thought. It is certainly true that we legitimately hold many beliefs as true while neither being able to nor being under compulsion to provide evidence for such beliefs. For example, I am quite confident that it is legitimate for me to believe there was a significant past even though I cannot give a sound argument as to why the universe may not have popped into being, complete with memories, history, and fossils, a mere five seconds ago. Anything that I could point to as evidence for a past could be attributed to the age attributes of this newly arrived universe. Many beliefs simply do not require further proofs. But others do.

One would think that the claim that a particular book is inspired revelation, when presented to an outsider of that particular religion, requires some evidence. I would not quibble with the demurrer that *within* a particular faith tradition believers are entitled to accept their holy writings as inspired without necessarily having proof—at least until there is a potent challenge from the outside. But it seems highly presumptuous to expect the same of someone coming to that tradition from the outside.

Richard Swinburne, a highly acclaimed contemporary philosopher, has created what he calls the "principle of credulity," which means, roughly, all other things being equal, we ought to believe other people's reports about their experience.[6] I would like to reverse this idea and claim that there is also a "principle of incredulity," namely, unless someone has been given good reasons, there is no obligation for him or her to accept another person's claim as true. To return to the example that began this section, I would need to give you some good reasons, in fact, some extremely powerful ones, before you should feel any obligation to accept what I am writing here as inspired.

Keep in mind that this book contains a solid amount of evidence for the inspiration of the Bible. Intellectually speaking, the Bible is supported by evidence for the existence of God, archaeological and historical discoveries, and ultimately, the testimony of Jesus Christ, who is God incarnate, through his teaching and resurrection. There is good reason to accept the factuality of his resurrection from the dead, and that gives his endorsement of the Bible high priority.

But how do other scriptures fare when it comes to the question of evidence. When I am presented with an alleged inspired writing, the "principle of incredulity" leads me to ask, "Where is the evidence that might lead me to accept this writing?" Given that I already have good reasons to embrace the Bible and to know that other scriptures conflict with the Bible's testimony, I better have good reasons to turn from the Bible to another piece of writing, for it has to be a switch and not just an addition.

SURVEYING THE COMPETITION

Once again, I wish to underscore that a survey of all the writings for which inspiration has been claimed at one time or another is not possible. In the preceding argument, I tried to show that one is not necessary either. Further, one could even question that such a survey is desirable for reasons other than the quest for knowledge, once it has been established that there is one exclusively inspired Scripture. Still, we can learn a great deal that will enhance our case for the Bible by looking at the scriptures of various religions.

Another preliminary point needs to be made. Many of the world's religions have sacred writings, but their purported nature and function within the religions vary widely. In Christianity, particularly on the Protestant side, the Bible is treated primarily as a source of information about God, Christ, and salvation. Theoretically, someone who has never had any contact with Christianity should be able to formulate the fundamental Christian beliefs simply by reading the Bible. In other religions, however, scriptures may not have such a fundamental informational role. The role of the writings in question might primarily be

- to be chanted or recited
- to give instructions to a priesthood
- to provide illustrations in stories of the religion in question
- to be the object of worship or veneration in its own right

There are other possibilities as well. Thus, we can already see that not all alleged scriptures are on a par in terms of how they are used within their religion, and many religions use their holy writings very differently from the way Christianity uses the Bible.

What follows is a brief description of the scriptures of some other religions, emphasizing the differences between them and the Bible. For the sake of manageability, each description is composed of the following items: name of religion, description, author and history, textual integrity, function within the community, content relationship to the Bible, and an "incredulity rating." The list is limited to those writings that are popularly available and occupy an important place in their religious community.

The Qur'an

Religion: Islam

Brief Description: Roughly the size of the New Testament, the Qur'an contains 114 chapters (*suras*) that are transcriptions of Muhammad's recitations in Mecca and Medina, which are based on his alleged revelations. The main teachings of the Qur'an are the unity and oneness of God, the inevitability of the last judgment, and rules for the Islamic community.

Author and History: The content of the Qur'an is attributed to Muhammad (A.D. 570–622) himself. The recitations were delivered in Mecca and in Medina. The Qur'an began to be collected during Muhammad's lifetime and reached its final form under Caliph Uthman.

Textual Integrity: There is good reason to believe that the Qur'an as it exists today is for the most part what Muhammad taught. Unfortunately, there is little opportunity to evaluate the textual integrity of the Qur'an any further since Caliph Uthman, third in line as successor to Muhammad, destroyed all manuscripts he did not consider correct. Muslims generally claim that the present Qur'an is pure, but even with Uthman's heavy-handed treatment, there are a few known variants.[7]

Function within the Community: The Qur'an is, of course, the central content revelation for Islam and, thus, the primary source for teaching and practice. However, its most central function may be its recitation, thus demonstrating Allah's presence in the Islamic community.

Content Relationship to the Bible: Muhammad derived many of his teachings from Jews and Christians, and the Qur'an contains various pieces derived from the Old and New Testaments (e.g., episodes from the lives of the patriarchs or Christ's virgin birth). Some of these were altered to suit Muhammad's purposes and audience. The Qur'an specifically denies the deity of Christ[8] and his atoning death on the cross.[9] Consequently, since these are two central teachings of the New Testament, acceptance of the Bible and acceptance of the Qur'an are mutually exclusive.

Incredulity Rating: Even though there is no particularly good reason to deny that the Qur'an is a fairly accurate record of Muhammad's teachings, there is also no particularly good reason to accept it as inspired scripture. Even if we grant that Muhammad was a particularly holy man and profound teacher, that does not mean we need to accept his recitations as divinely inspired over against the New Testament, which is corroborated by Jesus Christ, who authenticated his claims of divinity with a resurrection.

The Avesta

Religion: Zoroastrianism (Parsiism)

Brief Description: The Avesta is a complex set of writings that arose out of the life and history of Zoroastrianism. The oldest parts are in a very ancient language called Avestan, while the rest is in various forms of ancient Iranian language. It contains prayers and recitations as well as (in the latest part) magic incantations.

Author and History: Some of the oldest hymns in the Avesta, the Gathas, most likely go back to Zoroaster (sixth century B.C.[10]). The authors of the later parts are unknown. Zoroastrianism was an important religion in Persia during two periods, the Achaemenid (sixth through fourth centuries B.C.) and the Sassanid (third through seventh centuries A.D.). Both time periods produced Avestan writings. Thus, the Avesta was not complete until possibly as late as a thousand years after Zoroaster.

Textual Integrity: The oldest known manuscript of the Avesta stems from the 1200s A.D., a fairly long time since its composition, and it has been estimated that approximately 75 percent of the original Avesta has been lost.[11] Furthermore, because Avestan is such a difficult language, many sentences in it seem to make no sense.[12] At such points, it is always possible that the text became corrupt, but this is difficult to prove. (Claiming that there must be a scribal error when a scholar does not understand a text, and then changing it to read what the scholar thinks it should say can be a precarious enterprise.) There is no question that the majority of the Avesta, though claiming to stem from Zoroaster, was produced much later.

Function within the Community: The Avesta is the central revelation for Zoroastrianism. Its primary use is as a source of recitations in temple worship, but it is also used for private recitations and as a source of information about life and practice.

Content Relationship to the Bible: As far as they can be reconstructed, the early Gathas contain teachings that are fairly compatible with the Old Testament, espousing monotheism and a set of ethical standards upholding truth and righteousness. The later sections become increasingly speculative and—by the very end—downright bizarre. These later portions emphasize a dualism between God and Satan as equals that is not compatible with biblical teaching.

Incredulity Rating: The origins of the Avesta are, for the most part, shrouded in mystery. Any information concerning Zoroaster's revelations is so deeply rooted in late mythology that it cannot constitute compelling evidence that the Avesta is inspired scripture.

THE ADI GRANTH

Religion: Sikhism

Brief Description: The Adi Granth is a collection of hymns and poems.

Author and History: The Adi Granth contains six thousand hymns, amassed primarily by the fifth guru (divine teacher) of Sikhism, Arjan Dev, whose writings also constitute roughly a third of the collection. It also contains hymns of the founding guru, Nanak, and of his spiritual predecessors in Sufi Islam and Bhakti Hinduism. The tenth and last human guru, Gobind Singh, added a few more hymns, primarily those of his father, but only Arjan Dev's collection is considered completely authoritative.

Textual Integrity: The original copy of the Adi Granth is preserved in the "Golden Temple" in the city of Amritsar, India. Thus, there can be no uncertainty concerning the correctness of later copies, some of which contain deviations.

Function within the Community: The Adi Granth serves as the central object of veneration among Sikhs. It rests on the altar in the front of a Sikh temple every day. At night it is literally put to bed, complete with silk sheets in nicer temples, and brought out again in the morning. Sikh worship consists primarily of chants from the Granth.

Content Relationship to the Bible: The writings of the Granth express a mixture of Islam and Hinduism. They teach there is only one God, known by many names, including the "True Name" (sat nam) and "Only One" (ekankar). A soul that purifies itself through many rebirths may eventually merge itself with God. These doctrines of reincarnation and pantheism make an accommodation with the Bible impossible.

Incredulity Rating: The Adi Granth contains much beautiful poetry. Nevertheless, one looks in vain for a reason to accept this collection as inspired.

THE VEDAS

Religion: Hinduism (its earliest phase)

Brief Description: There are four Vedas (Rig, Sama, Yajur, Atharva). Together they comprise a set of writings many times the size of the Bible. The first Veda is a collection of hymns to the gods of early Hinduism, the next two combine hymns with ritual sayings and offering formulas. The last, which is considered somewhat inferior, includes magic formulas.

Author and History: The Vedas were written roughly between 1500 and 800 B.C. They represent the religion of the Aryan invaders who came into India and during this time span slowly conquered the entire subcontinent. The Vedas are not tied to any known person for authorship, though they were undoubtedly created by members of the emerging priesthood, the Brahman caste. Subsequently, the Vedas were supplemented by other writings, such as the Upanishads and various Brahmanas (priestly manuals), which are also frequently reckoned along with the Vedas.

Texual Integrity: The Vedas have been preserved orally as well as in writing, but there are virtually no ancient manuscripts. At the same time, since these books do not specify historical events or tie themselves to factual matters, how accurate they are textually really makes little difference.

Function within the Community: It is incumbent upon every person who wishes to be a Hindu to accept the Vedas as divinely revealed to a group of semidivine persons, called the *rishis*, in the remote past. However, doing so does not imply the need to (1) know what is in them, (2) understand them,

(3) practice what they teach, or (4) worship the gods referred to in them. Recognizing the Vedas as inspired is, in a sense, a pure religious formality.[13]

Content Relationship to the Bible: Other than possibly some references in the earliest Veda, the Rig Veda, to an ancient practice of the worship of a God in the sky with animal sacrifices, there is virtually no common ground between the Bible and the teachings of the Vedas. The Vedas are polytheistic,[14] focused on sacrificial rituals and the gods arising out of those sacrifices, and later on various forms of magic. The religion of the Vedas represents precisely the religion denounced in the Old Testament.

Incredulity Rating: There are no rational reasons to accept the Vedas as inspired. These are ancient documents that reflect, particularly later on, the political ramifications of the Brahman priesthood establishing its power in society. To accept the Vedas as divinely revealed involves a leap in the dark.

THE UPANISHADS

Religion: Hinduism (the middle phase)

Brief Description: The Upanishads are writings of devotional and philosophical nature, intended to supplement the Vedas.

Author and History: The Upanishads were composed by anonymous sages from about 500 B.C. on. Initially, they were not conceived of as independent writings but as continuations of the Vedas. There is no consensus as to how many there actually are; estimates go as high as 108—a symbolic number of completion in Hinduism. Many of these pieces actually exist independently of the Vedas, and only either twelve or thirteen are considered "classical." Each of these main Upanishads is associated with one of the four Vedas. Thus, they are also known as the Vedanta (the supplements to the Vedas).

Textual Integrity: There is little material with which to do textual study. Although scholarly consensus argues that the time of composition dates to roughly 500 B.C., nothing was written down until A.D. 1656.[15] This is not the date of the earliest manuscript copy but of the first original writing of what had supposedly been preserved only orally until then. As a result, it is not at all possible to undertake a study of the textual integrity of the Upanishads—there are no texts before this relatively recent date.

Function within the Community: The Upanishads are diverse in their teachings. Many simply carry on the fundamental doctrines of the Vedas, but the most original ones reflect a phase of Hinduism that is mystical and philosophical. For some Hindus, the pantheistic teaching represents the very essence of Hinduism. Many other Hindus know of the teaching of the Upanishads that the soul (atman) is identical with god (Brahman), but it does not have a direct impact on their religious lives.

Content Relationship to the Bible: The philosophical teaching of the Upanishads reveals an impersonal god, which is diametrically opposed to the biblical teaching in which a personal God and a human being can be in direct relationship, but based only on God's saving acts.

Incredulity Rating: Many people outside Hinduism find the Upanishads attractive because of their mystical teaching. In fact, they are sometimes considered the epitome of the *philosophia perennis*, an allegedly universal form of god-soul mysticism. Even if that is the case, they are still only a product of the human creative genius, not necessarily divinely inspired.

THE BHAGAVAD GITA

Religion: Hinduism (the later phase)

Brief Description: The Gita is part of a much larger epic work, the Mahabharata. This epic tells the story of the struggle between two branches of a family. In the eighteen chapters of the Gita, the god Krishna, acting as chariot driver, instructs the archer Arjuna that he can gain salvation simply by devoting himself to this god and by performing the duties of his caste.

Author and History: The author of the Bhagavad Gita is unknown. Together with the rest of the Mahabharata, it originated most likely sometime between 400 and 100 B.C.—a wide latitude, though some writers have stretched these boundaries even more.[16] Although one cannot rule out that the setting of the Mahabharata has historical roots, there is no clue, let alone evidence, for any further historical corroboration.

Textual Integrity: As we have already reported with other ancient Indian texts, textual integrity was not an issue until the influence of Western scholars. There really are no significant data even to attempt an assessment.

Function within the Community: The Gita is a widely accepted and popular scripture in contemporary Hinduism. Even though the fundamental teaching seems to focus on a personal god (Krishna), even pantheistically oriented groups try to claim the Gita for themselves. Among some groups such as ISKCON (Hare Krishna), it is accepted as the primary scripture, and they refer to it as Vedic.

Content Relationship to the Bible: There is no overlap with biblical teaching. It is impossible to equate Krishna with any understanding of God or Christ in the Bible. Even Krishna's instructions to Arjuna, which emphasize Krishna's love and mercy, fall far short of the New Testament's teaching of God's grace in Christ.

Incredulity Rating: The Bhagavad Gita is beautiful poetry. Its teaching, within its own setting, is lofty and marks a humanizing trend in the development of Hinduism. Nonetheless, there is no historical confirmation, and—apart from simply submitting to religious authority—it cannot rationally command acceptance.

THE PALI CANON

Religion: Buddhism (early [Theravada] stage)

Brief Description: This collection of writings of truly encyclopedic proportion is named after Pali, the language of its only surviving version and possibly the language of the Buddha. It is also called Tripitaka, the "Three Baskets," because it has three divisions: rules for Buddhist monks, teachings of the Buddha, and scholarly analysis of Buddhist teachings.

Author and History: According to tradition, some of the teaching material was assembled by the Buddha's own disciples at the first Buddhist council in the early fifth century B.C. Thus, it would most likely be fairly faithful to what Buddha himself taught. Over the centuries, the Tripitaka swelled by constant addition of new material. Some of it consists of the rewriting of popular traditions into Buddhist thought forms. The complete Pali canon stems from no earlier than the first century B.C.

Textual Integrity: Although the Pali version of the Tripitaka is the most complete and possibly the original, there are other less complete versions of it, several in Sanskrit and others translated into Chinese, Korean, and Tibetan. Once again, the overarching problem is not textual accuracy—that is a lost cause—but simply identifying texts that may have been part of the original. Wooden print blocks in Chinese and Korean exist from roughly the thirteenth century, so from that point on the translations into those languages are stable. Nevertheless, we are left with a sizeable gap between the thirteenth century and the time of the Buddha.

Function within the Community: Theravada Buddhism focuses primarily on its monks and their search for enlightenment. The Pali canon provides the theoretical and inspirational basis for their quest. The laity particularly profits from the Jataka tales, which are stories about the Buddha's former lives and illustrate specific Buddhist virtues such as generosity and filial piety.

Content Relationship to the Bible: Because the Pali canon is so strongly steeped in a philosophy that is alien to a biblical worldview, there are simply no plausible parallels. The two are utterly incompatible.

Incredulity Rating: The Tripitaka is a collection of writings that was constantly added to and taken away from, to the point at which we do not know what should in fact be a part of it. Unless one were already a Theravada Buddhist, one would have no reason to select the Pali canon as one's scripture.

THE LOTUS SUTRA

Religion: Buddhism (the later [Mahayana] version)

Brief Description: The Lotus Sutra is a purported account of teachings that the Buddha gave toward the end of his life. It provides the basis for the main beliefs of later Buddhism, particularly the universal salvation of all human beings and the proliferation of Buddhas and Bodhisattvas (Buddhas in the making).

Author and History: Although the text claims to be written by the Buddha himself, there is every reason to believe he was neither its author nor the source of its teachings. For one thing, it clearly contradicts what we can reasonably claim to know of Buddha's teachings from the Pali canon. It is a collection of various Buddhist writings that finally came together by roughly A.D. 200.

Textual Integrity: There are several ancient versions and translations of the Lotus Sutra. Since it is clearly a patchwork of multiple writings, there is no clear original. Of course, since it is fairly certain that the Lotus Sutra does not go back to the Buddha anyway, even an original version of any of its parts would not be greatly significant.

Function within the Community: Mahayana consists of virtually a countless number of schools, each emphasizing its own scriptures but usually acknowledging those of the other schools (frequently merely as a courtesy). The Lotus Sutra, as one of the fountainheads of Mahayana, is regarded as central by many schools. Among the rationalist (Tendai) Buddhists, it occupies a central place. Adherents of the Japanese Nichiren Shoshu school (which exists now primarily as the Soka Gakkai movement) believe that merely chanting the title of the Lotus Sutra (*namu myo horengekyo*) will bring about Buddhahood.

Content Relationship to the Bible: There are no direct parallels to the Bible, but there are some interesting contrasts. For example, in the biblical story of the prodigal son, the son is welcomed by the father unconditionally (Luke 15:11–32). In the Lotus Sutra, the Buddha comes into the stable alongside the son to show him how to work himself out of his predicament, a clear antithesis to the doctrine of grace exemplified by Christ's parable.[17]

Incredulity Rating: As alluded to above, in Buddhism, scriptures constitute a veritable cafeteria counter of wisdom from which one may select to suit one's appetite. Furthermore, since the Lotus Sutra contains a clear historical falsehood, namely, its origin from the Buddha himself,[18] to accept it as divinely inspired writing would be irrational.

The Daodejing (Tao-Te-Ching in Earlier Transcriptions)[19]

Religion: Daoism (Taoism), a strong component of Chinese popular religion

Brief Description: The Daodejing is a relatively short collection of sayings, commending the Daoist philosophy of *wu-wei* ("letting alone" or "actionless action"). The fundamental idea is that by performing as few deliberate actions as possible, the Way (dao) will manifest itself and provide its virtue and power (de).

Author and History: According to the legend, the founder of Daoism, Laozu, in roughly the year 600 B.C., wrote down the epitome of his wisdom in this book in order to be permitted to leave China. Broader scholarly opinion attributes it to anonymous sages sometime around 300 B.C.[20] Even though it is a very philosophical text, eventually it became the central text for the Daoist religion, which focuses on magic, alchemy, ancestor worship, and personal deities, none of which are mentioned in the Daodejing.

Textual Integrity: The oldest known manuscript dates to about 200 B.C. Thus, there is a relatively short time between its composition and our first textual evidence, and we can be fairly certain that what we have now is an accurate reproduction of the ancient form of the Daodejing.

Function within the Community: Even though Daoism recognizes the Daode jing as its primary scripture, the book has virtually nothing to do with reli gious Daoism, except for the notion that metaphysical balance produces spir itual power.

Content Relationship to the Bible: There are no discernable parallels. The Daodejing is primarily a philosophical treatise based on an impersonalist phi losophy, and, thus, no direct relationship is conceivable.

Incredulity Rating: The first groups to accept the Daodejing as revelation probably did so more out of spite for the dominant Confucian regime than out of a desire to practice its teachings (which they did not do). More rationally, how can a book be divinely inspired if it does not even fit into a worldview in which gods have a role to play? One can admire the philosophy of Daoism (up to a point, after which it becomes incredible), but there is no separate rea son to accept it as revelation.

THE ANALECTS (CONVERSATIONS)

Religion: Confucianism (an integral part of Chinese, Korean, and Japanese culture)

Brief Description: The Analects present the teachings of Confucius of the sixth century B.C. Primarily in conversational form, they bring out the main themes of his philosophy, including the occasional observation on religious matters.

Author and History: Undoubtedly, the content of the Analects goes back to Confucius himself, though none of it was written down until a century or more after his death. When the Han dynasty came to power in China in roughly 200 B.C., they made Confucianism the official dogma of China, and the Analects were established as one of the founding works of Eastern culture. Its study was mandated by the Chinese civil service, and it has set the pattern of behavior in traditional Asian cultures for more than two millennia.

Textual Integrity: Apparently there were several versions of the Analects in ancient times. The one we have now is the only one that survived. Thus, there is no way of testing to what extent other variants may have been closer to Confucius's original sayings.

Function within the Community: The Analects is not a religious book, and it does not function as such. One looks in vain for more than sporadic references to god, heaven, or the spirit world. It is a manual on leading a virtuous and humanitarian life and is studied for the sake of learning how to act properly.

Content Relationship to the Bible: The only overlap between the Analects and the Bible is their emphasis on virtuous lives. However, in the Bible this behavior is the result of a relationship with God; in the Analects it is for the purpose of relationships with people.

Incredulity Rating: The followers of Confucius saw the Analects as crucial and important. They revered it as stemming from the esteemed master him self, but they did not see it as divine revelation. Therefore, neither should we.

JAPANESE WRITINGS: KOJIKI, NIHONGI, AMATSU NORITO

Religion: Shinto

Brief Description: These three relatively short works are important books for Shinto, the indigenous religion of Japan. The Kojiki is the mythological story of the beginnings of Japan, the Nihongi provides variations on the myth, and the Amatsu Norito is a manual for prayers and rituals.

Author and History: According to tradition, a public servant named Yasumaro traveled throughout Japan to collect components of the national myth as it was recited orally. In A.D. 712, he presented the finished Kojiki to the emperor. At his regent's behest, Yasumaro then collected variations on the stories that he published in A.D. 720 as the Nihongi. The Amatsu Norito arose anonymously in the tenth century.

Textual Integrity: As an ancient work of literature, the Kojiki stands alone, insofar as the Nihongi provides multiple variants on its content.[21] Of course, those are variations on the myth presumably as Yasumaro heard it told; they are not actual changes in the completed text of the Kojiki. Nonetheless, against the backdrop of the Nihongi, it seems reasonable to accept both of these books as carefully transmitted. The same is most likely true of the Amatsu Norito.

Function within the Community: The Amatsu Norito functions in a practical way as a guide to prayers. It is not a Bible in the Christian sense, as it is not considered to have been revealed by a god. The two narrative collections are legitimation for Japanese society and religion, particularly the status of the emperor as having descended from the sun goddess.

Content Relationship to the Bible: There are no parallels, only mutually exclusive assertions.

Incredulity Rating: As already indicated, the members of this religion accept these writings as "sacred" in the sense of contributing to their religious culture, but they are not thought of as divinely revealed scripture.

A PERSONAL CONCLUSION

In this chapter, I have attempted to provide good reasons to believe that the Bible, and the Bible alone, is properly considered to be the Word of God. But this chapter bears a more personal title, "Why *I* believe . . ." Someone might very understandably respond to all this and say, "Come now, that's not really why you believe the Bible. Isn't it true that you were brought up as a Christian, and so from very early on you were taught that the Bible is the Word of God and other religious books are false?" This seems to be a legitimate challenge.

Certainly, the person challenging me in this way has some legitimate grounds. I am happy to say that God blessed me with godly parents and that I did indeed learn to treasure the Bible as the Word of God from early on. But that observation only describes the *origin* of that particular belief; it does not address the reasons why I accept the belief *now*.

The distinction between a source of a belief and a reason for a belief is a common one. Many times we hear of a belief but do not accept it until much later, when we find reasons why the belief is true. Do you believe everything everyone tells you? Do you later on find reasons for believing something that at one time you simply accepted at face value?

There certainly was a time when I accepted the Bible as the Word of God simply because my parents told me it was. The source for the belief and its reasons were identical because of my parents' authority. But I definitely no longer believe that the Bible is God's Word just because my mom told me so. My childish faith has become adult faith. In between were periods of searching and discovery and times of soberly assessing the evidence. I was not programmed by my parents to maintain their belief system, but I did so because the more I assessed the evidence on its behalf, the more true I found it to be. I do not give myself an argument every morning to keep myself believing in the Bible, but when I do reflect on the veracity of what I believe, the arguments of the present chapter are what come to mind.

PART 5

WHY
I BELIEVE
JESUS IS THE
MESSIAH AND
SON OF GOD

There are very few people who do not acknowledge that Jesus of Nazareth was the most extraordinarily good and wise man who ever lived. Interestingly, one of the few was Bertrand Russell, whose famous essay,

"Why I Am Not a Christian," admittedly played at least some minor role in rallying the contributors to this book. The purpose of this particular section of the book, however, is not to respond to Russell. It is actually the inverse: to present a stark challenge to those who hold that Jesus was *merely* a supremely good and wise man.

Jesus had already performed many miracles and had done a great deal of preaching and teaching when he called his disciples together and asked them, "Who do people say that I am?"

To paraphrase, the disciples replied, "Some say John the Baptist (come back from the dead), . . . others say Elijah (whose sweet chariot swung low, allowing him to circumvent death), . . . and still others, Jeremiah or one of the prophets. But one thing's for sure, they all agree you're an amazing individual!"

Not satisfied with hearing of his general positive acclaim, Jesus responded with a piercing question that still echoes in the universe and falls on the ears of every seeker of truth: "But who do *you* say that I am?"

This is truly *the* question, and it is personally directed at you and me. "I say you are just a good man" is a valid response if that is what you truly believe. But the answer that resounds throughout the centuries is that of Peter: "Thou art the Christ, the Son of the living God."

"Blessed art thou," responded Jesus. Peter had drawn the right conclusion, not from what others said but from the evidence he had witnessed. And more importantly, he had assimilated the truth of who Christ was into a personal conviction and so found the blessing of God.

Who do you say Jesus is?

This can be a gnawing question for believers and unbelievers alike, but especially for those who are born Jews into a nominally Christian culture. Whether Jesus is or is not the promised Messiah may mean little to you if your name is Russell. But it means a great deal if your name is Leventhal. In chapter 12, Dr. Barry Leventhal gives a scholar's explanation of why Jesus truly is the Messiah prophesied in the Hebrew Scriptures (i.e., the Old Testament) as well as a conservative Jew's personal account of all that it means to come to Jesus as Messiah, Savior, and Lord.

Having already demonstrated the historical reliability of the New Testament, we find in chapter 13 that our options for responding to *the* question are few and, in all honesty, a bit troubling. Dr. Peter Kreeft shows that Jesus left no room for a neutral answer. You will see that Jesus was either (1) a very bad man or (2) exactly who he claimed to be, the very Son of God.

TWELVE

WHY I BELIEVE JESUS IS THE PROMISED MESSIAH

BARRY R. LEVENTHAL

It would be so much easier just to throw in the towel and admit that Yeshua[1] was not really the Messiah promised to the Jews, that he never made such an audacious claim, and that there is certainly no historical evidence for such an assertion. After all, wouldn't this go a long way in furthering ecumenical dialogue as well as peace and harmony in our pluralistic society? It would certainly eliminate much of the antagonism and hostility that the Jewish community holds against most Messianic Jews,[2] as well as others who claim to be followers of Jesus Christ.[3] In fact, why not just claim, as some have, that Yeshua certainly *is* the Messiah, but not for the Jewish people. One well-known rabbi maintains that Yeshua was literally raised from the dead bodily, but only for the Gentiles.[4] Obviously, that is one easy way out of the painful dilemma of the messiahship of Yeshua.

But such a personal repudiation of the messiahship of Yeshua would not be right, safe, or honorable. First, it would not be *right* because it flies in the face of the historical evidence itself. Second, it would not be *safe*, for if the historical evidence is true, then Yeshua the Messiah controls the destinies of all men, as he himself and his first followers claimed.[5] Third, if the historical evidence truly does validate Yeshua's messianic authority, then such a rejection would not be *honorable* either, for as the risen and glorified Messiah, all honor and glory belong to him alone.[6]

Thus, we are left with the now famous trilemma proposed by the literary scholar C. S. Lewis when he concluded his own research into the messiahship of Jesus:

> I am trying here to prevent anyone saying the really foolish thing that people often say about Him: "I'm ready to accept Jesus as a great moral teacher, but I don't accept His claim to be God." That is the one thing we must not say. A man who was merely a man and said the sort of things Jesus said would not be a great moral teacher. He would either be a lunatic—on a level with the man who says he is a poached egg—or else he would be the Devil of Hell. You must make your choice. Either this man was, and is, the Son of God: or else a madman or something worse. You can shut Him up for a fool, you can spit at Him and kill Him as a demon; or you can fall at His feet and call Him Lord and God. But let us not come with any patronising nonsense about His being a great human teacher. He has not left that open to us. He did not intend to.[7]

And make no mistake about it, Jesus *did* claim to be the promised Messiah, and his earliest followers, all Jews, held him to be nothing less than the Messiah of Israel and the Savior of the world.[8]

So now we come to the crucial issue: What is the historical evidence for the messiahship of Jesus? If we believe that Jesus is the promised Messiah, both for the nation of Israel as well as for the entire world, then upon what kind of testimony does such a conviction rest? In light of the enormity of the evidence as well as the limitation of space, I will focus on only three major factors that demonstrate his messiahship.[9] The first piece of evidence is Jesus' fulfillment of messianic prophecy. Second is the impact of his messianic resurrection from the dead. Third is his messianic transformation of lives.

JESUS' FULFILLMENT OF MESSIANIC PROPHECY

Before investigating two specific messianic prophecies, a few introductory comments are necessary. First, when God called Abraham to himself in order to begin a new program with a new people, a universal program that would ultimately reach into eternity (Gen. 12:1–3), he granted to Abraham's descendants, the Jewish people, a fourfold mission.[10] The first aspect of the Jews' divine mission was that their prophets were to receive and write down God's revelation of himself and his will for humankind. The second aspect of their mission was to protect and preserve for posterity the textual purity of the Scriptures God inspired them to write. The third aspect of the Jewish calling was that they were to be a witness to a darkened world that there was only one true God, a God of light and life who loved humankind and wanted it to be reconciled to himself. The fourth and most important aspect of this divine election was that this strange and unique nation was to be the ethnic people through which the Messiah, the Savior of the world, would be born.

Second, with this final aspect of Israel's mission in mind, God progressively unfolded in the Hebrew Bible, commonly referred to as the Old Testament, a clear and distinct body of messianic prophecy.[11] The progressive nature of this messianic revelation unfolded in such a way that some aspects of the Hebrew prophets' messages were clear and others were not until a future time (cf. 1 Peter 1:10–12).

This growing corpus of messianic prophecy in the Hebrew Scriptures was also clearly recognized in the older rabbinic tradition. According to Alfred Edersheim, an earlier messianic believer and scholar, in some 558 rabbinic writings there are 456 separate Old Testament passages used to refer to the Messiah and the messianic times.[12] More recently, J. Barton Payne cited 574 verses in the Old Testament that were direct, personal messianic predictions. He found 103 in eighteen books of the Old Testament, including 25 in Isaiah, 24 in the Psalms, and 20 in Zechariah.[13]

Third, this raises the interesting and convicting question: What are the odds of one man—in this case, Jesus Christ—fulfilling each and every one of these prophecies? Biblical scholar John Phillips makes the following pertinent remarks:

> The Bible is the only book which challenges unbelief by foretelling the future, staking its authority on the ultimate, certain, and complete fulfillment of its detailed predictions. It has been said that there were some 109 Old Testament predictions literally fulfilled at Christ's first coming, and that, of the 845 quotations from the Old Testament in the New Testament, 333 refer to Christ. There are some 25 prophecies concerning the betrayal, trial, death, burial, and resurrection of Jesus uttered by various prophets over a period of some five hundred years. These were literally fulfilled although the chances against such fulfillment have been shown to be one chance in 33,554,438. If the law of Compound Probabilities is applied similarly to all 109 predictions fulfilled at Christ's first coming, the chances that they could accidentally be fulfilled in the history of one person is one in billions.[14]

It would appear, then, if one were to take these messianic prophecies seriously, and if Jesus fulfilled them at his first coming, that his messiahship would certainly be validated.

Fourth, Yeshua himself continued to press this same point. His consistent testimony was that the Old Testament Scriptures pointed forward to his own messiahship (cf. Luke 16:31; John 5:39). He even challenged his own disciples with similar pointed remarks about their refusal to believe the inspired words of the Old Testament concerning his messianic person and mission (Luke 24:25–27, 44–48). Not only did Yeshua press home this matter but so did his earliest followers (e.g., Acts 2:22–32; 13:26–31; Rom. 15:2–4; 1 Cor. 15:1–8).

Yeshua did indeed come in direct fulfillment of Old Testament messianic prophecy.

The conclusion, therefore, seems obvious: Yeshua himself and his earliest followers, as well as the myriads of true believers down through the centuries, saw and continue to see in him the final and ultimate fulfillment of all the messianic prophecies in the Hebrew Scriptures.

Out of all of these messianic prophecies, we will focus our attention on only two of the direct predictions: (1) the birthplace of the Messiah and (2) the nature and meaning of his death.[15]

THE BIRTHPLACE OF THE MESSIAH (MICAH 5:2)

According to Micah, a seventh-century B.C. prophet of God, the birthplace of the Messiah was to be in the little town of Bethlehem: "But as for you, Bethlehem Ephrathah,[16] too little to be among the clans of Judah, from you One will go forth for Me to be ruler in Israel. His goings forth are from long ago, from the days of eternity" (Micah 5:2 NASB).

Under the inspiration of the Holy Spirit, Micah predicted four crucial aspects regarding the birthplace of the Messiah. First, the birthplace was to be uniquely connected to the Davidic dynasty and its eternal kingdom, for Bethlehem was the city vitally linked to King David.[17] God had drafted a special unconditional covenant with David, called the Davidic covenant.[18] Along with the personal promises to David himself, God unilaterally committed himself to the eternal perpetuity of the Davidic dynasty: (1) an eternal throne, (2) an eternal kingdom, and, most important, (3) an eternal King.

Second, although uniquely connected with the Davidic dynasty, the birthplace of the Messiah was to be a place of humble beginnings, a town forgotten by history's power brokers. When God brings his Messiah into the world, it is through the backdoor of history. This has always been the divine initiative: humble beginnings that ultimately lead to glorious finales.[19]

Third, from the birthplace of the Messiah, God's messianic Ruler will go forth to do the will of God "in Israel." He "goes forth" for God himself as his messianic King. This One alone was uniquely appointed as God's messianic King to the nation of Israel.[20] Again, this reflects the unconditional and eternal nature of the Davidic covenant. Micah's messianic prophecy certainly forms the backdrop to the birth announcements that rang out when Yeshua made his humble and yet glorious entrance into the world (cf. Matt. 1:18–25; Luke 1:26–56; 2:1–38).

And fourth, the birthplace of the Messiah was not to be the first "going forth" [i.e., origin] of the Messiah, for "his goings forth are from long ago, from *the days of eternity*" [emphasis added].[21] Hebrew scholar Arnold Fruchtenbaum makes the following comments concerning the forceful language used by Micah in describing the eternality of the Messiah:

As regards His human origin, He is to be born in Bethlehem, but regarding His divine origin, He is said to be "from long ago, from the days of eternity."

The Hebrew words for "from long ago, from the days of eternity" are the strongest Hebrew words ever used for eternity past. They are used of God the Father in Psalm 90:2. What is true of God the Father is also said to be true of this One who is to be born in Bethlehem.[22]

In other words, through his birth in Bethlehem this unique Ruler was to be the Son of Man, but through his place in eternity he was also the Son of God. Micah's contemporary, the prophet Isaiah, prophesied in a similar vein, bringing together in one unique portrait both the humanity and the deity of the Messiah: "For *a child* will be born to us, *a son* will be given to us; and the government will rest on His shoulders; and His name will be called Wonderful Counselor, *Mighty God*,[23] eternal Father,[24] Prince of Peace" (Isa. 9:6 NASB, emphasis added).[25]

Hebrew scholar Merrill Unger aptly summarized all the messianic prophecies leading up to and including Micah's passage on the birthplace of the Messiah:

> This great Messianic prophecy presents the Messiah's generation in the Son of Man's coming forth from God to do His will on earth from Bethlehem. But as God the Son, His goings forth are "from everlasting."
>
> This great prophecy is an important milestone in the revelation of the promised Redeemer. The protoevangelium [first gospel] (Gen. 3:15) was marvelously comprehensive, but necessarily vaguely general. Then the Redeemer was foreseen to come from the Semitic sector of the human race (9:26–27).
>
> Then the revelation became more and more specific, defining the race and nationality from which the Savior would come, namely the posterity of Abraham, the Hebrews (12:3); then the particular tribe, Judah (49:10); then the family of David (2 Sam. 7:16; Ps. 110:1); then, in this prophecy, the very town of His birth; and as the Messiah's advent drew nearer, His very parentage is indicated (Matt. 1:18–25; Luke 1:27–33). Then all the scattered rays of prophecy concentrate upon the Lord Jesus as their focus (Heb. 1:1–2).[26]

There is no question that the rabbinical authorities of the second temple period [i.e., the time of Yeshua and his first followers] clearly understood that Micah 5:2 established the birthplace of the Messiah (see Matt. 2:1–6; John 7:40–42). Likewise, the rabbinic oral and written traditions also bear witness to the certainty of the messianic nature of the Micah 5:2 passage.[27] If the birthplace of the Messiah played such an important role in the prophetic panorama of God, the nature and meaning of the Messiah's death played perhaps the most important role.

THE NATURE AND MEANING OF THE MESSIAH'S DEATH (ISAIAH 52:13–53:12)

The nature and meaning of the Messiah's death are nowhere more significantly described than in the majestic fifty-third chapter of the Book of Isaiah.[28] All biblical scholars, no matter their theological persuasion, recognize it as one of the truly high points of the biblical revelation. In the words of one scholar, it "may without any exaggeration be called the most important text in the Old Testament."[29] The late Old Testament commentator Franz Delitzsch called it "the most central, the deepest, and the most lofty thing that the Old Testament prophecy, outstripping itself, has ever achieved."[30]

As one might expect, this messianic prophecy is also quoted extensively in the New Testament.[31] One biblical scholar has observed concerning this chapter, "Perhaps the most distinguished thing about it is the fact that this very portion stands in the background of almost every New Testament treatment of the great events connected with our Lord's passion, death, burial, resurrection, ascension, exaltation, and second coming."[32]

Actually, the fifty-third chapter of Isaiah is the last of what has been called the four "Servant Songs" of Isaiah.[33] F. Duane Lindsey has entitled the four songs: (1) The Call of the Servant (Isa. 42:1–9); (2) The Commission of the Servant (Isa. 49:1–13); (3) The Commitment of the Servant (Isa. 50:4–11); and (4) The Career of the Servant (Isa. 52:13–53:12).[34]

It is clear from these four Servant Songs of Isaiah, as well as other messianic prophecies, that the Jewish Messiah is clearly to be the Redeemer of *both* Jews and Gentiles alike. And since the evidence continues to point to Yeshua as this Jewish Messiah, Rabbi Lapide's assertion that he is the Messiah only of the Gentiles must be rejected.[35] No such teaching appears anywhere in the Hebrew Scriptures, let alone in the New Testament. If Yeshua has been raised from the dead (as Lapide asserts), then he is the very Lord of heaven and earth, of both Jew and Gentile alike!

Old Testament expositor Larry Helyer summarized the contents of the four Servant Songs in a list of the characteristics and accomplishments of Isaiah's Servant of the Lord:

1. He is elected by the Lord, anointed by the Spirit, and promised success in his endeavor (42:1, 4).
2. Justice is a prime concern of his ministry (42:1, 4).
3. His ministry has an international scope (42:1, 6).
4. God predestined him to his calling (49:1).
5. He is a gifted teacher (49:2).
6. He experiences discouragement in his ministry (49:4).
7. His ministry extends to the Gentiles (49:6).
8. The Servant encounters strong opposition and resistance to his teaching, even of a physically violent nature (49:5–6).
9. He is determined to finish what God called him to do (49:7).
10. The Servant has humble origins with little outward prospects for success (53:1–2).
11. He experiences suffering and affliction (53:3).
12. The Servant accepts vicarious and substitutionary suffering on behalf of his people (53:4–6, 12).
13. He is put to death after being condemned (53:7–9).

14. Incredibly, he comes back to life and is exalted above all rulers (53:11–12; 52:15).[36]

When Isaiah received this divinely inspired portrait of the Messiah's career, he formatted it in a literary structure called a chiasmus or chiasm (i.e., inverted parallelism); in this kind of chiastic structure, the literary emphasis falls on the central member of the configuration (i.e., the "C" of Isa. 53:4–6 below):

A. The prologue of the song (an overview) God speaking (a proclamation): "I value my servant!" (52:13–15)
The body of the song: the nation Israel speaking (a confession): "We utterly rejected the servant!" (53:1–9)
B. "We rejected him in his life!" (vv. 1–3)
C. A theological parenthesis (the ultimate reason for the rejection): "We thought he died for his own sins rather than our own!" (vv. 4–6)
B'. "We rejected him in his death!" (vv. 7–9)
A'. The epilogue of the song (a final view) God speaking (a declaration): "My servant is victorious!" (vv. 10–12)

A summary of Isaiah's classic passage is as follows:[37]

1. In the prologue of the song (Isa. 52:13–15), the prophet Isaiah asserted (on behalf of God) that the Servant of the Lord would ultimately be highly exalted (v. 13), as well as honored among the Gentiles (v. 15), but only after dreadful personal suffering (v. 14).
2. In the body of the song (53:1–9), Isaiah confessed (on behalf of his own people) that (1) Israel utterly rejected the Servant of the Lord in his life (vv. 1–3), (2) as well as in his death (vv. 7–9), because (3) the nation misjudged the meaning of his death by assuming that he died for his own sins rather than for the nation's (vv. 4–6).
3. In the epilogue of the song (53:10–12), the prophet asserted (on behalf of God) that by the Servant's completed work of atonement, God would be exalted (v. 10), believers would be justified (v. 11), and the Servant himself would be honored (v. 12).[38]

The one central image of the Servant in this passage is his suffering as a lamb without spot or blemish, going to his death as a vicarious atonement without hesitancy or resistance (Isa. 53:7–9). He is truly the Lamb of God who takes away the sins of the world![39]

Of course, the hotly debated issue of Isaiah 52:13–53:12, as well as the other three Servant Songs, is the identity of the Servant of the Lord.[40] It is almost universally maintained by modern Jewish authorities that the Suffering Servant of which Isaiah 53 speaks is the nation Israel. It is argued that as the Jewish people, the so-called Suffering Servant of the Lord, suffers innocently at the hands of the Gentiles, the Gentiles will eventually see the error of their ways and repent before God for their years of Jewish persecution. Even further, these modern rabbinic authorities contend that this is the *traditional* Jewish interpretation of Isaiah 53. This interpretation is impossible in light of the actual history of interpretation of Isaiah 53,[41] as well as the inherent meaning of the passage itself.

Old Testament authority Arnold Fruchtenbaum appropriately summarized the erroneous thinking of this modern rabbinic position:

> So to interpret Isaiah 53 as speaking of Messiah is not non-Jewish. In fact, if we are to speak of the *traditional* Jewish interpretation, it would be that the passage speaks of the Messiah. The first one to expound the view that this referred to Israel rather than the Messiah was Shlomo Yizchaki, better known as Rashi (c. 1040–1105). He was followed by David Kimchi (1160–1235). But this was to go contrary to all rabbinic teaching of that day and of the preceding one thousand years. Today Rashi's view has become dominant in Jewish and rabbinical theology. But that is not *the* Jewish view. Nor is it the *traditional* Jewish view. Those closer to the time of the original writings, and who had less contact with the Christian apologists, interpreted it as speaking of the Messiah.[42]

In terms of both the internal evidence as well as the external evidence, Isaiah 52:13–53:12 cannot be speaking about a corporate Messiah but rather about an individual Messiah. In terms of the internal evidence, the passage itself argues against a corporate Messiah (i.e., the nation Israel as the Suffering Servant). Rather, the grammar, syntax, and theology argue for a personal Messiah (e.g., the significant pronoun shifts in 53:4–6), as does the larger context of the Book of Isaiah (i.e., the three other Servant passages). In terms of the external evidence as well, a personal Messiah seems obvious. For example, the *traditional* interpretation of the rabbinic authorities clearly refers to a personal Messiah, as does the consistent testimony of the New Testament and the early messianic community.[43]

In addition, the passage itself yields at least four arguments countering the claim that the nation Israel, or for that matter any other mere human being, is the promised Suffering Servant of the Lord. First is the Servant's sinlessness (52:13; 53:9): The Servant of Isaiah 53 is described as without sin, that is, completely innocent in thought, word, and deed. He is perfect in his actions as well as his reactions. Where is the Jew who would dare to proclaim Israel, or for that matter even Moses or Isaiah, to be without sin? Why the need for a national Day of Atonement (Leviticus 16)? Or for Isaiah's indictment against Israel's sinful rebellion against God (Isaiah 1)? Or for that matter, Isaiah's confession of his own sinfulness (Isa. 6:5–7)?

Second is the Servant's submission (53:7): The Servant of Isaiah 53 submits (without any resistance whatsoever) to be slaughtered like a lamb. He lays down his life as a sacrifice, willingly and voluntarily, in an absolute sense. There are few exceptions in secular history and none in biblical history that

Israel ever submitted passively to her fate. Quite the contrary, Israel's heroism is well documented in the annals of history.

Third is the Servant's cessation (death) (53:8–9, 12): The Servant of Isaiah 53 is "cut off out of the land of the living" (53:8 NASB). "He poured out himself to death" (53:12 NASB). The Servant is also portrayed as alive from the dead and enjoying fellowship with God and his faithful followers (52:13, 15; 53:10–12). Israel as a nation still exists and always has, even as God promised (cf. Leviticus 26; Deuteronomy 28). The nation has never ceased to exist, let alone been raised from the dead in any literal sense of the word.

Fourth is the Servant's substitution (52:14–15; 53:4–6, 8, 10–12): The Servant of Isaiah 53 is a substitutionary atonement for others, not for himself. He is pictured as dying vicariously, punished for the sins committed by others. Israel, as well as Isaiah and all other individuals, were punished for their own sins. Accordingly, it is not surprising that Jewish prayer books make continual confessions on behalf of the Jewish people.

I vividly remember the first time I seriously confronted Isaiah 53, or better still, the first time it seriously confronted me. Being rather confused over the identity of the Servant in Isaiah 53, I went to my local rabbi and said to him, "Rabbi, I have met some people at school who claim that the so-called Servant in Isaiah 53 is none other than Jesus of Nazareth. But I would like to know from you, who is this Servant in Isaiah 53?"

I was astonished at his response. "Barry, I must admit that as I read Isaiah 53 it does seem to be talking about Jesus, but since we Jews do not believe in Jesus, it can't be speaking about Jesus." Not only did his so-called reasoning sound circular, it also sounded evasive and even fearful. There are none who are as deaf as those who do not want to hear.[44]

In conclusion then, no one else in all of history can come even close to fulfilling these, as well as the many other, messianic prophecies, except Yeshua himself. He alone is the promised Messiah who was born in Bethlehem, the totally unique One who died as the final Lamb of God—a vicarious and substitutionary atonement—and who was raised from the grave to enter into all of his own splendor and glory!

Jesus' Impact as the Resurrected Messiah

We have already seen that Yeshua's life, death, and resurrection were clearly prophesied in the Hebrew Scriptures, but the impact of his resurrection cannot be overstated, especially in the lives of the thousands of his first followers, all of them Jewish.[45] We often forget that all of Yeshua's resurrection appearances were to Jewish believers alone, except for his sole appearance to an avowed enemy, Saul of Tarsus. We also often forget that all of the first believers were Jewish, thousands of them.[46] Historically, it can actually be demonstrated that many of these Jewish believers came out of the ranks of the Pharisees and the Levitical priesthood.[47]

In regard to these early resurrection appearances of Yeshua, Christian philosopher and apologist J. P. Moreland has developed five pieces of circumstantial evidence that support Yeshua's historical resurrection from the dead, that is, five supporting factors that are not in dispute by anyone.[48]

EXHIBIT 1: THE DISCIPLES DIED FOR THEIR BELIEFS

When Yeshua died, all of his followers, in despair and fear, went into hiding. They thought that Yeshua's entire messianic movement was over. Even though they knew that the Hebrew Scriptures had prophesied that the Messiah would not see bodily corruption in the grave[49] and that Yeshua had even predicted his own resurrection on at least three different occasions,[50] they thought his messianic program had collapsed in utter defeat.[51] And yet in a short time, these very same disciples appeared on the historical scene boldly proclaiming the good news of the gospel, that this Jesus who had been crucified, dead, and buried was now alive from the dead and the Lord of life and the sole determiner of men's eternal destinies.[52]

And what did they get for such an open and bold proclamation? They endured some of the worst abuse and punishment known in their own day. In fact, many of them were tortured and even martyred for their faith in this resurrected Messiah. Men may live for a lie, but to think that thousands will die for that same lie requires a stretch of the imagination.[53] In the words of theologian Clark Pinnock, "Hypocrites do not become martyrs. The disciples might have been deluded, but they were not liars."[54]

Even Jewish theologian Pinchas Lapide, although certainly arriving at the wrong conclusion,[55] at least is forced to grant the historicity of Yeshua's resurrection based on the transformation of his disciples:

> When this scared, frightened band of the apostles which was just about to throw away everything in order to flee in despair to Galilee; when these peasants, shepherds, and fishermen, who betrayed and denied their master and then failed him miserably, suddenly could be changed overnight into a confident mission society, convinced of salvation and able to work with much more success after Easter than before Easter, then no vision or hallucination is sufficient to explain such a revolutionary transformation. For a sect or school or an order, perhaps a single vision would have been sufficient—but not for a world religion which was able to conquer the Occident thanks to the Easter faith.[56]

Michael Green, former principal of St. John's College, Nottingham, observed that belief in the resurrection

> was the belief that turned heartbroken followers of a crucified rabbi into the courageous witnesses and martyrs of the early church. This was the one belief

that separated the followers of Jesus from the Jews and turned them into the community of the resurrection. You could imprison them, flog them, kill them, but you could not make them deny their conviction that "on the third day He rose again."[57]

The question then that must be asked is the question Michael Green asked: "How have [these early followers] turned, almost overnight, into the indomitable band of enthusiasts who braved opposition, cynicism, ridicule, hardship, prison, and death in three continents, as they preached everywhere Jesus and the resurrection?"[58] It was also the question on the lips of the late evangelist and teacher Paul Little: "Are these men, who helped transform the moral structure of society, consummate liars or deluded madmen? These alternatives are harder to believe than the fact of the Resurrection, and there is no shred of evidence to support them."[59]

EXHIBIT 2: THE CONVERSION OF SKEPTICS

It is recognized by all that there were hardened skeptics who did not believe in Yeshua before his crucifixion, as well as others who violently opposed the early messianic revolution of Yeshua. And yet, for some powerful and overwhelming reason, many of them were swept into the revolution itself and became some of its most able and ardent defenders, even willingly going to their deaths on its behalf. One such example was the early church leader James, the half brother of Jesus. He had great doubts and even skepticism about the messiahship of his half brother until the resurrected Yeshua personally appeared to him (see John 7:1–5; Acts 1:14; 1 Cor. 15:7). James not only became the recognized leader of the Jerusalem church (Acts 12:17; 15:13; 21:18; Gal. 1:19) but, according to both early Jewish as well as Christian traditions, he was martyred for the faith.[60] What did it take to bring this kind of a skeptic to saving faith and then to such a prominent position of leadership as well as to martyrdom for the faith? His testimony is forcefully clear: "I saw the resurrected Lord!"[61]

Or take, for example, the utterly unique experience of the apostle Paul, who according to his own words "was formerly a blasphemer and a persecutor and a violent aggressor" (1 Tim. 1:13 NASB; cf. Phil. 3:6). Before his conversion the sole passion of this Pharisee, who was also a son of Pharisees,[62] was to stamp out "the sect of the Nazarenes" once and for all.[63] No one hated Yeshua and his early messianic followers more than Saul of Tarsus. What did it take to blow this Hebrew of Hebrews, like a raging tornado, out of the camp of Pharisaical Judaism and into the camp of his most hated enemies? His own testimony speaks for itself: "The risen Messiah appeared to me."[64]

The late New Testament scholar and historian F. F. Bruce affirmed the immensity of the evidence for the transformation of Paul through Yeshua's resurrection:

> It is reasonable to believe that the evidence which convinced such a man of the out-and-out wrong-ness of his former course, and led him so decisively to

abandon previously cherished beliefs for a movement which he had so vigorously opposed, must have been of a singularly impressive quality. The conversion of Paul has for long been regarded as a weighty evidence for the truth of Christianity.[65]

Josh McDowell suggested that the apostle Paul's life was radically transformed in at least four major ways: (1) His character was transformed (Acts 20:33–35); (2) his relationship with the followers of Jesus was transformed (Acts 9:19); (3) his message was transformed (Acts 9:20; 17:3); and (4) his mission was transformed (Acts 9:15–16, 19–22; 22:14–15; 26:16–18).[66]

The only reasonable answer as to what transformed Christianity's greatest antagonist into its greatest protagonist is that the resurrected Messiah himself sovereignly and graciously appeared to Saul of Tarsus and changed him forever into the apostle Paul.

EXHIBIT 3: CHANGES TO KEY SOCIAL STRUCTURES

J. P. Moreland explained why the social structures of Judaism were so important and how they were turned upside down by the resurrection of Yeshua:

> And there is another reason why these social institutions were so important: [The Jewish people] believed that these institutions were entrusted to them by God. They believed that to abandon these institutions would be to risk their souls being damned to hell after death.
>
> Now a rabbi named Jesus appears from a lower-class region. He teaches for three years, gathers a following of lower- and middle-class people, gets in trouble with the authorities, and gets crucified along with thirty thousand other Jewish men who are executed during this time period.
>
> But five weeks after he's crucified, over ten thousand Jews are following him and claiming that he is the initiator of a new religion. And get this: they're willing to give up or alter all five of the social institutions that they have been taught since childhood have such importance both sociologically and theologically.[67]

What were these five alterations that abrogated the old covenant (i.e., the law of Moses) and initiated the new covenant (i.e., the law of Messiah), which was predicted by the prophet Jeremiah and others in the Hebrew Scriptures?[68] First, these early messianic believers never offered another animal sacrifice for sin after the day they came to know the resurrected Messiah, for the day that Yeshua died on the cross, every animal sacrifice became redundant at best and blasphemous at worst (cf. John 19:30; Heb. 10:26–31). Second, they no longer felt obligated to keep the Mosaic law in its entirety, the law that, among other things, kept them separated exclusively from the noncircumcised. Jews and Gentiles were now uniquely *one* in the new covenant established through the covenant sacrifice of Yeshua (cf. Acts 15:14–29; Eph. 2:11–22; 3:1–12).

Third, these early believers no longer scrupulously kept the Sabbath. In fact, after the death and resurrection of Yeshua, they actually met on the first day of the week, on Sunday, apparently in honor of Yeshua's day of resurrection.[69] This was no minor matter, for like refusing to offer the Mosaically prescribed animal sacrifices, to violate the Sabbath under the old covenant was a capital offense.[70] Fourth, while the Hebrew Scriptures certainly gave intimations of the concept of the Triune nature of God,[71] after Yeshua's resurrection and his fuller new covenant revelation, the early messianic believers became a Trinitarian (i.e., Triunity) worshiping community: They believed in one God who was to be loved, honored, and worshiped in three Persons.[72] Fifth, while the first-century Jewish community had bound itself to the view that the coming Messiah would be a political and military deliverer, after Yeshua's resurrection and his postresurrection instructions, the early messianic believers understood that the Messiah had to come first, as the Hebrew Bible clearly taught, to suffer for sins, and then to enter into his glory (Luke 24:25–27, 44–48). Even further, although his kingdom in some initial sense had been inaugurated at his first advent, its full and glorious appearing would have to await his second advent (Luke 19:11–27).

EXHIBIT 4: COMMUNION AND BAPTISM

The emergence of the ordinances or sacraments of communion and baptism in the early messianic community also supply further circumstantial evidence that Yeshua's resurrection is true. These two ordinances were initiated into the new covenant community by Yeshua himself (Matt. 26:17–30; 28:16–20). Among other meanings, these two ordinances were experienced by that early community primarily as celebrations of the Messiah's death (Rom. 6:1–5; 1 Cor. 5:7–8; 11:17–34). But the obvious question arises: Why *celebrate* a death? The answer is because of his resurrection! A dead messiah is hardly the kind of messiah to be worshiped or for whom to live and die. On the other hand, a resurrected Messiah is something and someone to celebrate! In fact, these two ordinances are actually celebrations *with* him as well as *about* him, for the fact of his resurrection is God's validation of his substitutionary atonement for our sins. When Yeshua died on the cross, he cried out, "It is finished" (literally, "paid in full once and for all") (John 19:30)! Yeshua's resurrection is not only God's validation, it is also our celebration.

EXHIBIT 5: THE EMERGENCE OF THE CHURCH

The final piece of circumstantial evidence for the resurrection of Jesus is the radical emergence of the Christian church, the true body of believers in him. How else does one explain the emergence of such a vast number of believers, well into the thousands, out of a sect of Jewish believers called the Nazarenes (Acts 24:5)? In the space of approximately twenty years, this early messianic movement, founded on the resurrection of its leader, moved out from the city of Jerusalem right into the very heart of the city of Rome, the capital of the Roman Empire (Acts 1:8; 28:16–25; Phil. 4:22). In the words of J. P. Moreland, "Not only that, but this movement triumphed over a number of competing ideologies and eventually overwhelmed the entire Roman empire."[73]

The well-known historian Philip Schaff testified to the essential fact of Yeshua's resurrection as the sole basis for the existence of the church:

> The Christian church rests on the resurrection of its Founder. Without this fact the church could never have been born, or if born, it would soon have died a natural death. The miracle of the resurrection and the existence of Christianity are so closely connected that they must stand or fall together.[74]

Likewise, H. D. A. Major, former principal of Rippon Hall, Oxford, also emphasized the uniqueness of Yeshua's resurrection as the basis for the very existence of the church:

> Had the crucifixion of Jesus ended His disciples' experience of Him, it is hard to see how the Christian church could have come into existence. That church was founded on faith in the Messiahship of Jesus. A crucified messiah is no messiah at all. He was one rejected by Judaism and accursed by God. It was the Resurrection of Jesus, as St. Paul declares in Romans 1:4, which proclaimed Him to be the Son of God with power.[75]

The challenging words of C. F. D. Moule, the former Cambridge New Testament scholar, seem overtly appropriate: "If the coming into existence of the Nazarenes, a phenomenon undeniably attested by the New Testament, rips a great hole in history, a hole the size and shape of Resurrection, what does the secular historian propose to stop it up with?"[76]

Again, it is J. P. Moreland who concluded his interview with the following words concerning the cumulative impact of all of this circumstantial evidence:

> If someone wants to consider this circumstantial evidence and reach the verdict that Jesus did not rise from the dead—fair enough. But they've got to offer an alternative explanation that is plausible for all five of these facts.
>
> Remember, there's no doubt these facts are true; what's in question is how to explain them. And I've never seen a better explanation than the Resurrection.[77]

So the question remains: Does the supporting evidence cited above point to the unique space-time resurrection of Yeshua the Messiah? Whatever our response, it cannot be denied that the early messianic community thought so—and many of them gave their lives rather than deny any part of it. The fact of his resurrection was the hope of their own resurrection. Jesus' impact as the resurrected Messiah seems as certain as any fact can be. And so is his transformation of individual lives—and one in particular.

JESUS' MESSIANIC TRANSFORMATION OF LIVES

As has been demonstrated, Yeshua impacted that first messianic community in a most unique way. And his impact has continued down through history to this very time and place. In fact, he is committed to transforming any life that is placed in his hands. My own life is a case in point.

I was born in Los Angeles, California, on May 7, 1943, the grandson of Jewish immigrants from Russia and Hungary. I grew up in a typical Jewish home, believing in God and hoping for a happy life. My high school years were full years as I enjoyed studies, music, and athletics. When I graduated, I accepted a full scholarship to play football at UCLA. I moved to the campus and immediately joined a Jewish fraternity. Again, my college years were full as I continued to pursue my studies, music, and most of all, my athletic career. In the fall of 1965, the beginning of my last year at UCLA, my teammates elected me the offensive captain of the team. Touted to finish last, to the surprise of everyone, we proceeded to win our conference as well as the Rose Bowl championship on January 1, 1966. This was UCLA's first Rose Bowl victory. My life was great! I was a hero. People loved me. My Jewish fraternity chose me as the national athlete of the year. And I basked in the glory of it all.

Not too long after the Rose Bowl victory, my best friend, Kent, began to tell me that he had come to know Jesus Christ in a personal way. I had no idea what he was talking about. I thought he had always been a Christian. After all, he had been born into a Christian home, just as I had been born into a Jewish home. Isn't that how a person got his particular religion? You inherited it from your parents. But the more we talked, the more I realized that something significant was happening in Kent's life. His life was being transformed, and I could see it.

On one occasion, Kent said to me, "Barry, I want you to know that I thank God every day for the Jews." I responded, "Why in the world would you do that?" His answer utterly surprised me. He said, "I thank God every day for the Jews for two reasons. First, God used them to give me my Bible. And second, and most important, God used the Jews to bring his Messiah into the world, the One who died for the sins of the whole world and especially for all of my sins." To this day I remember the impact of those few simple but true statements. *Genuine* Christians don't hate the Jews after all. In fact, they truly love us and are grateful and honored that God has included them by faith into his forever family.

Kent introduced me to a man who worked with a campus ministry involving students and professors at UCLA. After several weeks of pouring over the messianic prophecies in the Old Testament, I became convinced that Jesus must be the promised Messiah of the Jews, and therefore, for me as well. No one else could have possibly fulfilled all the messianic prophecies. Yeshua alone must be the Messiah!

So having investigated the Old Testament messianic prophecies, I now turned my attention to the New Testament. What did Yeshua say about himself? What did those closest to him say about him? Although friends had given me a few New Testaments over the years, like most Jewish people, I had never read them, having been warned by my rabbis and family that it was the Bible of the Gentiles. To my surprise, I found it to be a very Jewish book: Jewish people, Jewish terrain, Jewish holidays, and most important, the Jewish Messiah!

After several days on my pursuit of the truth, two basic claims by Yeshua laid the entire matter before me. First, as the Lamb of God who takes away the sin of the world, he offers himself as a free gift to anyone who would believe on him and receive him into his life (John 1:10–13; Eph. 2:8–9). Salvation is a free gift of God's grace. All of his divine gifts—forgiveness of sins, eternal life, personal fellowship with him and his forever family, the invasion of the supernatural, the Spirit's transformation—are freely given as the gifts of his loving grace. Everything I ever wanted out of life I had to earn myself. And yet, here was Yeshua offering himself and all his best gifts for time and eternity as a free gift of his love. Who wouldn't want to embrace such an offer?

The second basic claim of Yeshua that propelled me into a life of continual transformation was the fact that if I received him into my life as a free gift of his love and mercy, he would not only invade my feeble life but he would never leave nor forsake me (John 3:16–18; 5:24; Heb. 13:5–6). When Yeshua offers us eternal life, he means *forever, unending life*—eternal life with him and his forever family. To have the Son was to have eternal life (1 John 5:9–13). I suddenly realized that I had nothing that withstood the test of time, let alone the test of eternity. And this was most graphically demonstrated to me by the Rose Bowl victory itself. Just a few mere months after the most significant event in my life, and perhaps in my entire life, all the glory, everything involved, was slowly fading away into a distant memory.

My course of action seemed all too obvious. I had to receive Yeshua into my life as my own personal Messiah, Lord, and Savior. So I found a quiet place—alone with God—and prayed a very simple, childlike prayer: "Jesus, I believe that you are the promised Messiah for the Jewish people and for the whole world, and so, for me as well, and that you died for my sins and that you are alive from the dead forevermore. So I now receive you into my life as my own personal Lord and Savior. Thank you for dying in my place." No lightning, no thunder—only his personal presence and peace as he promised, which has not left me to this very day (John 16:33; Phil. 4:7). Blaise Pascal (1623–1662), the French philosopher and mathematician, was certainly right when he said, "Jesus Christ is a God whom we approach without pride, and before whom we humble ourselves without despair."[78]

No one has better captured the ongoing impact and transformation of this one and only messianic Savior than the respected historian Philip Schaff. After a lifetime of researching the impact of Yeshua, he penned these words:

> This Jesus of Nazareth, without money and arms, conquered more millions than Alexander, Caesar, Mohammed, and Napoleon; without science and learning,

He shed more light on things human and divine than all philosophers and scholars combined; without the eloquence of schools, He spoke such words of life as
were never spoken before or since, and produced effects which lie beyond the
reach of orator or poet; without writing a single line, He set more pens in motion,
and furnished themes for more sermons, orations, discussions, learned volumes,
works of art, and songs of praise than the whole army of great men of ancient
and modern times.[79]

No, we must never throw in the towel and recant our confession that Jesus
is the promised Messiah, no matter what it costs, for he alone fulfilled all the
messianic prophecies of the Hebrew Scriptures. He alone, through his bodily
resurrection from the grave, impacted the first thousands of Jewish believers.
And he alone is the only One who continues to transform lives from the inside
out, for both time and eternity. Like the apostle Paul and the thousands of
other messianic Jews down through the centuries, "I admit that I worship the
God of our fathers as a follower of the Way, which they call a sect. I believe
everything that agrees with the Law and that is written in the Prophets, and
I have the same hope in God as these men, that there will be a resurrection
of both the righteous and the wicked. So I strive always to keep my conscience
clear before God and man" (Acts 24:14–16).

THIRTEEN

WHY I BELIEVE JESUS IS THE SON OF GOD

PETER KREEFT

W hy do you believe Jesus is the Son of God?" Instead of plunging directly into my answer to this all-important question, let me first confess something about myself. I am biased. That is not to say I am prejudiced. My belief that Jesus is the Son of God is based on evidence—both objective and subjective, both impersonal and personal, both logical and experiential. So I am not prejudiced. But I am biased.

When I say I am biased, I mean that I am not only totally convinced but also personally committed to this belief or, to be more precise, to the object of this belief, to Jesus Christ as the Son of God. As Thomas Aquinas said, "The primary object of faith is not a proposition but the reality it designates."

When defending the belief that Jesus is the Son of God, I am at least as biased as a husband defending his wife. I am a lover defending his beloved, not a scientist defending his hypothesis. A foolish and fickle lover, a weak and wimpy lover, but a lover nevertheless, and therefore biased. If I were allowed only one sentence to answer an inquiring unbeliever's question, "Why do you believe Jesus is the Son of God?" I would not try to summarize my syllogism in one sentence. Rather, I would offer a personal testimony.

However, this is a book of Christian apologetics, not an autobiography. It is *the* faith I am defending, not *my* faith. The reasons I am about to give cannot be dismissed as "true for him but not true for me," for they are objective, universally valid reasons, logical reasons, philosophical reasons.

We are commanded to "be prepared to give . . . the reason for the hope that you have" (1 Peter 3:15), and I am not at all uncomfortable with this task. I am a philosopher by vocation and profession, so my reasons for believing what two billion other Christians also believe are probably somewhat more philosophically explicit, more logically thought out than the reasons others would give. So please excuse me for writing like a philosophy professor at times, especially in the next section, where I shall undertake the tedious but necessary task of defining our terms.

What the Doctrine Means

If two people are to understand each other, it is not enough that they use the same words. The meanings of their words must also be the same. We must, therefore, define what we mean when we say Jesus is the Son of God.

Muhammad, in the Qur'an, rejected this belief as blasphemous and ridiculous. He apparently thought Christians believed God had a son *biologically* and rightly thought that idea to be blasphemous. This is a misunderstanding of what the doctrine means, of course. Misunderstandings must be distinguished from disagreements. Many educated Jews, Muslims, Unitarians, and others understand what Christians believe but do not agree that it is true. They think it is logically impossible that one God is three Persons or that one person, Jesus, is both God and man. That is a very different matter. I will deal with both matters, but I must first try to explain what I mean by the doctrine before I say why I believe it is true.

What did Jesus mean when he called himself the "Son of God"? His audience was familiar with the term "God," and Jesus, as a Jew, meant by "God" what the Jewish Scriptures meant by "God." That was not in question. The phrase "Son of God," however, was very much in question. No Jew had ever called himself or any other human being by that title. The title does occur in the Jewish Scriptures a few times, but it is always in the plural ("sons of God") and always refers to angels.

What did Jesus mean when he called himself the "Son of God"? The son of a man is a man. (Both "son" and "man," in traditional language, mean males and females equally.) The son of an ape is an ape. The son of a dog is a dog. The son of a shark is a shark. And so the Son of God is God. "Son of God" is a divine title.

223

Jesus claimed to have two natures, human and divine, for he called himself both "Son of Man" and "Son of God." The "Son of Man" is *a* man, but the "Son of God" is not *a* God but *God*, for Jesus was a Jew, and therefore, a strict monotheist. The most certain truth for a Jew, and the most familiar prayer, was, "Hear, O Israel: The LORD our God, the LORD God is one" (Deut. 6:4).

What any father gives to his son is first of all his nature, his species, his life. The son is equal to the father in species, in nature. Of course the word *son* is a metaphor when applied to God. God, not having a body (John 4:24), does not literally and physically father sons. Jesus never defined God but called him his Father. I think most Christian theologians and philosophers would agree that the only time God ever told us what he is in literal, non-analogical language was when he spoke to Moses in the burning bush and said simply, "I AM" (Exod. 3:14). But that did not tell us *what* he is, only *that* he is. Or—if Aquinas's interpretation of this infinitely profound revelation is right—God was telling us (among other things) that *what* he is (his essence) is not really distinct from his existence (*that* he is). He exists necessarily, by the necessity of his own nature or essence, and needs no cause.

In any case, "Jesus is the Son of God" means that Jesus is divine. In Jesus we find one person with two natures (human and divine). Theologians have labeled this uniquely Christian belief the incarnation, which means, quite literally, that God took on human flesh. Of course, God, the eternal "I AM," did not *become* human in nature, for God's nature cannot change. He did, however, *take on* a second nature. So it is that Jesus, the Son of God, had a God-nature and a human-nature.

My main task here is to explain why I find this believable, but we have to go into these difficult and abstract definitions of what "Son of God" means because it is not believable if it is not thinkable. It would be a meaningless and unthinkable self-contradiction to say that Jesus was one person and two persons, or to say that he had only one nature and also had two natures. But it is a mystery rather than a contradiction to say that he is one person with two natures, even if those two natures are opposites.

And of course they are opposites. To be divine is to be infinite, beginningless, and endless; to be human is to be limited, to have a beginning (birth), and to have an ending (death). But opposite natures can coexist in a single person. Each one of us, in a different way, is one person with two opposite natures: body and soul, visible and invisible, in space and not in space. Your soul has no size, shape, weight, or color. Though both your body and soul are in time, only your body is in space.

We have been doing the difficult but necessary task of defining the doctrine that Jesus is the Son of God. But most Christians, when they say, "I believe that Jesus is the Son of God," are not thinking of abstract definitions, just as we do not think "H₂O" when we ask for a glass of water. We believe that Jesus really is the Son of God when we believe *in* Jesus as the

Son of God and act on that belief by worshiping him and acknowledging him as Lord.

The apostle Paul's formula "Jesus is Lord" (e.g., Phil. 2:11) is probably the earliest of all Christian creeds. The Greek word used here, *Kyrios*, always meant "God." This creed was the most basic and essential way to distinguish what all Christians believed from what everyone else believed. No Christian denies that Jesus is Lord; if he does, he is no longer a Christian. Likewise, no non-Christian believes that Jesus is Lord in the same sense that Paul meant; if he does, he is arguably a Christian.

WHY THIS DOCTRINE IS CRUCIALLY IMPORTANT

Why is the doctrine that Jesus is the Son of God so important? We have already come across one reason: It is the touchstone of Christianity; it is the belief that most essentially and clearly distinguishes Christians from non-Christians.

Second, it is the reason for everything else Christians believe. If Christ is divine, his authority is supreme and infallible. Christianity is not a philosophy but a religion; it rests first of all not on human reason but on divine revelation. Christians have not reasoned their way into each of their beliefs, nor do they base their beliefs on their own experiences, whether mystical experiences or human feelings. Rather, they base them on authority—the authority of God himself, the God who took on human flesh in Christ and who commissioned his apostles to teach in his name and with his authority, to perpetuate the church Christ founded, and to write the Scriptures (the New Testament), and to communicate Christ to all generations.

The third and greatest importance of this doctrine is "existential," or personal. If Jesus is Lord, he is the Lord of all, and therefore, the Lord of me, of my life, and of everything in it: my thoughts, my choices, my morals, my body, my money, my relationships, my career, my death, my hope of eternity. (J. P. Moreland addresses this important principle in chapter 15, "Why I Have Made Jesus Christ Lord of My Life.")

Fourth, if Christ is both God and man, then he reveals to us, in a final and unsurpassable way, both who God is and who we are. God holds nothing back in Christ; the Son is equal to the Father in all things (Col. 1:19). If Christ is pure love, this shows that the Father is pure love. "Philip said to him, 'Lord, show us the Father, and we shall be satisfied.' Jesus said to him, 'Have I been with you so long, and yet you do not know me, Philip? He who has seen me has seen the Father'" (John 14:8–9 RSV). Christ also shows us the true nature of humankind—our true identity. Here is what we were made for; here is "success"; here is a complete human being and a perfect human life; here is the ultimate standard for everything human. Christ shows true God to man and shows true man to man.

WHY THIS DOCTRINE IS DIFFICULT TO BELIEVE

Christians tend to forget how difficult it is to believe the doctrine that Christ is divine. It is, quite literally, the most astonishing idea that any mind has ever conceived of in all of history. This man, this carpenter's son who was born from a woman like any other man, who had to learn to speak and walk, who got tired and hungry, who suffered pain and weakness and death as a crucified criminal, is God, the infinitely perfect, eternal, transcendent Spirit who created the universe!

I will not try to prove the doctrine obvious, easy, or probable. It is anything but. I have great sympathy for the non-Christian who understands what the doctrine means and shakes his head in amazement, wondering how two billion otherwise sane and rational people, many of them among the most intelligent people in the world, can believe such a thing.

That very puzzle should make it impossible for any honest truth seeker to do what most non-Christians do: dismiss the idea as either myth or exaggeration, something not to be taken seriously. Whatever else it is, the doctrine is serious. If it is not ultimate truth, it is ultimate lunacy. The non-Christian who thinks Christians are insane is far closer to Christian faith than the non-Christian who thinks Christians are just nice people who happen to believe some unimportant, meaningless piece of ancient theological nonsense. Those who crucified Christ for blasphemy were closer to faith than modern humanists who praise what he said about others, about how they should live, but ignore what he said about himself.

WHY IT IS NOT IMPOSSIBLE TO BELIEVE THIS DOCTRINE

Though difficult, it is not impossible to believe that Jesus is the Son of God. What makes it possible, however improbable it may be?

We have already seen that it is not a self-contradiction. The Trinity does not mean that there is one God and three Gods, or that God is one person and three persons, or that God has one nature and three natures. Rather, there is one God, one divine nature, and three divine Persons. The incarnation does not mean that Christ is one person and two persons, or has one nature and two natures. He is one person (the Second Person of the Trinity) with two natures (divine and human).

As R. Douglas Geivett explained in chapter 6, it is reasonable to believe that if there is a God who created the universe, this God is powerful enough to perform miracles in it if he wishes. If God is omnipotent, if God can do anything, how can we limit what he can do and declare that he could not do this deed Christians call the incarnation? If he is free, how can we know he would not choose to do it?

Non-Christians often call Christians arrogant and closed-minded for believing their dogmas, especially this one, but Christians are in reality humble and open-minded enough to receive the surprise. It is, in fact, the non-Christian who is closed-minded and arrogant if he assumes that there is no God or that God would never or could never do such a thing.

STANDARDS FOR JUDGING WHETHER THE DOCTRINE IS TRUE

Granted that the doctrine, though difficult, is possible, how shall we judge whether it is true? What standards shall we use?

We all naturally know and use at least two standards for judging ideas, especially religious ideas: truth and goodness. Most of us innately know the basic standards for judging whether an idea is true or false, and these include the laws of logic and commonsense scientific rules for evidence. We also innately know standards for judging goodness. We are not infallible, but we all have truth detectors and goodness detectors.

Our Western culture has emphasized and perfected the first of these standards, the intellectual, logical, and scientific standard. I will, therefore, spend the majority of the rest of this chapter applying this first standard and explaining the fundamental intellectual argument for believing Christ's claim to divinity. Then I will touch briefly on the moral argument.

THE LOGICAL ARGUMENT

Arguments need data. The information we have about Jesus comes mainly from the New Testament and the historical existence of the church, the community of believers who have passed on Jesus' story.

The information shows us a person who made more of an impact on others, on history, than any other man who ever lived. Yet he never entered politics, never fought a battle, and never wrote a book. He lived in a backwater nation, never went more than one hundred miles from his home, and was executed by crucifixion as a dangerous criminal. His moral teachings were not completely new. Nearly every piece of advice he gave us about how to live can be found in his own Jewish tradition, as well as in the philosophies of Socrates, Buddha, Lao Tzu, and Confucius.

What caused his unparalleled impact? Was it his personality? That was not unparalleled: There have been other wise, good, and creative human teachers. Was it his claim to divinity? That was not totally unique: There are hundreds of people who claim to be God, and most of them can be found in insane asylums. What was unique was the combination of these two things: No other sage ever claimed to be God, and no other person who ever claimed to be God was a sage. What was unique was the combination of his attractive personality and his unattractive teachings: Never has such an attractive and believable person given us teachings that are so apparently unattractive and unbelievable. In short, the seemingly incongruous combination of his person and teachings truly makes Jesus one of a kind in human history, and history's primary puzzle. We can solve the puzzle only by accepting his teachings because we accept his person, his personal trustability and authority, or by rejecting his person because we reject his teachings.

But what kind of person was he? According to all the data we have, he was a sage, a wise man, a trustable teacher. That is, he was neither deceiver nor deceived; neither an immoral, selfish, lying conniver nor a sincere but naive, out-of-touch, insane idiot. He made an almost unbelievable claim: He was God. But he was a believable person. To those who met him, this was the fundamental challenge: They had either to believe his almost unbelievable claim or disbelieve his very believable person.

The data also shows us a man who claimed to be God—in many ways and in all four Gospels:

> He called himself the "Son of God" (many times, in all four Gospels).
>
> He changed people's names ("Simon" to "Peter" in John 1:42)—something Jews believed only God could do. (God designed us and our destiny and knows our true identity; the Jews, like most ancient peoples, believed that a name was bound up with one's destiny and true identity.)
>
> He claimed to be sinless (John 8:46).
>
> He forgave all sins (Mark 2:5–12; Luke 24:45–47). No one can do this but God. I have a right to forgive you for your sins against me but not for your sins against others.
>
> He performed many miracles. He raised the dead (John 11) and even rose from the dead himself.
>
> He accepted the title "my Lord and my God" and accepted worship (John 20:28).
>
> He uttered the divine name "I AM" in his own name (John 8:58).
>
> He promised to send the Holy Spirit (John 14:25–26; 16:7–15).
>
> He claimed to give eternal life (John 3:16; 5:39–40).
>
> He claimed the authority to change the Mosaic law (Matt. 5:21–48; 19:3–9; Mark 10:2–12).
>
> He foretold the future (Matthew 24; Luke 24:1–7; John 6:64).
>
> He called himself "your Lord and Teacher" (John 13:14).
>
> He said he will come at the end of time to judge the world (Matt. 25:31–33).
>
> He said we will be judged by how we have treated him (Matt. 25:31–46).

This is the data. How shall we interpret it? There are only two possible interpretations: Jesus is God, or Jesus is not God.

The argument in its simplest form looks like this: Jesus was either (1) God, if his claim about himself was true, or (2) a bad man, if what he said was not true, for good men do not claim to be God. But he was not a bad man. (If anyone in history was not a bad man, Jesus was not a bad man.) Therefore, he was (and is) God.

This is the essential Christian argument. Why do people not accept it? Obviously, because Jesus' teaching is as difficult to accept as his personality is difficult to deny. On the one hand, what trustable people teach is trustable teaching, and Jesus was a trustable person if anyone ever was. Therefore, what he taught is trustable teaching. On the other hand, if someone teaches unbelievable things, especially about himself, he is an unbelievable person. And Jesus taught unbelievable things about himself. (What is more unbelievable than that a man is God?) Therefore, he is an unbelievable person. But one of these two conclusions must be false. Either his teaching is trustable, because he is, or he is not trustable, because his teaching is not. His teachings about himself and his person as a trustable authority go together as a package deal.

The earliest Christian apologists clearly saw that this was the heart of the issue and came up with an argument—one of the earliest arguments in Christian apologetics—that has been called the *aut deus aut homo malus* argument: Christ was either God or a bad man. Nearly every non-Christian who ever lived has believed that Jesus was neither God nor a bad man but just a good man. But just a good man is the one thing he could not possibly have been. If he was the God he claimed to be, then he was not just a good man but more than a man. And if he was not the God he claimed to be, then he was not a good man at all but a bad man. A man who claims to be God and is not cannot be called "a good man." He is either insane (if he believes that he is God) or a blasphemous liar (if he does not believe he is God but claims that he is).

Let's look at the logic again. Jesus was either God or not. If he was not, he either knew or did not know that he was not. Therefore, there are logically only three possibilities. (1) The first possibility is that Jesus was (and is) the Lord; he really did have the divine nature and authority he claimed for himself. (2) The second possibility is that Jesus was a liar; what he said (that he was God) was not true, and he knew it was not true. (3) The third possibility is that Jesus was a lunatic; he sincerely believed he was God but was really only a man. Lord, liar, or lunatic—those are the only possible options.

Neither "Jesus the lunatic" nor "Jesus the liar" are popular alternatives today to "Jesus the Lord." How then do thoughtful non-Christians escape the choice of "Lord, liar, or lunatic"? By two new options, two new views of who Jesus was.

According to one view, Jesus was a guru, a mystic, a kind of misplaced Hindu pantheist. Therefore, Jesus is God, just as he said he is (so he is neither a liar nor a lunatic), but by "God" he did not mean the God of the Jews, the unique, transcendent Person who created the universe. Rather, he meant that we are all God, or parts of God, or manifestations of God. There is only one being—God—and this God never created anything distinct from himself. So everyone and everything, from Jesus to Judas, from angels to atoms, is God. This view sees Jesus as a pantheist (pantheism is the belief ["ism"] that everything ["pan"] is God ["theos"]).

This view seems plausible at first because throughout the history of human thought there have been many pantheists, mainly in Hinduism but also elsewhere. Buddhism could be described as pantheism without a God. The New Age movement today is basically Hinduism dumbed down by pop psychology. Many Western philosophers, such as Benedict de Spinoza and Georg Hegel, were pantheists. Pantheism originated in the ancient Orient, but it is becoming much more popular in the modern West, where pantheists often emerge as rebels against the Western tradition, the view we could call theism, or creationism, or supernaturalism. The three great strands of supernaturalism in Western thought are Judaism, Christianity, and Islam. All three traditions have spawned pantheist "heretics": Spinoza came out of Judaism, the Sufis out of Islam, and Hegel out of Christianity.

It is not impossible, therefore, that Jesus was a pantheist, whether he arrived at this conclusion by reason (like Spinoza and Hegel) or by mystical experience (like the Sufis). If he was a pantheist, then his claim to be God would not be a unique claim at all. We know that no other sane and truthful human being ever claimed he was the God of the Jews, the God who created the universe, and no other person who ever claimed he was this God was sane and truthful. So perhaps Jesus did not mean that he was the God of the Jews at all. Perhaps Jesus was an early New Age thinker.

There are two problems with this view. First, it is utterly unhistorical: Jesus was a Jew, not a Hindu. He never left Israel, and there were no Hindus in Israel. There were many sects in the Judaism of Jesus' day, but none of them taught pantheism.

Another problem is that if Jesus were a guru, then he was the worst teacher in the history of the world, for no one, not his friends nor his enemies, ever understood what he taught—until a few clever persons finally figured it out in the twentieth century. These clever persons did not live in Jesus' time or place or culture, they never met him, they were not intimately familiar with his Jewish tradition and language, and they did not adhere to either Judaism or Christianity. But (if this view is true) they alone understand Jesus, and all others who ever met him, from those who crucified him to those who worshiped him, simply misunderstood him. Jesus tried to teach the Jews Hinduism but failed so badly that he did not leave a single disciple who grasped a single pantheistic point of his teaching.

On every single issue on which Judaism and Hinduism conflict, Jesus' teachings, from start to finish, both explicitly and implicitly, were 100 percent Jewish and 0 percent Hindu: God's personality, God's will, God's creation, the goodness of matter, the reality of the material world, the reality of the individual human soul, the importance of the body, human free will, human sin, the need for repentance, the reality of final judgment, the possibility of an eternal hell, individual immortality, resurrection rather than reincarnation, worship rather than mystical experience, prayer rather than meditation, even the name of God. He reinforced every one of these Jewish ideas, whereas pantheists disbelieve *all* of them.

There is one last possible escape from the dilemma, and it is so popular today among "educated" people that it is routinely assumed by the secular media to be true and is taught in many theology departments in so-called Christian colleges and universities. This is the view that the New Testament texts are not historically true. The Jesus of the Gospels, the Jesus who claimed to be God and to save us from sin, the Jesus who performed miracles and rose from the dead is a myth very different from "the historical Jesus." According to this position, the New Testament texts tell the truth about Jesus' remarkable human personality but not about his divine claims or his miracles. Those who hold this position take out of the Gospels what they dislike and declare that only what remains is the historical Jesus. Thus, Jesus was neither God nor a bad man because he never claimed to be God, as the New Testament says he did. His claim is neither true nor false; it simply does not exist.

That is the only way out of the dilemma: to deny the data. Once you admit the data, you have to deal with Jesus' claim to be God, for that is the very essence of the New Testament. And then you have only two options: If his claim is true, you had better become a Christian and worship him; if his claim is false, you had better crucify him as a blasphemer or lock him up as a madman.

Thus, we now have a massive effort to discredit the historical accuracy of the New Testament—an effort that has, ironically and tragically, come almost entirely from Christian theologians. These "modernist" theologians have spilled much ink in their attempts to justify their approach to the Bible. Instead of responding to these attempts in detail (an arduous task that, thankfully, has been well addressed by Gary Habermas in chapter 9), let's look at the conclusion of the enterprise and see how reasonable it is.

The conclusion of modernist historical textual criticism is that the New Testament is not historically accurate, that the historical Jesus is radically different from the Jesus of faith (i.e., the Jesus concocted by early Christians and the New Testament writers), that Christianity—the teaching of the New Testament—is a myth. In other words, rather than one liar or lunatic (Jesus), there are thousands: Jesus' friends, his enemies, the fabricators of the Jesus myth, whoever they were.

Let's look first at Matthew, Mark, Luke, John, and Paul. Matthew and John claim to be eyewitnesses. Luke and Paul claim to have interviewed eyewitnesses to the historical Jesus. The early church fathers tell us that Mark was a disciple of Peter and that his Gospel recounts Peter's firsthand observations. All the historical data we have confirm, rather than deny, refute, or disconfirm, these claims. All documents by or about Christians, from the beginning, both Christian and anti-Christian, assume that all Christians have always literally believed what we today define as Christianity, in other words, what the New Testament teaches.

Thus, the dating of the New Testament is crucial. If the Gospels were written during the lifetime of those who knew Jesus, it is impossible that such a "myth"— the divine Jesus—could have arisen and been believed. There would have been too many people alive to refute it. Imagine millions of Americans today believing that George Washington claimed to be God, forgave all sins, performed miracles, and rose from the dead, and then putting that claim in a book. No one would believe it. There is too much evidence to the contrary. But although there is a great deal of written evidence about Washington, no one is alive today who actually knew him. Some enterprisingly clever scholar could conceivably invent a new myth about Washington that contradicts the Washington of history, and many people could conceivably believe it today, over two centuries later.

But there is not one shred of evidence that the New Testament was written after Jesus' apostles died. There is speculation, and theory, and abstract hypothesis, but all the positive evidence, all the hard data both inside and outside the texts, points to the fact that the Gospels were written well within the lifetime of Jesus' contemporaries. Further, not one respectable scholar denies that the letters of Paul were written before A.D. 60. Yet these early letters already reveal a Christianity, shared by Paul and all the other apostles, that centers on Christ's divinity, atonement, and literal resurrection. If his divinity is a myth, if the story in the Gospels is a myth, if the historical Jesus never claimed divinity, forgave sins, performed miracles, or rose from the dead, then this myth was invented by Jesus' apostles themselves, not by later generations or the early Christian community.

But why would the apostles lie? What would motivate such a massive conspiracy of deceit? Liars always lie for selfish reasons. If they lied, what was their motive, what did they get out of it? What they got out of it was misunderstanding, rejection, persecution, torture, and martyrdom. Hardly a list of perks! And if they lied, why did not one of the liars ever confess this, even under torture? Martyrdom does not prove truth, but it certainly proves sincerity.

Perhaps it was not a lie but a sincere illusion, a hallucination, a collective insanity. Hallucinations happen, of course, but usually to only one person at a time, and even mass hallucinations never last long. Further, hallucinations never produce powerful moral progress, joy, hope, love, and saintly behavior. If the gospel is a lunacy, it is the only beautiful one in history.

Most modernists, however, do not say that the New Testament writers, whoever they were, were liars or lunatics but mythmakers. They claim that the miraculous, supernatural elements in New Testament Christianity are not supposed to be taken literally but rather symbolically, like Aesop's fables. As Aesop's talking ant and grasshopper are symbols of thrift and recklessness, so Jesus is a symbol for goodness, or the resurrection is a symbol for the triumph of life over death. The gospel story is a myth. It isn't true, but it's good. If people believe the story, they will live better lives and be better people.

This view, however, presents several problems. First, the texts themselves do not have the literary quality of myth; they are eyewitness descriptions.

Second, the texts themselves explicitly claim to be literal eyewitness descriptions (e.g., John 19:35) and deliberately insist, in so many words, that the Gospel events are not myths but literal, eyewitness accounts (2 Peter 1:16; 1 John 1:1). If they are myths, as they claim *not* to be, they are deliberate lies, fabrications, and deceptions rather than moral myths.

Third, reducing the Gospels to myths means reducing Christianity to another form of paganism, Christ to another god like Zeus. But all Christ's disciples were Jews, not pagans. They were the least likely people in the history of the world to use pagan myths, or to believe them, especially the pagan notion of many gods.

Fourth, no mythic symbol has ever so revolutionized the world and millions of lives. What softened hard Roman hearts and hardened cowards into heroes? What put hymns on the lips of martyrs? What made saints out of sinners? How can so many amazing life transformations be explained by a myth?

Fifth, what mythic symbol is Jesus supposed to be? Goodness, love, and compassion is the usual answer. But that is not "the good news" because it is not news at all. These characteristics are not new, not revolutionary. They are just moral common sense. The idea that it's good to be good is certainly not what made saints out of sinners. If the Christ of the Gospels is mere myth and not the Christ of history, then the (mythical) cause is far too weak to produce the (historical) effect.

Sixth, it is incredibly arrogant to claim that Christians and non-Christians, Jews and Gentiles alike fundamentally misunderstood the claim of the most read and studied book in the history of the world, mistaking myth for history, until a few clever scholars centuries later finally understood it for the first time.

Seventh, how can a lie be the basis for a good life? How can a misunderstanding of what is true be the greatest producer of what is good?

THE MORAL ARGUMENT

This brings us to the moral argument. I think this is the most effective argument of all for the claims of Christ. More people have been converted to Christ by saints than by theologians, by the argument from moral fruits than by the argument from logical possibilities.

The moral argument for Christianity can be stated as follows: How could Christ be good without being true? How could Christianity be so morally right if it is intellectually wrong? How could the best man who ever lived also be the most insane? How could the religion of love, the religion of the saints, be based on a lie? If Christ is not God, why has this lie made people better people than any truth has ever made them? How could it be that two things we need and want the most—goodness and truth—so contradict each other?

Those two ideals, truth and goodness, are the two things God himself is, two things that are in themselves infinite and eternal (since they are divine attributes), and therefore, two things that we can and should pursue without limit. Anything else we pursue without limit stunts us, narrows us, and makes us fanatics. But truth and goodness make us mature, broaden us, and make us more beautiful the more we pursue them. If they are divine attributes, they cannot contradict each other unless God contradicts himself—unless the very nature of God contradicts itself.

Here is another kind of moral argument for Christ's divinity. To some it will seem weak, but to others it will seem striking.

(1) If there is a God, he is infinitely perfect. That is what "God" means.

(2) The most important perfection is moral perfection: goodness, love, unselfishness.

(3) God showed his goodness by creating a universe—beautiful, complex, brilliant—and giving it to us. It will die, but we will not. When every star and galaxy blinks out, every one of us will still be alive.

(4) Your response to this must be total gratitude. Gratitude is the attitude that matches reality. To be grateful is to be realistic, to be sane. Gratitude is true, for truth is the correspondence with reality, and gratitude is truth in the emotions.

(5) Love is the other true response to reality, for ultimate reality is God, and God is love. God showed that he is love by giving us existence, life, and the universe. To love is therefore to be sane, to be in accord with ultimate reality, to be like God.

(6) The central claim of Christianity, the Christian gospel, is that "God so loved the world, that he gave his only begotten Son, that whosoever believeth in him should not perish, but have everlasting life" (John 3:16 KJV). The claim perfectly fits and fulfills the picture above: that God is amazing love, unpredictable love. The incarnation is the capstone to the self-revelation of the God who had already revealed himself as goodness, love, and self-giving. The incarnation and the atonement are exactly the kind of thing, the too-good-to-be-true thing, that this God would do.

The moral argument is an argument based on "fittingness." To explain such an argument, imagine we had the first eight of Beethoven's symphonies but not the Ninth. Then someone discovered the missing manuscript of the Ninth Symphony and claimed it was Beethoven's. If you knew the music of Beethoven, when you heard the missing symphony performed, you would know it was authentic, for you would recognize the master's touch, and you would recognize it as the capstone of Beethoven's career. In a similar way, Christ "fits" everything else we know of God. He is the culmination of God's revelation.

For some people, the moral argument based on "fittingness" can be as striking as juxtaposing two pictures and suddenly seeing an identity: "Why, that's *him!*" I find as I grow older and (hopefully) become a little more familiar with God that this is the argument that convinces me the most: "Why, that's *him!*" It's what Jesus himself predicted in his parable of the Good Shepherd: "The sheep hear his voice, and he calls his own sheep by name and leads them out. . . . The sheep follow him, for they know his voice. A stranger they will not follow, . . . for they do not know the voice of strangers" (John 10:3–5 KJV).

PART 6

WHY I HAVE CHOSEN TO FOLLOW CHRIST

I f Christianity were merely a belief system or a collection of pious doctrines, we could have concluded this book with Dr. Kreeft's chapter on the divinity of Jesus. But there is more to be told. Christianity is a religion; it is a combination of belief and conduct. Jesus' brother James put it well: "Faith without works is dead" (James 2:26 NASB).

Please don't misunderstand. When asked, "What shall we do, that we may work the works of God?" (John 6:28 NASB), Jesus made it clear that what brings us into true relationship with God is not works but faith, and only a particular kind of faith: "This is the work of God, that you believe in Him whom He has sent" (John 6:29 NASB). So the *work* of God is *belief in Christ*. We do not work our way into God's favor; we receive his favor through belief in Jesus. In this respect Christianity is arguably the most peculiar of all religions. One does not *do* anything to obtain salvation; one simply believes. This is God's grace, and it truly is amazing.

Nonetheless, Jesus did not say, "Believe in me," and leave it at that. He also said, "Follow me," and, "If you love me, keep my commandments," and, "Go unto all the world and preach the gospel." Follow me . . . keep my commandments . . . go. Believers in Jesus are clearly called to action. All new saints are promptly given marching orders.

Follow me, even when it hurts. And it will. Evil and suffering befall each of us, and never proportionately. Someone always seems to suffer more than his or her fair share. This can rock the faith and devotion of even the fortunate observer. All the more for those who must directly endure inequitable pain, people such as John S. Feinberg and his family. Even as an expert in the intellectual problem of evil, Dr. Feinberg was not fully prepared for firsthand experience. Though staggered, still he follows, and certainly not from mindless commitment. He has found, and presents in chapter 14, a real resolution to the experiential problem of evil, and this in the context of a Christian faith that thoroughly embraces the loving sovereignty of God.

Follow me with all your heart and mind and strength. Anything less is service unfit for the one who is both your Master and Savior. "Sell all you own, and give to the poor," he told the rich young man. To the newly bereaved he said, "Let the dead bury the dead"; in other words, demonstrate your sincerity by following me now. Tough words from a man known for his kindness. But true words from a man who sacrificed more than we can ever know. In chapter 15, Dr. J. P. Moreland tells you of his personal journey toward complete discipleship and encourages you to join him in total devotion to the Savior.

Follow me and no other, for there is no other: "There is no other name under heaven that has been given among men, by which we must be saved" (Acts 4:12 NASB). Nothing is more offensive to the modern ear than a claim to exclusive truth, particularly *ultimate* truth. Yet this is precisely what we have in the words and person of Jesus Christ: exclusive ultimate truth. As a native of India, raised in the Hindu culture, Ravi Zacharias intimately and personally knows both sides of the "one way" versus "many ways" argument. He shows in chapter 16 that they cannot both be right and why Jesus Christ truly is the ultimate source for meaning and the only person we should follow.

FOURTEEN

WHY I STILL BELIEVE IN CHRIST, IN SPITE OF EVIL AND SUFFERING

JOHN S. FEINBERG

Probe an atheist or agnostic deeply enough about why they doubt God's existence, and he or she will likely recount for you the problem of evil. This problem keeps many from faith in God altogether and rattles the faith of even the staunchest believers. It is an intellectual problem that has occupied much of my attention for all of my adult life. Even more, for the last thirteen years, wrestling with the reality of evil has been a personal challenge for me and my family. Things have happened that I must deal with every day for the rest of my life.

Though many religious believers and nonbelievers struggle with this problem, it is especially acute for adherents of a religion such as evangelical Christianity, which believes in an all-powerful and all-loving God. How can a God with those traits allow evil to beset his creatures? If evil is retribution for some horrendous sin, then perhaps its presence in the world is understandable. But even in cases of the most egregious sinners, some punishments seem to exceed the crime by quite a bit. For those who live a godly life, suffering from certain afflictions seems especially unjustified. In light of these things and my own experiences with suffering, you may wonder why I still believe in God at all, let alone remain a Christian. In the pages that follow, I want to explain why, but before I can, I must raise several preliminary items.

PRELIMINARY CONSIDERATIONS

I have argued at length elsewhere that the usual conception of the problem of evil is too simplistic. Traditionally, this problem is portrayed as a dilemma centering on the logical consistency of three propositions: (1) God is all-loving; (2) God is all-powerful; and (3) evil exists in a world created by this God. Philosophers and theologians have assumed that this problem is the only problem of evil and that it confronts equally all theological systems that believe in an omnipotent and all-loving God. I have argued that this is not so, for there are many different problems of evil. I needn't recount all of them here,[1] but I should distinguish several of them.

First, there is a difference between the strictly intellectual questions that evil raises and the more personal crises of faith it precipitates. Those dealing with the intellectual questions of evil usually question whether evil's existence is logically consistent with Christian doctrine about God. One could pose such questions in complete abstraction from actual evils being suffered. One could even ask these questions if one didn't believe there is a God or that evil exists in our world. These are the problems that professional theologians and philosophers write about and debate. There are distinct intellectual questions raised by the existence of any evil, the amounts of evil in our world, the intensity of certain evils, and the apparent purposelessness of some evils.[2] If theists cannot successfully answer such questions, continuing to believe in God (and holding to theologies that cannot solve these problems) seems unwarranted.

In contrast to the intellectual questions is the personal struggle that people have with suffering and affliction. Such experienced evils precipitate a crisis of faith. The afflicted person asks how a God of love can allow this to happen when he or she has faithfully followed God all of his or her life. Since God doesn't remove the evil, it is difficult to worship him and even more difficult to serve him. Clearly, the relationship this person has with God is strained, and it isn't likely that it can be restored merely by offering the afflicted information about how the experienced evil is consistent with an all-loving, all-powerful God, let alone simple platitudes about how God knows that this is ultimately for the best.

A further distinction relates to the intellectual problems. In recent decades, philosophers have argued that these questions can be posed in either a logical form or an evidential form. The former is the more traditional way the problem of evil has been conceived. In that case, the critic accuses a theistic system of containing views that collectively contradict one another. If any two of the three key propositions for theism mentioned above are true, the third must be false. Of course, any set of ideas that is internally self-contradictory cannot as a whole be true. Hence, if theistic systems are guilty of this error, they are false and should be abandoned. Since the charge of contradiction means there is no possible way the set of propositions can all be true, the theist needs only to show that there is a possible way for the three central propositions about God and evil to be true. Thus, it hasn't been shown that the theist contradicts himself.

In recent years, largely because of the work of Alvin Plantinga in elaborating and defending the freewill defense, many atheists as well as theists have agreed that it is possible to hold the three propositions central to theism without contradicting oneself. However, critics have launched the attack on a second front. Even if a theological system isn't guilty of contradicting itself over its views on God and evil, critics still argue that the mere facts of evil in our world make it unlikely that theism is true. Because instances of evil are seen as evidence against theism, this form of the problem of evil is called the evidential problem. Moreover, because the evidential problem claims that evil makes theism improbable, this form of the problem is also called the probabilistic problem of evil. In contrast to the logical problem of evil, one doesn't explain why one's theology is self-consistent. Instead, the theist must explain why, despite the evil in our world, theism isn't improbable.

As shown elsewhere, the kind of answers appropriate for the logical problem are different from those needed to solve the evidential problem.[3] Due to space limitations, I cannot respond to both forms of the problem in this essay. Since the logical problem is the one with the longest history and is most frequently discussed, I will focus on it. Moreover, the problem most frequently raised throughout the history of this discussion is the problem of moral evil. That question asks why an all-loving and omnipotent God allows moral evil, sin, in our world. Exactly how this problem confronts a given theological system depends on its account of metaphysics and ethics. Before turning to that matter, however, I should pause to clarify the basic strategy that most defenses and theodicies follow when attempting to solve the various intellectual problems of evil in their logical form. It is a fourfold strategy.

STRATEGY OF DEFENSES AND THEODICIES

First, for the theist divine omnipotence means that God has power to do all things logically possible for a being with his attributes. Actualizing contradictory states of affairs isn't logically possible. Moreover, given God's nature, he can't sin, catch a cold, fail a test, and so on. But the crucial point in defining omnipotence is to exclude the logically impossible. If a theist believes that God can actualize contradictory states of affairs, then the language used to describe our world (the theist's theology) will, of course, contain contradictions, but that will in no way prove that his system succumbs to the problem of evil. Hence, in order for the logical problem to be a significant challenge to the theist's views, the theist must hold that no one, including God, can do the logically contradictory.

Second, the theist appeals to a commonly held moral principle: No one can be held morally accountable for failing to do what they couldn't do or for doing what they couldn't fail to do. That is, moral praise or blame can be correctly assessed only to someone who acts freely. In God's case, if he can't do something, he can't be held morally culpable for failing to do it.

Third, the theist offers an explanation as to why God can't (isn't free to) both remove moral evil *and* accomplish some other valuable goal in our world. In other words, when contemplating which world to create, God could have chosen either a world with no moral evil or a world with some other value. According to the theist, God couldn't have done both conjointly without generating a contradiction. The two options were mutually exclusive. Therefore, God could have done one or the other but not both. Depending on the theology in question, this other value might be creating the best of a possible world, making creatures with libertarian free will, or building the souls of his human creatures so that they grow from mere creaturehood to children of God.

The definition of omnipotence excludes the logically contradictory. God can't actualize both of these values (removing moral evil and the other value) at the same time. But the ethical principle says that if one can't do something, one isn't guilty for failing to do it. It appears, therefore, that God is justified, but not quite. Critics may grant that God couldn't conjointly remove evil and put some other value in our world, but they may complain that God chose the lesser of the two values for our world, and hence, he still isn't justified. At that point, the theist adds the final element in the strategy. He argues that the item God put in our world is a value of such great magnitude that it either counterbalances or outweighs the moral evil that accompanies that value. Hence, God has done nothing wrong in creating our world; it is a good world.

Answers to the Logical Problem of Moral Evil

Given this strategy, how might one solve the problem of moral evil in its logical form? As suggested above, the problem confronts each theology differently. There are as many of these problems of moral evil as there are theological systems committed to the ideas that God is all-loving and omnipotent and that evil exists. Each theology has its own account of God and evil, and since the problem in its logical form is about whether the theist's system contradicts itself, we must first clarify the system's views on God and evil (i.e., its metaphysic and ethics).

While many distinct theologies fall under the rubric of evangelical Christianity, for our purposes I want to show how a traditional Arminian system and a moderate Calvinistic system (my own) would solve the logical problem of moral evil. Both theologies have the same general metaphysic and account of ethics, which I have elsewhere labeled modified rationalism,[4] though they do differ in their understanding of free will.

Modified rationalism holds that God's existence is the highest good in and of itself. Hence, by creating a world, God in no way enhances his value, for he is already the supreme value. On the other hand, God is free either to create or not create a world. Creating is a fitting thing for God to do, but not the only fitting thing; a decision to create nothing would in no way have decreased God's value. In addition, modified rationalists believe that there is an infinite number of contingent, finite, possible worlds. Some are inherently evil, and God had better not create any of them, but more than one of those possible worlds is a good world. God is free either to create one of the good worlds or refrain from creating altogether. Modified rationalists reject the idea of a best possible world. Finally, according to modified rationalism, some things can be known by pure reason alone, whereas others can be known only by revelation. Many forms of evangelical Christianity incorporate a system of modified rationalist metaphysics.

As to ethics, modified rationalist systems hold one of two broad kinds, consequentialism or non-consequentialism. Consequentialist theories determine which acts are right or wrong on the basis of the results of the action. Non-consequentialist theories hold that something other than consequences (e.g., God commands it; therefore, it is our duty) makes an act morally right or wrong. As this relates to the problem of evil, a consequentialist theory says that the world as created had evil in it. However, that produces no moral stain on God, for he will ultimately use evil to maximize good. Non-consequentialism demands that the world as created contained no evil. Evil was introduced instead by the actions of God's creatures.

Given such a metaphysic and an account of ethics, we can now specify exactly how the logical problem of moral evil would arise for a modified rationalist theology. The problem can be posed as the following question: Is the evil in our world ("evil" as the modified rationalist defines it) such as to refute the claim that our world is one of the good possible worlds God could have created? If the answer is yes, then the theological system is guilty of contradicting itself. On the other hand, if ours is a good world, despite the evil in it, then God's goodness and power are consistent with the existence of evil.

Modified rationalists defend their theology by pointing to some feature of our world that shows it is one of the good possible worlds God could have created. In line with the four-step strategy already described, the modified rationalist argues that the aspect of our world that makes it a good world also makes it logically impossible for God to remove moral evil. Since he can't both remove evil and create a world with the positive value to which the theologian points, he isn't guilty for failing to do so. In what follows, I will present two such defenses to show that modified rationalists can in fact solve this problem in its logical form. One will be a defense a theological Arminian could use, and the other a defense a Calvinist could use.

THE FREEWILL DEFENSE

Perhaps the most frequently used Christian defense is the freewill defense. In contemporary discussions, its ablest defender has been Alvin Plantinga.[5] Though this defense has its detractors, it successfully answers the problem of moral evil that confronts an Arminian theology. Many Calvinists have also invoked the freewill defense, but its notion of free will doesn't fit Calvinistic systems committed to a strong sense of divine sovereignty.

The freewill defense presupposes a modified rationalist metaphysic and is nonconsequentialist in its ethics. Hence, it holds that God didn't originate evil—the introduction of sin into our world is entirely due to God's creatures, human and angelic. These evil deeds weren't done or caused by God but were performed by the free acts of his creatures.

Some critics complain that even though humans in particular are responsible for sin in our world, God must also bear some responsibility, for he must have foreseen that we would abuse our free will to do evil, and yet he gave it to us anyway. Freewill defenders have a ready reply. For one thing, it is possible that free creatures will use their freedom to choose good, but there are no guarantees with creatures who possess genuine freedom. Good or evil acts must always be possible, and sadly, humans have frequently chosen to do evil. However, God knew when he gave us freedom that we could also use our freedom to do good. God reasoned that it is better to have creatures who do what is right (including love and obey him) freely because they want to, rather than doing right because they are forced or determined to do what is right. Hence, free will is a value of the highest order, one that God was surely right in putting into this world. Free will makes ours a good world, but, of course, if humans are genuinely free, there are no guarantees that they will never use their freedom to sin. God, therefore, cannot both give us free will and guarantee that there will be no sin, and since he can't do both, he isn't guilty for failing to do both.

Atheists such as J. L. Mackie aren't convinced that the freewill defense succeeds. Since Mackie's objection helps us understand the freewill defense better, it is worth raising. The freewill defense rests on the idea that there are no guarantees that humans will not sin if humans have genuine freedom. Mackie thinks otherwise. It is possible that someone will do moral good on one occasion. Freewill defenders grant this, but Mackie adds that it must also be possible that someone will use his or her free will on every occasion to do moral good. This is also possible, but then Mackie adds that this is possible for all human beings. If so, however, then an omnipotent God should be able to make it the case that all of us always freely choose to do what is morally good. The freewill defense says that if humans are truly free, there are no guarantees that they will do only good. Mackie's objection says otherwise.[6]

Though the answers to Mackie offered by Plantinga and other freewill defenders are quite intricate, they rest on a fundamental idea that seems difficult to resist. If God makes it the case or brings it about that we do anything, then we don't do it freely. In essence, this suggests that Mackie's proposal doesn't incorporate "real" freedom (or that somehow he has misunderstood what freedom means). We might be inclined to leave the matter, merely thinking that Mackie has incorrectly defined "free will," but the issue is more subtle than this. The fact is that Mackie's notion of freedom differs from the freewill defender's concept.

The concept of freedom espoused by the freewill defense is known as libertarian, contra-causal, or incompatibilistic free will. This notion of freedom holds that genuine free human action is incompatible with causal determinism. Hence, in spite of the direction causal forces point in a given situation, and in spite of how strong or weak the causes are, the agent can always do other than he or she does. The only way to guarantee a particular outcome is to causally determine the agent to do one thing or another. Since determinism rules out libertarian free will, however, no one, including God, can guarantee that someone will do moral good freely. Therefore, assuming that God gave us libertarian free will, without overturning our freedom, he can't also guarantee that we will never sin. Did God do something wrong in giving us this kind of freedom? Not at all, since we can use it to love and obey him. Further, since nothing moves us to do good but ourselves, we know that our good deeds are what we really want to do. They aren't forced upon us.

In contrast to libertarian free will, Mackie's brand of freedom is known as compatibilism or soft deterministic free will. According to this definition of freedom, genuine free human action is compatible with causal conditions that decisively incline the will, so long as those conditions don't constrain the will. To act without constraint means that one acts in accord with one's wishes or desires. Acting under constraint means that one acts contrary to one's wishes. It should be clear now why Mackie thinks God could bring it about that humans freely do good. According to compatibilism, factors decisively incline the will in one direction or another; there can be guarantees about what we do. But as long as we act in agreement with our wishes or desires, our act is free even though causally determined.

Based on the preceding, several things should be clear. First, compatibilism and incompatibilism contradict one another. Second, any theological position that holds that God is absolutely sovereign and exercises that sovereignty to decree and accomplish whatever he wills cannot at the same time hold that our actions are done with libertarian free will. If God exercises his sovereign power to guarantee certain outcomes, then many actions must be causally determined, which rules out libertarian free will. Most typically,

Calvinistic theologies hold this strong notion of divine sovereign control over the world.

This discussion of different notions of free will raises another issue, and it is crucial for the logical problem of evil. Since the logical problem is about whether the theist contradicts himself, we must ask what views freewill defenders hold. Do they hold Mackie's compatibilistic free will? Not at all; they are incompatibilists. But then it should be clear that if one defines freedom as freewill defenders do, Mackie's objection has broken the ground rules for handling the logical problem of evil. Mackie attributes his notion of freedom to the freewill defense and then accuses it of failing. Indeed, if freewill defenders are compatibilists, their freewill defense doesn't work for precisely the reason Mackie stated. But since Mackie's view of freedom isn't the same as that of the freewill defender, Mackie hasn't shown that freewill defenders contradict themselves. The message is clear: If one holds incompatibilism and offers the freewill defense as the answer to the logical problem of moral evil, one's system is logically consistent. The freewill defense solves this problem for systems committed to libertarian free will.

INTEGRITY OF HUMANS DEFENSE

The freewill defense answers the logical problem of moral evil for theologies that incorporate libertarian free will, but what if one's theology is Calvinistic and/or incorporates compatibilistic free will? My Calvinistic theology presupposes modified rationalism and non-consequentialist ethics. There are three stages to this defense.

I begin by asking what sort of beings God intended to create when he made humans. Here I am referring to the basic abilities and capacities God gave human beings. At a minimum, I believe he intended to create beings with the ability to reason, with emotions, with wills that are compatibilistically free (although freedom isn't the emphasis of this defense), with desires, with intentions, and with the capacity for bodily movement. God did not intend for individuals to be identical in respect to these capacities. God also intended to make beings who are finite both metaphysically and morally (as to the moral aspect, our finitude doesn't necessitate doing evil but only that we don't have God's infinite moral perfection). Thus, human beings are not superhuman beings or even gods. Moreover, God intended for us to use our capacities to live and function in a world suited to beings like us. Hence, he created our world, which is run according to the natural laws we observe, and he evidently didn't intend to annihilate what he had created once he created it.

None of these features were removed by the race's fall into sin, but because of our fall into sin, these capacities don't function as well as they would have without sin. Likewise, the fall didn't overturn the basic laws of nature and physics by which our world runs. The fundamental features of humanity and the world are still as God created them.

How do I know this is what God intended? By looking at the sort of being he created when he created us, and by noting that the world in which we live is suited to our capacities. Some might think this same line of thinking could be used to show that God also intended to create moral evil, because it exists. However, that is not so. Moral evil is not something God created. God created substances, including the world and the people in it. God intended for us to act, for he made us capable of acting. But he neither created our actions nor does he perform them. Hence, we cannot say God intended for moral evil to exist. God intended to create and did create agents who can act; he didn't create their acts (good or evil).

How do we know, though, by looking at what God did that he really intended to do it? Don't people at times act without fully understanding their intentions? While human beings don't always know what they intend to do, that is not true of an omniscient being. By seeing what God did, we can be sure what he intended to do.

If humans are the type of creatures I have described, how do they come to do moral evil (sin)? This brings us to the second stage of the defense: consideration of the ultimate source of evil actions. In accord with James 1:13–15, I hold that morally evil actions stem from human desires. Desires in and of themselves aren't evil, nor do they perform the evil. James says, however, that desires (*epithumia*) are carried away (*exelkomenos*) and enticed (*deleazomenos*) to the point where sin is actually committed (conceived).[7] Many moral philosophers would agree that the point of "conception" is when a person wills to do the act if he or she could. Once that choice is made, it remains only for that person to translate the choice into overt public action.[8]

Morally evil acts, then, ultimately begin with our desires. Desires in and of themselves aren't evil, but when they are aroused to lead us to disobey God's prescribed moral norms, then we have sinned. Desires are not the only culprit, however, for will, reason, and emotion, for example, also enter into the process. But James says that individual acts of sin ultimately stem from desires that go astray.

If humans are the sort of creatures described, and if moral evil arises as suggested, what would God have to do to get rid of moral evil? This brings us to the final stage of the defense. Clearly, if removing moral evil is God's only goal, he can accomplish it. However, my view of divine omnipotence doesn't allow God to actualize contradictions. Hence, if by removing evil God contradicts some other goal(s) he wants to accomplish, that explains why God can't remove evil.

It is my contention that if God did what is necessary to remove moral evil from the world, he would (1) contradict his intentions to create human beings and the world as he has, causing us to wonder if he has one or more of the attributes ascribed to him, and/or (2) do something we would not expect or want him to do, because it would produce greater evil than there already is. To see this, let's consider how God might get rid of moral evil.

Some may think all God needs to do to remove moral evil is arrange affairs so that his compatibilistically free creatures are causally determined to have desires only for good and to choose only good without being constrained at all. For each of us, God should know what it would take, and he should be powerful enough to do it.

However, this isn't as simple as it sounds. If people are naturally inclined to do what God wants, God may need to do very little rearranging of our world to accomplish this goal. If people are stubborn and resist his will, it may take a great deal more rearranging. God would have to do this for every one of us every time we resist his will. But changes in circumstances for one of us would affect circumstances for others. What might be necessary to get us to do good might disrupt others' lives, constrain them to do something that serves God's purposes in regard to us, and perhaps even turn them toward doing evil. Upholding everyone's freedom may be more difficult than we suppose. It is likely that the free will of many will be abridged as a result of God's attempts to convince certain people to do good.

There is another reason why it may be more difficult than we think for God to get us to do right. God didn't create us with an inclination toward sin, but even Adam in ideal surroundings and circumstances sinned. According to biblical teaching, the race inherited from Adam a sin nature that disposes us toward evil. In light of that sin nature, it isn't likely that a minimal rearranging of events, actions, and circumstances would achieve the goal of getting us to do good without constraining us. God would have to constrain many people in order to rearrange circumstances to convince a few of us to do the right thing without constraining us. Of course, that would contradict compatibilistic free will. We may begin to wonder how wise this God is if he must do all this just to bring it about that his human creatures do good. Why not make a different creature who would be unable to do evil? But, of course, this would contradict God's decision to make humans, not subhumans or superhumans.

There is yet a further problem with this method of getting rid of evil. It assumes that if God rearranged the world, all of us would draw the right conclusion from our circumstances and do right. Our desires, intentions, emotions, and will would all fall into place as they should without abridging freedom at all. This is most dubious, given our finite minds and wills as well as the sin nature within us that inclines us toward evil.

Perhaps there is a simpler, more direct way for God to get rid of evil. First, he could remove moral evil by doing away with humankind. Not only is this a drastic solution none of us would think acceptable, but it would also contradict his intention to create humans who aren't annihilated by his further actions.

Second, God could eliminate all objects of desire. Without objects of desire, humans would not be led astray to do moral evil. However, to eradicate all objects of desire, God would have to destroy the world and everything in it.

Since sin ultimately stems from desires, a third way for God to remove moral evil would be to remove human desires. Problems with this solution again are obvious. God intended to create creatures who have desires, but if he removed all human desires, such an act would contradict his intentions about the creature he wanted to create. Moreover, removing desires would also remove the ultimate basis of action so that people wouldn't act. This would contradict God's intention to create beings who perform the various actions necessary to remain alive.

Fourth, God could allow us to have desires but never allow them to be aroused to the point at which we would do moral evil. If God chose this option, he could accomplish it in one of two ways. He could perform a miracle to stop our desires whenever they started to run rampant, or he could give us the capacity to have desires that can be aroused only to a certain degree, a degree that would never be or lead to evil.

I shall address the former option when I discuss in general the option of God removing evil by performing a miracle. As for the second option, there are several problems. For one thing, it contradicts God's intention to create people who aren't stereotypes of one another. Whenever someone's desires would be allured in regard to something forbidden, those desires could be enticed only up to a point that would not be or lead to evil. What would be true of one person would be true of all. In every case, we would have to be pre-programmed to squelch the desire before it went too far.

There is another problem with God making us this way. When a desire would start to run amuck, one would have to stop having the desire (or at least not follow it), change desires, and begin a new course of action. A person's daily routine would be constantly interrupted (if not stopped altogether) and new courses of action implemented only to be interrupted again. Life as we know it would come to a standstill, contradicting God's intention to create us so as to function in this world.

Perhaps the greatest objection to this option is that for us to function this way God would have to make us superhuman both morally and intellectually. We would have to be willing to squelch our desires whenever they would lead to evil, and we would also need to know when desires would lead to evil so that we could stop them from being overly enticed. To do so, we would need to be more than human. Of course, such a situation would contradict God's intention to make non-glorified human beings, not superhuman beings.

Fifth, God could remove evil by removing intentions that lead to evil in either of the ways mentioned for handling evil-producing desires (by miracles or by making us so we would never develop intentions that lead to evil). However, this option creates the same problems raised with respect to desires.

Sixth, God could eliminate evil by removing any act of the will that would produce evil. We could will good things freely, but whenever we willed evil, the willing would be eliminated. God could do this either by miraculous intervention or by making us so we would never will evil. However, this option again faces the same objections that confront the desire and intention options.

Seventh, God could eliminate moral evil by stopping our bodily movement whenever we try to carry out evil. He could do this either by a miracle or by making us in such a way that we would stop our bodily movement when it would lead to evil. The same problems result as with the desire, intention, and will options.

If all of these options are problematic, perhaps God could remove evil through miraculous intervention. Several problems beset this method, however. First, if God did this, it would greatly change life as we know it. At any moment, God could miraculously stop desires, intentions, acts of the will, or bodily movements if he knew they would lead to evil. Since we wouldn't always know when our actions would lead to evil,[9] we wouldn't always know when to expect God to interfere. We might become too afraid to do, try, or even think anything, realizing that at any moment our movements or thoughts could be eliminated. Under those circumstances, life as we know it would come to a standstill, contradicting God's desire to create people who live and function in this world.

Second, it is one thing to speak of God miraculously intervening to prevent evil, but it is another to specify exactly what that means. Take bodily movement, for instance. God would probably have to paralyze a person as long as necessary to stop bodily movements that would carry out an evil act. Of course, such an act would alter the nature of life altogether and again contradict God's intention to make creatures who can live and function in this world.

In addition, it is difficult to imagine what miracle God would have to perform to remove a desire, an intention, or an act of willing that would lead to evil. Would God have to knock us unconscious or take away our memory for as long and as often as needed to remove evil-producing thoughts? Such acts would bring life to a standstill and be inconsistent with God's intention to make us so that we can live and function in this world.

A final objection to removing evil miraculously is that it would give us reason to question God's wisdom. Would a wise God go to all the trouble to make human beings as they are and then perform miracles to counteract them when they express that humanness in ways that would produce evil? Of course, had God made us differently so that he wouldn't have to remove evil by miracles, that would contradict his intention to make the sort of beings he has made. So either God must perform miracles and thereby cause us to question his wisdom, or he must change our nature as human beings. But that would contradict his goal of making humans rather than superhumans or subhumans.[10]

This discussion about what God would have to do to remove moral evil shows that God cannot remove it without contradicting his intentions to make the kind of creatures and world he has made, which would cause us to doubt his wisdom.

Someone may suggest that God could avoid these problems if he made creatures without desires, intentions, will, and bodily movement. This would likely remove moral evil, but it would also remove human beings as we know them.

Anyone who thinks there is any worth in being human would find this option unacceptable.

Someone else might suggest that moral evil could be avoided if God made us superhuman. But humans as we know them are a value of the first order. Scripture says humans are created in God's image (Gen. 1:26–27). When God finished his creative work, he saw that all of it, including human beings, was very good (Gen. 1:31). Psalm 8:5–8 speaks of God crowning us with glory and honor and giving us dominion over his creation. In light of this evaluation by God, who are we to say that human beings as created by God aren't valuable?

As a modified rationalist, all I need to show is that our world is one of those good possible worlds God could have created. It seems clear that a world with human beings in it is a good world. Neither I nor any other modified rationalist needs to show that our world is the best or even better than some other good world God might have created. We need only show that ours is one of those good worlds God could have created. I have done that by pointing to human beings and arguing that God cannot both create them and remove evil. Hence, I have solved my theology's logical problem of moral evil.[11]

Can God remove moral evil from our world? I believe he can, if he creates creatures different from human beings. He also can if he creates humans and then removes evil in any of the ways described above. But we have seen the problems that arise if God follows any of those options.

Has God done something wrong in creating human beings? Not at all, when we consider the great value human beings have and the great worth God places on us. We can say that moral evil has come as a concomitant of a world populated with non-glorified human beings. Still, it is one of those good possible worlds God could have created. God is a good God. Our world with human beings demonstrates his goodness.

THE RELIGIOUS PROBLEM OF EVIL

In the preceding pages, we have seen that it is possible to solve the intellectual problem of moral evil in its logical form and to do so for more than one theology.[12] Because this and other intellectual problems of evil are capable of solution, I see no reason to reject Christianity on the grounds that it succumbs to these intellectual problems. However, that isn't the end of the story. What about the experience of evil? Is Christianity sufficient to see someone through even the most difficult of trials? Is Christianity religiously bankrupt at a moment of personal crisis?

These questions have confronted me in vivid and unpleasant ways over the last ten to fifteen years. I have been interested in the problem of evil for much of my life, and in various degree programs I wrote theses and dissertations addressing the intellectual problems evil raises for a theist. For many years, I thought the intellectual answers I had constructed would be sufficient for someone in the midst of trials and afflictions. All of that changed for me in 1987 when my wife was diagnosed with Huntington's disease.

Huntington's disease is a genetically transmitted disease that attacks both mind and body and involves the premature deterioration of the caudate nucleus of the brain. On the physical side, the symptoms involve a growing inability to control voluntary movements. Among other things, this results in a loss of balance, difficulty in swallowing, slurred speech, and involuntary twitches in various parts of the body. Psychological symptoms can include memory loss, deterioration of attention span and mental function, depression, hallucination, and finally paranoid schizophrenia. The disease develops slowly, but over a period of decades it takes its toll, and it is fatal. In my wife's case, symptoms first appeared when she was twenty-eight. As bad as this is, however, just as bad is the fact that Huntington's is controlled by a dominant gene, so each of our children has a 50-50 chance of getting the disease. At the time we received this diagnosis, we already had three children. Since that time, progress has been made in research about this disease, but to date there is still no cure.

When news of this disease came, a host of emotions came with it: bewilderment, a sense of hopelessness and helplessness, a feeling of abandonment, and anger. As a Christian, I knew we aren't promised exemption from problems and trials, but I never expected something like this. With one diagnosis, a dark cloud had formed above my family that would not dissipate for the rest of our lives. At that point, the problem of evil moved from an intellectual problem that I could calmly reflect on in the solitude of my study to a real-life trauma that has to be confronted every day of my life.

One of the reasons for my confusion over what was happening was the previous thinking and writing I had done about the problem of evil. If anyone should have been ready for this crisis, it was I. But during this time of emotional and spiritual turmoil, none of the intellectual answers proved to be even the least comforting. As I thought about that, I came to an important realization. The religious problem of evil, the crisis of faith precipitated by suffering, at rock bottom is not primarily an intellectual question but an emotional problem. There are, of course, intellectual questions that the sufferer asks, and at an appropriate point in the grieving process when the afflicted is ready to hear the answers, it is appropriate to offer them. However, that point rarely comes during the shock of the terrible news. At that point, the sufferer needs comfort and care, not a dissertation on the logical consistency of God's existence and evil.

While there are many things one can say and do that won't help the afflicted cope with trials, other things can and do help.[13] In what follows, I will present what helped in my case, not as a how-to for comforting the afflicted but rather as a personal testimony and explanation of why I am still a Christian in spite of the evil that has befallen my family.

One of the first things that helped came in a conversation with my father. I was bemoaning the fact that this had happened and that I had no idea how

I would be able to cope as my wife's condition became progressively worse. My dad responded, "John, God never promises us tomorrow's grace for today. He only promises today's grace, and that is all you need." Though at the time I wasn't handling well the reality of my wife's situation, I hadn't completely collapsed. More importantly, my wife was still quite capable of functioning. Part of the grace for those early days was finding out the diagnosis at a time when the full burden of my wife's care didn't fall on me.

With this reminder from my dad, I began to readjust my focus from imagining what the disease would be like in the future to dealing with it in the present. I began to ask God each morning for the grace I would need to make it through that day. As I saw those prayers answered each day, I became more confident that when things got worse, I would still need only one day's grace at a time, and it would be there.

At other times during my struggles with this disease, I am reminded that despite what is happening, God has been gracious to us in other ways. First Peter 5:7 tells us to cast our problems on God, because he cares for us. At times it doesn't seem this is true, but it is. In our case, I realize that despite my wife's disease, there are other problems that God has kept from us. Some people lose their spouse to cancer or a heart attack or in an automobile accident, but that has not happened to us. God doesn't owe us such protection, but he has graciously given it to us. That is a sign that he really does care.

There is another realization that is difficult to swallow, but it is true. When tragedy strikes, we often blame God, but God didn't give my wife this disease. In Romans 5:12, Paul explains that through Adam sin entered the human race, and death resulted from sin. In other words, people die as a consequence of sin. I am not suggesting that this has happened to my wife as recompense for being a horrendous sinner. Rather, we live in a fallen world, and death is a consequence of sin. The particular death that befalls a person doesn't come from a specific sin he or she commits, but rather from the fact that the human race as a whole has fallen into sin. But if people die because of sin, they must die of something. One of the causes is disease, and some of those diseases are genetically controlled.

So while it is human nature to blame God for what happens, Scripture is clear that these things happen because we live in a fallen, sinful world. If we are going to be angry, our anger should be directed toward sin, not God. Our problem ultimately stems from not seeing the gravity of sin. But when we stand at the graveside of a relative or friend, or when we receive a diagnosis, we begin to see just how serious a matter sin is. The realization that something bad has happened because we live in a fallen world is not likely to comfort the afflicted, but it can help to assuage our anger at God, and it should help us redirect that anger to the proper target.

Some may grant the point about the cause of affliction but still object that an all-loving, all-powerful, all-gracious God should prevent evil from happening. Such a suggestion reflects a misunderstanding of what God's attributes obligate him to do. Many think that because God is all-loving, he is obligated to do every loving thing possible. His grace obligates him to do every gracious thing possible, and so on. However, this is an incorrect assessment of God's obligations. In my judgment, it would be very loving for God to make us all multimillionaires, but I can't think of anything that obligates him to do so. God's love doesn't obligate him to do every loving thing possible. Rather, everything he chooses to do (though he isn't obliged to do everything he can do) must exhibit his attribute of love. As to God's grace, at most it means that the things he chooses to do will exhibit his grace, but even here we must be careful. Grace as undeserved favor is by definition never owed, so we can hardly demand that God act graciously toward us. The key point is that before we mount a case against God for failing to do what his character requires, we must be sure that we understand what he is obligated to do.

In spite of this point about God's attributes, I still felt something was amiss. Granted, my wife's disease resulted from the sinfulness of the human race, and granted, God didn't owe us exemption from this problem because of his attributes, but still, not everyone has to deal with such a burden, so why should we? It seems God has been unfair in letting this burden fall on us when others escape such problems.

I believe this complaint is at the heart of why many believers and nonbelievers alike turn from God in the midst of affliction and feel justified in doing so. God hasn't treated them fairly, so he doesn't deserve their worship and devotion. As I reflected on this matter, several things came to mind. First, as I reflected on God's fairness or justice, I began to think of my philosophical training about matters of justice. Philosophers often distinguish between distributive and egalitarian justice. Distributive justice gives to each person exactly what they are owed, reward or punishment. Egalitarian justice requires that each person receive exactly the same thing.

With this distinction in hand, I realized the nature of my complaint. I was angry because God gave me something different from what he gave others. Egalitarian justice requires that each of us get the same thing. Others escape such problems, so we should have too. As logical as this sounds, no matter how hard I tried, I couldn't think of any biblical or nonbiblical principle that requires God to deal with us according to egalitarian justice.

In contrast, Scripture teaches that God functions in his relations with us in accord with distributive justice. Distributive justice is about what we have earned—what we deserve and what is owed to us. If we want God to treat us justly, that means we want what we deserve. But what do we deserve? Given God's moral governance of our world and the fact that we have broken his laws, we deserve punishment. None of us deserves exemption from problems and punishment for sin, for all of us have sinned against God. We may chafe under this system of moral government, but God as Creator has a right to set things up this way. And given this setup, he has done nothing unjust by not exempting my family from this affliction. If we are speaking in terms of justice, God owes none of us egalitarian justice, and in terms of distributive justice, he owes none of us blessing.

Still, I harbored residual anger toward God. Though I came to see that my desire for egalitarian justice was wrong and that according to distributive justice I didn't merit exemption from affliction, it seemed unfair that others who don't deserve exemption from problems have not been asked to bear this burden. Eventually I came to see that my complaint was that God has dealt with others in grace, and I felt that I should get the same grace.

As I pondered such thoughts, however, I came to see how wrong they are. I was demanding grace as though God owed it to me because he gave it to others. But grace is unmerited, undeserved, unearned favor. That is, you get something good that you don't deserve, haven't merited, and aren't owed. Grace is not given to reward good deeds or upright character; it's not a reward at all. It is given out of the generosity of God's heart. As unmerited blessing, grace is never owed—that's why it's grace and not justice. So God has done nothing wrong if he gives you grace that he doesn't give me.

One of Jesus' parables beautifully illustrates this principle. In the parable of the workers in the vineyard (Matt. 20:1–16), a landowner hired workers at various times in the day. Those hired early in the day were promised a denarius for the day's work. Others were promised only that the owner would do right by them, and still other workers were simply told to go to work. At quitting time, those hired last were paid first. The landowner paid them each a denarius, even though they had been hired a mere hour or two before the end of the day. In fact, he paid every worker a denarius. When the landowner paid those hired first the denarius he had promised, they were angry. They had worked the entire day, but those hired near the end of the day had received the same wage. Their complaint amounted to the following: Somebody got a better deal than I did, and that's not fair!

The landowner replied that he had not treated them unfairly. They had made a deal, and he had given them exactly what he had promised. Justice says you give people what they earn and what you owe. But if the landowner wanted to be generous with the others, what's wrong with that? If he wanted to extend them grace, why is that wrong? Whose money (whose grace) is it anyway? The message of the parable is clear: Our standing in the kingdom of heaven depends on God's grace, and God has a right to give grace and withhold it as he chooses. Never begrudge someone the grace that God gives them, especially when he doesn't give you the same grace.

Coming to this realization about whether God owed me exemption from this trial was a major breakthrough in my experience. It made me realize that if I were to mount a complaint against God over what he had or hadn't done, I had no ground for such a case. I had been angry at God without adequate reason. While this realization did not remove the affliction, it made me feel more comfortable with God. After all, he had not caused the affliction, and he didn't owe me release from it. But he hadn't abandoned me either. He gives me grace to sustain me through each day. I don't deserve that either, but it is there!

A final major factor in helping me adjust to what had happened and removing my anger were the many tangible signs of God's love and care for us. Many people displayed generosity and kindness, showing us that there are people who care and who will help when things grow worse. But why do these people show us this love and concern? I know it is ultimately because God moves them to do so, and hence, we have periodic reminders that God cares for us and loves us.

There is much more to our story and many other things that also helped me cope with this affliction.[14] I would not delude myself into thinking that everyone's situation is like mine or that what I have said will solve the personal crises of faith others confront. However, much of what I have said touches on very common, human themes, so others may find it helpful.

Though the intellectual problems of evil and the experience of affliction can be major detriments to belief in God, they needn't be. Of course, one can choose to remain angry at God, but I hope this chapter will help you to see that in the face of the intellectual and personal problems of evil, one need not sacrifice intellect to continue believing in God, nor does one need to hold on to God in blind faith without any explanation as to why afflictions happen and without any comfort or relief of the pain. Undoubtedly, it is easier to write about these things than to live them, but through God's sustaining grace, it is possible to cope with evils and to do so in ways that are pleasing to God and a positive testimony to others.

FIFTEEN

WHY I HAVE MADE JESUS CHRIST LORD OF MY LIFE

J. P. MORELAND

I was born on March 9, 1948, in Kansas City, Missouri, and was raised in Grandview, Missouri, a Kansas City suburb. My father died when I was in second grade, and I was raised largely by my mother, though she did marry again during my seventh-grade year. My mother and stepfather were good to me, though neither could help much with my religious instruction. My mother worked in a paper cup factory, and my stepfather was a welder. Throughout high school I attended a mildly liberal United Methodist church, and, as a result, I saw Jesus as a fairly boring, middle-class white person who espoused a somewhat benign set of moral platitudes. Since I was an honor student and a decent athlete with a good social life, I was simply uninterested in learning anything more about Jesus Christ. It seemed likely to me that there was a God, but my religious affections toward him lay unawakened in my breast.

I received a scholarship to study chemistry at the University of Missouri, so in the fall of 1966 I set out for Columbia, Missouri, not knowing that during my tenure there I would make a decision that would forever alter the course of my life. I had two goals for college: to prepare for Ph.D. work in chemistry so I could become a university professor in the discipline and to date as many attractive girls as possible to increase my chances of obtaining a wife. So I joined a social fraternity and took all the chemistry, physics, and math courses I could. I had a disdain for the humanities, but, like most undergraduates then and now, I was virtually ignorant of what they were.

It was the '60s, and I lived a fairly typical pagan lifestyle. I never took drugs, but I drank and partied hard. Even so, I still managed to be successful in school, graduating with honors in chemistry. On occasion I would pray to a vague father figure whose depiction I had managed to glean from the watered-down instruction I had received in Sunday school prior to college. Church attendance was out of the question. I recall the unrest on campus, as well as the desperate need for ultimate meaning that social/political causes afforded to many of my friends. I remember asking one friend, Carol, why she was marching against the Vietnam War. She replied that she really didn't know the issues and didn't actually have much of an opinion about the war, but she felt a need to count for something, and the antiwar rallies satisfied that need.

Encounters such as the one with Carol regularly shook me out of my lethargy about life. As a chemistry major, it was easy to hide in the lab and feel a sense of superiority without giving much thought to larger, ultimate questions. But I regularly sensed an emptiness inside me, and I knew that if there were no God, life in general, and my life in particular, had no ultimate significance. One tragedy of religious liberalism, which due to my upbringing was my only reference point, lies precisely in its inability to provide reasonable answers to the sort of hunger I regularly suppressed inside me. So I simply did not know where to go with my doubts and desires. Thus, I redoubled my efforts in school and social life, not knowing that they were like Turkish delight—the more I got of them, the more I was addicted to what could not satisfy the emptiness in my heart.

In November of my junior year (1968), some Campus Crusade for Christ speakers came to my fraternity house and shared an apologetic case for the deity of Jesus Christ, along with a presentation of the gospel. I was simply shocked. Here were attractive, intelligent people talking about Jesus outside the church walls. It was apparent to me that they had something I knew not of, so I began to meet weekly with Bob Farnsley, a Campus Crusade worker. I asked questions, read the New Testament, and after about a month and a half became convinced that the New Testament was probably true and that Jesus of Nazareth was the Son of God. One evening, I went up to my dorm room, closed and locked the door, and knelt by my bed. I accepted Jesus Christ as my Savior and set my heart to being his disciple for the rest of my life. I asked him simply never to leave me and to walk with me wherever I went, a request, I would learn, he was quite eager to grant.

That very evening I had a sense of Christ's presence that was so vivid I was afraid to open my eyes for fear that I would see a form standing in the room!

Since that day, I have had numerous additional visits from the Lord Jesus, and they have continued to strengthen my life as his follower. In the next weeks and months, my life changed dramatically. A new power, calm, strength, direction, and reality came into my life. I instantly became celibate and refrained from sexual activity until I was married in 1977. I also became an underground radical for Jesus, speaking at free speech rallies, distributing Christian literature on campus, and seeking to evangelize others. The Bible came alive to me and it, along with the fellowship I discovered with other believers, provided such sustenance to me that I have never recovered from the life-changing power of God I experienced in those early years of my newfound knowledge of God.

Upon graduation in 1970, I turned down a fellowship to do doctoral studies in nuclear chemistry and joined the staff of Campus Crusade, serving in the states of Colorado and Vermont from 1970 to 1972 and 1972 to 1975, respectively. Those were incredible days of growth and ministry. Apologetics was a real source of strength for me in my early years as a Christian, and I read widely in apologetics, theology, and devotional literature. I also witnessed genuine acts of God in my ministry. I will share one of them.

In 1972, I and two staff women went to the University of Vermont to start Campus Crusade. We had no student contacts at all, so we started doing evangelism. We desired to make a substantial, initial impact for Christ on the campus, so during the first week of classes, the three of us knelt in prayer in my apartment and asked the Lord Jesus to lead us to a fraternity or sorority house in which he had prepared hearts to respond to his gospel. There were roughly thirty fraternity and sorority houses at the university, and after prayer I opened the university catalog and picked the Alpha Chi house for our first meeting. That evening, we talked to the Alpha Chi president and set up a team meeting for the next week.

At the meeting, twenty-five out of forty-five women in the house became Christians. Three different women confessed to me that during the week before the meeting, they had been dreaming about God at night and had been talking about how to find God. Those twenty-five converts all stayed strong in the faith the rest of their college days, and five of them went into missionary work. In a little over a year, we had won over 150 students to Christ on a campus of 8,000, and our Christian group was three to four times larger than any other group on campus. The gospel of Jesus Christ was the single most discussed issue on campus, and a spiritual revolution came to pass.

In my evangelistic and discipleship ministry, I saw that if evangelical Christianity was going to make an impact on individuals and social structures, there needed to be more leaders who were spiritually vibrant and intellectually trained. So I left Campus Crusade and attended Dallas Seminary from 1975 to 1979. There I made the second greatest decision of my life, my decision to marry Hope Coleman. I had met Hope in 1971 at a Campus Crusade training conference. She was on Crusade staff and was a dedicated disciple whose life exuded the spirit and kindness of Christ himself. The year before I left for seminary, Hope was reassigned by Crusade to live in Dallas, and shortly before I arrived, God spoke to her in clear terms that she and I were to be married. She never put it to me in those terms (she merely said that God had given her a desire to be with me), but during the next year and a half we had a rocky dating experience (the death of my father made me fearful of intimacy and commitment).

I finally worked through my psychological difficulties, and we were married in May 1977. We now have two lovely daughters who currently attend the university at which I teach, and Hope and I are more convinced than ever that a marriage in which husband and wife individually seek Jesus Christ with all their hearts is far richer than anything that can be achieved without his lordship.

Since graduation from seminary in 1979, Hope and I have helped to plant two churches, and I have taught at various institutions, including Talbot School of Theology since 1990. From 1981 to 1985, I studied for my M.A. and Ph.D. in philosophy. I have always believed that philosophy, properly approached, is simply a way of enriching the life of discipleship unto Jesus, and when I teach or write on philosophical themes, that belief is always somewhere in the background.

In the last fifteen years of my life as one of Jesus' students, four values have informed my sense of vocation: (1) the value of love and devotion to the Triune God, with special focus on Jesus Christ, along with an intentional plan to make progress in spiritual formation; (2) the value of the mind and a developed intellectual life in which truth and reason are central; (3) the importance of being a Christian activist, one who seeks to penetrate the world with a Christian worldview, with special emphasis on the Great Commission; and (4) the value of friendship and community in the body of Christ in which one learns to give honor to others and to be genuinely enthusiastic about their successes and concerned about their hardships. These four values are expressions of a central truth I have learned over the years of being one of Jesus' followers: Being a Christian was never meant to be a separate compartment added to an otherwise secular life. Rather, being a Christian is a way of being present in the world, and it informs, permeates, and shapes every aspect of one's thinking, feeling, and acting. Throughout it all, being enraptured with Jesus himself is the central core to growing as his follower, and because Jesus is completely worthy of such devotion, I have without reservation continued to make him Lord of my life as best I can and within the limits of my own frailties. I have come to know that following Jesus is the wisest and best thing a person can do with his or her life.

INTELLECTUAL REFLECTIONS ON MY JOURNEY

The Christian life is a life of trust based on knowledge. Among other things, growth in the way of Jesus requires learning how to maintain and strengthen the beliefs central to the nature of that way. It may be helpful, therefore, to share why I am a Christian from an intellectual point of view.

My purpose here is not to argue for Christianity or to provide a detailed case for its truth—I have sought to do that elsewhere.[1] Instead, I want to give a very brief glimpse into my own life that, I trust, will be helpful to inquirers and fellow sojourners.

My approach to the rational justification of Christianity is threefold: (1) justification for the existence of a monotheistic God, (2) justification for the truth of Christianity, and (3) the evidence of religious experience for Christian theism.

THE EXISTENCE OF A MONOTHEISTIC GOD

There are a number of reasons why I believe in God. I am convinced that the cosmos of space, time, and matter had a beginning and that something outside the cosmos and, in that sense, supernatural, with the power of free choice brought it into existence. I am also persuaded that different forms of the design argument provide justification for belief in God. I am particularly impressed by the fine-tuning of the universe, the informational content and so-called specified complexity in biological organisms, the fact that our rational and sensory faculties allow us to gather truth in our intellectual environment, often with regard to immaterial entities (e.g., knowledge of universals, moral knowledge, self knowledge of one's own soul and mental states, aesthetic knowledge, knowledge of mathematics and logic) that have little or nothing to do with the demands for reproductive advantage and have much to do with the gratuitous beauty in the world.

Third, several features of the moral life and the objectivity of purpose in life are, in my view, best explained by the sort of monotheistic God the Bible describes and who creates human persons in his image: the fact that value properties came to be exemplified in the world, the imperative force of moral law that is best explained by a moral commander, the existence and appropriateness of moral shame and guilt that goes beyond what is owed to other human persons, the fact that human persons have incredibly high value compared with other entities in the cosmos and that they have equal value as human persons, the fact that our faculties are such that we have knowledge of value, the fact that our desire structure causes us to want to do what is right, even when it is not in our self-interest, the fact that we are so constructed that we can actually make moral progress, and the fact that it is rational to adopt the moral point of view in the first place.

Finally, the existence of immaterial souls, the reality of libertarian freedom, and the nature of consciousness and intentionality are, in my view, best explained by the notion that we were created by a God who has these features himself. It seems clear to me that none of these items could come from pure matter, nor do I believe that panpsychism is adequate to explain the unity of the self and its power of choice. There are other things I could cite here. I mention only a few items to give a feel for the main sorts of considerations that have been powerful in my own reflection about Christian monotheism. I also believe that God's own Spirit has testified to me of God's reality, though I believe this to be an aspect of religious experience, and I wish to postpone a discussion of this until later.

THE MOVE FROM MONOTHEISM TO CHRISTIANITY

The considerations just mentioned justify belief in God, but not belief in Christianity, at least not by themselves. I still have to ask why I am a Christian monotheist. I have never been able to respect people who approach this question by way of what I call the smorgasbord approach. When one goes to a smorgasbord, one picks and chooses food according to one's tastes, so the plate of food that results is a creation of the desires of the one who goes to the smorgasbord. Similarly, one who approaches the question of the existence and nature of God with inordinate reliance on one's feelings, one's desires, one's personal likes and dislikes will invariably end up with a picture of God that looks suspiciously like the person who went looking for him/her/it. Isn't it incredible how the supreme being happens to change his views on things at the same time that politically correct culture changes its opinions? How surprising that God's views on tolerance, truth, sexuality, egalitarianism, and a host of other things have evolved at precisely the same time that our culture has changed its views on these things!

A better approach is to assess the various options regarding monotheism and see which one is most likely to be true. Three criteria are central for choosing (and not losing!) one's religion: (1) Does the depiction of the supreme being in a given religion harmonize with what we already know about God from creation, for example, from considerations about monotheism listed above? If not, the religion is false; if so, it may be true. (2) Does the religion provide the most profound diagnosis of the human condition and the most adequate solution to that diagnosis? I cannot argue this point here, but while I would admit that most religions contain truths, the person, deeds, and teachings of Jesus of Nazareth and his apostles, found in the New Testament, simply tower over all other ideologies and religious systems. This is true both in intrinsic content and in historical impact. Regarding intrinsic content, all one needs to do is read the rich devotional, theological, and ethical literature found throughout the history of Christianity to see that, when it accurately expounds the New Testament, this literature is without rival. Regarding historical influence, wherever genuine Christianity has thrived, humans have flourished. (3) Is the best explanation of both the origin and continued history of the religion one that employs supernatural activity on God's part? Is the signature of the divine on that religion? I am convinced by arguments from prophecy and historical evidence that the Bible is, indeed, a divine revelation and that Jesus of Nazareth is the risen Son of God.

260

The Evidence of Religious Experience

At this point, I believe the testimony of God's Holy Spirit and, more generally, the value of religious experience enters the picture. I believe it is fruitful to consider four sorts of religious experiences as evidence for the truth of Christianity.

Biblical Wisdom

My experience, and that of my Christian brothers and sisters, is one in which I constantly find that biblical teaching accurately describes me, my family, and the social/ethical/aesthetic world in which I seek to live a good life. Time and time again, I come away from Scripture with the deep impression that it is absolutely correct in its insights into virtue and vice, individual and structural good and evil, parenting, sexual love in marriage, and a host of other issues. Moreover, I find that when I internalize biblical wisdom, my life changes for the better and I become a better person, father, husband, friend, and professor. I don't know how many times I and my Christian friends have said that we have no idea how people live without Jesus Christ and the Scriptures. When we say this, our hearts are not filled with arrogance and pride, nor are we trying to put others down or say that no one can do anything good without being a Christian. Rather, we are expressing the fact that most of us have lived on both sides—we were all unbelievers at some point—and having tasted the goodness of Jesus and his Word, we realize that life without him is mere biological existence compared to the deep flourishing that comes from knowing and living the wisdom in the Bible.

Specific Changes in One's Life

In his masterful work on religious experience, William James argued that real effects require real causes adequate to explain those effects and, moreover, that the real changed lives of religious believers is best explained by the existence of God.[2] In a similar way, Patrick Sherry argued that a careful study of the Christian church as a collective whole and as a group of individuals justifies the claim that distinctively New Testament conversion and discipleship is simply far superior in producing virtuous heroes and saints who have changed the world, often at great personal cost, and who have flourished as humans in a way unparalleled.[3] This does not mean that no moral heroes exist outside the church or that everyone in the church is a moral hero. It does mean, however, that an honest evaluation of history justifies the conclusion that authentic Christianity changes lives in an unparalleled way.

Specific Religious Experiences

In my own life, I have experienced times when God has been directly present to me in one way or another. I have also experienced times when God has spoken to me. A few years ago, I entered a three-month period during which

Jesus Christ came to me vividly on several occasions. One morning I was at home studying when I became overwhelmed with the presence of God. For the next hour, I just sat alone in my living room and wept with joy. On another occasion I was on a plane to Illinois to deliver an academic paper. I had the strong sense that God was asking me if there was something specific he could do for me. The evening before, my daughter had come down with a migraine headache, which, in her case, usually lasted one to two days. I asked God to take her headache away that very moment, and the sense came back to me that it had been done. That evening I arrived at my hotel and called my wife, and she informed me that my daughter's headache had left that morning, the time I was praying.

At the end of the three-month period, I had the distinct sense that God was going to hide his presence from me so I would seek him during a dark period, and since that time, I have had other periods of intense awareness of God's presence followed by times of dryness. Other mature believers have told me that this sort of thing happens to them regularly. I believe many people experience times during which the Lord Jesus manifests his presence to them in a special way, whether or not they recognize it. The experiences are difficult to explain away, and in my view, only a defective epistemology renders impotent the intellectual value of religious experiences such as these.

Answers to Prayer

I have already shared examples of answered prayer, and I have been strengthened considerably in my faith by their presence in my life. I, along with others, experience unanswered prayer as well, but in all honesty, I have seen enough specific answers to prayer that it is no longer reasonable for me to doubt that prayer actually works. Recently, William Dembski wrote a book in which he analyzed cases in which it was legitimate to infer that a phenomenon was the result of a purposive, intelligent act by an agent.[4] Among other things, Dembski analyzed cases in which insurance employees, police, and forensic scientists had to determine whether a death was an accident (no intelligent cause) or was brought about intentionally (done on purpose by an intelligent agent). According to Dembski, whenever three factors are present, investigators are rationally obligated to conclude that the event was brought about intentionally: (1) The event was contingent, that is, even though it took place, it did not have to happen; (2) the event had a small probability of happening; and (3) the event is capable of independent specifiability.

To illustrate, consider a game of bridge in which two people receive a hand of cards. One hand is a random set of cards—call it hand A—and the other is a perfect bridge hand dealt to the dealer himself. If that happened, we would immediately infer that while A was not dealt intentionally, the perfect bridge hand was and, in fact, represents a case of cheating on the part of the dealer. What justifies our suspicion?

First, neither hand had to happen. There are no laws of nature, logic, or mathematics that necessitate that either hand had to come about in the history of the cosmos. In this sense, each hand, indeed, the very card game itself, is a contingent event that did not have to take place. Second, since hand A and the perfect bridge hand have the same number of cards, each is equally improbable. So the small probability of an event is not sufficient to raise suspicions that the event came about by the intentional action of an agent. The third criterion makes this clear. The perfect bridge hand can be specified as special independently of the fact that it happened to be the hand that came about, but this is not so for hand A. Hand A can be specified as "some random hand or other that someone happens to get." That specification applies to all hands and does not mark out as special any particular hand that comes about. So understood, A is no more special than any other random deal. But this is not so for the perfect bridge hand. This hand can be characterized as a special sort of combination of cards by the rules of bridge quite independently of the fact that it is the hand that the dealer received. It is the combination of contingency (this hand did not have to be dealt), small probability (this particular arrangement of cards was quite unlikely to have occurred), and independent specifiability (according to the rules, this is a pretty special hand for the dealer to receive) that justifies the accusation that the dealer cheated.

The same considerations apply to specific answers to prayer. Early in my ministry I attended a seminar on how to pray specifically. A few weeks later, I was to return to Colorado to start my ministry at the Colorado School of Mines in Golden with Ray Womack, a fellow Campus Crusade worker. Unknown to anyone, I wrote a prayer request in my prayer notebook and began to pray specifically that God would provide for me and Ray a white house with a white picket fence and a grassy front yard, within two or three miles from campus, for no more that $130 per month. I told the Lord that this request was a reasonable one on the grounds that (1) we wanted a place that provided a home atmosphere for students, was accessible from campus, and we could afford, and (2) I was experimenting with specific prayer and wanted my faith to be strengthened.

I returned to the Golden area and looked for three days at several places to live. I found nothing in Golden, and, in fact, found only one apartment for rent for $135 per month about twelve miles from campus. I told the manager I would take it. She informed me that a couple had looked at the place that morning, and they had until that afternoon to make a decision. If they did not want it, I could move in the next day. I called late that afternoon and was informed that the couple had taken the apartment. I was literally back to square one. That evening, Kaylon Carr (a Crusade friend) called me to ask if I still needed a place to stay. When I said yes, she informed me that earlier that day she had been at Denver Seminary. While there, she had seen an advertisement for a house a pastor hoped to rent to seminary students or Christian workers. Kaylon gave me his phone number, and I called and set up an appointment to meet the pastor at his house. The next day I drove up to a white house with a white picket fence, a nice grassy front yard, located roughly two miles from campus. He asked for $110 per month. Needless to say, I took it, and Ray and I had a home that year in which to minister.

This answer to prayer—along with hundreds of others I and my Christian friends have experienced—was an event that was (1) contingent and did not have to happen according to natural law, (2) very improbable, and (3) independently specifiable (a number of features of the event were specified in my prayer prior to and independent of the event itself taking place). Meeting these three criteria are not necessary conditions for an event to be judged an action by God, but they do seem to be sufficient. As such, answers to prayer in my life have increased the rational justification of my confidence in Jesus Christ.

SPIRITUAL REFLECTIONS ON MY JOURNEY

It should be obvious by now that the division between the intellectual and spiritual aspects of one's Christian life is somewhat arbitrary. The so-called intellectual parts of the Christian life are crucial to a vibrant spirituality, and, conversely, the spiritual insights, practices, and habits of a person are important for informing a distinctively Christian intellectual life. Having said that, however, it still remains fruitful to reflect on factors central to one's spiritual progress in a way that does not make explicit reference to the intellectual relevance of those factors.

A host of things have been helpful to me in my own spiritual life, and some of them are pretty typical—worship, Bible study, and so forth. But certain ideas and activities are of special importance to me.

For one thing, I repeatedly return to the conviction that Jesus of Nazareth is simply peerless. He is the wisest, most virtuous, most influential person in history. I can't even imagine what the last two thousand years would have been like without his influence. There is no one remotely like him. The power of his ideas, the quality of his character, the beauty of his personality, the uniqueness of his life, miracles, crucifixion, and resurrection are so far removed from any other person or ideology that, in my view, it is the greatest honor ever bestowed on me to be counted among his followers.

Not only is it an unspeakable honor to be one of his followers, it is also by far the greatest opportunity to gain a life of meaning and to become what we all know we ought to be. Sometimes people say that following Jesus is difficult. In a sense I agree, but in a more fundamental sense I could not disagree more. Following Jesus is, indeed, difficult in the sense that exemplifying the traits characteristic of his teaching and kingdom takes more effort and practice than doing what comes naturally. But if by difficult one means a life that is painful, sad, lonely, depressing, and anxiety-filled, then a really difficult life is one lived contrary to the way of Jesus. All one needs to do is compare the lives of those who live in conformity with the New Testament with those who live contrary to it and ask, soberly and honestly, which ones flourish in a distinctively human way. It will become obvious that the way of Jesus is far easier than the path in the opposite direction. To take one simple example, it is actually much easier to love one's enemies than to hate them. Hating one's enemies causes one to be upset, angry, anxious, and controlled by others. Loving one's enemies creates a life in which God is trusted.

Second, the history of God's people is a history of the richest community the world has ever seen. The greatest music, the best literature, the most profound ethics and philosophy, the most influential moral saints and heroes, the richest treasures on spiritual formation are found among the followers of Jesus. I am not saying the church has been perfect. However, I would argue that when the church has been ugly and hideous in her actions, she has strayed from the New Testament charter given to her by the Master himself. Nor am I saying that no good things have come from outside the church. As John Wesley noted, "To imagine none can teach you but those who are themselves saved from sin, is a very great and dangerous mistake. Give not place to it for a moment."[5] I heartily agree. Still, Christians need to remind themselves regularly that, by and large, it was our people who started the universities; nurtured art, music, literature, and philosophy; sacrificially went to the four corners of the world to establish orphanages, care for the sick, and champion human rights (advocacy of human rights did not come from atheistic cultures but from the Christian West).

A few weeks ago, I attended a Talbot School of Theology graduation banquet. After dinner, a slide show was presented in which slide after slide depicted in chronological order some of the great followers in the way: Justin Martyr, Augustine, St. Francis, and on and on. A deep sense of pride and gratitude rose up in all our hearts that evening as the gathering contemplated afresh what a wonderful community of which it is our privilege to be a part.

Finally, Christian marriage and Christian friendship is so rich that I cannot imagine living without it. To be sure, my marriage has problems and struggles just like everyone else's, and my close band of Christian friends has its own share of interpersonal conflict and difficulty. Still, I know that these problems would be far worse if I (and we) were not Christians. And I have tasted the tremendous benefits of knowing Christ Jesus in these two areas of life.

At the end of the day, we all need to have a worthy purpose in life sufficient to justify our four score and ten on this earth. And as Jesus reminded us in Matthew 16:24–27, in order to gain a life of spiritual vitality and flourishing, one needs to develop the practice of giving oneself away to others for Jesus' sake. While I certainly have a distance to go in my journey, one thing has become abundantly clear: When it comes to a life of purpose, when it comes to finding something worth living and dying for, discipleship unto Jesus is the only game in town. Because of the spiritual richness and intellectual credibility of the Christian religion, I have made Jesus Lord of my life and sought to live out that commitment with others of similar passion as best I know how. And with God's help, I plan to enlist to that way as many as I can before this stage of my journey passes into the next one.

In closing, I urge you to ponder your own standing with Jesus Christ. Have you made him your Lord and Savior? If not, do not let this matter rest until you have. Are you one of his disciples? If so, dedicate yourself more firmly than ever to love and serve him with all your heart, soul, mind, and strength. I make these pleas for at least three reasons. First, for a number of reasons, including historical evidence, I believe there are more than adequate grounds to believe that Jesus Christ was and is the incarnate, risen Son of God. As our Creator God, he has the right to be Lord of our lives. Second, Jesus Christ is simply incomparable. The uniqueness of his claims, the depth and power of his teachings, the miraculous nature of his life and resurrection, the beauty of his character, the unique grace and forgiveness his death provides, and the profundity of his impact on world history unite to justify the claim that no one else comes close to offering what he does to those who submit to him. Finally, my own life and the lives of countless others have been immeasurably benefited by devotion to Jesus. True, there are ways in which it is difficult to be his follower. But it is also true that it is more difficult to live without being his follower, as those of us who know him can attest.

SIXTEEN

WHY I BELIEVE JESUS CHRIST IS THE ULTIMATE SOURCE FOR MEANING

RAVI ZACHARIAS

In the 1950s, *Encyclopedia Britannica* published its fifty-five-volume set, The Great Books of the Western World. One of the gifted minds behind the series was Mortimer Adler. The opening volume is a compilation of the great themes addressed by seminal thinkers during the last two millennia. Fascinatingly, the longest essay is on God. When Adler was asked why that particular theme merited the lengthiest treatment, he answered without apology: "Because more consequences for life follow from this one issue than any other issue you can think of," he said. He was right. Every life is built fundamentally and finally on one's view of God. For the Christian, the foundation is not built merely on the assertion that God exists but on the added claim that God was revealed in the person of Jesus Christ. A commitment of mind and heart affirming that Jesus Christ is who he claimed to be, that is, the Son of the living God, is at the heart of the Christian faith.

Right at the outset, I want to dispel a couple of commonly held errors. First, critics of Christianity falsely assume that only Christians make an audacious claim of exclusivity. Such critics often assert, "We all come through different routes and end up in the same place. There are many roads but just one destination." It sounds so all-encompassing and pleasing to the ear. However, it does not take long to recognize what is smuggled in with these statements.

The truth is that all religions are not the same. All religions do not point to God. All religions *do not say* that all religions are the same. In fact, some religions do not even believe in God. At the heart of *every* religion is an uncompromising commitment to a particular way of defining who God is or is not. Buddhism, for example, was based on Buddha's rejection of two of Hinduism's fundamental doctrines. Islam rejects both Buddhism and Hinduism. So it does no good to put a halo on the notion of tolerance and act as if everything is equally true. In fact, even all-inclusive religions such as Bahaism end up being exclusivistic by excluding the exclusivists!

Therefore, the statement that Christians are arrogant because they claim absoluteness ignores the reality that members of every other major religion do so as well. And it stands to reason. As Norman Geisler explained in chapter 2, inherent in any truth claim is the belief that something contrary to it is false. Truth excludes its opposite. The person who *denies* the exclusive nature of truth is *also* making a truth claim. The question is whether the truth claim being made can be sustained by the tests for truth.

The other commonly held error comes in the form of a plea: "Why can't we leave everybody alone to follow the religion within which they were born? Why all this proclamation and propagation?" Once again, this demand challenges the very core of the Christian faith, because no one is born a Christian. The relationship a Christian claims is one that comes not by culture but by virtue of a personal choice to follow Jesus Christ. Christian ideas may be inherited within a culture, but the Christian commitment is a personal affirmation. I made that commitment at the age of seventeen. While the moment of my commitment was based on a hunger to know God, the years that have followed have taken me through an intellectual journey. That journey culminated in the conclusion that in Jesus I find not only every hunger of the heart met but also every pursuit of the mind.

The Search for Meaning

One might well ask what those pursuits are that bridge the existential and the rigorously intellectual? At the center of life lie four questions of origin, meaning, morality, and destiny. How did I come to be? What brings life meaning? How do I determine right from wrong? What happens to a person when he or she dies? These are the questions that dig deep into our thinking, the answers to which we must find if life is to be defined correctly.

But there is a caution. First and foremost, the answer to each of these four questions must be established as true by its correspondence to reality. Further, all the answers when put together must cohere without contradiction. For example, the naturalist tries to explain our origin by saying that life evolved purely by accident and that we are here due to the cumulative effect of time plus matter plus chance. If that is true, there is no way to establish any point of reference for either meaning or morality. In other words, in a naturalistic framework, any constructed meaning is as equally valid as any other espoused meaning. The words of G. K. Chesterton ring true: The tragedy of disbelieving in God, he said, is not that a person ends up believing in nothing. It is much worse. He may end up believing in anything. There is no way within naturalism to arrive at an objective moral law or an ontic referent for meaning. Anything goes! Therefore, it does not suffice to offer just a view on origins. The entailments must be justified as well.

Another example is pantheism. If all is one and all is God, how can pantheism explain either origin or morality? And what about Buddha, who said that every birth is a rebirth and a payment for the previous birth? Was there ever a first birth? And if so, what was it paying for? It is not sufficient to explain merely origin or destiny. The questions of meaning and morality must also have equally coherent answers because they stand in interdependence to each other.

For me personally, the only one whose answers correspond to reality and cohere in their sum and substance is Jesus Christ. His gospel tells me that I am a moral being made for his purpose. My meaning is found in knowing and loving him. My moral choices are based on his character. My destiny is to live in eternity with him. In this chapter, I will address only one of these questions—what meaning means in the Christian context. In that meaning I find both a rational and an existential defense of Jesus' unique claims.

The search for meaning is as old as humanity. Even those who have dabbled lightly in the vast corpus of Greek mythology know the story of Sisyphus. Poor Sisyphus suffered the wrath of the gods when he revealed to mere mortals secrets that were known only within the Greek pantheon. He was sentenced to roll a massive stone to the top of a hill, watch it roll down again, and then repeat the process endlessly. His was a life consigned to futility.

Many intriguing suggestions have been made by philosophers in their attempts to rescue Sisyphus from this futility. "If only Sisyphus could have changed the way he viewed his task, so that he enjoyed rolling the stone," opined one. "Could he not have rolled up a different stone each time, so that someone else could have built a monument with it?" "Could he not have found some distraction that would take away the monotony?" It does not take a genius to grasp the reason behind the futility that holds Sisyphus in its grasp.

As times have changed and possibilities abound, one would think we should have come a long way from Sisyphus's malady. Instead, we deal with the same problem, only now it is the busyness of life. No amount of distraction has cured boredom. No variety changes the question of ultimate futility.

Not long ago, *Life* published a book on how individuals cope with this quest for meaning. The publication is a fascinating cross section of words and pictures—from philosophers to drug addicts, from painters to plumbers. José Martinez, a taxi driver in New York, provided this gripping sound bite of despair:

> We're here to die, just live and die. I live driving a cab. I do some fishing, take my girl out, pay taxes, do a little reading, then get ready to drop dead. Life is a big fake. . . . You're rich or you're poor. You're here, you're gone. You're like the wind. After you're gone, other people will come. It's too late to make it better. Everyone's fed up, can't believe in nothing no more. People have no pride. People have no fear. . . . People only care about one thing and that's money. We're gonna destroy ourselves, nothing we can do about it. The only cure for the world's illness is nuclear war—wipe everything out and start over. We've become like a cornered animal, fighting for survival. Life is nothing.[1]

There is a disturbing candor behind his admission. But we are quick to rationalize his predicament, fearful of seeing ourselves reflected in his portrait. "Of course a man struggling to make a living and stressed by an unrewarding job is bound to seem hopeless. If he were given limitless freedom and a limitless bank account, his meaninglessness would vanish." The errant assumption that meaning can be found by merely changing one's circumstances is endemic to our human condition.

Credited to the pen of King Solomon, no piece of ancient literature is more forthright and more penetrating in its treatment of this struggle than the Book of Ecclesiastes. The opening lines claim, "Meaningless, meaningless! All is meaningless!" Then Solomon takes a regressive journey, cataloguing his path to that cynicism—wisdom, pleasure, work, material gain, and much else. He came away empty.

> I denied myself nothing my eyes desired;
>   I refused my heart no pleasure.
> My heart took delight in all my work,
>   and this was the reward for all my labor.
> Yet when I surveyed all that my hands had done
>   and what I had toiled to achieve,
> everything was meaningless, a chasing after the wind;
>   nothing was gained under the sun.
>
> 2:10–11

This was no Sisyphus or taxi driver speaking. At Solomon's command, others rolled stones up steep hills so that he could build his stables, palaces, and temples. He was a man who boasted unparalleled intellect and imagination that made him the envy of many and who presided over the most pompous court of his time. In the end, he groaned that "under the sun" there was a monotony, a circularity, and a fatality to all human endeavor.

Solomon's assessment presents a startling even fearsome reality: The worst kind of meaninglessness does not come from being weary of pain or poverty but from being weary of pleasure amid plenty. Solomon is not the only one, surrounded by wealth and success, who talked of such disappointment at the end of the road. The refrain is repeated constantly yet often seems to fall on deaf ears. A modern-day writer, Jack Higgins, was asked at the pinnacle of his success what he now knows that he wished he had known as a younger man: "I wish I had known that when you get to the top, there is nothing there."[2]

Many scientists have recently entered the fray. Some have castigated philosophers and theologians for raising the problem in the first place and creating a need that ought never to have been manufactured. Their solution staggers the imagination. Here, for example, is the suggestion of Harvard paleontologist Stephen Jay Gould.

> The human species has inhabited this planet for only 250,000 years or so— roughly .0015 percent of the history of life, the last inch of the cosmic mile. The world fared perfectly well without us for all but the last moment of earthly time—and this fact makes our appearance look more like an accidental afterthought than the culmination of a prefigured plan.
>
> Moreover, and more important, the pathways that have led to our evolution are quirky, improbable, unrepeatable and utterly unpredictable. Human evolution is not random; it makes sense and can be explained after the fact. But wind back life's tape to the dawn of time and let it play again—and you will never get humans a second time. We are here because one odd group of fishes had a peculiar fin anatomy that could transform into legs for terrestrial creatures; because comets struck the earth and wiped out dinosaurs, thereby giving mammals a chance not otherwise available . . . because the earth never froze entirely during an ice age; because a small and tenuous species, arising in Africa a quarter of a million years ago, has managed so far by hook and by crook. We may yearn for a higher answer—but none exists. . . . We cannot read the meaning of life passively in the facts of nature. We must construct these answers ourselves—from our own wisdom and ethical sense. There is no other way.[3]

The naturalist's contribution is to assert that the search for higher meaning is itself a pointless one because it creates the need for objective metaphysical certainty, when in truth the empirical world does not offer us such assurances. If nature and matter are all that exist, higher meaning simply cannot be found and should not be sought.

To his credit, Gould correctly recognizes that the "what" of life and the "why" of life are inextricably connected. In a philosophy that defines life apart from God there is a plethora of options, each in one way or another forfeiting the right to judge anyone else's choice. But as we move from infancy to maturity, the "whys" of life proliferate, and we seek coherent answers that rise above mere speculation. By contrast, when God is in the picture, life gains an intrinsically sacred nature—based on who he is and why he has made us in the first place.

Stephen Hawking reinforces this impact at the end of his book, *A Brief History of Time*. After discussing the "what" of life, he says, "If we knew the why, then we will have the mind of God."[4] There it is again: More consequences follow from the reality of God than we are often willing to admit. It is the mind of God to which we turn in seeking an answer to meaning. The gospel of Jesus Christ deals precisely with the question why. Jesus says, "I have come that they may have life, and have it to the full" (John 10:10). He tells his disciples that he wanted their joy to be full. The wealthy and the poor, the young and the old came and drew life and joy from him. How did he give life meaning?

There are many approaches to take to find the answer. I shall take an indirect route. For our purposes, let's divide life into four stages—childhood, adolescence, young adulthood, and maturity—and in that context demonstrate and explore how at each stage meaning is pursued, attained, and sometimes lost.

THE ROMANCE OF ENCHANTMENT—WONDER

We will consider first the world of a child. I am greatly indebted here to the writings of G. K. Chesterton, who unabashedly proclaimed that he learned more about life by observing children in a nursery than he ever did by reflecting on the writings of any of the philosophers.

What is it about a child that fascinates us? Is it not the sense of wonder that pervades much of what the child sees and experiences? Listen to young fathers or mothers who have just welcomed a little one into their arms and their home. They themselves are starry-eyed, enveloped in the wonder of the bundle of life that has immeasurably enriched their lives.

I recall seeing our little boy, Nathan, when he was just three or four years old, playing with a helium balloon in the living room. He would let it go, watch it float to the ceiling, gleefully step up onto the sofa, grab the string, and get it down. This was fun. So he repeated the exercise. Stand on the floor, let the balloon go, climb up onto the sofa, grab the string, and get down. Chesterton has said that part of God's infinitude is revealed in a child's capacity to exult in the monotonous.

But gradually the monotonous is given complexity. So the next step Nathan took was to go outdoors and let the balloon go. It startled him to find that there was no sofa big enough to climb on so he could reach the string. His delight suddenly gave way to despair, until I stepped outside the house. He asked if I could grab it for him. When he knew it was too far even for my reach, he suddenly exclaimed, "I know what, Daddy. The next time you are in a plane you can get it back for me." What could I tell him? Within that child was a world so wonderful that the imagination knew no limits. That is how the childhood years make their impact. The fertile soil of the child's imagination is enchanted by the romance of possibilities.

I remember another occasion several years ago when I was speaking in the Middle East. My wife, our two-year-old daughter Sarah, and I were traveling from Jordan to Israel by way of the West Bank, crossing over at the Allenby Bridge. Once on Israeli soil, we were taken into a highly secured immigration building for routine but rigorous questioning, which was to precede our procurement of a visitor's visa. The three of us stood in one of the lines, having been warned to expect an emotionally taxing day. The room was full of machine-gun-clutching soldiers. There were sandbags piled against every wall, and a real sense of unease pervaded the room.

Finally, it was our turn to be interrogated. Unknown to me, as she was surveying the room, Sarah had locked eyes with a young Israeli soldier who was staring back at her in "eye-to-eye combat." Suddenly and strangely there was a moment of silence in the room, broken by the squeaky little voice of my daughter asking the soldier, "Excuse me, do you have any bubblegum?"

Words cannot fully express what that little voice and her request did for everyone in the room, where hitherto the weapons of war and the world of "adult ideas" had held everyone at bay. Those who understood English could not repress a smile, and those who did not understand English knew a soldier's heart had been irresistibly touched. All eyes were now on him.

He paused for a moment, then carefully handed his machine gun to a colleague. He came over to where we were standing, looked endearingly at Sarah, and picked her up in his arms. He took her into a back room and returned a few minutes later with her in one arm and in his other hand a tray with three glasses of lemonade—one for my wife, one for Sarah, and one for me. Our interrogation was short. In fact, the young soldier brought his jeep to the door and drove us to the taxi stand, sending us on our way to Jericho. I have often remarked that Sarah earned her year's keep with one little question voiced at the right time.

The incredible power of a child! The wonder-filled face of a little boy with a balloon, the wonder-imparting face of a two-year-old girl who changed the feel in a room from fear to fondness. The very strength of that child's influence was only bolstered by the fact that she was not even aware of the power she wielded or what she had accomplished.

Childhood is such a precious time in life. But, then, as a child gets older, that world of wonder begins to fade. As the years go by, something significant happens. The world becomes commonplace. Balloons burst and the harsh reality of conflicts, wars, hate, and power take the mind captive. The second stage has arrived. One cannot live in a world of fairy tales at this stage. The harder questions of life surface. What is true? What is good? What is evil? What is worth living for and what is worth dying for? In fact, why is there death at all?

Before we move on, I want to draw one conclusion. Wonder is a necessary component of meaning at every stage in life. But how does one find that wonder when fantasy is shattered? I suggest to you that wonder is not found in the pen of an author writing fantasy. It is not found in the continuation of some fantastic thrill. In fact, even the child begins to realize this in subtle ways. Every fairy tale does not contain just fantasy. There is always a condition— "If you do not come back by such and such, you will become a such and such." Chesterton adds this powerful reminder: "Have you noticed," says he, "that the person never ever says to the fairy godmother, 'How come?'"[5] Chances are that if the person asked that of the fairy godmother, adds Chesterton, the question would merit a counter. "If that is the way you want it, tell me how come there is a fairyland at all?" The point is well taken. There is not a world of limitless fantasy. There is a world of intelligibility and wonder, but certain boundaries pertain.

Here, then, is our first clue. The wonder that endures is not found in the things to play with but in the ones who are there with you—in relationships. Look into the face of a mother nursing her little infant. Look at the tears of a loved one, weeping at the pain of another. Read the account of anyone with minutes to live and one message to send to someone they love. Life's most tender and awe-inspiring significance comes not in the stories of "wonderland" but by way of precious relationships with those who share that wonder. That is our first clue.

In the person of Jesus Christ, God offers us an ultimate relationship with himself. The unique and marvelous truth of the Christian message is that God himself is a being-in-relationship. We, then, his offspring, long to live in relationship. But no relationship can find a blueprint until that individual is first related to his Creator. In Christ, we find that God himself has come to us, to dwell in us in fellowship, making us his children and extending to us his care. That, in turn, opens the world of the legitimately fantastic. I shall develop this further, but for now let me just make the assertion that the ultimate answer to the search for wonder is in a relationship with Christ. This is not mere fairy-tale talk. Jesus Christ went beyond the fantastic: He pointed to the fantastically true. How did he do this? That takes us to the next stage.

Truth—An Endangered Species

As the years pass and the wonder of childhood imagination is eroded in the face of reality and in the recognition that life may not be lived in an imaginary world, the search for truth becomes all-pervasive, drawing implications for the essence and destiny of life itself—connecting the what and the why. No thinking person can avoid this search, and it can end only when one is convinced that the answers espoused are true. Aristotle was right when he said that all philosophy begins with wonder, but the journey, I suggest, can progress only through truth. And so we move away from the world of imagination to the cerebral world of knowledge and truth. We move from the childhood sounds of ecstasy to the young world that seeks in language to explain the struggles of the heart and mind. Why this? Why that?

Scripture provides a fascinating discussion between the Roman governor Pontius Pilate and Jesus in the eighteenth chapter of John's Gospel. Jesus has been brought to him by the high priests, who want to execute him because of his claim to be equal with God. Pilate asks Jesus, "Are you a king?" We can well imagine a sardonic grin planted on the face of this nervous puppet of Caesar's, as he inquires into the kingship of a Jewish carpenter. Jesus responds with a question: "Are you asking this on your own or has someone else set you up?" Pilate is somewhat exasperated by this seeming insolence. "Look," he answers, "I did not bring you here—your own people have done that." Then Jesus says, "My kingdom is not of this world. If it were, my servants would fight to prevent my arrest. But now my kingdom is from another place." Pilate says, "Ah! So you are a king!"

The response of Jesus discloses Pilate's real predicament. "You are right in saying I am a king. In fact, for this reason I was born, and for this I came into the world, to testify to the truth. Everyone on the side of truth listens to me."

Pilate mutters, "What is truth?" and walks away.

The answer of Jesus is both subtle and daring. The fundamental problem Jesus was exposing to Pilate and to the world is not the paucity of available truth; it is more often the hypocrisy of our search. Truthfulness in the heart, said Jesus, precedes truth in the objective realm. Intent is prior to content. How can one deny that at the core of so much conflict today is the untruthfulness in our hearts? Wars are fought over lies. Peace treaties are concluded, laden with lies. It is truth that has died, not God. Humanity loves to chase a lie till it believes the lie, which frees the individual from any impinging moral reality.

After disclosing the true nature of the human heart, Jesus makes the most provocative statement during that penetrating conversation with Pilate. He affirms that the truthfulness or falsity of an individual's heart is revealed by that person's response to him. The implication is uncompromising. He was and is the truth. What you do with him defines the truthfulness of your search.

But that could be a rather presumptuous claim. Was this statement made in a vacuum? Not by any stretch of the imagination. From his birth to his death, from the way he lived to what he taught, from the wealth of prophecy to the completion of fulfillment, from the historicity of Scripture to the transformation Scripture brings about in lives, by his death and his resurrection— he sustained that massive claim. The coeditor of this book, Norman Geisler, succinctly states and defends the uniqueness of Christ in his exhaustive work, *Baker Encyclopedia of Christian Apologetics*.

Christ is absolutely unique among all who ever lived. He is unique in his supernatural nature, in his superlative character, and in his life and teaching.

275

No other world teacher claimed to be God. Even when the followers of some prophet deified their teacher, there is no proof given for that claim that can be compared to the fulfillment of prophecy, the sinless and miraculous life, and the resurrection. . . . Jesus is absolutely unique among all human beings who ever lived.[6]

Never has a life been lived the way Jesus lived it. Even the skeptic and famed historian W. E. H. Lecky grants this when he says:

The character of Jesus has not only been the highest pattern of virtue, but the strongest incentive in its practice, and has exerted so deep an influence, that it may be truly said that the simple record of three short years of active life has done more to regenerate and to soften mankind than all the disquisitions of philosophers and all the exhortations of moralists.[7]

There you have it from even one who has no prejudicial commitment to him—no one ever spoke like him or lived like him. That immediately sets him apart from everyone else who has ever lived. Contrast his life to that of Mohammed or Krishna and you will see there is a world of difference. From his pure life comes the reminder that if the heart is not truthful, then the very truth of Christ is missed. But like Pilate of old, we miss the striking force of truth. We miss seeing who he is because we are blinded by the power of preconceived notions. We come determined not to find his claim to truth.

Jon Krakauer, in his book *Into Thin Air*, tells a gripping story. His book recounts the ill-fated ascent of Mount Everest in 1996, in which many lives were lost, including those of the most adept leaders. At one point he recounts an episode with Andy Harris, one of the expedition guides, who had been exhausted by his conquest of the summit. On his descent, he had started to run out of oxygen, when he came across a cache of oxygen canisters. But Harris, already starved for oxygen, argued with his fellow climbers, mistakenly insisting that all the canisters were empty. Those to whom he was speaking repeatedly assured him that the canisters were indeed full. They themselves had left them there. But Harris was beguiled by a brain devoid of oxygen and made the false judgment that what he held in his hand could not help him.

What a remarkable parable of life that is! In a similar way, Pilate was standing face-to-face with the truth, but snared by the disorientation of power, he walked away from the source of all life.

If that is all Jesus had asserted—that our response to him betrayed our own prejudice—the argument would at best be circular and at worst no better than anyone else's claim. But Jesus had a basis on which to make such a statement. When a life is so lived that we see how life is meant to be lived, we must at least give ear to what that person says about what living means. And here, his description of reality moves us to a closer understanding that in him alone the ideal and the embodiment were unbroken. He was God incarnate, who never broke the demands of his own proclamation. He took us beyond words to himself.

Any other claimant to divine or prophetic status separates himself from the ideal. Jesus, by contrast, identified himself with his teaching. "I am the way, the truth, and the life," he said.

He was born in the context of three great cultures—the Hebrew, the Greek, and the Roman. For the Hebrews, the ideal was symbolized by light. For the Greeks, the ideal was in knowledge. For the Romans, the ideal was in glory. Light, knowledge, and glory—the three great abstractions of cultural pursuits. The apostle Paul was a Hebrew by birth, a citizen of Rome, raised in a Greek city. He well understood the pluralism of his time. Writing to the church in Corinth, he said, "God, who said, 'Let light shine out of darkness,' made his light shine in our hearts to give us *the light of the knowledge of the glory of God in the face of Christ*" (2 Cor. 4:6, emphasis added). Every ideal was demonstrated and lived out. This could not be said of anyone else.

Here we come to the next realization. Just as wonder was found in a person, so the Scriptures claim and prove that truth is fully embodied in a person, the person of Jesus Christ. It is not merely that he has the answers to life's questions; he *is* the answer. We find the truth not merely in platitudes or in creedal affirmations but in knowing him. When his questioners asked him for bread that would satisfy, he pointed to himself—"I am the bread of life," he said. As we study his claims and his teaching, we find a message that beautifully unfolds, encompassing the breadth of human need and the depth of human intellect. Truth was in his very person. In a world starved for truth, he stands as the eternal example of what ultimate truth and reality are all about.

But just as wonder fades with the search for truth, so truth longs for that which is not merely propositional or demonstrated but which gives relevance. Here we move to the third component.

LOVE'S LABOR WON

I have so far presented two essential components for meaning—the pursuit of wonder and the knowledge of truth—and suggested that they are both fulfilled in a person. I now suggest that the third component essential to meaning is love. From the wonder of childhood to the search for truth in adolescence, we come to the consummation of love in young adulthood. Christopher Morley said, "If we all discovered that we had only five minutes left to say all that we wanted to say, every telephone booth would be occupied by people calling other people to stammer that we love them."[8]

The greatest institution God gave to humanity is the institution of the family, based on the need for unconditional love. On love and marriage, G. K. Chesterton made this poignant observation: "They have invented a new phrase that is a black-and-white contradiction in two words—'free love.' As if a lover had been, or ever could be, free. It is the nature of love to bind itself."[9] Those words seem totally foreign to our disposable society: "It is the nature of love to bind itself." Realistically, what passes for love today could be more aptly described as self-gratification or indulgence.

How strange that we call the sexual act "making love." In actuality, if that act is without commitment, it is a literal and figurative denuding of love by which the individual is degraded to an object. In short, love is not love when it has been manufactured for the moment. Love is the posture of the soul, and its entailments are binding. When love is shallow, the heart is empty, but if the sacrifice of love is understood, one can drink deeply from its cup and be completely fulfilled. The more one consumes love selfishly, the more wretched and impoverished one becomes. But how do we know this? Through the message of Christ.

At the heart of the gospel is a Savior who loves us and offered himself for us. Once more, a unique truth emerges. Even Mahatma Gandhi, who was a Hindu, stated that the cross of Jesus constantly showed itself as an unparalleled expression of God's grace. Dr. E. Stanley Jones, a famed and noted missionary to India, used to tell the story of a man, a devout Hindu government official, to whom he was trying to explain the concept of the cross. The man kept reiterating to Dr. Jones that he could not possibly make sense of the crucifixion of Jesus Christ and the offer of salvation by virtue of the cross. Their conversations on this subject were circular and seemingly unsolvable to his satisfaction.

One day, through a series of circumstances, the man involved himself in an extramarital affair that tormented his conscience. He could live with himself no longer, and finally, looking into the eyes of his devoted wife, he told her the heartrending story of his betrayal. The hours and days of anguish and pain became weeks of heaviness in her heart. Yet, as she weathered the early shock, she confessed to him not only her deep sense of hurt but also the promise of her undying commitment and love.

Suddenly, almost like a flash of lightning illuminating the night sky, he found himself muttering, "Now I know what it means to see love crucified by sin." He bent his knee in repentance to the Christ who went to the cross for him, binding his heart with a new commitment to his Lord and to his wife.

If there is one description that captures the purpose of the cross, it is this: forgiveness that has been just and merciful at the same time. Christ did not die just as an example or as a martyr. He died so that the very ones who crucified him could have a way provided for their forgiveness. The cross conveys a message that is unquestionably unique. It stands in stark contrast to every other human power and human solution. This cross defines what love's entailments are.

But there is something more, and here we get to the crux of meaning. In Christian terms, love does not stand merely as an emotion or even as an expression of being reconciled to God. In a relationship with God, it ultimately flowers into worship. It is in worship alone that wonder and truth coalesce and our expression prefigures the consummation of an eternal communion. The enrichment that results from worship feeds all other relationships and helps us to hold sacred all of life's needed commitments.

D. H. Lawrence was right when he said that the deepest hunger of the human heart goes beyond love. And Thomas Wolfe was right—there is that sense of cosmic loneliness apart from God. In Christ that loneliness is conquered as the hungers of the human heart are met and the struggles of the intellect are answered.

"How is that so?" one might ask. Archbishop William Temple defined worship in these terms:

> Worship is the submission of all of our nature to God. It is the quickening of conscience by His holiness, nourishment of mind by His truth, purifying of imagination by His beauty, opening of the heart to His love, and submission of will to His purpose. All this gathered up in adoration is the greatest of all expressions of which we are capable.[10]

Life is bereft of meaning because of the essential fragmentation that results when life is viewed as nothing more than matter. But if our lives are in truth designed for the supreme purpose of worship, then the sacred binds our lives and fuses every activity with meaning, even as it enables us to resist that which desacralizes life. Thomas Merton was right when he said that man is not at peace with his fellow man because he is not at peace with himself. And he is not at peace with himself because he is not at peace with God. That inner fragmentation is corrected only by the integrity of worship. It is not accidental that in one of the most notable of all Jesus' conversations, with the woman at the well, the conversation began with her disintegrated life, littered with five broken marriages, and ended with the fulfillment of worship that sent her running back home to tell her people that she had found the source of her mending. It is vital to know that this is not worship that is just a "spiritual" act. This is worship that takes its cue from truth that has been tested against reality. In that combination, wonder blossoms into fullness.

Is there a difference between this worship and worship in other religions? Indeed, yes. At its heart and in its goals Hinduism, for example, teaches us that we are to seek union with the divine. Why union? Because the Hindu claims that we are part and parcel of this divine universe. The goal of the individual is, therefore, to discover that divinity and live it out. This is the heart of philosophical Hinduism—self-deification. One of India's premier philosophers stated forthrightly, "Man is God in a temporary state of self-forgetfulness."

This is the reason the "you" disappears in Hinduism and the meditative process is enjoined, so that we can, as individuals, merge with the one impersonal absolute—the capital "I," because there is no significant other. Union with the impersonal absolute defies language, reason, and existential realities. It does not satisfy the longing for communion. However much one may respect the intent of such teaching, we deceive ourselves if we believe that it is philosophically coherent. It is not. That is why some of the most respected Hindu philosophers and thinkers have brandished it as one of the most contradictory systems of life's purpose ever espoused.[11] Not only that, Hinduism could not survive the sterility of this kind of self-deification. Personal deities are erupted by the millions, and the temples are crowded with people seeking to *worship*. No, the suggestion of inward divinity is psychologically imprisoning, and the individual breaks away to find another.

While Hinduism goes to one extreme—the deification of the self—Islam is at the other extreme. In Islam, the distance between God and humanity is so vast that the "I" never gets close to the "him" in God. And because this distance between the two is impossible to cross, worship takes on an incredible clutter of activity, designed to bring the worshiper close. Repetition and submission take the place of the warmth of a relationship. One only need glimpse a Muslim at worship to see the difference. Yet, with all that he observes and all the rules he keeps, there is never a certainty of heaven for the common person in Islam. It is all in the will of God, they say. One's destiny is left at the mercy of an unknown will. When relationship is swallowed up by rules, political power and enforcement become the means of containment.

In the Christian message, the God who is distinct and distant came close so that we who are weak may be made strong and may be drawn close in communion with him, even while our identity is retained. The individual retains his individuality while dwelling in community. The physical retains its physicality but is transcended by the spiritual. Meaning finds its consummate purpose.

CROSSING THE BAR

Beginning with wonder in childhood and after pursuing truth in adolescence and the fulfillment of love in the adult years, all culminating in a relationship, we finally face in the end an old age that longs for hope and security.

The question that must be answered if all other answers of Jesus are to be justified is the question of life beyond the grave. The writings of Albert Camus reveal that for him death is philosophy's only problem. By contrast, at the graveside of a friend he loved, Jesus spoke these words: "I am the resurrection and the life. He who believes in me will live, even though he dies; and whoever lives and believes in me will never die" (John 11:25–26). Outside the resurrection, there is no transcending view of life. Hope ceases if there is no hope beyond the grave.

I found new life in Jesus. The Jesus I know and love today I encountered at the age of seventeen. I can now enjoy the benefit of time's distant view. Over three decades later his name and his tug in my life mean infinitely more than they did when I first surrendered my life to him. I came to him because I did not know which way to turn. I have remained with him because there is no other way I wish to turn. I came to him longing for something I did not have. I remain with him because I have something I will not trade. I came to him as a stranger. I remain with him in the most intimate of friendships. I came to him unsure about the future. I remain with him certain about my destiny. I came amid the thunderous cries of a culture that has three hundred thirty million deities. I remain with him knowing that truth cannot be all-inclusive.

I close with those glorious words of Malcolm Muggeridge on his discovery of a personal relationship with Jesus Christ:

> I may, I suppose, regard myself as a relatively successful man. People occasionally stare at me in the streets, that's fame; I can fairly easily earn enough money to qualify for admission to the higher slopes of the Internal Revenue Service. That's success. Furnished with money and a little fame, even the elderly, if they care to, may partake of friendly diversions. That's pleasure. It might happen once in a while that something I said or wrote was sufficiently heeded for me to persuade myself that it represented a serious impact on our time. That's fulfillment. Yet, I say to you, and I beg you to believe me, multiply these tiny triumphs by millions, add them all up together, and they are nothing, less than nothing. Indeed, a positive impediment measured against one drop of that living water Christ offers to the spiritually thirsty, irrespective of who or what they are.[12]

Solomon also came to the same postscript. "Under the sun"—that is, in a closed system—all is meaningless. With the relationship God offers in the Son, a relationship that opens up the eternal, wonder, truth, love, and security connect. When one claims to have found meaning, that meaning must bring together these four elements. And all four are found in the person of Jesus Christ, who alone brings life meaning by meeting the test at every age of life.

We have moved from the world of a child to the sunset years of life in our pursuit of meaning, and we have seen how this search for meaning fails if our lives are lived without God. Augustine said it well: "You have made us for yourself, and our hearts are restless until they find their rest in thee." The apostle Paul triumphantly reminded us that because of who we are in Christ, every deed can be done with purpose: "Whatever you do, do it all for the glory of God" (1 Cor. 10:31).

Without such glorious purpose in life, the search for meaning can leave us like Sisyphus, weak, burdened, and despairing. But the Savior, Jesus, calls to us, saying, "Come to me, all you who are weary and burdened, and I will give you rest" (Matt. 11:28). Those who respond to the call of Christ know what meaning is. Those who do not still bear the burden of Sisyphus.

AFTERWORD

JOSH MCDOWELL

There is a principle of law that says that a witness may give testimony only about matters for which he or she has had personal experience. "I saw that the light was red" is competent and admissible testimony; "I heard him say the light was red," with some exceptions, is not. The law favors and values eyewitnesses, people who give their own accounts of what they have actually seen and experienced. Moreover, there is something about the report of a personal experience that is difficult to challenge or deny. One may attempt on cross-examination to prove the witness who saw the red light was color blind or perhaps biased, but a healthy and disinterested witness who says the light was red is a significant obstacle to proving it was green.

This principle holds true out of court as well. Personal testimony of personal experience is both compelling and difficult to challenge. If Tom were to tell you that he caught a ten-pound largemouth bass yesterday, you would probably judge the veracity of his story based on what you knew of his reputation for truthfulness. On the other hand, if he said he was walking on water at the time he caught the fish, you might question his sanity. But what if you knew Tom to be a perfectly sane and scrupulously honest person? And what if several other honest and sane people told you they had witnessed the event? This is not unlike the predicament faced by skeptics who hear the accounts of people who have found Jesus. Billions of sane and honest people have reported a truly incredible story, the story of passing from death to life, of being lost and then found, of being blind and then seeing. There are billions of eyewitnesses to the life-changing power of the gospel. And many were once skeptics themselves. One such former skeptic is Josh McDowell, a man whose personal testimony is both compelling and difficult to challenge. This successful author and international speaker, who is clearly a sane and honest man, reports that a miracle occurred in his life and that he is now a new creature because of Jesus Christ. The good news is that you too can share in this miracle. Having considered the evidence in support of the Christian faith, we invite you now to consider these closing words of our final eyewitness to the life-changing power of Jesus Christ.

A SKEPTIC'S QUEST: JOSH McDOWELL'S TESTIMONY

Thomas Aquinas wrote, "There is within every soul a thirst for happiness and meaning." As a teenager, I exemplified that statement. I wanted to be happy and to find meaning for my life. I wanted the answers to three basic questions: Who am I? Why am I here? Where am I going? I would estimate that 90 percent of people age forty and younger cannot answer those three questions. But I was thirsty to know what life was about. So as a young student, I started looking for answers.

Where I was brought up, everyone seemed to be into religion. I thought maybe I would find my answers in being religious, so I started attending church. I went to church morning, afternoon, and evening. But I felt worse inside church than I did outside. I was brought up on a farm in Michigan, and most farmers are very practical. My dad, who was a farmer, taught me, "If something doesn't work, chuck it." So I chucked religion.

Then I thought that education might have the answers to my quest for happiness and meaning, so I enrolled in a university. What a disappointment! You can find a lot of things at a university, but enrolling there to find truth and meaning in life is virtually a lost cause.

I was by far the most unpopular student among the faculty of the first university I attended. I used to buttonhole professors in their offices, seeking the answers to my questions. When they saw me coming, they would turn out the lights, pull down the shades, and lock the door so they wouldn't have to talk to me. I soon realized that the university didn't have the answers I was seeking. Faculty members and my fellow students had just as many problems, frustrations, and unanswered questions about life as I did. A few years ago I saw a student walking around campus with a sign on his back: "Don't follow me. I'm lost." That is how everyone in the university seemed to me. Education was not the answer.

Prestige must be the way to go, I decided. It just seemed right to find a noble cause, give yourself to it, and become well known. The people with the most prestige in the university were the student leaders, who also controlled the purse strings. So I ran for various student offices and got elected. It was great to know everyone on campus, make important decisions, and spend the university's money doing what I wanted to do. But the thrill soon wore off as with everything else I had tried.

Every Monday morning I woke with a headache because of the night before. My attitude was, *Here we go again, another five boring days.* Happiness for me revolved around my three party nights a week: Friday, Saturday, and Sunday. Then the whole boring cycle started over again. I felt so frustrated, even desperate. My goal was to find my identity and purpose in life, but everything I tried left me empty, without answers.

About that time I noticed a small group of people on campus—eight students and two faculty—and there was something different about them. They seemed to know where they were going in life. And they had a quality I deeply admire in people: conviction.

But there was something more about this group that caught my attention. Love. These students and professors not only loved each other, they loved and cared for people outside their group. They didn't just talk about love; they got involved in loving others. It was something totally foreign to me, and I wanted it. So I decided to make friends with this group of people.

About two weeks later, I was sitting at a table in the student union talking with some members of this group. Soon the conversation turned to the topic of God. I was pretty insecure about this subject, so I put on a big front to cover it up. I leaned back in my chair acting like I couldn't care less. "Christianity, ha!" I blustered. "That's for the weaklings, not the intellectuals." Down deep, I really wanted what they had. But with my pride and my position in the university, I didn't want *them* to know that I wanted what they had. Then I turned to one of the girls in the group and said, "Tell me, what changed your lives? Why are you so different from the other students and faculty?"

She looked me straight in the eye and said two words I never expected to hear in an intelligent discussion on a university campus: "Jesus Christ."

"Jesus Christ?" I snapped. "Don't give me that kind of garbage. I'm fed up with religion, the Bible, and the church."

She quickly shot back, "I didn't say 'religion.' I said 'Jesus Christ.'"

Taken aback by the girl's courage and conviction, I apologized for my attitude. "But I'm sick and tired of religion and religious people," I added. "I don't want anything to do with it."

Then my new friends issued a challenge I couldn't believe. They challenged me, a pre-law student, to examine intellectually the claim that Jesus Christ is God's Son. I thought it was a joke. These Christians were so dumb. How could something as flimsy as Christianity stand up to an intellectual examination? So I scoffed at their challenge.

But they didn't let up. They kept challenging me day after day, and finally they backed me into the corner. I became so irritated at their insistence that I finally accepted their challenge, not to prove anything but to refute them. I decided to write a book that would make an intellectual joke of Christianity. So I left the university and traveled throughout the United States and Europe to seek the evidence that Christianity was a sham.

One day I was sitting in a library in London, England, and I sensed a voice within me say, "Josh, you don't have a leg to stand on." I immediately suppressed it. But just about every day after that I heard that inner voice. The more I researched, the more I heard that voice. I returned to the United States and to the university, but I couldn't sleep at night. I would go to bed at ten o'clock and lie awake until four in the morning trying to refute the overwhelming evidence that Jesus Christ is God's Son.

I began to realize that I was being intellectually dishonest. My mind told me that the claims of Christ were indeed true, but my will was being pulled in another direction. I had placed so much emphasis on finding the truth, but I wasn't willing to follow it once I saw it. I had sensed Christ's personal challenge to me in Revelation 3:20: "Here I am! I stand at the door and knock. If anyone hears my voice and opens the door, I will come in and eat with him, and he with me." But becoming a Christian seemed so ego shattering to me. I couldn't think of a faster way to ruin my good times.

I knew I had to resolve this inner conflict because it was driving me crazy. I had always considered myself an open-minded person, so I decided to put Christ's claims to the supreme test. One night at home in Union City, Michigan, at the end of my second year at the university, I became a Christian. Someone may say, "How do you know you became a Christian?" I was there! I got alone with a Christian friend, and I prayed four things that established my relationship with God.

First, I said, "Lord Jesus, thank you for dying on the cross for me." I realized that if I were the only person on earth, Christ would have still died for me. You may think the irrefutable intellectual evidence brought me to Christ, but the evidence was only God's way of getting his foot in the door of my life. What brought me to Christ was the realization that he loved me enough to die for me.

Second, I said, "I confess that I am a sinner." No one had to tell me that. I knew there were things in my life that were incompatible with a holy, just, righteous God. The Bible says, "If we confess our sins, he is faithful and just and will forgive us our sins and purify us from all unrighteousness" (1 John 1:9). So I said, "Lord, forgive me."

Third, I said, "Right now, in the best way I know how, I open the door of my life and I place my trust in you as Savior and Lord. Take over the control of my life. Change me from the inside out. Make me the type of person you created me to be."

The last thing I prayed was, "Thank you for coming into my life."

After I prayed, nothing happened. There was no bolt of lightning. I didn't sprout angel's wings. If anything, I actually felt worse after I prayed, almost physically sick. I was afraid I had made an emotional decision I would later regret intellectually. But more than that, I was afraid of what my friends would say when they found out. I really felt I had gone off the deep end.

But over the next eighteen months, my entire life was changed. One of the biggest changes occurred in how I viewed people. At the university, I had mapped out the next twenty-five years of my life. My ultimate goal was to become governor of Michigan. I planned to accomplish my goal by using people in order to climb the ladder of political success, because I figured people were to be used. But after I placed my trust in Christ, my thinking changed. Instead of using others to serve me, I wanted to be used to serve others. Becoming other-centered instead of self-centered was a dramatic change in my life.

Another area that started to change was my bad temper. I used to blow my stack if somebody just looked at me wrong. I still have the scars from almost killing a man during my first year at the university. My bad temper was so ingrained that I didn't consciously seek to change it. Then one day I was faced with a crisis that ordinarily would have set me off, but my bad temper was gone. I'm not perfect in this area, but the change in my life has been significant and dramatic.

Perhaps the most significant change has been in the area of hatred and bitterness. I grew up filled with hatred, primarily aimed at one man whom I hated more than anyone else on the face of the earth. I despised everything that this man stood for. I can remember as a young boy lying in bed at night plotting how I could kill this man without being caught by the police. That man was my father.

When I was growing up, my father was the town drunk. I hardly ever knew him sober. My friends at school joked about my dad lying in the gutter downtown, making a fool of himself. Their jokes hurt me deeply, but I never let anyone know. I laughed along with them. It was a very secret pain.

I would sometimes find my mother in the barn, lying in the manure behind the cows where my dad had beaten her with a hose until she couldn't get up. My hatred seethed as I vowed to myself, "When I am strong enough, I'm going to kill him." When Dad was drunk and visitors were coming over, I would grab him around the neck, pull him out to the barn, and tie him up. Then I would park his truck behind the silo and tell everyone he had gone to a meeting so we wouldn't be embarrassed as a family. When I tied up his hands and feet, I looped part of the rope around his neck. I just hoped he would try to get away and choke himself.

Two months before I graduated from high school, I walked into the house after a date to hear my mother sobbing. I ran into her room, and she sat up in bed. "Son, your father has broken my heart," she said. Then she put her arms around me and pulled me close. "I have lost the will to live. All I want to do is live until you graduate, then I want to die."

I graduated two months later, and the next Friday my mother died. I believe she died of a broken heart. I hated my father for that. Had I not left home a few months after the funeral to attend college, I might have killed him.

But after I made a decision to place my trust in Jesus as Savior and Lord, the love of God inundated my life. He took my hatred for my father and turned it upside down. Five months after becoming a Christian, I found myself looking my dad right in the eye and saying, "Dad, I love you." I did not want to love that man, but I did. God's love had changed my heart.

After I transferred to Wheaton University, I was in a serious car accident, the victim of a drunk driver. I was moved home from the hospital to recover, and my father came to see me. Remarkably, he was sober that day. He seemed uneasy, pacing in my room. Then he blurted out, "How can you love a father like me?"

I said, "Dad, six months ago I hated you; I despised you. But I have put my trust in Jesus Christ, received God's forgiveness, and he has changed my life. I can't explain it all, Dad. But God has taken away my hatred for you and replaced it with love."

We talked for nearly an hour, then he said, "Son, if God can do in my life what I've seen him do in yours, then I want to give him the opportunity." He prayed, "God, if you're really God and Jesus died on the cross to forgive me for what I've done to my family, I need you. If Jesus can do in my life what I've seen him do in the life of my son, then I want to trust him as Savior and Lord." Hearing my dad pray that prayer from his heart was one of the greatest joys of my life.

After I trusted Christ, my life was changed in six to eighteen months. But my father's life was changed right before my eyes. It was as if someone reached down and switched on a light inside him. He touched alcohol only once after that. He got the drink as far as his lips, and that was it—after forty years of drinking! He didn't need it anymore. Fourteen months later, he died from complications of his alcoholism. But in that fourteen-month period, over a hundred people in the area around my tiny hometown committed their lives to Jesus Christ because of the change they saw in the town drunk, my dad.

You can laugh at Christianity. You can mock and ridicule it. But it works. If you trust Christ, start watching your attitudes and actions, because Jesus Christ is in the business of changing lives. But Christianity is not something I can shove down your throat or force on you. All I can do is tell you what I have learned and experienced. After that, what you do with Christ is your decision.

Here are four principles that clearly explain the gospel message and the truth of what God has done through his Son Jesus Christ for each and every human being.

1. God loves you personally and created you to know him personally.

While the Bible is filled with assurances of God's love, perhaps the most telling verse is John 3:16: "For God so loved the world that he gave his one and only Son, that whoever believes in him shall not perish but have eternal life."

God not only loves each of us enough to give his only Son for us, but he desires that we come to know him personally: "Now this is eternal life: that they may know you, the only true God, and Jesus Christ, whom you have sent" (John 17:3).

What, then, prevents us from knowing God personally?

2. Men and women are sinful and separated from God, so we cannot know him personally or experience his love.

We were all created to have fellowship with God, but because of humankind's stubborn self-will, we chose to go our own independent way, and fellowship with God was broken. This self-will, characterized by an attitude of active rebellion or passive indifference, is evidence of what the Bible calls sin. "For all have sinned and fall short of the glory of God" (Rom. 3:23).

The Bible also tells us that "the wages of sin is death" (Rom. 6:23), or spiritual separation from God. When we are in this state, a great gulf separates us from God, because he cannot tolerate sin. People often try to bridge the gulf by doing good works or devoting themselves to religious practices, but the Bible clearly teaches that there is only one way to bridge this gulf.

3. Jesus Christ is God's only provision for our sin. Through him alone we can know God personally and experience his love.

God's Word records three important facts to verify this principle: (1) Jesus Christ died in our place; (2) he rose from the dead; and (3) he is our only way to God:

But God demonstrates his own love for us in this: While we were still sinners, Christ died for us.

Romans 5:8

Christ died for our sins. . . . He was buried. . . . He was raised on the third day according to the Scriptures. . . . He appeared to Peter, and then to the Twelve. After that, he appeared to more than five hundred.

1 Corinthians 15:3–6

Jesus answered, "I am the way and the truth and the life. No one comes to the Father except through me."

John 14:6

Thus, God has taken the loving initiative to bridge the gulf that separates us from him by sending his Son Jesus Christ to die on the cross in our place to pay the penalty for our sin. But it is not enough just to know these truths.

4. We must individually receive Jesus Christ as Savior and Lord; then we can know God personally and experience his love.

John 1:12 records, "Yet to all who received him, to those who believed in his name, he gave the right to become children of God." What does it mean to receive Christ? Scripture tells us that we receive Christ through faith—not through good works or religious endeavors: "For it is by grace you have been saved, through faith—and this not from yourselves, it is the gift of God—not by works, so that no one can boast" (Eph. 2:8–9). We're also told that receiving Christ means to invite him personally into our lives: Christ said, "Here I am! I stand at the door and knock. If anyone hears my voice and opens the door, I will come in and eat with him" (Rev. 3:20). Thus, receiving Christ involves turning to God from self and trusting Christ to come into our lives to forgive our sins and to make us the kind of people he wants us to be.

If you are not sure whether you have ever committed your life to Jesus Christ, I encourage you to do so today! Perhaps the prayer I prayed would help you: "Lord Jesus, I need you. Thank you for dying on the cross for me. I confess that I am a sinner. Forgive me and cleanse me. Right this moment I trust you as Savior and Lord. Make me the type of person you created me to be. Thank you for coming into my life. In Christ's name, amen."

If this prayer expresses the desire of your heart, why not pray it now? If you mean it sincerely, Jesus Christ will come into your life, just as he promised in Revelation 3:20. He keeps his promises! And there is another key promise to write indelibly in your mind:

> And this is the testimony: God has given us eternal life, and this life is in his Son. He who has the Son has life; he who does not have the Son of God does not have life. I write these things to you who believe in the name of the Son of God so that you may know that you have eternal life.
>
> 1 John 5:11–13

That's right—the man or woman who personally receives Christ as Savior and Lord is assured of everlasting life with him in heaven. And he or she will also discover that a relationship with Jesus Christ also gives life purpose and meaning.

For years I searched for the answer to the question, What will bring happiness and meaning to my life? I thought I would find the answer in organized religion, education, and prestige, but each time I ended up disappointed and unfulfilled. Ultimately, I discovered that the answer could be found only in the Lord Jesus Christ.

If today the truth became clear to you and you made the decision to receive Jesus Christ as your Savior and Lord, let me be the first to welcome you into the family of God. I heartily encourage you to attend and participate in a church where the Lord Jesus Christ is glorified, where the Bible is honored and taught, and where believers love, encourage, and pray for one another. Study God's Word regularly and apply it to your daily life. Share his love with your family, friends, and neighbors. And remember, when you received Christ by faith, many wonderful things happened:

1. Christ came into your life (Col. 1:27; Rev. 3:20).
2. Your sins were forgiven (Col. 1:14).
3. You became a child of God (John 1:12).
4. You received eternal life (John 5:24).
5. You began the great adventure for which God created you (John 10:10; 1 Thess. 5:18).

I can't think of anything more wonderful than that!

NOTES

Introduction

1. Admittedly, the first generalization may be true, but in all fairness it probably applies to everyone, not just Christians. In general, most people are not very intellectual and are often anti-intellectual.

2. The many Christian denominations, from Roman Catholics to Quakers, may formulate the definition of *Christian* with varying degrees of specificity or doctrinal emphasis. But we all accept as true and foundational the words of the apostle Paul: "That if you confess with your mouth, 'Jesus is Lord,' and believe in your heart that God raised him from the dead, you will be saved" (Rom. 10:9). The particular expression of faith described here by Paul, if genuine, brings with it a supernatural transaction that truly changes us. Jesus himself described it as being "born again" (John 3:7), and Paul said, "If anyone is in Christ, he is a new creation; the old has gone, the new has come! All this is from God" (2 Cor. 5:17–18).

Chapter 1

1. Allan Bloom, *The Closing of the American Mind* (New York: Simon & Schuster, 1987), 25.

2. There are many works that defend the notion that the Bible teaches objective moral norms. See, for example, Norman L. Geisler, *Christian Ethics: Options and Issues* (Grand Rapids: Baker, 1989).

3. Materialism is the worldview that holds that matter is all that exists. Since the God of the Bible is nonmaterial, if materialism is true, the Christian God does not exist.

4. Hadley Arkes's work, *First Things: An Inquiry into the First Principles of Morality and Justice* (Princeton, N.J.: Princeton University Press, 1986), was instrumental in helping to better understand the difference between the two statements.

5. For an overview of the abortion debate from different sides, see Louis P. Pojman and Francis J. Beckwith, eds., *The Abortion Controversy 25 Years After Roe v. Wade: A Reader*, 2d ed. (Belmont, Calif.: Wadworth, 1998).

6. See, for example, Louis P. Pojman, *Ethics: Discovering Right and Wrong*, 2d ed. (Belmont, Calif.: Wadsworth, 1995). Pojman, a supporter of abortion rights, is a critic of moral relativism as well as a defender of moral objectivism. For his defense of the pro-choice position, see Pojman, "Abortion: A Defense of the Personhood Argument," in *Abortion Controversy*, 275–90.

7. Arkes, *First Things*, 149.

8. Ibid., 132.

9. See C. S. Lewis, *Mere Christianity* (New York: Simon & Schuster, 1996), 26.

10. See James Rachels, "A Critique of Ethical Relativism," in *Philosophy: The Quest for Truth*, ed. Louis P. Pojman (Belmont, Calif.: Wadsworth, 1989), 317–25.

11. Ibid., 322–23.

12. Sophisticated pro-choice advocates argue that fetuses are not human persons, and for this reason, fetuses do not have a right to life if their life hinders the liberty of a being who is a person (i.e., the pregnant woman). See H. Tristram Englehardt Jr., "The Ontology of Abortion," *Ethics* 84 (1973–74): 217–34; Michael Tooley, *Abortion and Infanticide* (New York: Oxford, 1983); Michael Tooley, "In Defense of Abortion and Infanticide," in *Abortion Controversy*, 209–33; Pojman, "Abortion: A Defense of the Personhood Argument," in *Abortion Controversy*, 275–90; and Mary Ann Warren, "On the Moral and Legal Status of Abortion," in *Problem of Abortion*, 2d ed., ed. Joel Feinberg (Belmont, Calif.: Wadsworth,

1984), 102–19. For critiques of these and other views, see Francis J. Beckwith, *Politically Correct Death: Answering the Arguments for Abortion Rights* (Grand Rapids: Baker, 1993); Francis J. Beckwith, *Abortion and the Sanctity of Human Life* (Joplin, Mo.: College Press, 2000); Patrick Lee, *Abortion and Unborn Human Life* (Washington, D.C.: The Catholic University of America Press, 1996); J. P. Moreland and Scott B. Rae, *Body and Soul* (Downers Grove, Ill.: InterVarsity Press, 2000); Stephen Schwarz, *The Moral Question of Abortion* (Chicago: Loyola University Press, 1990); and Don Marquis, "Why Abortion Is Immoral," *The Journal of Philosophy* 86 (April 1989): 183–202.

13. J. P. Moreland, *Scaling the Secular City* (Grand Rapids: Baker, 1987), 92.

14. Ibid., 243.

15. Tom L. Beauchamp, *Philosophical Ethics: An Introduction to Moral Philosophy* (New York: McGraw-Hill, 1982), 42.

16. This dialogue is presented in slightly different form in Francis J. Beckwith and Gregory P. Koukl, *Relativism: Feet Firmly Planted in Mid-Air* (Grand Rapids: Baker, 1998), 74.

17. Xiaorong Li, "Postmodernism and Universal Human Rights: Why Theory and Reality Don't Mix," *Free Inquiry* 18, no. 4 (fall 1998): 28.

18. The argument I am presenting in this section was developed by Gregory P. Koukl in *Relativism*, chapters 14 and 15. My presentation in this chapter differs slightly from Koukl's version of the argument. The argument also has affinities with C. S. Lewis's argument in *Mere Christianity* (New York: Macmillan, 1948), chaps. 1–5.

19. Paul Copan, "Can Michael Martin Be a Moral Realist?: *Sic et Non*," *Philosophia Christi* series 2, 1, no. 2 (1999): 58.

20. Koukl, *Relativism*, 166.

21. Ibid., 167.

22. Robert Wright, *The Moral Animal—Why We Are the Way We Are: The New Science of Evolutionary Psychology* (New York: Pantheon, 1994), 23.

Chapter 2

1. This follows the discussion in "Truth, Nature of," in *Baker Encyclopedia of Christian Apologetics*, ed. Norman L. Geisler (Grand Rapids: Baker, 1999), 741–45.

2. William James, *Pragmatism and Other Essays* (New York: Washington Square Press, 1963), 160–61.

3. Søren Kierkegaard, *Concluding Unscientific Postscripts* (Princeton, N.J.: Princeton University Press, 1968), 169ff.

4. Popular New Ager Shirley MacLaine wrote, "Stop judging and evaluating what you're getting at. Leave your mind out of this. Just get out of your intellectual ways" (MacLaine, *Dancing in the Light* [New York: Bantam, 1985], 328).

5. For a classic defense of the correspondence view of truth, see Thomas Aquinas, *On Truth*, trans. J. V. McGlynn (Chicago: H. Regnery, 1952–54); and St. Anselm, *Truth, Freedom, and Evil: Three Philosophical Dialogues*, trans. Jasper Hopkins et al. (New York: Harper & Row, 1967).

6. David Hume, *Enquiry Concerning Human Understanding*, ed. Chas. W. Hendel (New York: Liberal Arts, 1955), last lines of the book.

7. Ibid., IV.2.

8. David Hume, *Dialogues Concerning Natural Religion* (1779; reprint, Indianapolis: Bobbs-Merril, 1962).

9. Immanuel Kant, *Critique of Pure Reason*, trans. Norman Kemp Smith (New York: St. Martin's, 1965).

10. Ibid., 173–74.

11. Ibid., 393–94.

12. By now it is probably clear that logical positivism is also self-defeating. How do we verify that the proposition "The means of verification determine the meaningfulness of a proposition" is true? Certainly not by mathematics or science! Hence, logical positivism is, by its own standards, meaningless.

13. For a good critique of agnosticism, see Robert Flint, *Agnosticism* (New York: Scribner's, 1903).

14. N. L. Geisler, "Finite Godism," in *Baker Encyclopedia of Christian Apologetics*, 246–49.

15. For a penetrating critque of Kant, see Stuart Hackett, *The Resurrection of Theism* (Chicago: Moody, 1957), part 1.

16. See the discussion in N. L. Geisler, "Hume, David," in *Baker Encyclopedia of Christian Apologetics*, 342–44.

17. David Hume, *The Letters of David Hume*, 2 vols., ed. J. Y. T. Greig (Oxford: Clarendon Press, 1932), I.187

18. For further discussion, see N. L. Geisler, "Kant, Immanuel," in *Baker Encyclopedia of Christian Apologetics*, 401–5.

Chapter 3

1. A more conventional personal testimony, from which I have adapted several sentences and paragraphs, may be found in the preface to my book *Revenge of Conscience: Politics and the Fall of Man* (Dallas: Spence Publishing, 1999).

2. James Q. Wilson, *The Moral Sense* (New York: Free Press, 1993), xiii, 10–11, 18, 72, 82, 218, and 225–26: "Let me . . . stress that these are four aspects of the moral *sense*, not rules or laws. . . . [M]y saying that people have a moral sense is not the same thing as saying that they have direct, intuitive knowledge of certain moral rules. . . . If we find such common inclinations, we will not have found a set of moral rules. . . . Deciding that mankind has at some level a shared moral nature is not the same thing as deciding that men are everywhere in possession of a set of moral absolutes. . . . [T]he existence of a natural moral sense does not require the existence of universal moral rules. . . . [Parents care for children] not because a rule is being enforced, but because an impulse is being obeyed. . . . I agree that there is a universal human nature, but disagree that one can deduce from it more than a handful of rules or solutions to any but the most elemental (albeit vitally important) human problems. . . . I am reckless enough to think that many conducting [the search for moral universals] have looked in the wrong places for the wrong things because they have sought for universal rules rather than universal dispositions."

3. "By a moral sense," he says, "I mean an intuitive or directly felt belief about how one *ought* to act when one is free to act voluntarily." As though to remove any doubt that *ought* means rules to him too, he adds, "by 'ought,' I mean an obligation binding on all people similarly situated." On a later page he seems to concede the point himself. "What [researchers] find to be binding everywhere are those *rules* governing the fundamental conflicts of everyday, intimate life—keeping promises, respecting property, acting fairly, and avoiding unprovoked assaults—*that have been the subject of earlier chapters in this book*" (ibid., 12, 142, emphasis added).

4. Neale Donald Walsch, *Conversations with God*, bk. 1 (New York: G. P. Putnam's Sons, 1995), 124.

5. G. K. Chesterton, *Orthodoxy* (New York: John Lane, 1909), chap. 5, "The Flag of the World."

Chapter 4

1. James Collins, *God in Modern Philosophy* (Chicago: Henry Regnery, 1959).

2. David Hilbert, "On the Infinite," in *Philosophy of Mathematics*, ed. with an introduction by Paul Benacerraf and Hillary Putnam (Englewood Cliffs, N.J.: Prentice-Hall, 1964), 139, 141.

3. Fred Hoyle, *Astronomy and Cosmology* (San Francisco: W. H. Freeman, 1975), 658.

4. Anthony Kenny, *The Five Ways: St. Thomas Aquinas' Proofs of God's Existence* (New York: Schocken Books, 1969), 66.

5. David Hume, *The Letters of David Hume*, 2 vols., ed. J. Y. T. Greig (Oxford: Clarendon Press, 1932), I:187, letter to John Stewart, February 1754.

6. Kai Nielsen, *Reason and Practice* (New York: Harper & Row, 1971), 48.

7. Arthur Eddington, *The Expanding Universe* (New York: Macmillan, 1933), 124.

8. See James T. Cushing, Arthur Fine, and Sheldon Goldstein, *Bohmian Mechanics and Quantum Theory: An Appraisal*, Boston Studies in the Philosophy of Science 184 (Dordrecht, Holland: Kluwer Academic Publishers, 1996).

9. See John Barrow and Frank Tipler, *The Anthropic Cosmological Principle* (Oxford: Clarendon Press, 1986), 441.

10. See Bernulf Kanitscheider, "Does Physical Cosmology Transcend the Limits of Naturalistic Reasoning?" in *Studies on Mario Bunge's "Treatise,"* ed. P. Weingartner and G. J. W. Dorn (Amsterdam: Rodopi, 1990), 346–47.

11. Robert Deltete, critical notice of *Theism, Atheism, and Big Bang Cosmology*, *Zygon* 30 (1995): 656 (the review was attributed to J. Leslie due to an editorial mistake at *Zygon*).

12. J. L. Mackie, *Times Literary Supplement* (5 February 1982): 126.

13. See, for example, Abraham Robinson, "Metamathematical Problems," *Journal of Symbolic Logic* 38 (1973): 500–516.

14. See Alexander Abian, *The Theory of Sets and Transfinite Arithmetic* (Philadelphia: W. B. Saunders, 1965), 68; B. Rotman and G. T. Kneebone, *The Theory of Sets and Transfinite Numbers* (London: Oldbourne, 1966), 61.

15. See I. D. Novikov and Ya. B. Zeldovich, "Physical Processes near Cosmological Singularities," *Annual Review of Astronomy and Astrophysics* 11 (1973): 401–2; A. Borde and A. Vilenkin, "Eternal Inflation and the Initial Singularity," *Physical Review Letters* 72 (1994): 3305, 3307.

16. Christopher Isham, "Creation of the Universe as a Quantum Process," in *Physics, Philosophy and Theology: A Common Quest for Understanding*, ed. R. J. Russell, W. R. Stoeger, and G. V. Coyne (Vatican City: Vatican Observatory, 1988), 385–87.

17. See John D. Barrow, *Theories of Everything* (Oxford: Clarendon Press, 1991), 67–68.

18. Stephen Hawking and Roger Penrose, *The Nature of Space and Time*, The Isaac Newton Institute Series of Lectures (Princeton, N.J.: Princeton University Press, 1996), 20.

19. On this distinction, see the discussion by Richard Swinburne, *The Existence of God*, rev. ed. (Oxford: Clarendon Press, 1991), 32–48.

20. Stephen W. Hawking, *A Brief History of Time* (New York: Bantam Books, 1988), 123.

21. P. C. W. Davies, *Other Worlds* (London: Dent, 1980), 160–61, 168–69.

22. P. C. W. Davies, "The Anthropic Principle," *Particle and Nuclear Physics* 10 (1983): 28.

23. John Leslie, *Universes* (London: Routledge, 1989), 202.

24. P. C. W. Davies, *The Mind of God* (New York: Simon & Schuster, 1992), 169.

25. Barrow and Tipler, *Anthropic Cosmological Principle*, 15.

26. See William A. Dembski, *The Design Inference: Eliminating Chance through Small Probabilities*, Cambridge Studies in Probability, Induction, and Decision Theory (Cambridge: Cambridge University Press, 1998), 167–74.

27. J. C. Polkinghorne, *Serious Talk: Science and Religion in Dialogue* (Valley Forge, Pa.: Trinity Press International, 1995), 6.

28. Robert Brandenburger, personal communication.

29. See Michael Behe, *Darwin's Black Box* (New York: Free Press, 1996), 51–73.

30. Bertrand Russell, *Human Society in Ethics and Politics* (New York: Simon & Schuster, 1955), 124.

31. Michael Ruse, "Evolutionary Theory and Christian Ethics," in *The Darwinian Paradigm*, ed. Michael Ruse (London: Routledge, 1989), 262–69.

32. John Healey, fund-raising letter, 1991.

33. Richard Taylor, *Ethics, Faith, and Reason* (Englewood Cliffs, N.J.: Prentice-Hall, 1985), 83.

34. Ibid., 83–84.

35. See Douglas Geivett, *Can a Good God Allow Evil?* in this same series.

36. John Hick, introduction to *The Existence of God*, ed. with an introduction by John Hick, Problems of Philosophy Series (New York: Macmillan, 1964), 13–14.

37. William Alston, "Religious Diversity and Perceptual Knowledge of God," *Faith and Philosophy* 5 (1988): 433–48.

Chapter 5

1. Tertullian, *The Prescription against Heretics*, 7.

2. Some of these attributes (e.g., immutability, eternality, and simplicity) have been challenged by recent evangelicals called Neotheists. See Clark Pinnock et al., *The Openness of God* (Downers Grove, Ill.: InterVarsity Press, 1994). However, they agree that God is an eternal, infinite, and necessary being who created the universe out of nothing *(ex nihilo)*, which is all that is necessary to establish that the God of the Bible is the one true God.

3. See William Lane Craig's discussion in chapter 4.

4. God's necessity follows logically from his pure actuality, for pure act has no potential not to exist. And what has no potential for nonexistence must exist (necessary existence). Further, necessity follows from aseity, for a self-existent being is an independent being. And what has an independent existence is a necessary existence. Finally, God's necessity follows from his uncausality, for what is uncaused exists independently, and what exists independently is a necessary existence.

5. See discussion below.

6. See Hugh Ross's contribution to this book in chapter 8, and John D. Barrow and Frank J.

Tipler, *The Anthropic Cosmological Principle* (New York: Oxford University Press, 1989).

7. See William Lane Craig, *The Kalam Cosmological Argument* (London: Macmillan, 1979).

8. See Thomas Aquinas, *Summa Theologica*, 1.2.3.

9. If all beings that exist are contingent, then they could all not exist. But if they did, then nonexistence could have been the cause of their existence. But nothing cannot produce something. It takes something to produce something.

10. Of course, since God created the temporal world, he can relate to time without being in time, the same way the Creator can relate to his creation without being a creature.

11. Of course, God can make a finite being, and he is infinite. But finitude is not being; it is a mode or condition under which a finite being has being. The same is true of contingency, createdness, and so on. Since the uncreated cannot make another uncreated being, it follows that only created beings can be created.

12. See William Paley, *Evidence of Christianity* (London, 1851).

13. Michael J. Behe, *Darwin's Black Box* (New York: Free Press, 1996), 187.

14. Ibid., 160.

15. Ibid., 232–33.

16. This argument does not show that everything said about this God in the Bible is true. It merely demonstrates that the kind of God described in the Bible actually exists.

17. See St. Augustine, *City of God*, 8.6; 11:10; Thomas Aquinas, *Summa Theologica*, 1.3.1–3.

18. God has power he has not used, but he has no capacity that is not actualized. In fact, he has nothing that has been actualized. He is the unactualized actuality and actualizer of all other things.

19. See Paul Tillich, *Systematic Theology* (Chicago: University of Chicago Press, 1951), 1.18–28.

Chapter 6

1. J. L. Mackie, *The Miracle of Theism* (Oxford: Clarendon Press, 1982), 11–12.

2. See, for example, Nicholas Humphrey, *Leaps of Faith: Science, Miracles, and the Search for Supernatural Consolation* (New York: Basic Books, 1996).

3. William P. Alston, "God's Action in the World," in *Divine and Human Language: Essays in Philosophical Theology* (Ithaca, N.Y.: Cornell University Press, 1989), 207.

4. For a positive account of "The Evidential Value of Miracles," see my essay by that title in *In Defense of Miracles: A Comprehensive Case for God's Action in History*, ed. R. Douglas Geivett and Gary R. Habermas (Downers Grove, Ill.: InterVarsity Press, 1997), 178–95.

5. This places us in the neighborhood of other distinctions leading to the identification of yet more varieties of skepticism about miracles. The main difference is between (1) those skeptics who allow that an actual event could prove to be miraculous on the basis of historical evidence that is in some sense available but so far not yet fully appreciated or known, and (2) those skeptics who allow that testimonial and historical evidence could in principle support belief in the actuality of miracles but suppose or suspect that the actual testimonial and historical evidence that exists is such that it does not support belief in the actuality of miracles.

6. Claude Lévi-Strauss, *De Près et de Loin* (Paris: n.p., 1988), quoted in Eric Hobsbawm, *The Age of Extremes: A History of the World, 1914–1991* (New York: Vintage Books, 1994), 522.

7. Roger Trigg, *Rationality and Science: Can Science Explain Everything?* (Oxford: Blackwell, 1993), 13.

8. T. H. Huxley, quoted in Alan H. Guth, *The Inflationary Universe: The Quest for a New Theory of Cosmic Origins* (Reading, Mass.: Perseus Books, 1997), xiii.

9. Stephen W. Hawking, *A Brief History of Time: From the Big Bang to Black Holes* (Toronto: Bantam Books, 1988).

10. See Jerry Adler, "Reading God's Mind," *Newsweek*, 13 June 1988, 56.

11. Hawking, *Brief History*, 175.

12. H. D. Lewis, *Philosophy of Religion* (London: Cox & Wyman, 1965), 301.

13. Martin Curd, "Miracles as Violations of Laws of Nature," in *Faith, Freedom, and Rationality: Philosophy of Religion Today*, ed. Jeff Jordan and Daniel Howard-Snyder (Lanham, Md.: Rowman & Littlefield, 1996), 171.

14. Mackie, *Miracle of Theism*, 19.

15. Ibid. See also Curd, "Miracles as Violations," 172.

16. R. F. Holland, "The Miraculous," *American Philosophical Quarterly* 2 (1965): 43.

17. Alastair McKinnon, "'Miracle' and 'Paradox,'" *American Philosophical Quarterly* 4 (1967): 309.

18. Curd, "Miracles as Violations," 174–75.

19. Mackie, *Miracle of Theism*, 23.

20. Ibid., 26.

21. Ibid., emphasis added.

22. I use the present tense here as a natural literary convention in my exposition of Mackie's views, but the very book from which I have been quoting was published posthumously.

23. John Macquarrie, *Principles of Christian Theology*, 2d ed. (New York: Scribner's, 1977), 248.

24. This type of analysis is developed in Richard Swinburne, *The Concept of Miracle* (London: Macmillan, 1970); and in Richard Swinburne, *The Existence of God* (Oxford: Clarendon Press, 1979), 228–36.

25. See Mackie, *Miracle of Theism*, 23.

26. See also Geivett and Habermas, *In Defense of Miracles*.

Chapter 7

1. Jarl Fossum, "Understanding Jesus' Miracles," *Bible Review*, 10, no. 2 (April 1994): 17.

2. For a more in-depth treatment of the issues in this section, see Gary R. Habermas, "Did Jesus Perform Miracles?" in *Jesus Under Fire*, ed. Michael Wilkins and J. P. Moreland (Grand Rapids: Zondervan, 1995), 117–40.

3. Israel W. Slotki, ed., *The Babylonian Talmud*, trans. S. Daiches (n.p.: Rebecca Bennet Publications, 1959), Berakot 34b. Fossum includes another example (18).

4. Flavius Philostratus, *The Life of Apollonius of Tyana*, trans. F. C. Conybeare, 2 vols. (Cambridge: Harvard University Press, 1912), 4:20.

5. For numerous details on this initial point, see Habermas, "Did Jesus Perform Miracles?" 119–23.

6. Rudolf Bultmann, "The Study of the Synoptic Gospels," in *Form Criticism: Two Essays on New Testament Research*, trans. Frederick C. Grant (New York: Harper & Row, 1962), 38.

7. Michael Grant, *Jesus: An Historian's Review of the Gospels* (New York: Macmillan, 1977), 199.

8. Reginald Fuller, *The Foundations of New Testament Christology* (New York: Scribner's, 1965), 93, 97–98.

9. Barry L. Blackburn, "Miracle Working θεῖοι ἄνδρες in Hellenism (and Hellenistic Judaism)," in *The Miracles of Jesus*, vol. 6, Gospel Perspectives, ed. David Wenham and Craig Blomberg (Sheffield: JSOT, 1986), 199–202.

10. Ibid., 198–206.

11. Martin Hengel, *The Atonement: The Origins of the Doctrine in the New Testament*, trans. John Bowden (Philadelphia: Fortress, 1981), 31. Hengel enumerates three uniquely Christian aspects of atonement on pages 31–32.

12. Fuller, *Jesus*, 90; cf. 142–43.

13. Details can be found in Howard Clark Kee, *Miracle in the Early Christian World* (New Haven: Yale University, 1983), 253; S. A. Cook, *The Cambridge Ancient History*, vol. 12 (Cambridge: Cambridge University, 1965), 611.

14. James Ferguson, *The Religions of the Roman Empire* (Ithaca, N.Y.: Cornell University, 1970), 51; cf. Cook, *Cambridge Ancient History*, 613.

15. See Conybeare's introduction to Philostratus, *Life of Apollonius*, vol. 1, vii–x.

16. For more details and sources on each of the above critiques of Apollonius of Tyana, see Gary R. Habermas, "Resurrection Claims in Non-Christian Religions," *Religious Studies* 25 (1989): 167–77; cf. Habermas, "Did Jesus Perform Miracles?" 123–24.

17. Marcus Borg, *Jesus—A New Vision: Spirit, Culture, and the Life of Discipleship* (San Francisco: HarperCollins, 1987), 61; cf. 60–67.

18. John Dominic Crossan, *Jesus: A Revolutionary Biography* (San Francisco: HarperCollins, 1994), 82.

19. Ibid., 95.

20. Fossum, "Understanding Jesus' Miracles," 50.

21. John Dominic Crossan, *The Historical Jesus: The Life of a Mediterranean Jewish Peasant* (San Francisco: HarperCollins, 1991), 404.

22. Borg, *Jesus*, 70; cf. 66–71.

23. Such as Robert W. Funk, Roy W. Hoover, and the Jesus Seminar, *The Five Gospels: The Search for the Authentic Words of Jesus* (New York: Macmillan, 1993), 16; Fossum, "Understanding Jesus' Miracles," 23.

24. Paul L. Maier, *In the Fullness of Time: A Historian Looks at Christmas, Easter, and the*

Early Church (San Francisco: HarperCollins, 1991), 197.

25. Funk, Hoover, and the Jesus Seminar, *Five Gospels*, 26.

26. These critical sources are Mark, M (material distinctive to Matthew), L (material distinctive to Luke), Q (material found in both Matthew and Luke, but not in Mark), and John.

27. Borg, *Jesus*, 61.

28. Maier, *In the Fullness of Time*, 198–99.

29. Borg, *Jesus*, 61.

30. Ibid.

31. See the detailed study by Graham Twelftree, *Jesus the Miracle Worker* (Downers Grove, Ill.: InterVarsity Press, 1999), especially chaps. 11–17. For these specific examples, see pages 288, 300. Cf. Graham Twelftree, "Εἰ δὲ . . . ἐγὼ ἐκβάλλω τὰ δαιμόνια," in *Miracles of Jesus*, vol. 6, 361–400.

32. B. D. Chilton, "Exorcism and History: Mark 1:21–28," in *Miracles of Jesus*, vol. 6, 260–61.

33. Twelftree, *Jesus*, chaps. 14, 16. For discussions of some early and eyewitness source material, see 305–8, 316–17, 321–22, 326; for dissimilarity (defined in chap. 9), see 306; for coherence, see 315.

34. John P. Meier, *A Marginal Jew: Rethinking the Historical Jesus*, vol. 2 (Garden City, N.Y.: Doubleday, 1994), 682–83, 690, 758, 792–95. Many other details are contained in the following essays from *Miracles of Jesus*: P. W. Barnett, "The Feeding of the Multitude," 273–93; Murray J. Harris, "The Dead Are Raised," 298–99, 310–14; Craig Blomberg, "The Miracles as Parables," 347–48; Stephen T. Davis, "The Miracle at Cana," 429.

35. Crossan, *Historical Jesus*, 404.

36. Crossan, *Jesus*, 80–88; Borg, *Jesus*, 63.

37. Randolph C. Byrd, "Positive Therapeutic Effects of Intercessory Prayer in a Coronary Care Unit Population," *Southern Medical Journal* 81, no. 7 (July 1988): 826–29; Randolph C. Byrd and John Sherrill, "On a Wing and a Prayer," *Physician* 5, no. 3 (May–June 1993): 14–16.

38. M. Scott Peck, *People of the Lie* (New York: Simon & Schuster, 1983), 182–211.

39. Borg, *Jesus*, 72, note 16; cf. 66–70.

40. We will provide a list (with explanations) of these critical rules in chapter 9.

41. Amazingly, the critical rules treated in chapter 9 can *all* be applied several times each

to the three categories of Gospel miracle accounts that Twelftree and others defended as historical.

42. Borg, *Jesus*, 61.

43. Twelftree lists a total of twenty-two Gospel accounts (including all three miracle categories) in which he has "high confidence" that a miracle occurred (*Jesus*, 328–29).

44. This section follows several other similar discussions by the author. For more details, see especially Gary R. Habermas, *The Historical Jesus* (Joplin, Mo.: College Press, 1996), esp. chap. 7; "The Resurrection of Jesus," in *Beyond Death: Exploring the Evidence for Immortality*, coauthored with J. P. Moreland (Wheaton: Crossway Books, 1998), chap. 5; cf. chap. 6; "The Resurrection Appearances of Jesus," in *In Defense of Miracles*, ed. R. Douglas Geivett and Gary R. Habermas (Downers Grove, Ill.: InterVarsity Press, 1997), chap. 16; "Jesus' Resurrection and Contemporary Criticism: An Apologetic," *Criswell Theological Review* part 2, 4, no. 2 (spring 1990): 373–85.

45. For just a few examples of those who provide these details, see especially Pinchas Lapide, *The Resurrection of Jesus: A Jewish Perspective* (Minneapolis: Augsburg, 1983), 97–99; Reginald Fuller, *The Formation of the Resurrection Narratives* (New York: Macmillan, 1971), 10–11; Hans Conzelmann, *1 Corinthians*, trans. James Leitch (Philadelphia: Fortress, 1975), 251, 254, 257; Raymond E. Brown, *The Virginal Conception and Bodily Resurrection of Jesus* (New York: Paulist, 1973), 81, 92; Willi Marxsen, *The Resurrection of Jesus of Nazareth*, trans. Margaret Kohl (Philadelphia: Fortress, 1970), 80; Gunther Bornkamm, *Jesus of Nazareth*, trans. Irene and Fraser McLuskey with James M. Robinson (New York: Harper & Row, 1960), 182; Joachim Jeremias, *New Testament Theology: The Proclamation of Jesus*, trans. John Bowden (New York: Scribner's, 1971), 306.

46. Ulrich Wilckens, *Resurrection*, trans. A. M. Stewart (Edinburgh: St. Andrew, 1977), 2.

47. Jeremias, *New Testament Theology*, 306.

48. Most of those in the previous note endorse this Jerusalem scenario. Hans Grass thinks that Paul received this instruction at Damascus, which places it about three years earlier (*Ostergeschehen und Osterberichte*, 2d ed. [Gottingen: Vandenhoeck und Ruprecht,

1962], 96). Thomas Sheehan does not venture a date in the immediate context.

49. For a number of these scholars, see Grass, *Ostergeschehen und Osterberichte*, 96; Fuller, *Foundations of New Testament Christology*, 142, 161; Fuller, *Formation of the Resurrection Narratives*, 10, 14, 28, 48; Oscar Cullmann, *The Early Church: Studies in Early Christian History and Theology*, ed. A. J. B. Higgins (Philadelphia: Westminster, 1966), 65–66; Brown, *Virginal Conception*, 81; Leonard Goppelt, "The Easter Kerygma in the New Testament," in *The Easter Message Today*, trans. Salvator Attanasio and Darrell L. Guder (New York: Thomas Nelson, 1964), 36; John A. T. Robinson, *Can We Trust the New Testament?* (Grand Rapids: Eerdmans, 1977), 125; Thomas Sheehan, *First Coming: How the Kingdom of God Became Christianity* (New York: Random, 1986), 110, 118; Wolfhart Pannenberg, *Jesus: God and Man*, trans. Lewis Wilkins and Duane Priebe (Philadelphia: Westminster, 1968), 90; C. H. Dodd, *The Apostolic Preaching and Its Developments* (Grand Rapids: Baker, 1980), 16; George Eldon Ladd, *I Believe in the Resurrection of Jesus* (Grand Rapids: Eerdmans, 1975), 105. Gerald O'Collins is unaware of scholars who place Paul's reception of this creed after the 40s A.D. (*What Are They Saying about the Resurrection?* [New York: Paulist, 1978], 112). Although such would be a minority position, our major conclusions here would still follow even given such a date.

50. G. D. Kilpatrick, "Galatians 1:18 Ἱστορῆσαι Κηφᾶν," in *New Testament Essays: Studies in Memory of Thomas Walter Manson*, ed. A. J. B. Higgins (Manchester: Manchester University, 1959), 148–49.

51. William R. Farmer, "Peter and Paul, and the Tradition Concerning 'The Lord's Supper' in 1 Cor. 11:23–25," *Criswell Theological Review* 2 (1987): esp. 122–30. On the Petrine, apostolic nature of the creed that Paul received, see 135–38.

52. Some object that Paul claims in Galatians 1:11–17 that he didn't receive his message from anyone, including other apostles. But this certainly mistakes Paul's point. He is speaking here specifically about his initial, direct call by the Lord, before he ever met another apostle. Yet he is equally clear that his consultation with certain apostles came later. To say that he never conferred with another apostle, then, misses his very next point, especially when he tells us that his second trip to see the apostles in Jerusalem was specifically to ascertain if he had been preaching in vain (Gal. 2:2).

53. Dodd, *Apostolic Preaching*, 16.

54. Hans von Campenhausen, "The Events of Easter and the Empty Tomb," in *Tradition and Life in the Church* (Philadelphia: Fortress, 1968), 44.

55. A. M. Hunter, *Jesus: Lord and Saviour* (Grand Rapids: Eerdmans, 1976), 100.

56. Dodd, *Apostolic Preaching*, 16.

57. Michael Martin, *The Case against Christianity* (Philadelphia: Temple University, 1991), 81; cf. 89.

58. G. A. Wells, *The Historical Evidence for Jesus* (Buffalo: Prometheus, 1988), 43.

59. For critiques of both Martin's and Wells's positions, see Habermas, *Historical Jesus*, chap. 2. For other problems with Wells's thesis, see Gary R. Habermas, "Questioning the Existence of Jesus," *Christian Research Journal* 22, no. 3 (2000): 54–56.

60. Hans Dieter Betz, *Galatians* (Philadelphia: Fortress, 1979), 86.

61. Ibid., 100; cf. 82, 85–89, 95, 103.

62. See 1 Cor. 15:1–5, 14, 17; Rom. 1:1–4; 4:25; 10:9, for examples.

63. Lapide, *Resurrection of Jesus*, 99.

64. Details are contained in Daniel P. Fuller, *Easter Faith and History* (Grand Rapids: Eerdmans, 1965), chaps. 7–8; Habermas and Moreland, *Beyond Death*, 135, 405–6.

65. This resurrection theme is found in the early confessions in Acts 2:22–33; 3:14–15, 26; 4:10; 5:30; 10:39–43; 13:27–37. All of these are attributed to Peter, except the last one, to Paul.

66. For these quotations along with Dodd's influential discussion of the Acts texts, see *Apostolic Preaching*, 17–31.

67. John Drane, *Introducing the New Testament* (San Francisco: Harper & Row, 1986), 99.

68. Additional arguments of a specific, extended nature are supplied by William Lane Craig, *Assessing the New Testament Evidence for the Historicity of the Resurrection of Jesus*, vol. 16, Studies in the Bible and Early Christianity (Lewiston, N.Y.: Edwin Mellen, 1989), part 2, 161–347; Grant Osborne, *The Resurrection Narratives: A Redactional Study* (Grand Rapids: Baker, 1984), part 2, 41–192.

69. C. H. Dodd, "The Appearances of the Risen Christ: An Essay in Form-Criticism of the Gospels," in *More New Testament Studies* (Grand Rapids: Eerdmans, 1968), 102–33.

70. For examples, Romans 1:3–4; 4:25; 10:9; 1 Corinthians 15:3ff., Luke 24:34, plus the instances from the Acts texts (2:14–39; 3:12–26; 4:8–12; 5:29–32; 10:34–43; 13:16–41).

71. These critical sources are Mark, M (material unique to Matthew), L (material unique to Luke), and John.

72. See Matthew 28:17; Luke 24:12, 21, 36–43; John 20:9, 24–25; cf. 21:12.

73. See Mark 8:31–33; 9:31–32; 14:27–31. Also, Jesus told the disciples to meet him in Galilee after his resurrection (Mark 14:27–28), but they stayed in Jerusalem and had to be reminded of the earlier command (Mark 16:7–8).

74. For details, see Gary R. Habermas, *The Resurrection of Jesus: An Apologetic* (Grand Rapids: Baker, 1980; Lanham: University Press of America, 1984), esp. chaps. 3–5.

75. I spell out the details of such an approach in several places. For the most recent example, see Gary R. Habermas, "Evidential Apologetics," in *Five Views on Apologetics*, ed. Steven B. Cowan (Grand Rapids: Zondervan, 2000), esp. 99–120.

76. Dodd, *Apostolic Preaching*, 16.

77. Fuller, *Foundations of New Testament Christology*, 142.

78. James D. G. Dunn, *The Evidence for Jesus* (Philadelphia: Westminster, 1985), 73–75.

79. Grant, *Jesus*, 176.

80. Carl Braaten, *History and Hermeneutics*, vol. 2, *New Directions in Theology Today*, ed. William Hordern (Philadelphia: Westminster, 1966), 78.

81. Wolfhart Pannenberg, "The Historicity of the Resurrection: The Identity of Christ," in *The Intellectuals Speak Out about God*, ed. Roy Abraham Varghese (Chicago: Regnery Gateway, 1984), 260.

82. Gerd Luedemann, *The Resurrection of Jesus*, trans. John Bowden (Philadelphia: Fortress, 1994), 37, 50, 66; Gerd Luedemann, *What Really Happened to Jesus*, trans. John Bowden (Louisville: Westminster John Knox, 1995), 103.

83. Although much oversimplified, I will explain this briefly by using a few examples.

Neither here nor in the text is it my purpose to disprove completely the alternative views. Rather, I will argue that they don't even explain the appearance data alone, which is my chief emphasis. For example, charges that Jesus did not die on the cross are faced with several exceptionally weighty medical refutations. But the key is that, in his severely weakened, bloodied, limping condition, Jesus couldn't have convinced his disciples that he was raised at all, let alone in an eternal, glorified body! He would be alive, but raised? No! So the final blow is that a swoon fails to adequately account for the quality of Jesus' appearances. To say that the disciples stole Jesus' dead body can't account for their being totally transformed, convinced that they had really seen the risen Jesus. It especially fails to explain the disciples' willingness to die for this belief! If anyone else took the body, this does not even address the appearances, so another thesis must be employed in order to treat the appearance data. Legends and comparative mythology don't explain the testimony given by early eyewitnesses that they actually saw Jesus. Additionally, each naturalistic thesis also struggles to explain many added aspects of the resurrection evidence, such as the empty tomb, the apostles' radical transformations, the centrality of the resurrection proclamation, and the conversions of both James and Paul. Further, there is virtually no evidence for any of these other options. More detailed treatments of naturalistic hypotheses, their status in current studies, as well as additional refutations, can be found in Habermas and Moreland, *Beyond Death*, 55–65; Craig, *Assessing the New Testament Evidence*, 374–79, 397–404.

84. This view is taken, for example, in Luedemann's two books, above.

85. Clinical psychologist Gary R. Collins maintains, "Hallucinations are individual occurrences. By their very nature only one person can see a given hallucination at a time. They certainly are not something which can be seen by a group of people. Neither is it possible that one person could somehow induce an hallucination in somebody else. Since an hallucination exists only in this subjective, personal sense, it is obvious that others cannot witness it" (personal correspondence, 21 February 1977).

For this and other ideas discussed below, see Phillip H. Wiebe, *Visions of Jesus: Direct*

Encounters from the New Testament to Today (Oxford: Oxford University, 1997), chaps. 6–7; J. P. Brady, "The Veridicality of Hypnotic, Visual Hallucinations," in *Origin and Mechanisms of Hallucinations*, ed. Wolfram Keup (New York: Plenum, 1970), 181; Weston La Barre, "Anthropological Perspectives on Hallucinations and Hallucinogens," in *Hallucinations: Behavior, Experience and Theory*, ed. R. K. Siegel and L. J. West (New York: John Wiley, 1975), 9–10.

86. Using only examples from the early creeds, 1 Corinthians 15:3ff. names three group appearances ("to the twelve" [v. 5], the 500 [v. 6], "to all the apostles" [v 7]), while at least two Acts traditions imply group appearances (10:40–42; 13:30–31).

87. For many more details regarding subjective vision hypotheses, see Gary R. Habermas, *The Resurrection of Jesus: A Rational Inquiry* (Ann Arbor: University Microfilms, 1976), 127–45. For a much more succinct critique, see Habermas and Moreland, *Beyond Death*, 60–61.

88. For some examples, see Hans Grass, *Ostergeschehen und Osterberichte*, 96, 242; Raymond Brown, "The Resurrection and Biblical Criticism," *Commonweal* 87, no. 8 (24 November 1967): 233; Paul Tillich, *Systematic Theology* (Chicago: University of Chicago, 1971), vol. 2, 156; Bornkamm, *Jesus of Nazareth*, 185; Karl Barth, *Church Dogmatics*, ed. G. W. Bromiley and T. F. Torrance (Edinburgh: T & T Clark, 1956), vol. 4, 1:340; Wiebe, *Visions of Jesus*, 210; Lapide, *Resurrection of Jesus*, 124–26; Jeremias, *New Testament Theology*, 302; Fuller, *Formation of the Resurrection Narratives*, 46–49; Robinson, *Can We Trust?* 123–25; Dunn, *Evidence for Jesus*, 72; Pannenberg, *Jesus—God and Man*, 94–97; A. M. Ramsay, *The Resurrection of Christ* (London: Collins, 1961), 41, 49–50; Neville Clark, *Interpreting the Resurrection* (Philadelphia: Westminster, 1967), 100–101.

89. Pannenberg, *Jesus—God and Man*, 96.

90. Dunn, *Evidence for Jesus*, 76.

91. Brown, "The Resurrection and Biblical Criticism," 233. After listing several natural options, Karl Barth exclaimed: "To-day we rightly turn up our nose at this. . . ." Noting that they are beset by problems, Barth says that "these explanations . . . have now gone out of currency. . . ." (Barth, *Church Dogmatics*, vol. 4, 1:340).

92. Dunn, *Evidence for Jesus*, 74–76; Pannenberg, "The Historicity of the Resurrection," 260–62.

Chapter 8

1. A more complete account of my conversion to Christianity is available on a fifty-minute audiotape: Hugh Ross, *Beyond the Stars: An Astronomer's Quest* (Forest, Va.: Life Story Foundation, 1996).

2. Hugh Ross, *The Creator and the Cosmos*, 2d ed. (Colorado Springs: NavPress, 1995); Hugh Ross, *Beyond the Cosmos*, 2d ed. (Colorado Springs: NavPress, 1999); Hugh Ross, *Journey toward Creation* (Pasadena, Calif.: NavPress, 1998). This is a fifty-eight-minute video documentary.

3. Hugh Ross, *The Genesis Question* (Colorado Springs: NavPress, 1998).

4. Edwin Hubble, "A Relation between Distance and Radial Velocity among Extra-Galactic Nebulae," *Proceedings of the National Academy of Sciences* 15 (1929): 173.

5. Steven Weinberg, *Gravitation and Cosmology: Principles and Applications of the General Theory of Relativity* (New York: John Wiley & Sons, 1972), 198; C. C. Counselman III et al., "Solar Gravitational Deflection of Radio Waves Measured by Very-Long-Baseline Interferometry," *Physical Review Letters* 33 (1974): 1621–23; Irwin I. Shapiro et al., "Mercury's Perihelion Advance: Determination by Radar," *Physical Review Letters* 28 (1972): 1594–97; R. D. Reasonberg et al., "Viking Relativity Experiment: Verification of Signal Retardation by Solar Gravity," *Astrophysical Journal Letters* 234 (1979): 219–21; R. F. C. Vessot et al., "Test of Relativistic Gravitation with a Space-Borne Hydrogen Maser," *Physical Review Letters* 45 (1980): 2081–84.

6. Stephen Hawking and Roger Penrose, "The Singularities of Gravitational Collapse and Cosmology," *Proceedings of the Royal Society of London* series A, 314 (1970): 529–48.

7. Vessot, "Test of Relativistic Gravitation."

8. J. H. Taylor et al., "Experimental Constraints on Strong-Field Relativistic Gravity," *Nature* 355 (1992): 132–36.

9. Roger Penrose, *Shadows of the Mind* (New York: Oxford University Press, 1994), 230.

10. Irwin I. Shapiro, Charles C. Counselman III, and Robert W. King, "Verification of the Principle of Equivalence for Massive Bodies," *Physical Review Letters* 36 (1976): 555–58; Reasonberg, "Viking Relativity."

11. Ron Cowen, "Einstein's General Relativity: It's a Drag," *Science News* 152 (1997): 308.

12. Ibid.

13. G. S. Bisnovatyi-Kogan, "At the Border of Eternity," *Science* 279 (1998): 1321.

14. Ibid.

15. Stephen Battersby, "A Ring in Truth," *Nature* 392 (1998): 548.

16. Ignazio Ciufolini et al., "Test of General Relativity and Measurement of the Lense-Thirring Effect with Two Earth Satellites," *Science* 279 (1998): 2100–2103.

17. P. Kaaret et al., "Strong-Field Gravity and X-Ray Observations of 4U 1820–30," *Astrophysical Journal Letters* 520 (1999): L37–L40.

18. Ralph Wijers, "The Burst, the Burster, and Its Lair," *Nature* 393 (1998): 13–14; S. R. Kulkarni et al., "Identification of a Host Galaxy at Redshift $z = 3.42$ for the G-Ray Burst of 14 December 1997," *Nature* 393 (1998): 35–39.

19. J. C. Breckenridge et al., "Macroscopic and Microscopic Entropy of Near-Extremal Spinning Black Holes," *Physics Letters B* 381 (1996): 423–26; Curtis G. Callan Jr. and Juan M. Maldacena, "D-Brane Approach to Black Hole Quantum Mechanics," *Nuclear Physics B* 472 (1996): 591–608; Juan M. Maldacena and Andrew Strominger, "Statistical Entropy of Four-Dimensional Extremal Black Holes," *Physical Review Letters* 77 (1996): 428–29; Andrew Strominger and Cumrun Vafa, "Microscopic Origin of the Bekenstein-Hawking Entropy," *Physics Letters B* 379 (1996): 99–104; Gary Taubes, "How Black Holes May Get String Theory Out of a Bind," *Science* 268 (1995): 1699.

20. Ross, *Beyond the Cosmos*, 40–43.

21. George Gamow, "Expanding Universe and the Origin of the Elements," *Physical Review* 70 (1946): 572–73; Ralph A. Alpher and Robert C. Herman, "Evolution of the Universe," *Nature* 162 (1948): 774–75.

22. Arno A. Penzias and Robert W. Wilson, "A Measurement of Excess Antenna Temperature at 4080 Mc/s," *Astrophysical Journal* 142 (1965): 419–21.

23. Rainer Weiss, "Measurements of the Cosmic Background Radiation," *Annual Review of Astronomy and Astrophysics* 18 (1980): 489–535; George F. Smoot, "Comments and Summary on the Cosmic Background Radiation," *Proceedings of the International Astronomical Union Symposium*, no. 104; *Early Evolution of the Universe and Its Present Structure*, ed. G. O. Abell and G. Chincarini (Dordrecht-Holland, Boston-USA: D. Reidel, 1983), 153–58.

24. G. F. Smoot et al., "Structure in the COBE Differential Microwave Radiometer First-Year Maps," *Astrophysical Journal Letters* 396 (1992): L1–L6.

25. Ron Cowen, "Balloon Survey Backs COBE Cosmos Map," *Science News* 142 (1992): 420; S. Hancock et al., "Direct Observation of Structure in the Cosmic Background Radiation," *Nature* 367 (1994): 333–38; A. C. Clapp et al., "Measurements of Anisotropy in the Cosmic Microwave Background Radiation at Degree Angular Scales Near the Stars Sigma Herculis and Iota Draconis," *Astrophysical Journal Letters* 433 (1994): L57–L60.

26. David Briggs, "Science, Religion, Are Discovering Commonality in Big Bang Theory," *Los Angeles Times*, 2 May 1992, pp. B6–B7.

27. J. C. Mather et al., "Measurement of the Cosmic Microwave Background Spectrum by the COBE FIRAS Instrument," *Astrophysical Journal* 420 (1994): 439–44.

28. H. Guth Alan and Marc Sher, "The Impossibility of a Bouncing Universe," *Nature* 302 (1983): 505–7; Sidney A. Bludman, "Thermodynamics and the End of a Closed Universe," *Nature* 308 (1984): 319–22.

29. Ron Cowen, "COBE: A Match Made in Heaven," *Science News* 143 (1993): 43; Mather, "Cosmic Microwave."

30. Antoinette Songaila et al., "Measurement of the Microwave Background Temperature at Redshift 1.776," *Nature* 371 (1994): 43–45.

31. E. Torbet et al., "A Measurement of the Angular Power Spectrum of the Microwave Background Made from the High Chilean Andes," *Astrophysical Journal Letters* 521 (1999): L79–L82; C. M. Gutiérrez et al., "The Tenerife Cosmic Microwave Background Maps: Observations and First Analysis," *Astro-*

physical Journal 529 (2000): 47–55; Bharat Ratra et al., "Cosmic Microwave Background Anisotropy Constraints on Open and Flat-L Cold Dark Matter Cosmogonies from USSB South Pole, ARGO, MAX, White Dish, and SuZIE Data," *Astrophysical Journal* 517 (1999): 549–64; Graça Rocha et al., "Python I, II, and III Cosmic Microwave Background Anisotropy Measurement Constraints on Open and Flat-L Cold Dark Matter Cosmogonies," *Astrophysical Journal* 525 (1999): 1–9; James Glanz, "Microwave Hump Reveals Flat Universe," *Science* 283 (1999): 21.

32. P. De Barnardis et al., "A Flat Universe from High-Resolution Maps of the Cosmic Microwave Background Radiation," *Nature* 494 (2000): 955–59.

33. S. Perlmutter et al., "Measurements of Ω and L from 42 High-Redshift Supernovae," *Astrophysical Journal* 517 (1999): 565–86; Megan Donahue and G. Mark Voit, "Ω_m from the Temperature-Redshift Distribution of EMSS Clusters of Galaxies," *Astrophysical Journal Letters* 523 (1999): L37–L40; David H. Weinberg et al., "Closing in on Ω_M: The Amplitude of Mass Fluctuations from Galaxy Clusters and the Lya Forest," *Astrophysical Journal* 522 (1999): 563–68; G. Steigman and I. Tkachev, "Ω_B and Ω_0 from MACHOs and Local Group Dynamics," *Astrophysical Journal* 522 (1999): 793–801; J. Nevalainen, M. Markevitch, and W. Forman, "The Baryonic and Dark Matter Distribution in Abell 401," *Astrophysical Journal* 526 (1999): 1–9; Joseph J. Mohr, Benjamin Mathiesen, and August E. Evrard, "Properties of the Intercluster Medium in an Ensemble of Nearby Galaxy Clusters," *Astrophysical Journal* 517 (1999): 627–49; J. S. Alcaniz and J. A. S. Lima, "New Limits on Ω_L and Ω_M from Old Galaxies at High Redshift," *Astrophysical Journal Letters* 520 (1999): L87–L90.

34. S. Perlmutter, "High-Redshift Supernovae."

35. Persis S. Drell, Thomas J. Loredo, and Ira Wasserman, "Type Ia Supernovae, Evolution, and the Cosmological Constant," *Astrophysical Journal* 530 (2000): 593–617; Anthony Aguirre, "Intergalactic Dust and Observations of Type Ia Supernovae," *Astrophysical Journal* 525 (1999): 583–93; Hideyuki Umeda, Ken'ichi Nomoto, and Chiaki Kobayashi, "The Origin of the Diversity of Type Ia Supernovae and the

Environmental Effects," *Astrophysical Journal Letters* 522 (1999): L43–L47.

36. Lev R. Yungelson and Mario Livio, "Supernova Rates: A Cosmic History," *Astrophysical Journal* 528 (2000): 108–17; Adam G. Riess, Alexei V. Filippenko, Weidong Li, and Brian P. Schmidt, "Is There an Indication of Evolution of Type Ia Supernovae from Their Rise Times?" *Astronomical Journal* 118 (1999): 2668–74.

37. Idit Zehavi and Avishai Dekel, "Evidence for a Positive Cosmological Constant from Flows of Galaxies and Distant Supernovae," *Nature* 401 (1999): 252–54; Adam G. Riess, "Universal Peekaboo," *Nature* 401 (1999): 219, 221.

38. Lawrence M. Krauss, "The End of the Age Problem and the Case for a Cosmological Constant Revisited," *Astrophysical Journal* 501 (1998): 461.

39. Zehavi and Dekel, "Positive Cosmological Constant," 252.

40. N. Straumann, "The Mystery of the Cosmic Vacuum Energy Density and the Accelerated Expansion of the Universe," *European Journal of Physics* (2000).

41. Hugh Ross, *The Fingerprint of God*, 2d ed. (Orange, Calif.: Promise, 1991), 79–96; Ross, *Creator and the Cosmos*, 28–47.

42. James Glanz, "Microwave Hump," 21; P. De Barnardis et al., "A Flat Universe," 957–58; Wayne He, "Ringing in the New Cosmology," *Nature* 404 (2000): 939–40.

43. S. Perlmutter, "High-Redshift Supernovae," 584.

44. Hugh Ross, *The Fingerprint of God*, 1st ed. (Orange, Calif.: Promise, 1989), 121–28.

45. Hugh Ross, *Big Bang Refined by Fire* (Pasadena, Calif.: Reasons To Believe, 1998), 11–17.

46. Lawrence M. Krauss and Glenn D. Starkman, "Life, the Universe, and Nothing: Life and Death in an Ever-Expanding Universe," *Astrophysical Journal* 531 (2000): 22–30.

47. Yu N. Mishurov and L. A. Zenina, "Yes, the Sun Is Located Near the Corotation Circle," *Astronomy & Astrophysics* 341 (1999): 81–85.

48. Ross, *Beyond the Cosmos*, 217–28.

49. I list quotes in support of this conclusion from seventeen different astronomers and physicists who have done research on cosmic

characteristics in my book *Creator and the Cosmos*, 121–25.

50. Robert H. Dicke, "Dirac's Cosmology and Mach's Principle," *Nature* 192 (1961): 440–41.

51. Iosef S. Shklovskii and Carl Sagan, *Intelligent Life in the Universe* (San Francisco: Holden-Day, 1966), 343–50.

52. Ross, *Fingerprint of God*, 1st ed., 121–27, 129–31.

53. Ross, *Creator and the Cosmos*, 118–21, 138–44.

54. Ibid., 176–81; Ross, *Beyond the Cosmos*, 235–39; Ross, *Big Bang Refined by Fire*, 31–38.

55. Ed Harrison, *Masks of the Universe* (New York: Collier Books, Macmillan, 1985), 242, 263.

Chapter 9

1. Some of these subjects are addressed in other chapters, such as those by Walter Bradley and Winfried Corduan.

2. For information on New Testament manuscript evidence, see John A. T. Robinson, *Can We Trust the New Testament?* (Grand Rapids: Eerdmans, 1977), 33–38; F. F. Bruce, *The New Testament Documents: Are They Reliable?* (Grand Rapids: Eerdmans, 1960), 16–18; Henri Daniel-Rops, ed., *The Sources for the Life of Christ* (New York: Hawthorn, 1962), chap. 4 (by Daniel-Rops), 41–42.

3. Robinson, *Can We Trust?* 36. Atheist Antony Flew agrees in Gary R. Habermas and Antony G. N. Flew, *Did Jesus Rise from the Dead? The Resurrection Debate*, ed. Terry L. Miethe (San Francisco: Harper & Row, 1987), 66.

4. Helmut Koester, *History and Literature of Early Christianity*, 2 vols. (Philadelphia: Fortress, 1982), vol. 2, 16–17. Koester goes on to explain that this manuscript "richness" and "wealth" even raises difficulties not encountered in the classics, regarding families of manuscripts, their derivation, and readings.

5. John W. Wenham, *Christ and the Bible* (Grand Rapids: Baker, 1984), 180.

6. Ibid., 186–88.

7. In recent decades, a number of scholars have supported some of these options for the authorship of the Gospels and Acts. For examples, see John Drane, *Introducing the New Testament* (San Francisco: Harper & Row, 1986), 181–82, 191, 196–97; R. A. Cole, *The Gospel*

according to St. Mark (Grand Rapids: Eerdmans, 1970), 28–50; Robert Gundry, *Matthew* (Grand Rapids: Eerdmans, 1982); C. Stewart Petrie, "The Authorship of 'The Gospel according to Matthew': A Reconsideration of the External Evidence," *New Testament Studies* 14, no. 1 (October 1967): 15–33; Norval Geldenhuys, *Commentary on the Gospel of Luke* (Grand Rapids: Eerdmans, 1972), 15–22; E. J. Tinsley, *The Gospel according to Luke* (Cambridge: Cambridge University, 1965), 2–4; Ray Summers, *Commentary on Luke* (Waco: Word, 1972), 8–10; Raymond E. Brown, *The Gospel according to John* (Garden City, N.Y.: Doubleday, 1966), vol. 1, chap. 7; Raymond E. Brown, *New Testament Essays* (Milwaukee: Bruce, 1965), 129–31; Leon Morris, *The Gospel according to John* (Grand Rapids: Eerdmans, 1971), 8–35; R. V. G. Tasker, *The Gospel according to St. John* (Grand Rapids: Eerdmans, 1968), 11–20; F. F. Bruce, *Commentary on the Book of Acts* (Grand Rapids: Eerdmans, 1971), 19; Robinson, *Can We Trust?* 71–94; Bruce, *The New Testament Documents*, chap. 4; Paul Barnett, *Is the New Testament Reliable? A Look at the Historical Evidence* (Downers Grove, Ill.: InterVarsity Press, 1986); Donald Guthrie, *New Testament Introduction*, 4th rev. ed. (Downers Grove, Ill.: InterVarsity Press, 1990), 43–53, 81–84, 113–25, 252–83.

8. This is not an argument from silence, in light of the similar items (in both content and geography) that the author *does* record.

9. See Robinson, *Can We Trust?* 71–73; Gundry, *Matthew*, on the date of Matthew; Craig Blomberg, "The Historical Reliability of the New Testament," in *Reasonable Faith*, ed. William Lane Craig (Wheaton: Crossway, 1994), 206.

10. While it is true that secular references to Jesus are generally brief and sometimes derived from Christian sources, it does not follow that they should be largely ignored, as is often their fate.

11. For specific details, see Gary Habermas, *The Historical Jesus* (Joplin, Mo.: College Press, 1996), esp. chap. 9. Compare R. T. France, *The Evidence for Jesus* (Downers Grove, Ill.: InterVarsity Press, 1986); F. F. Bruce, *Jesus and Christian Origins outside the New Testament* (Grand Rapids: Eerdmans, 1974); Edwin Yamauchi, "Jesus outside the New Testament: What Is the Evidence?" in *Jesus under Fire*, ed.

Michael Wilkins and J. P. Moreland (Grand Rapids: Zondervan, 1995).

12. For details, see Habermas, *The Historical Jesus*, chap. 11.

13. See J. B. Lightfoot, ed. and trans., *The Apostolic Fathers* (Grand Rapids: Baker, 1891, 1956). A discussion of these and other early sources can be found in Habermas, *The Historical Jesus*, chap. 10.

14. France, *Evidence for Jesus*, chap. 4; Bruce, *New Testament Documents*, chap. 8.

15. A. N. Sherwin-White, *Roman Society and Roman Law in the New Testament* (Oxford: Oxford University, 1963; Grand Rapids: Baker, 1978).

16. Habermas, *Historical Jesus*, chap. 8.

17. A notable examination of this entire topic is C. Behan McCullagh's *Justifying Historical Descriptions* (Cambridge: Cambridge University, 1984), esp. 17–33. Other historical texts will be listed below.

18. This time frame is emphasized by Robert W. Funk, Roy W. Hoover, and the Jesus Seminar, *The Five Gospels: The Search for the Authentic Words of Jesus* (New York: Macmillan, 1993), 25–26.

19. David Hackett Fischer, *Historian's Fallacies: Toward a Logic of Historical Thought* (New York: Harper & Row, 1970), 62. Fischer includes here an event's archaeological "remains," placing this even above "direct observations." On the import of eyewitnesses in ancient Greek writing, see Ernst Breisach, *Historiography: Ancient, Medieval, and Modern*, 2d ed. (Chicago: University of Chicago, 1994), 38–39.

20. Paul L. Maier, *In the Fullness of Time: A Historian Looks at Christmas, Easter, and the Early Church* (San Francisco: HarperCollins, 1991), 197.

21. Funk, Hoover, and the Jesus Seminar, *Five Gospels*, 26.

22. Michael Grant, *Jesus: An Historian's Review of the Gospels* (New York: Macmillan, 1977; Collier Books Edition, 1992), 202–3. Cf. ibid., 23.

23. Maier, *In the Fullness of Time*, 198–99.

24. Grant, *Jesus*, 202.

25. Perhaps no one has done more on this subject than Joachim Jeremias. For example, see his famous work on the term *abba* in *The Central Message of the New Testament* (Philadelphia: Fortress, 1965), 9–30; also *The*

Parables of Jesus, 2d rev. ed., trans. S. H. Hooke (Upper Saddle River, N.J.: Prentice Hall, 1972), 100–114; cf. Norman Perrin, *Rediscovering the Teaching of Jesus* (New York: Harper & Row, 1967), 37–41.

26. Cf. W. B. Gallie, "Explanations in History and the Genetic Sciences," in *Theories of History: Readings from Classical and Contemporary Sources*, ed. Patrick Gardiner (New York: Macmillan, 1959), 397–98; the idea in critical New Testament research is pursued in Norman Perrin, *Rediscovering the Teaching of Jesus* (New York: Harper & Row, 1967), 43–45.

27. Christopher Blake, "Can History Be Objective?" in *Theories of History*, 331.

28. I employ this twofold test in all my publications on Jesus' resurrection. For example, see *Historical Jesus*, 158–67; and *Resurrection of Jesus* (Grand Rapids: Baker, 1980; Lanham: University Press of America, 1984), 24–26, 38–41.

29. For instance, some propose the presence of plural forms—an item is more likely to be historical if it is found in more than one literary pattern. Grant judges that this is "not very decisive" (*Jesus*, 201). We will also look below at a major indication of early material—the presence of creeds or traditions in the New Testament.

30. Again, the scope of this inquiry requires us to exclude from discussion a number of relevant details, especially regarding ancient historiography, such as those mentioned by Lucian of Samosata in *How to Write History* (Cambridge: Harvard University, 1959), esp. 7–15. Breisach includes other items on pages 64, 68–69, 72.

31. I will say very little concerning the literary aspects of this issue, involving, for example, an examination of the Gospel's genre as biography, history, or novel. For an overview, see L. W. Hurtado, "Gospel (Genre)," in *Dictionary of Jesus and the Gospels*, ed. Joel B. Green, Scott McNight, and I. H. Marshall (Downers Grove, Ill.: InterVarsity Press, 1992).

32. France, *Evidence for Jesus*, 124.

33. Ibid., 122–25.

34. See some of the more recent scholars in note 7 above.

35. Sherwin-White, *Roman Society*, 187.

36. Grant, *Jesus*, 199–200; cf. also 176.

37. Ibid., 201.

38. Plutarch, *The Lives of the Noble Grecians and Romans* (Dryden translation), Great

NOTES

Books of the Western World, ed. Robert Maynard (Chicago: Encyclopedia Britannica and University of Chicago, 1952), see 541, 553, 565, 575–76.

39. For some instances, see Tacitus, *Annals*, 1:11, 19, 28, 42, 55; 12:43; 14:22; *History*, 5:13.

40. Examples can be found in Suetonius, *The Twelve Caesars* (Baltimore: Penguin, 1957): Julius Caesar, 88; Augustus, 100; Tiberius, 74–75; Gaius Caligula, 57, 59; Claudius, 45–46; Nero, 56; Vespasian, 4, 25; Titus, 10; Domitian, 23.

41. Plutarch, *Lives*, 575–76; Tacitus, *Annals*, 1:28; Suetonius, *Twelve Caesars*: Nero, 56, Vespasian, 4.

42. For some examples, see Plutarch, *Lives*, 541; Tacitus, *Annals*, 1:55; 12:43; *History*, 5:13; Suetonius, *Twelve Caesars*: Claudius, 46; Vespasian, 25; Domitian, 23.

43. See Moses Hadas's point on this explicit issue of Tacitus's textual embellishments, where he concludes that, in terms of ancient methods, "Tacitus never consciously sacrifices historical truth," calling him Rome's "greatest historian." See Hadas's introduction to *The Complete Works of Tacitus*, in The Modern Library, trans. Alfred John Church and William Jackson Brodribb (New York: Random House, 1942), xvii–xviii, ix, respectively. Translator Robert Graves remarks similarly that it is possible to allow for Suetonius's extravagances and still conclude that he is "trustworthy." See Graves's foreword to *Twelve Caesars*, 7.

44. On both subjects, two helpful collections of essays are Richard Swinburne, ed., *Miracles* (New York: Macmillan, 1989); R. Douglas and Gary R. Habermas, eds., *In Defense of Miracles: A Comprehensive Case for God's Action in History* (Downers Grove, Ill.: InterVarsity Press, 1997).

45. Marcus Borg, *Jesus, A New Vision: Spirit, Culture, and the Life of Discipleship* (San Francisco: HarperCollins, 1987), 67–71. For some detailed textual evidence, see the massive text by Graham H. Twelftree, *Jesus the Miracle Worker* (Downers Grove, Ill.: InterVarsity Press, 1999).

46. Some of the following material, with far less detail, is contained in my chapter "The New Testament," in *Why Believe? God Exists!* ed. Terry L. Miethe and Gary R. Habermas (Joplin, Mo.: College Press, 1993), chap. 25.

47. Plutarch, *Lives*, 540–41.

48. Grant, *Jesus*, 182.

49. Sherwin-White, *Roman Society*, 189. This does not mean that the Gospels and Acts are precisely the same literary genre as ancient biographies and histories, only that some of the same standards should be applied.

50. Titus Livius, *The History of Rome*, trans. D. Spillan (London: Bell and Daldy, 1872), book I:1–3.

51. Even the table of contents of Plutarch's *Lives* illustrates this point quite well.

52. Two helpful works here are Norman Geisler and Thomas Howe, *When Critics Ask: A Popular Handbook on Bible Difficulties* (Wheaton: Victor Books, 1992); and Gleason L. Archer Jr., *Encyclopedia of Bible Difficulties* (Grand Rapids: Zondervan, 1982).

53. Sherwin-White, *Roman Society*, 187.

54. Maier, *In the Fullness of Time*, 180.

55. Grant, *Jesus*, 181–82; Maier, *In the Fullness of Time*, 179–80, 189, 196–98.

56. Sherwin-White, *Roman Society*, 189. Details of his claims are provided especially in chapters 3–5. See also the exhaustive work by classical scholar Colin Hemer, *The Book of Acts in the Setting of Hellenistic History*, ed. Conrad H. Gempf (Winona Lake, Ind.: Eisenbrauns, 1990).

57. Sherwin-White, *Roman Society*, 189–91; Grant, *Jesus*, 182.

58. For more details concerning these critiques, see Sherwin-White, *Roman Society*, 186–93; Grant, *Jesus*, esp. 180–84, 199–200.

59. Details are found in A. M. Hunter, *Jesus—Lord and Saviour* (Grand Rapids: Eerdmans, 1976), 39–41.

60. See France, *Evidence for Jesus*, 124.

61. Ephesians, Colossians, 2 Thessalonians, Timothy, and Titus.

62. N. T. Wright, *What Saint Paul Really Said: Was Paul of Tarsus the Real Founder of Christianity?* (Grand Rapids: Eerdmans, 1997), 8. Cf. similar comments by Ben Witherington III, *The Paul Quest: The Renewed Search for the Jew of Tarsus* (Downers Grove, Ill.: InterVarsity Press, 1998), who extends the core group of critically recognized Pauline writings to 1 Thessalonians and Philemon (109–10), and Wenham, who also includes 1 Thessalonians when referring to "the overwhelming majority of scholars" (*Christ and the Bible*, 24; cf. 13).

63. Koester, *History and Literature*, 52.

306

64. G. A. Wells, *The Historical Evidence for Jesus* (Buffalo: Prometheus, 1988), 19–22.

65. Although this could well refer to the incarnation rather than to Jesus' social condition.

66. For a recent, detailed discussion, see David Wenham, *Paul: Follower of Jesus or Founder of Christianity?* (Grand Rapids: Eerdmans, 1995), 3–7, 338–72, 380–92. For other lists, see Barnett, *Is the New Testament Reliable?* 131–36; Amedee Brunot, "The Gospel before the Gospels," in *The Sources for the Life of Christ*, ed. Henri Daniel-Rops, trans. P. J. Hepburne-Scott (New York: Hawthorn, 1962), 110–11; Habermas, *Historical Jesus*, 32–33.

67. One of the distinctives of Wenham's treatment of Paul is not only attempting to study the "Jesus traditions" found in this apostle's writings but to challenge those who are less positive about such a move (Wenham, *Christ and the Bible*, 18–19).

68. C. H. Dodd, *The Apostolic Preaching and Its Developments* (Grand Rapids: Baker, 1980), 31. Note here that Dodd is arguing from the primitive speeches in Acts (see below) rather than from the book as a whole.

69. Ibid., 26. For Dodd's entire argument, see 16–31.

70. Paul Barnett, *Jesus and the Logic of History* (Grand Rapids: Eerdmans, 1997), 91–102, 133, 164. The quoted words appear on pages 91 and 94, respectively.

71. Lightfoot's above edition of *The Apostolic Fathers* highlights citations of Scripture portions. For the actual figures provided here, I am indebted to an unpublished essay by one of my former graduate students, Kevin Smith ("References to Paul by Ignatius, Polycarp, and Clement," 30 April 1992).

72. Wells, *Historical Evidence for Jesus*, 21.

73. Guthrie argues for 53–57, with 57 the preferred date of most scholars (*New Testament Introduction*, 457–59); Koester places it at 52–55 (*History and Literature*, 103–4).

74. For our purposes here, it is not an issue whether 1 or 2 Corinthians contains parts of other letters written by Paul to this church (cf. Drane, *Introducing the New Testament*, 313–14).

75. Witherington, *Paul Quest*, 230–31.

76. The classic study on this topic is Oscar Cullmann's *The Earliest Christian Confessions*, trans. J. K. S. Reid (London: Lutterworth, 1949). Other major critical studies include Joachim Jeremias, *The Eucharistic Words of Jesus*, trans. Norman Perrin (London: SCM Press, 1966); Dodd, *Apostolic Preaching*. For additional details, see Habermas, *Historical Jesus*, 143–57.

77. Perhaps the clearest listing of what follows in the next paragraph is provided by Ethelbert Stauffer, *New Testament Theology*, trans. John Marsh (London: SCM Press, 1955), 338–39. See also Markus Barth, *Ephesians 1–3*, Anchor Bible Commentary (New York: Doubleday, 1974), 6–10.

78. See especially 1 Cor. 11:2, 23; 15:3; cf. 2 Thess. 3:6; 1 Tim. 1:15; 3:1; 4:9; 2 Tim. 2:11; Titus 1:9.

79. Examples that fit one or more of these patterns include Luke 24:34; Rom. 1:3–4; 10:9; 1 Cor. 16:22b; 2 Cor. 5:21; 8:9; Phil. 2:6–11; 1 Tim. 3:16; 2 Tim. 2:11–13; Rev. 1:4; cf. Mark 7:3. Further, the early apostolic preaching in Acts (2:14–39; 3:12–26; 4:8–12; 5:29–32; 10:34–43; 13:16–41) presents several examples of concise phrases that contain brief snippets of theology.

80. Some of the creedal material that summarizes these beliefs are Luke 24:34; Acts 2:22–24, 30–32; 3:13–15; 4:10–12; 5:29–32; 10:39–41; 13:37–39; Rom. 1:3–4; 4:25; 10:9; 1 Cor. 11:23ff.; 15:3–8; Phil. 2:6–11; 1 Tim. 2:6; 3:16; 6:13; 2 Tim. 2:8; 1 Peter 3:18; 1 John 4:2.

81. For a discussion of this data, see Habermas, *Historical Jesus*, chap. 7.

Chapter 10

1. David Briggs, "Science and Religion Are Discovering Commonality in Big Bang Theory," *Los Angeles Times*, 2 May 1992, pp. B6–B7.

2. Michael Shermer, *How We Believe: Search for God in an Age of Science* (New York: W. H. Freeman, 1999).

3. Edward J. Larson, *The Summer of the Gods: The Scopes Trial and America's Continuing Debate over Science and Religion* (Cambridge: Harvard University Press, 1998).

4. Franz Delitzsch, *Babel und Bible*, trans. Thomas J. McCormack and W. H. Carruth (Chicago: The Open Court Publishing, 1903), 45.

5. Steve Allen, *Steve Allen on the Bible, Religion, and Morality* (Buffalo: Prometheus, 1990), 155.

6. Isaac Asimov, *Asimov's Guide to the Bible: The Old and New Testament* (New York: Random House Value Publishing, 1988).

7. Issac Asimov, "Notes on Genesis 1:1–19," in *Creations: The Quest for Origins in Story and Science*, ed. Isaac Asimov, George Zebrowski, and Martin Greenberg (London: Harrap, 1984), 6.

8. Asimov, *Asimov's Guide*, 195.

9. Frank Press, *Science and Creationism: A View from the National Academy of Sciences* (Washington, D.C.: National Academy Press, 1984), 6.

10. Frank J. Tipler, *The Physics of Immortality* (New York: Doubleday, 1994), 7.

11. Francis Schaeffer, *Escape from Reason* (Downers Grove, Ill.: InterVarsity Press, 1968).

12. Isaac Newton, *Philosophiae Naturalis Principia Mathematica* (London: Henderson & Saplding, 1687), preface.

13. R. Hooykaas, *Religion and the Rise of Modern Science* (Grand Rapids: Eerdmans, 1972).

14. Gleason L. Archer, "A Response to the Trustworthiness of Scripture in Areas Relating to Natural Science," in *Hermeneutics, Inerrancy, and the Bible*, ed. Earl D. Radmacher and Robert D. Preus (Grand Rapids: Zondervan, 1983), 321–33.

15. Ibid.

16. Walter L. Bradley and Roger Olsen, "The Trustworthiness of Scripture in Areas Relating to Natural Science," in *Hermeneutics, Inerrancy, and the Bible*, 285–317; Paul Nelson, John Mark Reynolds, Robert C. Newman, and Howard J. Van Till, *Three Views on Creation and Evolution*, ed. J. P. Moreland and John Mark Reynolds (Grand Rapids: Zondervan, 1999).

17. Nelson et al., *Three Views*.

18. Archer, "Response to the Trustworthiness of Scripture."

19. Robert C. Newman and Herman J. Eckelmann Jr., *Genesis 1 and the Origin of the Earth* (Downers Grove, Ill.: InterVarsity Press, 1977).

20. Frank Press and Raymond Siever, *Planet Earth*, 3d ed. (San Francisco: W. H. Freeman, 1982), 68.

21. A. G. Mayor, "Growth Rate of Samoan Corals," Department of Marine Biology of Carnegie Institute of Washington, publication no. 340, vol. 19, 51–72; W. B. N. Berry and

R. M. Barker, "Fossil Bivalve Shells Indicate Longer Month and Year in Cretaceous Than Present," *Nature* 217 (1968): 938–39; S. K. Runeorn, "Corals as Paleontological Clocks," *Scientific American* 215 (1966): 26–33.

22. W. C. Pitmann III and M. Talwani, "Sea Floor Spreading in the North Atlantic," *Geological Society of America Bulletin* 83 (1972): 619–45.

23. Harry E. Cook, "North American Stratigraphic Principles as Applied to Deep-Sea Sediments," *American Association of Petroleum Geologists Bulletin* 59 (1975): 824; R. Y. Anderson, W. E. Dean Jr., D. W. Kirkland, and H. I. Snider, "Permian Castile Varied Evaporite Sequence," *Geological Society of America Bulletin* 83 (1972): 59–86.

24. Bradley and Olsen, "Trustworthiness of Scripture."

25. Archer, "Response to the Trustworthiness of Scripture"; Nelson et al., *Three Views*.

26. Michael Behe, *Darwin's Black Box* (New York: Free Press, 1996).

27. Richard Dawkins, *Climbing Mount Improbable* (New York: W. W. Norton, 1996).

28. Walter L. Bradley and Charles B. Thaxton, "Information and the Origin of Life," in *The Creation Hypothesis: Scientific Evidence for an Intelligent Designer*, ed. J. P. Moreland (Downers Grove, Ill.: InterVarsity Press, 1994), 173–210.

29. Paul R. and Anne H. Ehrlich, *Extinction: The Causes and Consequences of the Disappearance of Species* (New York: Ballantine, 1981), 19–38, 123–247; Robert M. May, John H. Lawton, and Nigel E. Stork, "Assessing Extinction Rates," in *Extinction Rates*, ed. John H. Lawton and Robert M. May (New York: Oxford University Press, 1995), 10–21; David W. Steadman, "Human-Caused Extinction of Birds," in *Biodiversity II: Understanding and Protecting Our Biological Resources*, ed. Marjorie L. Reaka-Kudla, Don E. Wilson, and Edward O. Wilson (Washington, D.C.: Joseph Henry Press, 1997), 139–58.

30. Ehrlich, *Extinction*, 23.

31. Peter D. Ward and Donald Brownlee, *Rare Earth: Why Complex Life Is Uncommon in the Universe* (New York: Springer-Verlag, 2000), 37–43.

32. Hugh Ross, *The Genesis Question* (Colorado Springs: NavPress, 1998), 26, 31.

33. Ibid., 34–35; Ward and Brownlee, *Rare Earth*, 117, 168–69.

34. Ibid.

35. Ross, *Genesis Question*, 34–35.

36. Ward and Brownlee, *Rare Earth*, 265.

37. Ross, *Genesis Question*, 39.

38. J. G. M. Thewissen et al., "Evolution of Cetacean Osmoregulation," *Nature* 381 (1996): 379–80.

39. Ross, *Genesis Question*, 59–63.

40. Francis Schaeffer, *No Final Conflict* (Downers Grove, Ill.: InterVarsity Press).

41. Bruce Bower, "Retooled Ancestors," *Science News* 133 (1988): 344–45; Bruce Bower, "Early Human Skeleton Apes Its Ancestors," *Science News* 131 (1987): 340; Bruce Bower, "Family Feud: Enter the 'Black Skull,'" *Science News* 131 (1987): 58–59.

42. C. Simon, "Stone-Age Sanctuary, Oldest Known Shrine, Discovered in Spain," *Science News* 120 (1981): 357; Bruce Bower, "When the Human Spirit Soared," *Science News* 130 (1986): 378–79.

43. J. S. Jones and S. Rouhani, "Human Evolution: How Small Was the Bottleneck?" *Nature* 319 (1986): 449–50; Bower, "Retooled Ancestors," 344–45; Jean-Jacques Hublin et al., "A Late Neanderthal Associated with Upper Paleolithic Artifacts," *Nature* 381 (1996): 224–26.

44. Jeffrey H. Schwartz and Ian Tattersall, "Significance of Some Previously Unrecognized Apomorphies in the Nasal Region of *Homo neanderthalensis*," *Proceedings of the National Academy of Sciences* 93 (1996): 10852–54; Ryk Ward and Chris Stringer, "Molecular Handle on the Neanderthals," *Nature* 388 (1997): 225–26.

45. Ross, *Genesis Question*, 115–22.

46. Ibid.

47. Ibid.

48. Ibid.

49. Ibid.

50. Ibid.

51. Scott A. Elias, Susan K. Short, C. Hans Nelson, and Hilary H. Birks, "Life and Times of the Bering Land Bridge," *Nature* 382 (1996): 61–63.

52. Frederick A. Filby, *The Flood Reconsidered* (Grand Rapids: Zondervan, 1970), 82.

53. R. Laird Harris, Gleason L. Archer, and Bruce K. Waltke, *Theological Wordbook of the Old Testament*, vol. 2 (Chicago: Moody, 1980), 800, 909, 923; William Gesenius, *Gesenius' Hebrew-Chaldee Lexicon to the Old Testament* (Grand Rapids: Baker, 1979), 407.

54. Robert Young, *Analytical Concordance to the Holy Bible* (London: Lutterworth Press, 1963).

55. Ross, *Genesis Question*, 143.

56. Filby, *Flood Reconsidered*, 120.

57. Ross, *Genesis Question*.

58. Filby, *Flood Reconsidered*; Ross, *Genesis Question*.

Chapter 11

1. Compare my discussion in *No Doubt about It* (Nashville: Broadman and Holman, 1997), 183–205.

2. "Tanakh" is an acronym based on the Hebrew names of the three divisions: the Law (Torah), the Prophets (Neviim), and the Writings (Ketuvim).

3. We could use others just as easily to make similar points: Matthew 4; 5:18; or John 5:46–47, to cite just a few.

4. The Pharisees were the strictest sect of the Jews in Jesus' day. They believed that a Jew should obey not only all of God's law but, to make sure God's law would never be violated, the human additions to the law as well.

5. Recognizing, of course, that we cannot refer to all Scriptures, but illustrations do not require that all members of a set be addressed.

6. Richard Swinburne, *The Existence of God* (New York: Oxford, 1979), 254–71.

7. Toby Lester, "What Is the Koran?" *Atlantic Monthly* 238, no. 1 (January 1999): 43–56.

8. Qur'an 5:117.

9. Qur'an 4:157.

10. See my article, "The Date of Zoroaster: Some Apologetic Considerations," *Presbyterion* 23, no. 1 (1997): 25–42.

11. Gherardo Gnoli, "Avesta," in *The Encyclopedia of Religion*, vol. 15, ed. Mircea Eliade (New York: Macmillan, 1987), 16–17.

12. A summary and critique of some of the outrageous liberties scholars have taken with the Avesta is provided by W. B. Henning, *Zoroaster: Politician or Witch Doctor?* (London: Cumberlege, 1957).

13. Nevertheless, it is an important "formality." For example, Jainism and Buddhism are not considered "orthodox" forms of Hinduism because, among other things, they reject the divine nature of the Vedas.

14. There is an interesting dynamic within the Vedas because many of the hymns and prayers addressed to specific deities make it sound as though, for the moment at least, a particular god or goddess is the only one. Thus, the religion of the Vedas also comes close to being henotheistic (recognizing many gods as real but worshiping only one at a time).

15. William K. Mahony, "Upanishads," in *Encyclopedia of Religion*, vol. 15, 148.

16. See the article "Bhagavad Gita," in *The Perennial Dictionary of World Religions*, ed. Keith Crim (San Francisco: Harper & Row, 1981), to get a feel for the amount of diversity.

17. Lotus Sutra, chap. 4.

18. The Lotus Sutra deals with the issue of falsehood in an ingenious way. It develops a notion in the second chapter, to which it makes reference from time to time throughout. This is the idea that it is permissible to tell what otherwise would be a falsehood in order to bring about someone's salvation. Thus, the idea of "expedient means" can justify many a falsehood or contradiction. Needless to say, to anyone interested in truth and not willing to capitulate to expediency, this move can hardly be considered legitimate.

19. The Romanization of Chinese terms has undergone several major shifts. The older Wade-Giles system is currently slowly being replaced by the Pinyin system, which I prefer.

20. Arthur Waley, *The Way and Its Power: A Study of the Tao Te Ching and Its Place in Chinese Thought* (New York: Grove Press, 1958).

21. Reading the Nihongi is a unique experience since episode after episode comes with five or six versions. One winds up reading the same narrative over and over again.

Chapter 12

1. "Yeshua" is the Hebrew name by which Jesus was known in the first century. The commonly used name "Jesus" is the Latinized rendering of his name in the Greek New Testament, which was "Iesous." The meaning of his Hebrew name is "the LORD is salvation" (cf. Matt. 1:21; Luke 1:31; 2:11).

2. The term "Messianic Jew" is used today for those Jews who believe that Jesus is the promised Messiah for the Jewish people as well as for the entire world.

3. The term "Christ" is not Jesus' last name but rather his title. It is a transliteration of the New Testament Greek term *Christos*, which is derived from the Greek verb *chrio*, meaning "to anoint." Thus, "Christ" is the English rendering of the Hebrew term *Mashiach*, used thirty-nine times in the Old Testament (derived from the Hebrew verb *mashach*, "to anoint"), meaning "the Anointed One" or "the Messiah."

4. See Pinchas Lapide, *The Resurrection of Jesus: A Jewish Perspective*, trans. Wilhelm C. Linss (Minneapolis: Augsburg, 1983); also, Pinchas Lapide, "The Resurrection of Jesus," *Time*, 7 May 1979.

5. For such unique messianic claims by Jesus himself, see John 5:21–24; 11:25–26; 14:6. For the claims of his first followers concerning his unique messianic authority, see Acts 4:12; 10:43; 1 Tim. 2:3–6.

6. See Heb. 13:20–21; Jude 24–25; Rev. 5:8–14.

7. C. S. Lewis, *Mere Christianity* (New York: Macmillan, 1943, 1945, 1952), 55–56.

8. For Jesus' own claim to be the Messiah of Israel, see Mark 14:61–64; Luke 24:25–27, 44–48; John 4:25–26. For his earliest Jewish followers' testimony to his messiahship, see Matt. 16:13–16; 21:9, 15; Mark 10:47ff.; John 1:29–41; Acts 2:31–38; 3:18–26; 4:24–28; 13:32–39; Rom. 1:1–4; Eph. 1:1–2; Phil. 2:5–11; Heb. 1:1–5; 5:5–6; 6:1–2; 9:13–14, 27–28; 10:4–10; 13:7–9, 20–21; James 1:1; 1 Peter 1:1–3; 1 John 2:1–2; Jude 1, 20–21, 24–25; Rev. 1:1–2. For two works by the same author that discuss the messianic thinking of Jesus' earliest followers, see Richard N. Longenecker, *Biblical Exegesis in the Apostolic Period* (Grand Rapids: Eerdmans, 1975); and *The Christology of Early Jewish Christianity*, Studies in Biblical Theology, Second Series, no. 17 (Naperville, Ill.: Alec R. Allenson, 1970).

9. For a fuller development of the massive apologetic evidence collected over the years in defense of the person and work of Jesus Christ, see Norman L. Geisler, ed., *Baker Encyclopedia of Christian Apologetics* (Grand Rapids: Baker, 1999); Josh McDowell, *The New Evidence That Demands a Verdict* (Nashville: Thomas Nelson, 1999); Lee Strobel, *The Case for Christ: A Journalist's Personal Investigation of the Evidence for Jesus* (Grand Rapids: Zondervan, 1998).

10. See Hal Lindsey, *The Promise* (Eugene, Ore.: Harvest House, 1982), 15–17.

11. For a concise treatment of the progressive revelation of messianic prophecy in the Hebrew Scriptures, see H. L. Ellison, *The Centrality of the Messianic Idea for the Old Testament* (London: Theological Students Fellowship, 1953); for a fuller treatment, see Walter C. Kaiser Jr., *The Messiah in the Old Testament*, Studies in Old Testament Biblical Theology (Grand Rapids: Zondervan, 1995); also by the same author, *Toward an Old Testament Theology* (Grand Rapids: Zondervan, 1978); plus, two older works, Franz Delitzsch, *Messianic Prophecies in Historical Succession* (Edinburgh: T & T Clark, 1891); and E. W. Hengstenberg, *Christology of the Old Testament*, rep. ed. (Grand Rapids: Kregel, 1970). For two more recent works, see James E. Smith, *What the Bible Teaches about the Promised Messiah* (Nashville: Thomas Nelson, 1993); and Gerard Van Groningen, *Messianic Revelation in the Old Testament* (Grand Rapids: Baker, 1990).

12. Alfred Edersheim, *The Life and Times of Jesus the Messiah*, 2 vols. (Grand Rapids: Eerdmans, 1953), 2:710–41.

13. J. Barton Payne, *Encyclopedia of Biblical Prophecy* (New York: Harper & Row, 1973), 667–68.

14. John Phillips, *Exploring the Scriptures* (Chicago: Moody, 1965, 1970), 124. For a fuller discussion on the use of the Old Testament in the New, see Gleason L. Archer and G. C. Chirichigno, *Old Testament Quotations in the New Testament: A Complete Survey* (Chicago: Moody, 1983); plus, R. T. France, *Jesus and the Old Testament: His Application of Old Testament Passages to Himself and His Mission* (London: The Tyndale Press, 1971); Walter C. Kaiser Jr., *The Uses of the Old Testament in the New* (Chicago: Moody, 1985); John W. Wenham, *Christ and the Bible* (Downers Grove, Ill.: InterVarsity Press, 1972). Also, for the remarkable statistical evidence on Yeshua's fulfillment of messianic prophecy, see Peter W. Stoner, *Science Speaks: Scientific Proof of the Accuracy of Prophecy and the Bible* (Chicago: Moody, 1969), 107–9.

15. In dealing with the biblical phenomenon of "the proof from prophecy," scholars have correctly recognized that many of the Old Testament messianic prophecies that find their fulfillment in the New Testament are *direct* predictions and others *indirect* predictions. The *direct* messianic prophecies are

straightforward predictions being fulfilled in a normal or literal fashion (e.g., Isa. 7.14 quoted in Matt. 1:22–23; Micah 5:2 quoted in Matt. 2:5–6). The *indirect* messianic prophecies are knowable only after the fact and are fulfilled in a broader and figurative fashion, such as in typology ["prophecy by parallelism"], illustration, allusion, summarization, application, and so on (e.g., Hosea 11:1 quoted in Matt. 2:15; Jer. 31:15 quoted in Matt. 2:17–18; also see the use of summarization in Matt. 2:23). Generally speaking, *direct* messianic prophecy is used in evangelistic contexts to proclaim the gospel to unbelievers (e.g., Acts 2:24–31 quoting Ps. 16:8–11; Acts 13:35–37 quoting Ps. 16:10). On the other hand, *indirect* messianic prophecy is used to instruct and edify believers who are in tune with the things of God and, thus being instructed by the Holy Spirit, can see the beginning from the end in all that the Spirit has inspired in the Word of God (e.g., Matthew writing to the early messianic community as an encouragement to steadfast discipleship; therefore, his use of *indirect* messianic prophecy in Matt. 2:15, 17–18, 23). For more on this subject, see France, *Jesus and the Old Testament*; Kaiser, *The Uses of the Old Testament in the New*; G. K. Beale, ed., *The Right Doctrine from the Wrong Texts: Essays on the Use of the Old Testament in the New* (Grand Rapids: Baker, 1994); S. Lewis Johnson, *The Old Testament in the New: An Argument for Biblical Inspiration*, Contemporary Evangelical Perspectives (Grand Rapids: Zondervan, 1980); R. V. G. Tasker, *The Old Testament in the New Testament* (Grand Rapids: Eerdmans, 1946, 1954). In this present essay I will deal with only *direct* messianic prophecy.

16. According to Kaiser, *Messiah in the Old Testament*, "Ephrathah was either the ancient name for Bethlehem (David's father was known as 'an Ephrathite from Bethlehem in Judah,' 1 Sam. 17:12; cf. Gen. 35:19; 48:7; Ruth 4:11) or the district in which Bethlehem was located" (153n). Micah's use of Ephrathah distinguishes the Bethlehem of Judah, the actual birthplace of the Messiah, from the Bethlehem of Galilee.

17. Cf. Ruth 4:11; 1 Sam. 16:1.

18. Cf. 2 Samuel 7; 1 Chronicles 17; Psalm 89; also, Isaiah 11; Jer. 23:5–6.

19. Everything about Yeshua was lowly and unassuming; for example: (1) his triumphal entry (Zech. 9:9, fulfilled in Matt. 21:1–5); (2) his own description of himself (Matt. 11:28–30); (3) his prayer on the same occasion as his description (Matt. 11:25–26). It is not surprising, therefore, that God chose, humanly speaking, such an insignificant place as Bethlehem to begin his messianic redemptive program for the whole world. God's ways are surely not our ways (cf. Isa. 55:6–11).

20. The timing of "the going forth" or arrival of the Messiah was also clearly predicted by the Hebrew prophets. His messianic career was scheduled by a divinely determined calendar that biblical scholars call Daniel's Seventy Weeks (Dan. 9:24–27). For a development of this messianic timetable, see Sir Robert Anderson, *The Coming Prince* (Grand Rapids: Kregel, 1954); Harold W. Hoehner, *Chronological Aspects of the Life of Christ* (Grand Rapids: Zondervan, 1978); Kaiser, *Messiah in the Old Testament*, 201–4; J. Alva McClain, *Daniel's Prophecy of the Seventy Weeks* (Grand Rapids: Zondervan, 1940); Robert C. Newman, "Fulfilled Prophecy as Miracle," in *In Defense of Miracles*, ed. R. Douglas Geivett and Gary R. Habermas (Downers Grove, Ill.: InterVarsity Press, 1997), 214–25.

21. Old Testament scholar Merrill Unger, in speaking of the eternality of the Messiah, says that the Hebrew for the phrase "days of eternity" means the "timelessness" of the Messiah (*Unger's Commentary on the Old Testament* [Chicago: Moody, 1981], 1863).

22. Arnold G. Fruchtenbaum, *Messianic Christology: A Study of Old Testament Prophecy Concerning the First Coming of the Messiah* (Tustin, Calif.: Ariel Ministries Press, 1998), 64.

23. In the Hebrew, *El Gibbor,* which is used elsewhere for "God" in the Book of Isaiah (cf. 10:21); for the same words reflecting God himself, see also Deut. 10:17; Neh. 9:32; Ps. 24:8; Jer. 32:18; Zeph. 3:17.

24. Literally in the Hebrew, "Father of Eternity" (i.e., the Messiah maintains an eternal as well as paternal relationship to his people, protecting and providing for them forever).

25. Further, on the nature of the Messiah's birth as a virgin birth, see also Isa. 7:14, which finds its fulfillment in Matt. 1:22–23. For a full discussion on the virgin birth, see Kaiser, *Messiah in the Old Testament,* 158–62; also see Geisler, *Baker Encyclopedia of Christian Apologetics,* 759–64; J. Gresham Machen, *The Virgin Birth of Christ* (Grand Rapids: Baker, 1930, 1977). Also, on the dual natures of the Messiah, see Ps. 110:1, quoted by Yeshua in Matt. 22:41–46; Mark 12:35–37; Luke 20:41–44, in defense of his own unique identity.

26. Unger, *Commentary,* 1863–64.

27. See for example the Targum of Jonathan [the Targum of the Prophets] quoted in Samson H. Levy, *The Messiah: An Aramaic Interpretation: The Messianic Exegesis of the Targum* (Cincinnati: Hebrew Union College Jewish Institute of Religion, 1974), 92. Also, Edersheim, in appendix 9 (*Life and Times of Jesus,* 2:735), refers to another reference in the Targum, in the Pirqe de Rabbi Eliezer, chapter 3, as well as other references by later rabbis.

28. I am greatly indebted to my former Hebrew professor, Dr. Bruce K. Waltke, who many years ago first introduced me to the grandeur of this passage.

29. Ivan Engnell, "The 'Ebed Yahweh Songs and the Suffering Messiah in Deutero-Isaiah," *Bulletin of John Rylands Library* 31 (January 1948): 73.

30. Franz J. Delitzsch, *Isaiah,* Commentary on the Old Testament (Grand Rapids: Eerdmans, 1973), 2:203.

31. E.g., Luke 22:37; Acts 8:30–35; 1 Peter 2:22–25.

32. Robert D. Culver, *The Sufferings and the Glory of the Lord's Righteous Servant* (Moline, Ill.: Christian Service Foundation, 1958), 20.

33. For a popular exposition of the four Servant Songs of Isaiah, see Henri Blocher, *The Songs of the Servant* (Downers Grove, Ill.: InterVarsity Press, 1975); H. L. Ellison, *The Servant of Jehovah* (Exeter, Eng.: Paternoster Press, 1983); F. Duane Lindsey, *The Servant Songs: A Study in Isaiah* (Chicago: Moody, 1985).

34. See Lindsey, *Servant Songs.* For a summary of the four songs, see Delitzsch, *Messianic Prophecies,* 2:165; and Roland K. Harrison, *Introduction to the Old Testament* (Grand Rapids: Eerdmans, 1969), 488–89.

35. See note 4 above.

36. Larry R. Helyer, *Yesterday, Today and Forever: The Continuing Relevance of the Old Testament* (Salem, Wis.: Sheffield Publishing, 1996), 318.

37. For a detailed exposition of Isaiah 52:13–53:12, see David Baron, *The Servant of Jehovah: The Sufferings of the Messiah and the Glory That Should Follow, An Exposition of Isaiah LIII* (Minneapolis: The James Family Christian Publishers, 1920, 1978); Culver, *The Sufferings and the Glory of the Lord's Righteous Servant*; and Sanford C. Mills, *A Hebrew Christian Looks at Isaiah Fifty-Three* (New York: The American Board of Missions to the Jews, 1971).

38. It is obvious that a dramatic transition occurs between Isaiah 53:9 and 53:10. The messianic Suffering Servant "was cut off out of the land of the living" [a Hebrew idiom for death] (53:8 NASB), "His *grave* was assigned to be with wicked men, . . . in His *death*" (53:9 NASB), and "He poured out Himself to *death*" (53:12 NASB). And yet in 53:10–12, he is alive and well, "prolong[ing] His days" (53:10), justifying the many who believe on him (53:11), and sharing in the spoils of his victorious war (53:12). Without question, this is the messianic Servant's triumphant resurrection from the dead! This transition is similar to the break in Psalm 22, "The Messianic Psalm of the Cross," between 22:21 and 22:22. This should not be surprising since the Messiah's resurrection from the dead was *directly* prophesied in the Hebrew Scriptures, specifically in Psalm 16. This psalm was used in the preaching of the early messianic community as an apologetic for the Messiah's resurrection, with the result that thousands of Jews became believers (cf. Acts 2:25–28; 13:35–37; also, Luke 24:25–27, 44–48; 1 Cor. 15:1, 3–8; 1 Peter 1:10–12). For a fuller development of Psalm 16 as a prophetic psalm of the Messiah's resurrection, by recent commentators, see Kaiser, *Messiah in the Old Testament*, 118–22; John Sailhamer, *The NIV Compact Bible Commentary* (Grand Rapids: Zondervan, 1994), 318; and Willem A. VanGemeren, "Psalms," in *The Expositor's Bible Commentary*, vol. 5, ed. Frank E. Gaebelein (Grand Rapids: Zondervan, 1991), 153–60.

39. See John 1:29, 36; also, Acts 8:32–33; 1 Cor. 5:7; 1 Peter 1:18–19; Rev. 5:6, 9, 12; 6:1; 13:8.

40. For a detailed survey of the history of the interpretation of Isaiah 53, see S. R. Driver and A. D. Neubauer, *The Fifty-Third Chapter of Isaiah according to Jewish Interpreters* (New York: KTAV Publishing House, 1969); Sam-

son H. Levy, *The Messiah: An Aramaic Interpretation: The Messianic Exegesis of the Targum* (Cincinnati: Hebrew Union College Jewish Institute of Religion, 1974); also, for a summary, see Edersheim, *Life and Times of Jesus*, 2:727; Mark Eastman and Chuck Smith, *The Search for Messiah*, rev. ed. (Fountain Valley, Calif.: Joy Publishing, 1993; Costa Mesa: The Word for Today, 1996), 257–74; and Fruchtenbaum, *Messianic Christology*, 123–34. For the identity of Isaiah's threefold use of the term "Servant of the Lord," see Lindsey, *Servant Songs*, 1–34.

41. See the sources cited in note 39 above.

42. Arnold G. Fruchtenbaum, *Jesus Was a Jew* (Tustin, Calif.: Ariel Ministries Press, 1974, 1981), 35.

43. E.g., Matt. 8:14–17; Acts 8:26–35; 1 Peter 2:18–25.

44. Concerning the messiahship of Jesus and the Jewish people, history continues to repeat itself, even as his words to the Jewish leaders of his own day bear testimony. "Jerusalem, Jerusalem, who kills the prophets and stones those who are sent to her! How often I wanted to gather your children together, the way a hen gathers her chicks under her wings, but you were *unwilling*" (Matt. 23:37 NASB, emphasis added).

45. For some of the more recent works on the historical evidences for the bodily resurrection of Jesus, see Geisler, *Baker Encyclopedia of Christian Apologetics*, 644–70; McDowell, *New Evidence*, 203–84; also, William L. Craig, *Knowing the Truth about the Resurrection: Our Response to the Empty Tomb*, rev. ed. (Ann Arbor, Mich.: Servant Books, 1981); also, by the same author, *The Son Rises: Historical Evidence for the Resurrection of Jesus* (Chicago: Moody, 1981); Norman L. Geisler, *The Battle for the Resurrection* (Nashville: Thomas Nelson, 1989); also, by the same author, *In Defense of the Resurrection*, rev. ed. (Clayton, Calif.: Witness, 1993); Gary R. Habermas, *The Resurrection of Jesus: An Apologetic* (Grand Rapids: Baker, 1980); George Eldon Ladd, *I Believe in the Resurrection of Jesus* (Grand Rapids: Eerdmans, 1975); Josh McDowell, *The Resurrection Factor* (San Bernardino, Calif.: Here's Life Publishers, 1981); Terry L. Miethe, ed., *Did Jesus Rise from the Dead? The Resurrection Debate: Gary R. Habermas and Anthony G. N. Flew* (San Francisco: Harper & Row, 1987); Frank

Morison, *Who Moved the Stone?* (Grand Rapids: Zondervan, 1930, 1958); Merrill C. Tenney, *The Reality of the Resurrection* (New York: Harper & Row, 1963); John W. Wenham, *Easter Enigma: Are the Resurrection Accounts in Conflict?* (Grand Rapids: Zondervan, 1984).

46. See Acts 2:41ff., 47; 4:4; 5:14; 6:1, 7; 9:31, 35, 42; 11:21, 24; 14:1, 21; 16:5; 17:12.

47. See John 3:1–21; 7:40–52; 19:38–42; also, 12:42–43; Acts 6:7; 15:5.

48. Adapted from an interview with J. P. Moreland in Strobel, *Case for Christ*, 244–57.

49. Psalms 16; 22; Isaiah 53; Daniel 9.

50. Mark 8:27–31; 9:30–32; 10:34.

51. See Luke 24:13–24.

52. See Acts 2:22–24, 36ff.; 3:11–21; 4:5–22; 5:27–33.

53. See Josh McDowell, *More Than a Carpenter* (Wheaton: Tyndale House, 1977), 60–71.

54. Clark H. Pinnock, *Set Forth Your Case: Studies in Christian Apologetics*, rev. ed. (Chicago: Moody, 1967, 1971), 95.

55. See note 4 above.

56. Lapide, *Resurrection of Jesus*, 125.

57. Michael Green, editor's preface in *I Believe in the Resurrection of Jesus*.

58. Michael Green, *Man Alive!* (Downers Grove, Ill.: InterVarsity Press, 1968), 23–24.

59. Paul Little, *Know Why You Believe* (Wheaton: Scripture Press, 1971), 63.

60. See Josephus, *Antiquities of the Jews*, xx.9.1 (200f.); and Eusebius, *Historia ecclesiastica* [Church History], ii.23.3–18.

61. Of course, the most famous "doubter" of all was none other than *doubting Thomas* himself, who became *believing Thomas* when he saw the risen Messiah (John 20:19–31). The earliest historical traditions also testify to Thomas's great faith. Like many others who saw the risen Lord, he died a martyr's death.

62. See Acts 23:6; also, 22:3; 26:4–5.

63. See Acts 7:58–60; 8:1–3; 9:1–2; 22:4–5; 26:9–11; cf. 9:13–19; Gal. 1:13.

64. For the historian Luke's account of Paul's actual conversion, see Acts 9:1–9; and for Paul's testimony in his own words first before a Jewish audience and then before a Gentile audience, see Acts 22:1–21; 26:1–29. For Paul's own testimony to seeing the risen Messiah, see 1 Cor. 9:1; 15:1–11; Gal. 1:1, 11–24; 1 Tim. 1:12–17.

65. F. F. Bruce, *The New Testament Documents: Are They Reliable?* rev. ed. (Leicester, Eng.: Inter-Varsity Press, 1943; Grand Rapids: Eerdmans, 1997), 77.

66. McDowell, *More Than a Carpenter*, 83–85.

67. Quoted in Strobel, *Case for Christ*, 250.

68. On the Old Testament prophecies pointing forward to the establishment of a new covenant, see Jer. 31:31–37; 32:37–40; also, Isa. 59:20–21; Ezek. 16:60–63; 37:21–28. On the abrogation of the old covenant and the actual establishment of the new covenant, see Mark 7:19; Luke 22:14–20; Acts 10:9–16; 11:4–10; 15:1–35; Rom. 7:1–4; 10:1–4; 14:1–23; 1 Cor. 11:17–34; 2 Cor. 3:1–11; Gal. 3:24–29; Col. 2:16–17; 1 Tim. 4:3–5; Heb. 7:15–22; 8:6–13; 9:11–28; 12:18–24.

69. See Matt. 28:1; Mark 16:2; Luke 24:1; John 20:1; Acts 20:7; 1 Cor. 16:2; Rev. 1:10; also, Rom. 14:1–23; Gal. 4:8–10; Col. 2:16.

70. See Exod. 20:8; 31:12–18; 35:1–3; Num. 15:32–36; Deut. 5:12.

71. See Gen. 1:1–27; Isa. 6:8; 22:11.

72. See John 14:1–20; cf. Matt. 28:19; 2 Cor. 13:14.

73. Quoted in Strobel, *Case for Christ*, 254.

74. Philip Schaff and David Schaff, *History of the Christian Church*, 8 vols., 5th ed. (Grand Rapids: Eerdmans, 1950), 172.

75. Quoted in Wilbur M. Smith, *Therefore Stand: Christian Apologetics* (Grand Rapids: Baker, 1945), 368.

76. C. F. D. Moule, *The Phenomenon of the New Testament* (London: SCM Press, 1967), 3.

77. Quoted in Strobel, *Case for Christ*, 254.

78. Blaise Pascal, *Pascal's Pensees*, trans. W. F. Trotter (New York: E. P. Dutton, 1958), 143.

79. Philip Schaff, *The Person of Christ* (American Tract Society, 1913).

Chapter 14

1. Interested readers can find the details of the many problems of evil in my *Many Faces of Evil* (Grand Rapids: Zondervan, 1994), chap. 1.

2. For details about the nature of each of these problems, see my *Many Faces of Evil*, esp. chap. 1.

3. In chapters 1–7 of *The Many Faces of Evil*, I discuss various answers to the logical

form of the problem, and in chapters 8–12, I address the evidential problem.

4. The other main metaphysical options are theonomy and Leibnizian rationalism. For details, see chapters 2 and 3 of *The Many Faces of Evil*.

5. See his *God, Freedom and Evil* (New York: Harper & Row, 1974).

6. J. L. Mackie, "Evil and Omnipotence," in *Philosophy of Religion*, ed. Basil Mitchell (Oxford: Oxford, 1971), 100–101.

7. Joseph B. Mayor, *The Epistle of St. James*, Classic Commentary Library (Grand Rapids: Zondervan, 1954), 54–55.

8. This interpretation of the point of sin's conception certainly squares with the tenor of Jesus' teachings, when he claimed that sin is committed in a person's thoughts first and made public later. Think, for example, of Matthew 5:27–28, where we find Jesus' teaching that if a man desires a woman in his heart, he has already committed adultery with her before doing any overt act.

9. In this case, people would not have to be capable of having such knowledge, since God would take care of any possible problems by means of miracles.

10. My defense focuses on evil that is voluntarily produced. If a world in which God removes intentionally evil actions is problematic, there is even more reason for concern when one realizes that involuntary and reflex actions can also produce evil. If it would disrupt normal life to remove evil-intentioned acts, it would be even more disruptive to remove also our good-intentioned and reflex actions that wind up producing evil.

11. I agree that this other world would be better morally, because there would be no moral evil in it. But God cannot make that world and also make the non-glorified human beings he has. Was God wrong in making non-glorified humans? Only if they are evil themselves, and they are not. Is God obligated to create this other world anyway? According to modified rationalism, God is free either to create or not create at all. If he creates, he is free to create any good possible world available. He is not obligated to forego our world in favor of the eternal state, so long as our world is a good world. And I have shown why ours is a good world.

12. Actually, many theologies can solve their problem of moral evil. For further details, see my *Many Faces of Evil*, chaps. 2–3, 5.

13. For a discussion of things that don't work (and why they don't) in comforting the afflicted, see my *Deceived by God? A Journey through Suffering* (Wheaton: Crossway, 1997), chap. 3.

14. Interested readers can read the rest of *Deceived by God?*

Chapter 15

1. For some of my writings in this area, see *Scaling the Secular City: A Defense of Christianity* (Grand Rapids: Baker, 1987); *Does God Exist?: The Debate between Atheists and Theists* (coauthored with Kai Nielsen) (Buffalo: Prometheus, 1993); *The Creation Hypothesis: Scientific Evidence for a Designer* (Downers Grove, Ill.: InterVarsity Press, 1994); *Jesus under Fire: Crucial Questions about Jesus* (coedited with Michael Wilkins) (Grand Rapids: Zondervan, 1995); *Love Your God with All Your Mind: The Role of Reason in the Life of the Soul* (Colorado Springs: NavPress, 1997); *Three Views on Creation and Evolution* (coedited with John Mark Reynolds) (Grand Rapids: Zondervan, 1999); *Body and Soul: Human Nature and the Crisis in Ethics* (coauthored with Scott Rae) (Downers Grove, Ill.: InterVarsity Press, 2000); *Naturalism: A Critical Analysis* (coedited with William Lane Craig) (London: Routledge, 2000). In my writings, I have sought to embody the value of community in which Christians band together to produce things of value that are better than they would be if done individually. I, and I hope others, have been enriched by the process. I encourage other Christian authors to seek to exhibit this virtue more widely in their publishing.

2. William James, *The Varieties of Religious Experience* (New York: Modern Library, 1902), esp. 506–7.

3. Patrick Sherry, *Spirit, Saints, and Immortality* (Albany, N.Y.: State University of New York Press, 1984).

4. William Dembski, *Intelligent Design* (Downers Grove, Ill.: InterVarsity Press, 1999).

5. John Wesley, *A Plain Account of Christian Perfection* (London: Epworth Press, 1952), 87.

Chapter 16

1. Quoted in David Friend, *The Meaning of Life* (Boston: Little, Brown, 1991), 90.

2. Quoted in Alister McGrath, *Intellectuals Don't Need God and Other Modern Myths* (Grand Rapids: Zondervan, 1993), 15.

3. Stephen Jay Gould, quoted in *The Meaning of Life*, 33.

4. Stephen Hawking, *A Brief History of Time* (London: Bantam Books, 1988), 175.

5. G. K. Chesterton, *Orthodoxy* (New York: Image Books, 1959), 57.

6. Norman L. Geisler, *Baker Encyclopedia of Christian Apologetics* (Grand Rapids: Baker, 2000), 140.

7. W. E. H. Lecky, *A History of European Morals from Augustus to Charlemagne II* (London: Longmans Green & Co., 1869); quoted in F. F. Bruce, *Jesus, Lord and Savior* (Downers Grove, Ill.: InterVarsity Press, 1986), 15.

8. Christopher Morley, quoted in a column by Ruth Walker in *Christian Science Monitor*, 20 November 1991.

9. G. K. Chesterton, *As I Was Saying,* ed. Robert Knille (Grand Rapids: Eerdmans, 1985), 267.

10. William Temple, quoted in David Watson, *I Believe in Evangelism* (Grand Rapids: Eerdmans, 1976), 157.

11. See Radhakrishnan in his *Hindu View of Life* (New Delhi, India: Indus, 1993); and Pandit Nehru on his comment on Hinduism, quoted in David Brown, *A Guide to Religions* (London: S.P.C.K., 1975), 63.

12. Malcolm Muggeridge, *Jesus Rediscovered* (Garden City, N.Y.: Doubleday, 1969), 77.

LIST OF CONTRIBUTORS

Beckwith, Francis J. (Ph.D., Fordham University; M.J.S., Washington University School of Law) is associate professor of philosophy, culture, and law at Trinity International University. He has published many articles in academic journals and has authored several books, including *Relativism: Feet Firmly Planted in Mid-Air* (Baker, 1998) and *Do the Right Thing: Readings in Applied Ethics and Social Philosophy*, 2d ed. (Wadsworth, 2002).

Bradley, Walter (Ph.D., University of Texas) recently retired from his position as professor of mechanical engineering at Texas A&M University. He has published dozens of articles in academic and professional journals and has coauthored or contributed to several books, including *The Creation Hypothesis: Scientific Evidence for an Intelligent Designer* (InterVarsity Press, 1994).

Budziszewski, J. (Ph.D., Yale University) is an associate professor in the departments of philosophy and government at the University of Texas at Austin. He has published many articles in academic journals and has authored several books, including *Written on the Heart: The Case for Natural Law* (InterVarsity Press, 1997).

Corduan, Winfried (Ph.D., Rice University) is professor of philosophy and religion at Taylor University. He has published numerous articles in academic journals and is the author of *Neighboring Faiths: A Christian Introduction to World Religions* (InterVarsity Press, 1998).

Craig, William Lane (Ph.D., University of Birmingham; D.Theol., University of Munich) is research professor of philosophy at Talbot School of Theology. He has published many articles in academic journals and has contributed to and authored several books, including *Reasonable Faith: Christian Truth and Apologetics* (Crossway, 1984).

Feinberg, John S. (Ph.D., University of Chicago) is professor of biblical and systematic theology at Trinity Evangelical Divinity School. He has published numerous articles in academic journals and is the author of *Deceived by God? A Journey through the Experience of Suffering* (Crossway, 1997).

Geisler, Norman L. (Ph.D., Loyola University of Chicago) is president of Southern Evangelical Seminary. He has published countless articles in academic journals and has authored over fifty books, including *Baker Encyclopedia of Christian Apologetics* (Baker, 1999).

Geivett, R. Douglas (Ph.D., University of Southern California) is professor of philosophy at Talbot School of Theology. He has published many articles in academic journals and has authored or contributed to several books, including *In Defense of Miracles* (InterVarsity Press, 1997).

Habermas, Gary R. (Ph.D., Michigan State University; D.D., Emmanuel College, Oxford, England) is distinguished professor of philosophy and theology at Liberty University. He has published many articles in academic journals and has authored or contributed to several books, including *The Historical Jesus* (College Press, 1996).

Hoffman, Paul K. (J.D., University of California at San Francisco) has been a trial lawyer for twenty years. He has authored articles in a variety of periodicals, including "A Jurisprudential Analysis of Hume's 'In Principle' Argument against Miracles," *Christian Apologetics Journal* 2, no. 1 (1999).

Kreeft, Peter (Ph.D., Fordham University) is professor of philosophy at Boston College. He has published many articles in academic journals and has authored, edited, and contributed to many books, including *Handbook of Christian Apologetics* (InterVarsity Press, 1994).

Leventhal, Barry R. (Ph.D., Dallas Theological Seminary) is academic dean and professor at Southern Evangelical Seminary. Dr. Leventhal has contributed chapters to several books, including "The Masada Suicides: The Making and Breaking of a Cultural Icon," in *Suicide: A Christian Response* (Kregel, 1998).

McDowell, Josh (M.Div., Talbot School of Theology) has spoken to millions of young people throughout the world as a traveling representative of Campus Crusade for Christ. He is the author and coauthor of more than seventy books and workbooks, including the best-selling *Evidence That Demands a Verdict* (Here's Life, 1979).

Moreland, J. P. (Ph.D., University of Southern California) is professor of philosophy at Talbot School of Theology. He has published many articles in academic journals and has authored and contributed to several books, including *Scaling the Secular City* (Baker, 1987).

Ross, Hugh (Ph.D., University of Toronto) is the founder and president of Reasons to Believe. Dr. Ross has served as a research fellow in astronomy at Cal Tech in Pasadena and has published articles in several academic journals. He is the author of several books, including *Fingerprint of God* (Promise, 1989).

Zacharias, Ravi (M.Div., Trinity Evangelical Divinity School, honorary doctorates from Houghton College, Asbury College, and Tyndale College and Seminary) is the founder and president of Ravi Zacharias International Ministries. He has spoken on hundreds of college campuses and has authored several books, including *Jesus among Other Gods* (Word, 2000).